DISCARD

DONATED BY EDITH FOSTER

As Grain Once Scattered

A view of the altar Palm Sunday, 1984.

Text by Roger K. Warlick • Photographs by Jeanne Papy

As Grain Once Scattered

*The History of Christ Church
Savannah, Georgia
1733-1983*

The State Printing Company, Columbia

One of the Central focal points is the high altar which was installed after the destructive fire of 1897.

©*Christ Church, Savannah, GA. 1987.*

ISBN 0-9619270-0-3

All Rights Reserved. No part of this publication may be reproduced, stored in a retrieval system, or transmitted in any form or by any means, electronic, mechanical, photocopying, recording or otherwise, without the prior permission of the Rector, Wardens, and Vestry of Christ (Episcopal) Church, Savannah, GA.

In Memoriam

Francis Bland Tucker, D.D.
Rector of Christ Church
1945-1967

Born Norfolk, Virginia January 6, 1895
Died Savannah, Georgia January 1, 1984

Priest • Poet • Scholar

Significant Contributor to English Hymnody

Foreword

At a meeting of the Vestry of Christ Church in February of 1982, it was suggested by the Rector, the Rev. George M. Maxwell, that an appropriate and memorable celebration of the upcoming 250th Anniversary (in 1983) might be a compilation of our church's long and interesting history — a book that would be worthy in every way of the oldest parish in the State of Georgia.

The Vestry received this suggestion with enthusiasm and, as Senior Warden at that time, it seemed incumbent upon me to assume leadership of this task without delay. My friend and fellow vestryman, **John B. Adams**, volunteered to be my *aide de camp*.

Finding the right person to do the enormous amount of research that would be required and to write the history was accomplished without undue agitation: he was in our midst — **Dr. Roger K. Warlick**, Head of the Department of History, Armstrong State College, a long-time Christ Church parishioner and choir member for 15 years. Roger accepted the assignment with alacrity. He understood clearly from the beginning that it was the Vestry's wish that the facts be marshalled in logical order and that, if warts there were, to make no attempt to hide them if they reflected the true nature of our very old congregation. The desire of the Vestry was only that a volume of lasting worth would result.

Getting started in a field that is far removed from my normal endeavors was eased considerably by my friends. **Malcolm Bell, Jr.**, as a published author himself, gave us some canny suggestions, and **Arthur Gordon**, also a published author, laid out some facts of the business which, while not minimizing the scope of the project, still made it seem entirely attainable, even by amateurs.

In these early months, I had support and assistance which I shall never forget, from friends like the late **Hugh ("Buck") Hill**, the late **Franklin Traub, David Barrow, Jr., Joe Harrison, David Johnson, Robert H. Demere, Eleanor (Mrs. Alex) Ormond**, the late **Jimmy Goethe** and **Jane Wright**. Then there were **Sarah (Mrs. Lewis) Little, Jeanne Garlington, Alice Myrick, Mrs. Sally (Alex) Sullivan, Gawin Corbin, Ted Erickson, Libby Kingston** and the **Women of Christ Church.**

Especially, I am indebted to **Jeanne Papy** and **Hansell ("Hank") Ramsey**, both Christ Church parishioners, who grasped the spirit of the project and whose extraordinary photographs enhance this volume.

My gratitude goes to **Betty Mercer** who generously made available suitable photographs which had been taken by the late **George A. Mercer III**, an outstanding photographer.

And in addition, there are three individuals who should receive their full deserts: **Lee Giffen**, whose advice and everyday help I leaned on heavily, was unfailingly encouraging and supportive. I owe to her, for her wise suggestion, her careful reading and re-reading, a debt I can scarcely express. To **Nellie Schmidt**, for executing the time consuming and tedious job of indexing, let me say "Thank You". I am also deeply grateful to **Pinny Morgan Crouch** who created and arranged the graphic art in this volume. Observing her at work taught this non-professional a great deal about the multitude of facets involved in putting together a book.

These lines cannot be brought to a close without deep expression of appreciation to the late **F. Bland Tucker**, our rector for so many years. Although he was ill, his fine mind was involved in the project and he let us draw upon his fabulous memory and legendary love for his last parish which he served with unequalled devotion and compassion.

I do not believe there was anyone who was called upon for a contribution to this volume, however small, who did not respond with enthusiasm and belief that the finished product would be worthy of our great church.

To Roger, and all who helped to illuminate these pages, "Thank You".

For my part, I can say with total honesty that the service has enriched and enlarged my life.

Edward H. Morgan
August 1985

Preface

Even the "History of Christ Church" has a considerable history. Some years ago the Diocese adopted a canon which prescribed that its Registrar "be responsible to collect the journals, files, papers, reports, title deeds, [and other historical records,] throwing light upon the history of the Church in this Diocese and in its parishes." The canon also made it the responsibility of each parish to write its history and place a copy on file with the Registrar. That was in 1872.[a] After much pleading by the Registrar the histories began slowly trickling into his office, but not until 1881 was the already sizable task of creating history for Christ Church undertaken by the Rector, Thomas Boone.[b] Subsequently, a number of sketches by the Rev. Messrs, Wing, Wright, Tucker, and probably Brown, were done in the 20th century for use in speeches, brochures, etc. Although some of these ran to 15 or 20 pages, and often had good entertainment value, none were documented histories and none of them made systematic use of the treasures hidden away in the archives of the Georgia Historical Society, or the more exotic ones in Washington, D.C., and London.

A major effort to make some of the more remote documents available locally was carried on by T.F. Screven and J.B. Lawrence, earlier this century, when they spent countless hours transcribing records from the British Library and Public Records Office and depositing them in the Georgia Historical Society. The parish itself has also felt a continuing concern over the care and conservation of its records, at least since 1890, when the Vestry appointed a committee to "classify, file. . . and find a safe place of storage for them."[c] This logic culminated eventually in placement of older Church records "on loan" at the Georgia Historical Society where they have been inventoried, preserved, and microfilmed.[d] Still other records were collected by individuals, such as Miss Edith Johnston, during the late 19th and early 20th centuries. These were given to the Church by her sister, Miss Eugenia Johnston, about 1940, in the "hope that someone at some future time will take up my sister's work and write a definitive history of Christ Church, [it being] her great desire to have a history of the parish in printed form."[e] Miss Johnston finally got her wish when the Rector, the **Rev. George Maxwell**, proposed publication of a history as part of the parish's 250th Anniversary observance.[f]

Whether the vision of our predecessors has been honorably fulfilled in the present volume is for you to judge, but it should be clear already that this history is founded in the heroic efforts and ardent wishes of many. The task has been immeasurably supported by **Edward H. Morgan**, former Senior Warden, through his energetic collection of documents, and also by his encouragement and forbearance during the three years of research and writing. This task has also been greatly supported by **Lilla Mills Hawes**, Director Emerita of the Georgia Historical Society, **Mary Lane Morrison**, **Jeanne Garlington** and the late **Franklin Traub**, who read all or part of the manuscript and offered helpful suggestions as well as encouragement. In addition, crucial contributions were made by the **Rev. Charles L. Hoskins**, who graciously made available several rare documents from his private collection; by **Nellie Hankins Schmidt**, who prepared the index; by **Eulalie McDowell Giffen** and **Lorraine VandenBout Warlick**, who proofread the entire text and surely, thereby, saved the author much embarrassment; and by the staff of the Georgia Historical Society — specifically, **Barbara S. Bennett**, **Anne P. Smith**, **Karen E. Osvald**, **Susan F. Murphy**, and **Tracy D. Bearden** — for their helpful suggestions and patience. Thanks are also due to the late **Hugh Hill**, a former Senior Warden of Christ Church, who made the first pioneering effort to dig out this semiquincentennial history of the parish.

I am also endebted most deeply to **A. Diane Wagner**, who prepared the entire typescript, deciphering a multitude of textual obscurities in the process. Finally, my wife, Lorraine, has earned a crown of laurel for her proofreading, patience, and all-purpose care and pampering through these years. She made my life manageable while I neglected hers.

The Rector, Wardens and Vestry of Christ Church, too,

deserve a note of appreciation. Surely their foresight in initiating the history project and forbearance in awaiting the final product are worthy in themselves. But even more notable has been their hands-off policy, strictly observed from the beginning, with never the slightest attempt to influence either the content or the perspective of the story that would emerge. This was to be history "as it was", not "as we wish." Thus, our predecessors have been allowed to show forth in their full humanity so that we might better know and more richly appreciate that which is common to us all.

Despite the generous help of so many, assuredly shortcomings remain. All of these are mine, alas, but a few are also deliberate. One such is brought about by the decision to by-pass secondary sources and turn directly to the original documents wherever possible. This has gained important economies of time, but has done so at the risk of ignoring assumptions and controversies that have been favorites for generations. (Unfortunately, severing pious tradition, or impious, from verifiable history often involves considerable pain.) Another conscious choice was to forego the use of oral history in compiling the present account. No doubt much could be gained from a systematic recording of the recollections and reminiscences of the parish's older members, but that would be a project of several years magnitude in itself and quite beyond the limits of the present undertaking.

With these points in mind, only a few additional niceties need be observed in order to read this volume with comfort. First, *dates* have been partially modernized. Specifically, years are rendered in the modern style (that is, according to the calendar revision of 1752), but months and days are left as they appear in the original sources, for the sake of easy reference, except where greater precision seemed crucial. Exceptions are noted. Second, *newspaper references* appear with the page and column noted parenthetically after the date of publication. For example, (3-2) indicates a citation on page 3, column 2. Beyond that, *abbreviations* have been minimized for the sake of reading comfort. The only other consistent exception to this rule is the use of CR to indicate the *Colonial Records of Georgia*. Third, all *manuscript references* (MS) are to collections in the Georgia Historical Society unless otherwise specified. Finally, *spelling* has been left as it appears in the original documents, if at all intelligible to the modern eye, for the sake of flavor. Our predecessors of all classes and degrees of education were a great deal more casual about spelling than we, even to the point where an individual might present his own name two or three different ways in the same letter! The sensible course would seem to be to relax and enjoy their imaginative, and often amusing, approach.

Roger K. Warlick

Reading this book left me with only one negative comment: It should have been written sooner!

I do commend it enthusiastically. It should be required reading for every member of Christ Church, Savannah. But it will have considerable interest for (and use by) a much wider audience. All Episcopalians in the State of Georgia should find the history of Georgia's Mother Church of personal significance. Methodists too will read with interest and profit — and occasional astonishment — those portions especially which deal with the brothers Wesley and George Whitefield. Any historically-conscious Savannahian will be rewarded as he learns more Savannah history.

I stand in awe of the research that lies behind this volume. The way the facts are presented is lively, the interpretations perceptive.

I thank and congratulate the sponsors of the project, as I do the author.

Paul Reeves
VII Bishop of Georgia

It is very important that we know from whence we have come, for then we should be better able to understand where we are and better prepared to chart our course into the future. God has richly blessed this parish which in my mind richly illustrates St. Paul's understanding of the church as unity in diversity. It truly amazes me that our gracious Lord has held us together and enabled us to grow in such a diverse pattern over the last twelve years. We at Christ Church are indebted to **Roger Warlick** for his untiring efforts and creative abilities in writing this history. We are also indebted to **Edward Morgan** and his many helpers in coordinating this project. May our Lord continue to bless us as we strive to faithfully write our history into the future.

G. M. Maxwell,
Rector

Contents

Mission to Utopia: 1732-1750 .... *11*

Revolutionary Fever: 1750-1785 .... *35*

Fire and Tempest: 1785-1835 .... *53*

The Mid-19th Century: 1835-1851 .... *67*

Crisis in Church and Nation: 1851-1867 .... *83*

Reconstruction, Reproach, and Recovery: 1867-1889 .... *95*

Flamboyant Preparation for the 20th Century: 1889-1914 .... *115*

War, Prosperity, Depression, & War: 1914-1945 .... *133*

An Era of Crisis: Race, Politics and Worship *155*

References *181*

Bishops of the Diocese of Georgia *183*

Selected Bibliography *185*

Footnotes *187*

Index *215*

I
Mission to Utopia
1732-1750

After years of effort the pieces of the puzzle fell together in 1732. The charter from the king was initiated[1] and promised to realize ideals unprecedented in Britain's colonial enterprise. Georgia was to be a place where

forever hereafter, there shall be a liberty of conscience allowed in the worship of God to all persons inhabiting . . . or resident within the said province, and . . . all persons, except papists, shall have a free exercise of their religion.[2]

Further defining the unique design of the new colony was the prohibition of large land holdings. To look after the spiritual welfare of the colonists the Trustees also took steps to procure a minister for Georgia.

The Rev. Mr. [Henry] Herbert . . . having offered his service to attend and officiate in Savannah until another minister should be found to succeed him, his offer was accepted[3]

and he sailed aboard the *Anne* with the first group of emigres.

Dr. Herbert's priestly duties commenced almost immediately. First he was called upon to baptize a son of one of the passengers, while they were still within sight of Isle of Wight. A few days later, it became his duty to bury a child at sea.[3a] Finally, after seven more wearisome, worrisome, sea-bobbing weeks they "came to anchor off [Charleston] bar, a ship with about 120 People for settling the new colony of Georgia."[3b] The visit was brief — just long enough for Mr. Oglethorpe to meet and secure the support of Governor Johnson of South Carolina. Then the colonists moved on to Port Royal and Beaufort where at last they came ashore and "refreshed themselves." Mr. Oglethorpe, meanwhile, went ahead to select the site for the new town.

He returned on the 24th day [of January]; and they celebrated the Sunday following as a day of Thanksgiving for their safe arrival; and a sermon was preached by the Rev'd Mr. [Lewis] Jones, (the Rev'd Dr. Herbert, who came with the colony, preaching that day at Beaufort town.) There was a great resort of the Gentlemen of that neighborhood, and their families, and a plentiful dinner provided for the colony, and all that came, by Mr. Oglethorpe: being four fat hogs, 8 turkies, besides fowls, English Beef, and other provisions, a hogshead of punch, a hogshead of beer, and a large quantity of wine; and all was disposed in so regular a manner that no person was drunk, nor any disorder happened.[3c]

A few days later on Yamacraw Bluff "we hade Divine Service performed in Mr. Oglethorpe's tent by the Rev'd Dr. Herbert with thanksgiving for our safe arrivall." Guests at that service were Mr. Musgrove, the Indian trader, and his wife, but most significantly,

Tomochichi, the Indian King, desired to be admitted, which Mr. Oglethorpe readily consented to, and he and his Queen were seated in the tent. During the time of Divine Service, severall of the Indian warriors . . . sat at a small distance from the tent . . . and behaved very decently.[3d]

Given Tomochichi's ecumenical attitude, prospects seemed bright indeed for the religious aspect of the Georgia enterprise. This was reinforced just a few weeks later at what was essentially a diplomatic meeting. At that time the assembled Creek chieftains expressed for themselves and their people willingness to be taught the ways of the English, including religion, since after all "He who had given the English breath, had given them breath also."[3e]

To place the Church in the new colony on a sound footing, Oglethorpe was empowered to set out sites for the Church building, the minister's house, a burial place, and 3000 acres for a glebe.[4] The Trustees then underscored their point in a letter to Mr. Oglethorpe by directing the execution of their design "as soon as possible."[5] To ease the strain on their limited finances the trustees turned for aid to the Society for the Propagation of the Gospel in Foreign Parts (SPG). Taking pains to note for the Society the committment they had made already themselves to the cause of religion in Georgia, in the form of glebe lands, etc., they requested money for a salary to support the missionary who would soon arrive there.[6] The SPG agreed and the Trustees then began the search for a permanent missionary. A Mr. Samuel Quincy, then in London for ordination, was recommended to them, and they agreed to direct him to the SPG for examination and approval.[6a] This same pattern held throughout the trusteeship of the colony — the Trustees did the selecting, the SPG met, endorsed, and with few exceptions provided the missionary's salary, typically £50 per year.

Mr. Herbert's visit to the new world was short-lived, as indeed was he. "Falling ill of a flux," he died and was buried at sea on the return voyage to England that same year.[6b] Whether the journey was part of the cause is inknown, but there is ample evidence that such trips did take their toll. Consider, for instance, that to replace him, Mr. Quincy embarked for Georgia in April[7] but did not arrive until July, 1733.[8] Added to difficult communications, problems such as short tenure, crossed purposes, and troubled and unproductive labors further burdened the missionary effort. As things turned out, Mr. Quincy was only the second of *nine* missionaries during the colony's first dozen years! Nothing, it seems, especially in matters of religion, came easily in those first years. One almost gets the feeling that the Indians were more positive in attitude than the average colonist.

The Trustees soon became distressed with Quincy for leaving them, as they felt, poorly informed. Their original instructions to him had made clear their desire that he report frequently and fully to them on the spiritual state of the colony. But having heard no such reports by November they were sufficiently upset to reiterate their wish in concise terms[9] and insist that he send a journal to better inform them of his activities.[10] Protesting ignorance of their desire did not soothe the Trustees as Mr. Quincy had hoped. Fortunately, one of his few letters to them does give us some glimpse of congregational conditions, although in its brevity one may wonder whether it tells us more of Mr. Quincy than of his congregation. In it he notes the existence of "a small society of seven or eight" who meet on Sunday evenings to read the Epistle and Gospel for the day, and hear the Evening Service, etc., "after the [manner of the] societies in London."[11] He felt such interest was exceptional apparently; for continuing his report, he expressed to the Trustees his doubt that there was any serious "Romish proselytizing" in Savannah, simply because "religion seems to be the least minded of anything in the place."[12]

None of this mattered too much, however, for minor irritants were soon obscured by major ones. Quincy for his part was unhappy because the 300 acres laid out for the glebe by Noble Jones' survey were as unattractive as the people of the congregation in his eyes, "a useless pine-barren, not at all as Oglethorpe had indicated" to him personally.[13] True or not, the Trustees were in no mood to listen to his complaint or even acknowledge his belated and poor attempt to report on the state of the parish. Word had reached them that he was once again "out of town," this time "abandoning the Province for seven months and leaving only a wheelright to bury the dead and console the sick."[13a] No wonder the Trustees got the distinct impression "he seems not to value his cure."[14]

One might plead that Quincy could have been too burdened with duties to do as the Trustees asked, or that their demands were unrealistic. Perhaps . . . but one wonders. He did, after all, have time to write Oglethorpe, when possibly he had heard a bit too much adulation of the General for the hardships endured. His point was that Oglethorpe's meticulous attention to countless details could not properly be called "hardships" because he took such great delight in them![14a]

Mr. Quincy's anxiety was made more complete by the fact that his wife refused to come to Georgia at all to join him![15] At least that was the reason he cited when requesting the Trustees to appoint him a successor. Perhaps he was truly unaware the Trustees were at that very moment in process of relieving him of his charge, feeling that he "does not attend his duty as he ought", and the religious disposition of the people is so cool that some Sundays there are not ten at Church![16] The Trustee's letter to Quincy makes even clearer both their thinking and their determination to change the situation.

For good and sufficient reason they have thought it proper to revoke the authority granted by them to you for performing the duty of clergyman in the town of Savannah, and that they have granted a license to the Rev. Mr. John Wesley for the said purpose. You are therefore hereby required not to give any interruption . . . in the performance of his duty.[17]

In any case, the letters of the two parties crossed in the mail causing the Earl of Egmont to comment in his *Journal*, with evident disgust, that by this means he "avoided disgrace."[18] We can only guess at the Earl's thoughts when one year later Quincy appeared in person to request a letter attesting to his good behavior and three month's pay for "lost time" after Wesley's arrival![19]

John Wesley's entry into the story is a real gift to us as we seek to recall the early years of Christ Church, regardless of the view we might take of his ministry. His time in Savannah was filled with matters of considerable human interest and is a rich mine for those concerned with the rise of Methodism. These topics have deservedly received great attention in the past. The special gift to our enterprise, however, is found in his generous correspondence and diligent keeping of a detailed and reflective journal. These writings give us access to the life of the town and congregation during the first years in a way which routine bureaucratic correspondence will not likely afford. On a larger scale, they furnish insight into the purposes

An early engraving showing John Wesley (on the left) on his way to America with Moravian brethren during a storm at sea, 1736.

of the Trustees, some of the motives behind the colonial enterprise itself, and even into the mind of the age, and to what it was really thinking when it called itself "Enlightened."

One impression the Wesleyan records make about his phase of the Georgia mission is the engaging sense of excitement with which it began. It is an excitement well worth our close examination for the opportunity it gives us to share in the reaction of his eighteenth century congregation. John's journal almost vibrates with expectation as he notes:

Tues, 14 October 1735: Benjamin Ingham (Queen's College), Charles Delamotte (son of a London merchant), who had offered himself some days before, my brother Charles and myself took boat for Gravesend in order to embark for Georgia. Our end in leaving our native country was . . . singly this — to save our own souls; to live wholly to the glory of God. In the afternoon we found the Simmonds *off Gravesend and immediately went on board.*[20]

The days on board ship were packed from their rising at 4 A.M. for private prayer till retirement at 9 or 10 each evening. Between came scripture readings, and study, Morning and Evening Prayer read for the passengers, joining with the Moravian passengers in their services, reading to "those in need", and sessions in which the four men shared their own thoughts, insights, and expectations with each other.

I began to learn German in order to converse with the [Moravians], six and twenty of whom we had on board. On Sunday, the weather being fair and calm, we had the morning service on the quarterdeck, I now first preached ex tempore *and then administered the Lord's Supper to six or seven communicants. A little flock, May God increase it!*[21]

Crossing in early winter, as the *Simmonds* did, the trip was not an easy one. Five weeks out, and after a series of storms, Wesley reflected on his own and the other passengers' inner strength and weakness. As he did, he was particularly struck with the Moravians on board who were also destined for Savannah.

I had long before observed the great seriousness of [the Moravians'] behavior. Of their great humility they had given continual proof . . . There was now opportunity of trying whether they were delivered from the spirit of fear as well as from that of pride, anger, and revenge. In the midst of the Psalm with which their service began, the sea broke over, split the mainsail in pieces, covered the ship and poured between the decks as if the great deep had already swallowed us up. A terrible screaming began among the English. The Germans calmly sang on.[22]

With calm finally restored, he gives us a glimpse of how much 18th and 20th century minds have in common, including our reactions to the sea and a good preacher's ability to recognize a promising text.

We enjoyed the calm. I can conceive of no difference comparable to that between a smooth and rough sea, except that which is between a mind calmed by the love of God, and one torn up by the storms of earthly passions.[23]

Although Wesley's initial impression of Georgia sounds like that of many a modern tourist, it is soon apparent he did not come for relaxation. The enthusiasm and eagerness his journal reveals to us during the voyage continue as he describes the welcome sight of land, just before the passengers briefly slipped ashore on Cockspur Island to give thanks.

Tuesday, February 5th, between two and three in the afternoon, God brought us all safe into the Savannah River. We cast anchor near Tybee Island where groves of pines, running along the shore, made an agreeable pros-

pect, showing .. the bloom of spring in the depth of winter.[24]

The first days included visits to Mr. Spangenberg, Moravian leader, and to Mr. Causton, the chief magistrate in Savannah, along with many others. The next weeks were filled with excitement and things went well generally. But Wesley reported to his mother, with a barely muffled chuckle of triumph, some were angry at him already . . .

> *for a gentleman, no longer ago than last night, made a ball, but the public prayers happening to begin about the same time, the church was full and the ballroom so empty that the entertainment could not go forward.*[24a]

Those same weeks also saw the emergence of Wesley's own liturgical style and the mainlines of a disagreement which was destined to cause much controversy. Indeed, what would become a controlling influence in the ultimate fate of his Georgia ministry appears in the journal as early as 14th March 1736, when "having before given notice of my design to do so every Sunday and Holy Day, according to the rules of our Church, I administered the holy communion to eighteen persons."[25] Wesley had already baptized his first native Georgian "according to the custom of the first church and the rule of the Church of England — by immersion."[26] Those few lines hold so much of what already happened in the life of the Church, and also of what was to come. They show us, for example, that the congregation in Savannah was sent a young priest zealously determined to observe every letter of the law of the Church of England. Even when the custom of the day differed sharply from the letter, as in Baptism, and even in the face of strong parental opposition, Wesley would make his point.

> *I was asked to baptise a child of Mr. Parker's, second bailiff of Savannah, but Mrs. Parker told me, "Neither Mr. Parker or I will consent to its being dipped." I answered, "If you certify that your child is weak, it will suffice." [the rubic says] "to pour water upon it." She replied, "Nay, the child is not weak; but I am resolved it shall not be dipped." This argument I could not confute. So I went home, and the child was baptized by another person.*[27]

This very literalism in interpreting and enforcing the rubrics and "apostolic constitutions" of the early church, as he understood them, lay beneath much of the unhappiness that surrounded Wesley's later ministry in Savannah. His opponents accused him of practising confession, penance, mortification, mixing wine with water in communion, etc., to support their suspicion.[28] They feared he was a "closet papist" of some sort. His turning one communicant away from the communion table because she had not given proper notice of her intent to receive, as the rubrics and Wesley required, tended to confirm all suspicions.[29]

Incidents such as these should remind us also that the congregation of the "church at Savannah" was typical of the 18th century in its mixture of people and beliefs — a diversity inherent in its being part of an established Church. Even its modern descendants might be surprised at such diversity. The range of devotion from zealous and disciplined to lackadaisical will surprise no one. That the "congregation" technically included many who shared little or none of the official belief of the established Church is, if not unprecedented, nevertheless unexpected. But that it also included those openly opposed in belief may indeed be surprising. This difference must be held in mind if the voices that speak to us from the early years are to make any sense, yet it is never spoken of directly, because it is surprising only to us. To the founders of the congregation it was routine and habitual, never having known any other way. To discover the reason we must remember that the

The New World paradise as it appeared in the minds of some early promoters and in a Georgia advertisement of 1733. Mr. Martyn was secretary to the Trustees, but along with many other supporters he seems to have entertained some rather unrealistic notions of their colony's true situation.

Church of England had become strongly identified with particular political and social views and parties in the era of controversy that immediately preceded the founding of Georgia. Indeed, advocacy of Anglican Churchmanship was taken to be sure proof of one's party affiliation, and party feelings ran high — high enough to break into civil war and revolution twice within living memory! This is one reason why, astonishing as it may sound, it did not occur to most people, did not seem acceptable or possible simply to become "inactive" in the life of the established Church and instead devote attention to their own Presbyterian or Baptist congregation. Even after the founding of other denominational congregations, their members were "involved" in the established Church, willy nilly, by law. Since ignoring it was therefore impossible, their inclination was to try influencing the style of the establishment in directions they found more compatible.

With these things in mind, it is easier to appreciate why each action of a missionary priest such as John Wesley brought such intense reactions both positive and negative. Even though the Church of England was not actually "established" in the colony, when Wesley "began dividing the public prayers according to the original appointment of the Church (still observed in a few places in England)", or began holding Sunday Morning Service at 5:00 A.M., Communion Office (and service) at 11:00 and Evening Service at 3:00 P.M.,[30] it is easy to imagine parishioners reading into those actions party views and positions about which they felt strongly. Had they chosen quietly to "retire" from the life of the established Church they would soon have heard a knock at the door when "I began visiting my parishioners in order, from house to house, for which I set apart from 12 to 3 in the afternoon (the time when they cannot work because of the heat)."[31] Diligence is so admirable if one approves of what is being done, but if not . . . .

The diversity of the parish was not only in its range of opinion about the Church of England, but also in its linguistic or broader cultural make-up. Wesley's thoughts, as recorded in his *Journal*, once again are helpful in bringing to mind a point we are likely to overlook or to weaken considerably. We might well miss, for example, the degree to which the rector of the Church at Savannah, would feel responsibility for all within the parish. This comes home as Wesley comments that he "began learning Spanish in order to converse with my Jewish parishioners." As he did the Salzburgers and Moravians, he admired greatly these Sephardim, "some of whom seem nearer the mind that was in Christ than many of those who call him Lord."[33]

Finally, the diversity of the parish was geographical, too. At one point, writing back to England, Wesley agonized at how a parish "above 200 miles in length laughs at the labour of one man!"[33a] Nevertheless, he and other early rectors journeyed to the outlying villages such as Highgate and Hampstead (4-5 miles SW of the town) and Vernonburgh and Acton (10-12 miles to the South) in order to read public prayers and counsel the French, German and Swiss settlers there.[34] What began there as occasional readings developed before long into a major enterprise as the need was more clearly recognized. One day, recalls Wesley, "being at Highgate, consisting (all but one) of French families, . . . I offered to read prayers there in French every Saturday afternoon. They embraced the offer gladly." The following week "I read prayers likewise to the German villagers at Hampstead . . . and so continued to do so once a week." As Wesley described them, the services were simple, probably of necessity. "We began the service with singing a Psalm. Then I read and explained a chapter in the French or German Testament, and concluded with prayers and another Psalm." Jobs well done, however, or needs well met have a way of growing. Some of the French who heard prayers at Highgate urged him to do the same in Savannah where there were many who knew little English. One Sunday "I began to do so, and I now had a full employment for that holy day." Pieced together, the rector of the "Church of Savannah" had a day that went like this:

5:00-6:30 English Prayers
9:00-10:00 Italian Prayers [. . ."read to a few Veaudois"]
10:30-12:30 English Communion and Service
1:00-2:00 French Prayers
2:00-3:00 Catechism of children
3:00-4:00 English Prayers

At 4:00 were joined together "as many as my largest room would hold in reading prayer and singing praise". Surely it was with some relief that he then was free to join the Moravians at 6:00 "Where I was glad to be present not as a teacher, but as a learner."[35]

Rectors of the Church in Savannah also felt both responsibility and a considerable curiosity to visit the more remote settlements at Abercorn, Ebenezer, and Frederica.[36] Comments on Ebenezer are universally positive. Only a year after its founding, for instance, Wesley visited the new Ebenezer with August Gottlieb Spangenberg, a well known international leader of the Salzburgers. He was amazed at what he saw: some sixty "huts", plantations laid out, and indian corn planted and flourishing in the main street that was presently wider than needed.[37] Frederica, on the other hand, had a very different reputation. Early rectors made the trip with some frequency, and much trepidation. John Wesley went usually on some special mission for Mr. Oglethorpe or to rescue his brother Charles from quarrels or other tangles at the outpost.[38] Those are fascinating stories of independent interest. The point in raising the subject here is simply to offer something comprehensible about the definition of parish responsibility as understood during the early years. That definition is given greater value when it is realized that the journey then required several days, perhaps as much as a week, of sailing, rowing, and pushing through the coastal marshes and channels, each way! Rather typical of such adventures is the one recounted by Wesley for 4th-10th April, 1736.

Having set out about 4 PM in a "pettiawga", the first night they anchored at Skidaway . . wrapped self in a cloak from head to foot to keep off the sand flies and lay down on the quarter deck. Between 1 and 2 I waked under water, being so fast asleep that I did not find where I was till my mouth was full of it. Having left my cloak, I know not how, upon deck, I swam round to the outside of the pettiawga, where a boat was tied and climbed up by the rope without any hurt, more than wetting my clothes.[39]

Trips such as this one also taught him the untruthfulness of some of the superstitions commonly circulated in Europe regarding life in the colonies.

In walking to Thunderbolt I was in so heavy a shower that all my clothes were as wet as if I had gone thru the river . . . [casting doubt on the] vulgar error concerning the hurtfulness of the rains and dews of America. I have been thoroughly wet with these rains more than once yet without any harm at all. And I have lain many nights in the open air, and received all the dews that fell, and so, I believe might anyone, if his constitution was not impaired by the softness of a genteel education.[40]

Occasionally, duty also might take one to Charleston as it did Wesley once in attempt to close a "marriage factory" being run by "one in Carolina who had married several of my parishioners without either banns or license, and declared he would [continue]."[41] Certainly the diversity and extent of the Georgia territory and the inherent hardships of frontier living have much to do with the rather labored quality that seems to characterize the early years of the Savannah Church. It is equally certain that the unprosperous beginning of the colony, the distressed recent history of the established Church of England, and the accidental circumstances that made for a series of short rectorships all further contributed to the situation. But one cannot escape the feeling, regarding at least those factors directly concerning the Church in Savannah, that they are symptoms as much as they are causes. Fundamentally, the cause appears to be that the Trustees, their chief executive figure, Mr. Oglethorpe, and the missionaries they sent to Georgia never reached a full understanding on what was to be accomplished by the mission. This may have been close to impossible in view of the controversy at that time complicating the relations of Anglicans and Dissenters — relations which were soon to be further confused by the emergence of the Methodist movement within the Church of England. Not only was opinion divided, it looks as though the matter was never openly discussed at all.

To begin with, no statements from the Trustees stating their expectations or purposes have surfaced. In their place are numerous signs of unresolved differences of view. Once again the more generous historical sources relating to Wesley show the matter with some clarity. For instance, when the brothers prepared to depart from England, Egmont described the team thus: "Mr. John Wesley in priest's orders, and Charles Wesley his brother in deacon's orders, who is to be minister at Savannah whilst his older brother (i.e. John) endeavors to convert the Indians."[42] This was substantially in accord with the Wesley's own wishes in the matter and distinctly contrary to the Trustees purposes apparently. No matter, for once in the new world Charles was settled at St. Simon's to mix the duties of pastor and Oglethorpe's "Secretary for Indian Affairs" while John was directed to care for the flock in Savannah. Oglethorpe understandably felt that the need was in the town itself, and aparently the Trustees agreed — or at least some of them did. Several weeks later John was still expectant, but "not finding, as yet, any door open for the pursuing of our main design, we considered in what manner we might be most useful to the little flock at Savannah."[44]

Certainly John did not think his primary mission was to serve in Savannah, yet it only very slowly dawned on him that Oglethorpe did. Months later, still waiting, he thought that finally

a door was opened for going up to the Choctaws, the least polished, . . . least corrupted of all the Indian nations. But upon my informing Mr. Oglethorpe of our design, he objected, not only the danger of being intercepted or killed by the French there, but much more, the inexpedience of leaving Savannah destitute of a minister.

Discussion with his associates produced the unhappy conclusion that "we ought not to go yet."[45] Yet opportunity would not knock forever. Tomochichi's touching lamentation to Wesley a few weeks before had made this uncomfortably clear.

When I was in England, I desired that some would speak the Great Word to me; and my nation then desired to hear it. But since that time we have all been put into confusion. The French have built a fort with a hundred men in it. . . . and the Spaniards are preparing war. The English traders too put us into confusion and have set our people against hearing the Great Word. For they speak with a double tongue."[45a]

Fortunately, even though Wesley was unable to reach the Indians, as he had hoped, occasionally they came to him, or at least to Savannah, where he had some further opportunity to talk with them.[46] The result of such "appetizers" was not satisfaction, however, but renewed conviction as to the validity of his original motive in coming to Georgia, and heightened anxiety at the frustration of it. Toward the end of Wesley's first year the problem finally came into the open when

Mr. Oglethorpe sailed for England leaving Mr. Ingham, Mr. Delamotte and me at Savannah, but with less prospect of preaching to the Indians than we had the first day we set foot in America. Whenever I mentioned [the matter], it was immediately replied, "you cannot leave Savannah without a minister." To this . . . my answer was . . "I never promised to stay here one month," "I openly declared both before, at, and ever since my coming hither that I neither would nor could take charge of the English any longer than

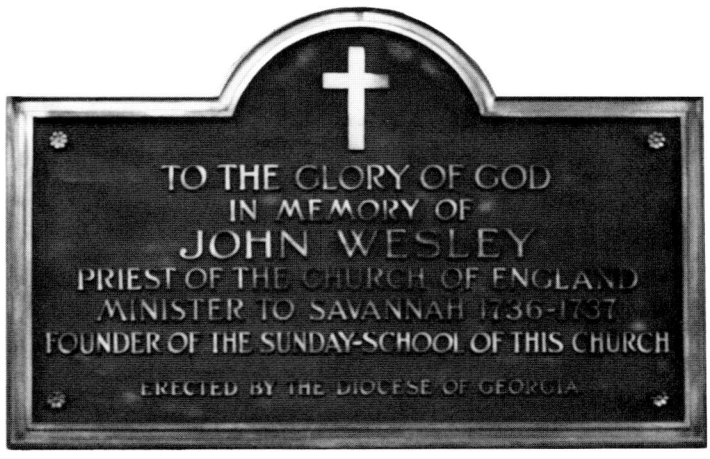

Although presented in this engraving some time after leaving Savannah, John Wesley's missionary tenacity and at times stubborn determination to fulfill what he earnestly believed to be his duty still show with striking clarity. The bronze plaque which commerates Wesley's work in the parish is located on the west porch of the Church.

till I could go among the Indians." "But did not the Trustees of Georgia appoint you to be minister of Savannah?" "They did . . . but it was done without either my desire or knowledge."[47]

The point in airing the problem here is simply that it sheds helpful light on the rather unhappy scene that one sees in examining the early years of the Church in Georgia. What we see through Wesley's letters, journals, etc. is probably not his difficulty only. It is years of difficulties that are attributable to poor communication, unreconciled or even unrecognized differences of purpose, as much as to the expected burdens of a frontier. How much more of what appears to be negligence by clergy, or brittle churchmanship, quarrelsomeness and sectarianism among parishioners should be attributed to the same causes? Certainly most of these weaknesses were present, but were they so general as sometimes appears?

What neither Oglethorpe nor the Trustees generally understood was the full reason Wesley wanted so much to preach to the Indians, and why he felt so deeply the deprivation of opportunity. He has already told us that his chief motive in going was "the hope of saving his own soul", but no mention has been made of how he envisioned this would happen. In fact, as Wesley saw the matter, the Indians were absolutely essential if his hope was to be realized. The clue is in a letter to a close confidant, dated just prior to his embarking for Georgia, which reveals

> *I hope to learn the true sense of the gospel of Christ by preaching it to the heathen. They have no comments to construe away the text; no vain philosophy to corrupt it; no luxurious, sensual, covetous, ambitious expounders to soften its unpleasing truths. . . They are as little children, humble, willing to learn and eager to do the will of God; and consequently they shall know of every doctrine I preach whether it be of God. By those [people], therefore, I hope to learn the priority of that faith once delivered to the saints, the genuine sense and full extent of those laws which none can understand who mind earthly things.*[48]

What emerges clearly here is an increasingly popular eighteenth century concept that man as a creature was naturally pure and good, but that civilization and its sophisticated ways were corrupt and corrupting. The opportunity to speak with pure uncorrupted humanity, "noble savages" European popular thought would later style them, was quite literally, the chance of a lifetime. For Wesley felt that in his corrupt condition he knew the words but did not truly sense the meaning of the gospel. Indeed, to him it meant the difference between life and death — eternal life and death!

While the details of Wesley's motivation have their own intrinsic interest, they also have a more general significance. They offer us the belated comfort, for instance, that 20th century folk are not the only ones with illusions about the southern life style — the 18th century had some too! More seriously, we are forced to ask to what degree the illusions, not only of Wesley and the other missionaries, but also of Oglethorpe, the Trustees, and their colonialist contemporaries in general, may account for the inauspicious early record of the Church in Savannah and the colony. Whatever the full story,[49] the jottings Wesley made in his journal on leaving Georgia somehow describe the mood that story creates, much more even than his individual experience.

> *I clearly saw the hour was come for leaving this place; and as soon as evening prayers were over, about 8 o'clock, the tide then serving, I shook off the dust from my feet and left Georgia after having preached the Gospel there (not as I ought but as I was able)*[50]

Reviews of Wesley's work in the colony were quite mixed, as could easily have been predicted. There was complaint that he "drenched them with the physick of an intolerant discipline."[50a] Fortunately, to balance the opinion of those who found him too brittle, there were others who saw positive outcome from his labors. His brother Charles, not surprisingly, was an admirer. When he returned to England later in 1736, Charles reported to the Trustees that although John's predecessor, Quincy, had miserably neglected the people, his brother had greatly improved the spiritual condition of the congregation and the practice of the town. In only a few months, he had brought them from a condition wherein only three took communion when he arrived to one which now had full assemblies, twice daily public prayers, and forty communicants.[51]

The fullest treatment of the matter is given by Mr. Garden in a letter to the Bishop of London. First he explained his surprise at the turn of events that precipitated Wesley's sudden departure, "for no one could be more approved of, or better reported of, by all the people of Georgia than this very gentleman was, till lately, that he presumed to repell the chief magistrate's niece from the Holy Communion." Then he itemized the complaints against Mr. Wesley, often inserting his own editorial comments in the process — Wesley's antagonists had labeled him "a setter forth of strange doctrine, a Jesuit, a spiritual tyrant, a mover of sedition, etc." The Grand Jury summoned to hear the case presented the following against Wesley:

1. *not having sufficiently declared himself of the Church of England;*
2. *refusing to christen otherwise than by dipping (except as in the Rubric excepted);*
3. *saying that he was ordinary in Georgia;*
4. *refusing to bury an Anabaptist (when he was at 100 miles distance and knew nothing of the matter);*
5. *reading the Litany at 6 and not at 10 o'clock on Litany Days; but above all for*
6. *repelling Mr. Williamson's niece, and for speaking and writing to her (on matters, he assures me, of his duty as her pastor) contrary to the commands of her husband."*

All but the last of these Mr. Garden regarded as "either impertinent, false, or frivolous," and nothing more than an "apparatus . . . to accummulate the accusation." On the final accusation, however, Wesley "may not be acquitted of some imprudence and unguarded conduct. Yet I verily believe him to be innocent of anything criminal, either in fact or intention." Closing his letter, Mr. Garden became more broadly reflective and offered his observation that "this gentlemen has met with full as hard usage as did his predecessor, Mr. Quincy, and it will be Pitty if any more clergymen be sent thither till your lordship's jurisdiction be . . . regularly extended to that colony, that they may not be obliged to cross the seas on every complaint made against them."[51.1] A year and a half later George Whitefield, too, praised his work.

> *Surely I must labor heartily since I come after such worthy predecessors. The good Mr. Wesley has done in America under God is inexpressible; and he has laid such a foundation that I hope neither men nor devils will ever be able to shake. Oh, that I may follow him as he has Christ!*[52]

Even the London *Times*, already known by its cautious approach to matters, in its obituary summary of his work described Wesley as "having done infinite good to the lower class of people." The *Times* then went on to assert that "as a man and as a writer he must be considered as one of the most extraordinary characters this or any age has produced."[53]

His successor in Savannah was to prove no less controversial. George Whitefield was much more likely to offend by his free interpretation of tradition than by sticking over-much to the letter of it. He also drew both admiration and condemnation for his constant travel, itinerating at a rate virtually unmatched in its time. At his first appearance in Georgia, however, in the Spring of 1738, he was only 23 years old, virtually unknown, and kept busy enough at home — having been assigned to serve as deacon at Savannah and Frederica until a replacement could be found for Mr. Wesley at Savannah.[54] Egmont reported the Trustees' pleasure in having secured his services and expressed their confidence in his ability to handle the spirit of dissention among the people.[55] The Trustees were especially anxious that matters not be neglected during Whitefield's required absences, however, and urged the people "not to absent themselves on Sundays, but to assemble together and cause prayers to be read to the people by some decent person who can read."[56] Whitefield began those prayers himself, with an exposition of the second lesson, at five in the morning to 17 adults and 25 children.[57]

Help was on the way, for the Trustees received word that the Primate of Ireland had discovered another volunteer for Georgia, and they urged that the Bishop of London "expedite his several ordinations with all convenient speed."[58] By August, 1738, Mr. William Norris set sail aboard the *Two Brothers*, a frequent caller at the port; he arrived in October.[59] No sooner were the new clergy in place than controversy and factionalism began to emerge once again. Whitefield and

Norris seem to be objects caught up in the quarrelling winds of the storm more than they are subjects who are driving them along. One is tempted to the conclusion that the factions were pre-established. All that remained to be done was to choose the field of battle and the issue. New personalities might affect the ammunition used but do little to alter the enmity or the sides. William Stephens saw the problem as a growing wish to discredit Norris in order that Whitefield might shine more brightly, at least in the minds of his followers.[60] The discreditors worked fast, too! Within days after reaching Savannah, it was already accepted as fact, way up river in Ebenezer, that Mr. Norris "does not have the spirit or the gifts of Mr. Whitefield . . . and he preaches very insipidly."[60a] Whitefield himself immediately departed for London to seek from the Trustees the commission which Norris already possessed.[61] then, quickly tiring of the lull while Whitefield was in England, his followers next accused Mr. Norris of scandalous conduct with a maid-servant. The story was, in Stephen's words, "industriously reported in several places without the least show of any foundation."[62] Whether the maid-servant was a cause or merely a casualty in the incident is unclear for a hearing determined Mr. Norris' innocence and ordered her to be whipped publicly — "a punishment she had tasted before", says Stephens. Our best glimpse of Mr. Norris is found in his response to the situation. Instead of allowing her to be whipped, he chose to accept such satisfaction as she could make by confessing her fault before the congregation and asking God's forgiveness.[63]

When Whitefield finaly returned to Georgia, the two men met and Whitefield presented his new credentials. Norris immediately deferred and promised no controversy "to the disappointment of some . . . who are pleased best with contention."[64] Further confounding those so pleased, Whitefield asked Norris to preside at Savannah during his expected absences; but Norris thought better of it, pointing out that his charge from the Trustees was now for Frederica.[65] Relations between the clerical rivals were not destined to remain so stiffly proper for long, however. Whitefield soon accused Norris of being "at work for the Devil, and capable of doing more harm than immoral livers." Indeed, in Whitefield's view, Norris *was* immoral since he "played on the Fiddle, and at cards with the Ladies, and kept polite Company." Furthermore, declared Whitefield, although Norris had twice assisted him in the Sacrament he would never again, "or receive it at his hands."[65a]

With their relationship at such a point as this, perhaps it was better that the whole question soon lost its importance. Whitefield hoped to be off on his travels again and apparently so notified the Trustees. By July they had procured the services of Mr. William Metcalf to replace Whitefield and were only waiting passage for the new incumbent to complete the change.[66] Several factors combined to frustrate the planned transition as it turned out. Simultaneously, rising controversy over the state of the colony led to an extensive review by the Trustees. This presents us with a unique opportunity to assess, with them, the state of the "Church at Savannah".

Along with his own reasons for desiring the change, Whitefield gives us some hint as to the concern which may have motivated the Trustees via a departing note in his *Journal*,

In the evening, I preached at Savannah, and took my final leave of the people, it being inconsistent with my other affairs to act as their pastor anymore. Another minister is not yet come, but one is expected daily. I gave the Trustees notice in January last of my design to give up the parsonage (i.e. the position) . . . I yet hope well of Georgia, though at present it is in a very declining and piteous state. It will flourish, I believe, when settled upon a religious foundation. Till then . . .[67]

Mr. Norris, too, had ideas about what was disturbing the health of the congregation and the town, and was good enough to tell us his thoughts in some detail. The disagreement may have distressed contemporaries but it is something of a gift to us. For in airing their viewpoints the principals tell us more of their daily practice than we learn through any other source. Mr. Norris recalls that when he arrived, the Church retained "little more than the titles of her most excellent institutions." Specifically, his complaint was that services commonly omitted the exhortation, absolution, Psalms, and even the first lesson, and that they abbreviated the collects, prayers for the royal family, etc.[68] Adding to the problem he felt were the hours at which services were held, so "unreasonable and disagreeable" as to prevent frequency and to encourage neglect. Whether the people at Highgate and Hampstead are the ones he had in mind when making this point we can only guess but they certainly seem to justify it to a degree. He found them so "unacquainted with our form of worship" they knew not even where to join with the minister! Moreover, they had not communicated, despite professing the faith and articles of the Church of England, for two years, having ever been excluded from it by Mr. Wesley. For all of that they had by this time erected a tabernacle, and have twelve children "more or less instructed".[69]

He also perceived what he described as a "spiritual pride" in previous pastors, whom he does not identify, "making principles of their delusions", and thus giving offense to many.[70] Egmont, too, had expressed similar thoughts, describing recent clergy (Wesley?) as "pious and zealous". He was especialy troubled by one trait he saw: "whatever they deliberate on and resolve, they fancy to be a motion of the Holy Spirit."[71]

As far as Mr. Norris was concerned, perhaps the most threatening manifestation of the spiritual pride he saw in his Savannah congregation was a "separate night assembly . . . at the Minister's House, which made up a communion of saints . . . distinguished by the name of the faithful". Such a practice invited two responses as he saw it: an abhorence of such "enthusiasm" which he feared had led some to contempt for all religion, or a spiritual pride which would surely consume the "faithful". Thus he summarizes, in a neat homiletical twist, "the one quite loses all devotion, and the other is quite lost in it . . . [and] religion [is] split on the very rock on which it was to be founded."[72] In his fears and observations, we can recognize both the eighteenth century phobia for "enthusiasm" and a distinctly Wesleyan style in the little "society" meeting at the minister's house. Such meetings were to become the trademark of the new movement which would shortly spring from Wesley.[73] Some of what Mr. Norris meant by neglect must surely be charged to his colleague, Mr. Whitefield, and his irrepressible urge to itinerate. It caused William Stephens to lament that on Good Friday and Easter (1740), for example, there was nothing at all at the Church, Mr. Whitefield "again being away". The distress he felt obviously goes deeper, however, than a simple absence would produce. True, the neglect is compounded since it was the rector's responsibility to see that his place was duly filled by another clergymen or the services read by a literate and exemplary layman. But Stephens' reflection in his journal reveals yet other facets visible in his view of the problem.

It is a sad truth that this place had little piety . . . yet it is to be hoped there may be some well-meaning persons in it who find comfort in frequenting the Church and joining in the public service when duly performed, [and] that are equally grieved when they see the liturgy mangled and giving way to — we know not what next.[74]

One wonders at times whether the spiritual life of the community may have been seized by something akin to the ailment that frequently gripped colonial digestion, what one resident described as "an American distemper called the 'dry gripes', which very few die of though some are severly dealt with in it . . ." In the current condition of the colony, however, Oglethorpe and the Trustees found little humor. For his part, the General was beginning to suspect that "the mutinous temper at Savannah shows itself to be fomented by the Spaniards."[74.1] But sworn testimony taken in the course of their inquest led the Trustees to a different theory of its cause. Most noteworthy here, the testimony included an almost poetic sketch of the frustration and disappointment that seemed to characterize the local mood. After listing the major public buildings it goes on to describe "a public garden of ten acres cleared, fenced, and planted with orange trees, mulberry-trees, vines, some olives, which thrive very well, peaches, apples, etc."[75] But the statement continues by admitting

It must be confessed that oranges have not so universally thriven . . . by reason of some severed blasts by frosts in spring.

The witness still had hope, however. "Because they do flourish to the north in Carolina, therefore, success is expected with further knowledge and experience.[76] Alas, subsequent comments make it too clear what "not thriving" actually meant: an irreversible debilitation from freezing back to ground-level nearly every year, revivifying in the spring only to face the same harsh pruning the following winter, until the plants finally lost their vitality altogether. The olives suffered also, for though the trees appeared to flourish, the fruit dropped prematurely each year for no reason that could be discovered. Thus despite the zealous effort of some, and the heroic tenacity of many, and even in spite of the grand idealism of the charter, the early years of the Church in Savannah and the colony around it became a lengthy and wearisome vigil . . . waiting for the seed to bear fruit — not unlike the wait for the orange trees and the olives. It was not that they were fools who had set them there, nor that they had planted mock-oranges or bitter olives which could never bear edible fruit. Yet somehow, they seemed not well conceived to bear good fruit in the place where they were set.

In a way, it is surprising that we are left so little information about public worship in the early days. Normally it was discussed only when a clergyman or practice became controversial, or a natural disaster provided occasion to offer details about the suitability of a structure considered for use. Otherwise, we get our information only through oblique references. Perhaps this is so because Anglican worship was such public knowledge and the currently used *Book of Common Prayer* (1662) so familiar to every Briton, even those in whom that familiarity bred contempt. Comment on unique sectarian practices would have been a different matter, but there was probably little that seemed noteworthy in the common practice of the Church of England. Most of what we can see through the records is similar in nature to Whitefield's description of his success when the courthouse was still the site of public worship. "The Courthouse is generally full, and I keep as near as possible to my old way of proceeding. We have the Sacrament every Sunday, and public prayer and exposition twice everyday in the week."[77] The same coin, viewed on its reverse side, is visible in William Stephens' journal. There he expresses his hope for better things to come since

. . . we might once again expect a regular divine of the church of England to be soon with us, whom the honorable Trustees had provided to succeed Mr. Whitefield . . . which occasions much joy and comfort to true lovers of the Church here. [They] have been at a great strait for a long while, not well knowing how to behave under such torrent of enthusiasm and strange doctrine brought among us by sectaries of diverse sorts. [Meanwhile] the liturgy in most parts of its several offices has been either curtailed, mangled, or omitted; the Psalms and ordinary lessons appointed have been disregarded to make room for extemporaneous expositions on any part of Holy Scripture which the expositor liked better for his purpose. Surplice, gown, cassock, and all such innocent decencies have been thrown aside as useless or worse . . .

"Worse," in this case, Stephens finds it impossible to leave unspoken, means that clergy have been maligned, *"by name, from this pulpit."*[78] It could also have been new fangled

The youthful Whitefield as he looked about the time of his arrival in Savannah. His popularity and reputation for eloquence grew very rapidly despite his inexperience and less-than-handsome physical appearance. He must, indeed, have been something to hear! The plaque is located on the Church's west portico.

"spiritual songs" used with the new-mangled liturgy that distressed him, for when Wesley published his *Collection of Psalms and Hymns* in 1737 it represented a major break with Anglican tradition.[79] The seventy texts, several of which are still in use, are all either metrical versions of Psalms or strongly Biblical in theme. Some of them may well have been the hymns Wesley recalls translating from the German while making his pastoral rounds or on his way to Thunderbolt.[79a] Yet the normal pattern for congregational music required a cantor to lead the worshippers in their Psalm-singing. In the 1740's, for example, we catch a glimpse of "a young lad", appointed by colonial authorities "to set the Psalm tunes in Divine Service for which he was allowed Ten Shillings a Quarter during the absence of Thomas Lee."[79b] Perhaps Wesley's deviation from traditional treatment of the Psalms, or his German chorales and texts were thought too susceptible to enthusiastic abuse. He was, as Pastor Bolzius observed,

> *a great enthusiast for good German songs, of which he . . . learned quite a number with their melodies; and he . . . translated some of these into English and had them printed in Charlestown, together with some psalms that had been done into English verse.*[79c]

For whatever reason, the songs did in fact upset many and thus stood high on the list of "offences" charged against Wesley.[80]

More probably, however, it was "irregularities" in vestments and liturgical usage that grated so. In this regard the real offender in Stephens' eyes was Whitefield, who "since his return this time thought fit to make use of the surplice again, that has some time before been laid aside by him."[81] But Stephens could never take more than cautious pleasure in anything agreeable in the preacher. Between Whitefield's Calvinist theology and his Methodist practice Stephens seemed always to fear "what next!" The disappointments were seldom unbearable, but felt keenly nevertheless, as on Christmas Day, 1740, when

> *Mr. Doble read the accustomed service of the day and a sermon after it; whilst Mr. Whitefield staid with his family at Bethesda, the better to avoid (as some thought) making any distinction of days.*[82]

A few days later the enthusiastic side of Whitefield broke loose when

> *in the evening he began the Common Service of the Church, then read the second lesson and so proceeded to give the congregation a lecture, off hand, on those topicks which he was always fond of concerning Election, Reprobations, etc . . . that . . . we were all in a State of Damnation.*

Stephens' recollection of the occasion continued at length to describe the tears Whitefield drew from himself and the congregation, and how at one point he laid aside the *Book of Common Prayer* and "fell into a long *ex tempore* prayer of his own, full of Flatus and Enthusiasm and uttered with a Stentor's voice."[83]

Even after five years, when Whitefield once again sought permission to preach to the congregation during a visit to town, Stephens found the prospect most unappetizing. He finally agreed, but only after extracting the preacher's promise that he would conform to the *Book of Common Prayer* and not use the occasion as a "handle for contention".[83a]

These reflections, however unflattering, have a double value for us. They give us a chance to view common practice of the day through its exceptions; they also give us some basis for treating the question of how typical was Stephens' reaction? Our answer to the latter will much affect our diagnosis of the less than flourishing state of the Church in Savannah.

A few months, later heavy rains precipitated remarks of great interest from the same author. They describe in detail the courthouse setting in which these spiritual calamities and much of congregational and community life took place.

The body of the House is one entire building, formed in the inside commodiously, with benches of different sorts, but only one distinguished from the rest in degree, beneath which stands a table — both of equal use for sacred purposes or civil. This was built in the year 1736, and soon after there was added to it a cloister or colonade encompassing the front and both ends of the house which was not only ornamental, but very useful likewise in breaking off the violence of the weather, more especially the heats which otherwise did beat so strong upon the house (being all built of timber) that when a number of people were in it, twas hardly to be born. This portico, so added, had only a flat roof which joyned the other a little above the eaves; but after so long a time, wherein . . . finding nothing sufficient to keep out the rains, (there was) apparent danger of the whole going to ruin. Upon due consultation . . . it was thought most adviseable to make a new roof for the whole, wide enough to span it all even to the extent of the colonade and enclosing the roof of the house, which work . . . is now in hand.[84]

Fortunately, there are a few exceptions to the rule that only storms of nature or of controversy brought much comment on common practice. From the beginning the records afford us tantalizing glimpses of common usage, often through acknowledgement of donations or almost accidental references. One of the first type occurred through thanks given Mr. Samuel Wesley for "a Pewter Chalice and Pattine for . . . use in Georgia until silver ones were had."[85] Another is a "candle branch given for use in devine worship" which received mention only because for some reason it had not been put into use and the Trustees wanted to know why.[86] Does its disuse tell us more than the giving of it? No answer is readily discernible, but happily there are a few more generous descriptions of the *Book of Common Prayer* (1662) in action.

George Whitefield recorded in 1740 that the congregation "buried this evening one of the women . . . The orphans sang before the corpse, from our house to the courthouse, where I preached and afterwards gave another word of exhortation" at the grave.[87] Curiosity wonders whether this represents widespread usage among Anglicans of the day or may itself be the "mangling" Mr. Stephens so lamented . . . , but again, there are no easy answers in sight. Stephens, however, tells us a good bit more in noting the activities of Easter Day, 1744: in the morning, Mr. Thomas Bosomworth, now the rector of a growing congregation, preached a sermon suitable for the day, on the Resurrection, and administered the sacrament to twenty or more. In the afternoon, after the prayers, he preached another sermon likewise adapted to the day as a *"Festival on the Incarnation of our Blessed Savior."*[88]

'Twas observed by some out of curiosity . . that his congregation consisted of a hundred or more, which was indeed surprizing, the like not having been seen in a long while (all English). . . . Considering how many dissent from us it could hardly have been expected besides too many to their shame rarely go to any public worship.[89]

Easter was more than a one day celebration, however. Its function as a popular spring festival in the British tradition was apparently quite well established by this time. Indeed, it is again Stephens who tells us so in noting the activities of an Eastern Monday.

Our common people never failed of punctually observing Easter holy days. [It was] beyond my imagination such a number of people could be put together any where except at St. Simon's in the province of Georgia as I saw this day at Savannah — men, women, and chidren of all ages and inspite of all obstacles . . . Diverse sports, cricket, and the like, was mostly the employment of the day.[90]

On a more mundane level, modern descendants of these Easter celebrants will be warmed to learn that even in this changing world, some of the lesser feasts were properly kept. Wesley's Journal for February of 1738 makes the point, for in addition to recording the events of that day, he recalls that it is also "the anniversary festival in Georgia for Mr. Oglethorpe's landing there."[91] Even more important than "Georgia Day" to the royalists among us, however, may be the evidence that colonial priorities were in proper order and that the hardships of a frontier had not seriously warped their perspective. This time it is William Stephens who provides the insight by noting in his *Journal* under 11th June (1744), "this being the anniversary of His Majestey's accession . . the occasion was marked with due solemnity." Ceremonies centered around the flag and included the militia under arms, a muster and exercises, the firing of the great guns in "three handsome vollies" then "all drank in ranks two or three glasses of wine each to the King's, the Royal Family's, the Trustees', and the General's healths!" Finally, "in the evening, Mr. Bosomworth called the congregation to church and read the public service appointed for the day."[92]

From the first some of the efforts of the Church at Savannah were directed toward a fairly broadly conceived idea of public service. Education and general reading were special matters of concern, and that meant books. On the founders' ship itself, the *Anne*, and on at least four succeeding ones during the six months that followed its arrival, books donated from all over the Kingdom came right along with the colonists and their possessions. Trustees' records note a great variety of generous philanthropies, parish collections, and individual copies from sources both named and nameless.

Typical was the order by the "Associates of Dr. Bray" "that a library shall be sent to Georgia for the use of the minister in the Town of Savannah as [soon as] the Trustees hear of the Rev. Mr. Quincy's arrival and settlement"[92a]

Along with the expected Bibles, Testaments, Book of Common Prayer and Psalms some real favorites emerge among the gifts which formed the core of the parish library. They include traditional "Hornbooks," primers, and spelling books, as well as such catechetical favorites as Lewis' *Catechism*, another known as *A, B, C, with the Church*; the *Young Instructed*, and the officially sponsored "Books of the Homilies". In addition, there are a number of titles frequently recurring in the lists of books collected which were apparently sent along for general family use. Typical among these were:

The [Whole] Duty of Man,
Bp. Gibson's *Family Devotion*,
Nelson's *Practice of Free Devotion*,
Guide to Christian Families,
The Great Importance of a Religious Life Considered, one known as the
Christian Monitor, with "Answers to Excuses" Annext, and the very handy
Two Hundred Friendly Admonitions to Drinkers of Brandy[93]

Yet no matter how generous the donations, useful books seem perpetually to have been in short supply. In correspondence between the early rectors and their London connections the need for more books is reiterated frequently, but never satisfied.[94] "Nine cases . . . containing the library of the late Dr. Crow to be added to the books in Georgia for composing a publick library"[95] helped, as did the tireless efforts of the "Associates of Dr. Bray," the SPG, and the Society for Promoting Christian Knowledge (SPCK). The books that were available, however, were not left idle. They were either distributed to families or put to use in school such as the one in which "Mr. Delamotte . . . has taken charge of between thirty and forty children." Writing to the SPG, Wesley described the work of teaching the children

to read, write and cast accounts. Before school in the morning and after school in the afternoon, he catechizes the lowest class . . . In the evening he instructs the larger children. On Saturday, in the afternoon, I catechize them all. The same I do on Sunday before the evening service. And in church, immediately after the second lesson, a select number of them having repeated the catechism and been examined in some part of it, I endeavor to explore at large, and enforce that part, both on them and the congregation.[96]

That work continued, apparently uninterrupted by personal conflict and controversy. Writing to the Trustees, Mr. Norris refers also to the "Public School of Savannah" which then had "forty boys which I catechize twice a week and every Sunday evening in Church using Lewis' Explanation."[97] Norris lingered to make the point more strongly: "These (Lewis' Explanations) with Books of Common Prayer and Bibles are much needed."

The reference to "forty boys" in the school raises the obvious question of the education of girls. Was there another school or were they neglected? Whitefield's *Journal* settles the question for us by a notation made just a few months before Mr. Norris' letter was written. In it Whitefield notes that he "opened a school today for the girls of Savannah, a friend whose heart God was pleased to touch on board the ship, having . . . undertaken to teach them"[98]

The school was but the first fruit of Whitefield's work in Savannah, however. When we hear his name we are more likely to think of Bethesda than anything else. This is properly so. When in Savannah Whitefield gave much of his energy to the orphan house project, even to the neglect of other duties at times, so vital a part of the ministry of the Church at Savannah did he consider it. Out of town it was just the same; for much of his itinerant preaching was devoted, materially at least, to the specific task of raising money for the project. The cause that literally became the center of his life for the next thirty years began as the dream of the Trustees, Charles Wesley, and Gen. Oglethorpe. Charles' own record appears to credit the Trustees for the idea, for it was they who "desired me to draw up a plan for an Orphan House."[99] Whitefield credits Wesley and Oglethorpe, who might well have sold the idea to the Trustees, but refuses credit for himself.

Some have thought that the erecting of [an orphange] was only the produce of my own brain, but they are much mistaken; for it was the first proposed to me by my dear friend, the Rev. Mr. Charles Wesley, who with his excellency Gen. Oglethorpe had concerted a scheme for carrying on such a design before I had any thoughts of going abroad myself.[100]

Regardless of its origin, the idea soon had broad backing from well placed people — Trustees, Archbishop of Canterbury and several other bishops, etc. — who were able to make it happen.[101] Whitefield's experience in Georgia, once he arrived, demonstrated the need for such a place beyond any doubt. Visiting the Franco-Swiss at the outlying villages of Highgate and Hampstead, for instance, he "found there were many who might prove useful members of the colony, if there were a proper place provided for their maintenance and education." Then, as if confirming the idea in his own mind, he adds: "Nothing can effect this but an Orphan House. . ."[102]

Once here, Whitefield had ready access to a successful example from which he hoped to learn. He journeyed to Ebenezer in the summer of 1738 where he was struck by the bounty he saw; and as preceding pilgrims had done, he also took note of the piety of their ministers. But, attracting special attention,

> *they likewise have an Orphan House, in which are seventeen children and one widow, and I was much delighted to see the regularity with which it is managed. Oh that God may stir up the hearts of His servants to contribute to that and another which we hope to have erected at Savannah.*[103]

Whitefield continued his efforts in the cause, taking a great step forward the next year, when during his travels, he

> *waited at noon upon the Honorable Trustees for Georgia. They received me with utmost civility, agreed to everything I asked, and gave a grant of five hundred acres of land to me and to my successors for ever, for the use of the Orphan House. My friend Habersham also writes me word today from Georgia that the General and officers are very kind to him on my acccount, so that there is a comfortable prospect of all things going on as I could wish.*[104]

His other activities that same day are so typical of Whitefield's style of doing all things, including the generation of funds for the project, that it is worth our while to follow him out to Kennington Common (near London). There he recalls,

> *after God had enabled me to preach to about twenty thousand, for above an hour. . . He inclined the hearers' hearts to contribute most cheerfully and liberally towards the Orphan House. I was one of the collectors, and it would have delighted anyone to have seen with what eagerness and cheerfulness the people gave their mites. Surely God must have touched their hearts. . . We found we had collected above £46, amongst them were £16 in halfpence.*[105]

A few days later on a similar occasion at Moorfields, he collected nearly £53 with over twenty of it in halfpence, so many "they almost wearied me in receiving their mites, and they were more than one man could carry home."

On this latter occasion Whitefield reports an incident which gives us a glimpse of the intense reaction differences in clerical style could arouse. Probably it tells us much of how strongly some Savannah churchmen felt about their clergy's behavior, too! It seems that one of his hearers muttered loudly in the crowd "how vile . . . is Mr. Whitefield!" Look at him "venting his enthusiastic ravings in a gown and cassock upon a common, and collecting mites from the poor people!"[106] But Whitefield knew his own mind, apparently, and remained undisturbed by such reactions. He merely appended a brief plea to the account in his journal. "If this is to be vile, Lord, grant that I may be more vile."[107]

Controversial or not, Whitefield could report to the Trustees when he met them that he had already collected over £700 in addition to annual subscriptions.[108] He collected even more before returning to the colony to take up the Orphan House project on this end. Early in the new year he could at last report that he "went this morning, with some friends to view a tract of land consisting of 300 acres, which Mr. Habersham, whom I left schoolmaster of Savannah, was directed (I hope by providence) to make choice of for the Orphan House." By the time Whitefield first viewed the land, some of it had already been cleared and Habersham had "also stocked it with cattle and poultry," built a hut and begun a fence.[109] Apparently, Whitefield had some say in its location, for he explains

> *I choose to have it so far off the town, because the children will be more free of bad examples, and can more conveniently go up on the land and work. For it is my design to have each of the children taught to labor so as to be qualified to get their own living. Lord, do Thou teach and excite them to labor for that meat which endureth to everlasting life!*[110]

A few days later, Whitefield expectantly took formal possession of the tract, calling it "Bethesda, that is, House of Mercy."[111] None too soon it was, either, for it seems he also had a talent for collecting orphans. The very next week he added three German children to the growing "family" he sheltered in his home, describing the new comers as "the most pitiful objects, I think, I ever saw."

> *They have been used to exceedingly hard labor, and though supplied with provisions from the Trustees, were treated in a manner unbecoming even heathens. Were all the money I have collected to be spent in freeing these three children from slavery, it would be well laid out. I have also in my house near twenty more, who . . . if not taken in, would be as ignorant of God and Christ as the Indians.*[112]

The orphan house was to be a school as much as a shelter and the plans for instructing the children were also moving ahead. One of the ways Whitefield hoped to accomplish this he noted in his journal the same day he wrote of the last three children.

> *This day I began the cotton manufacture, and agreed with a woman to teach the little ones to spin and card. I find annual cotton grows very well in Georgia; and to encourage the people, I bought today 300 lbs. weight, and have agreed to take all the cotton, hemp and flax that shall be produced the following year through the whole province.*[113]

Things went well enough that within a few months he could do more than fabricate grand hopes. He could claim accomplishments, *because the children are industrious. We have now in the house near 100 yards of cloth spun and woven. We have several tradesman belonging to the House, much cattle on our plantation, and I hope before long we shall live amongst ourselves. There are several masters set over the children, who watch over them both in and after school hours.*[114]

The hope expressed that they could soon "live amongst ourselves" was not an idle one either, for concurrent with the textile work the actual buildings for the "orphan house" were also progressing. Months before, Whitefield tells us, he

went with the carpenter and surveyor and laid out the ground whereon the Orphan Hosue is to be built. It is to be sixty feet long and forty feet wide. The foundation is to be brick, and is to bed sunk four feet within and raised three feet above the ground. The house is to be two stories high, with a hip roof: the first ten, the second nine feet high. In all there will be nearly twenty commodious rooms. Behind are to be two small houses, the one for an infirmary, the other for a work house. There is also to be a still-house for the apothecary; and I trust before my return to England I shall see the children and family quite settled.[115]

Another trip could not be far off for Whitefield's funds were running low and the goals were so worthy.

I find it will be an expensive work; but it is for the Lord Christ. He will take care to defray all charges. The money that will be spent . . . will keep many families from leaving the colony, and in all probability may bring many others over.[116]

Also the need was great and the time seemed right so that he saw no need for moderation in the matter.

There are nearly thirty working at the plantation already, and I would employ as many more if they were to be had. Whatsoever is done for God ought to be done speedily, as well as with all our might![117]

In the spring of 1740 actual construction was begun amid great expectation and an obvious need that seemed to grow daily as the project moved forward. Whitefield's jubilation is apparent as he wrote how he

went to Bethesda (25 March) and laid the first brick of the great house. The workmen attended, and with me kneeled down and prayed. After we had sung a hymn suitable to the occasion, I gave a word of exhortation to the laborers, and bid them remember to work heartily, knowing that they work for God . . . Nearly twenty acres of land are cleared and almost ready for planting. Two houses are already raised, and one nearly finished. All the timber of the great house is sawn, and most of it brought to the place where it is to be built. A good part of the foundation is dug and many thousands of bricks ready for use. Nearly forty children are now under my care, and nearly one hundred mouths are daily supplied with food from our store. The expense is great, but . . . as yet I am kept from the least doubting. And though what has been done hitherto . . . may be only like a grain of mustard seed, yet I believe it will, in God's good time, take root and fill the land, and many poor distressed souls will come and lodge under the branches of it . . .[118]

With its foundation, Bethesda increasingly assumed a life of its own, somewhat independent of the clergy and Church at Savannah. Before leaving the topic, however, we might enjoy one more surprise from the Rev. Mr. Whitefield. Despite his years of absorption in the "Orphan House" project, it is still difficult to tell how he really thought of Bethesda or conceived its primary mission. Perhaps the emphasis varied with the audience or it may be simply that he was always working on the next dream. In any case, on the occasion just cited he wrote to a friend "I laid a foundation for a university in Georgia."[119] Knowing Whitefield's penchant for "homiletical hyperbole", some caution is no doubt in order when we meet such statements.[120] Yet other references to Bethesda in later years do frequently describe it as an academy or as "the college". Indeed, a letter written shortly after Whitefield's death (in 1770) suggests just how general such an idea may have become. Since Whitefield's will had left the Countess of Huntingdon in charge, it was to her that John Wesley wrote urging her to pursue both parietal and academic goals with her new responsibility.[121] What neither correspondent knew yet was that Whitefield's Bethesda had burned to the ground a few months earlier. Indeed, another letter was at that moment on its way to the Countess, this one from James Habersham in Savannah, to inform her of the disastrous fate of "Bethesda College and its neat chapple adjoining."[122]

Tragic though the loss may have been, its very erection represents a real triumph for Whitefield, his supporters in the parish, and the Trustees. Things were happening. When added to other significant accomplishments, for example, the schools in Savannah, the library, and even an infirmary,[123] the record on the social side of the parish's ministry becomes notable.

The ecclesiastical side, on the other hand, did not fare as well. Two things in particular seemed to defy accomplishment despite all efforts: clerical stability and the building of a church structure. While Bethesda was still rising on its foundations in 1740 Whitefield's interests and travels increasigly removed him from Savannah. The Trustees, therefore, appointed Mr. William Metcalf to fill his post, requesting the usual £50 support from the SPG in July 1740.[124] They found themselves still in a quandry a few months later, however, when they had revoked Whitefield's power to perform eccleciastical offices in Georgia,[125] but Metcalf's illness had prevented his going over yet or even answering their letters to him.[126] Unfortunately, Metcalf would never make his journey, for the illness that had

The gate which now marks the entry to Bethesda commemorates the 200th anniversary of the founding of Whitefield's "orphan house." No wonder Whitefield, not normally given to verbal restraint, grew increasingly enthusiastic as he watched his ambitious plan for Bethesda take shape.

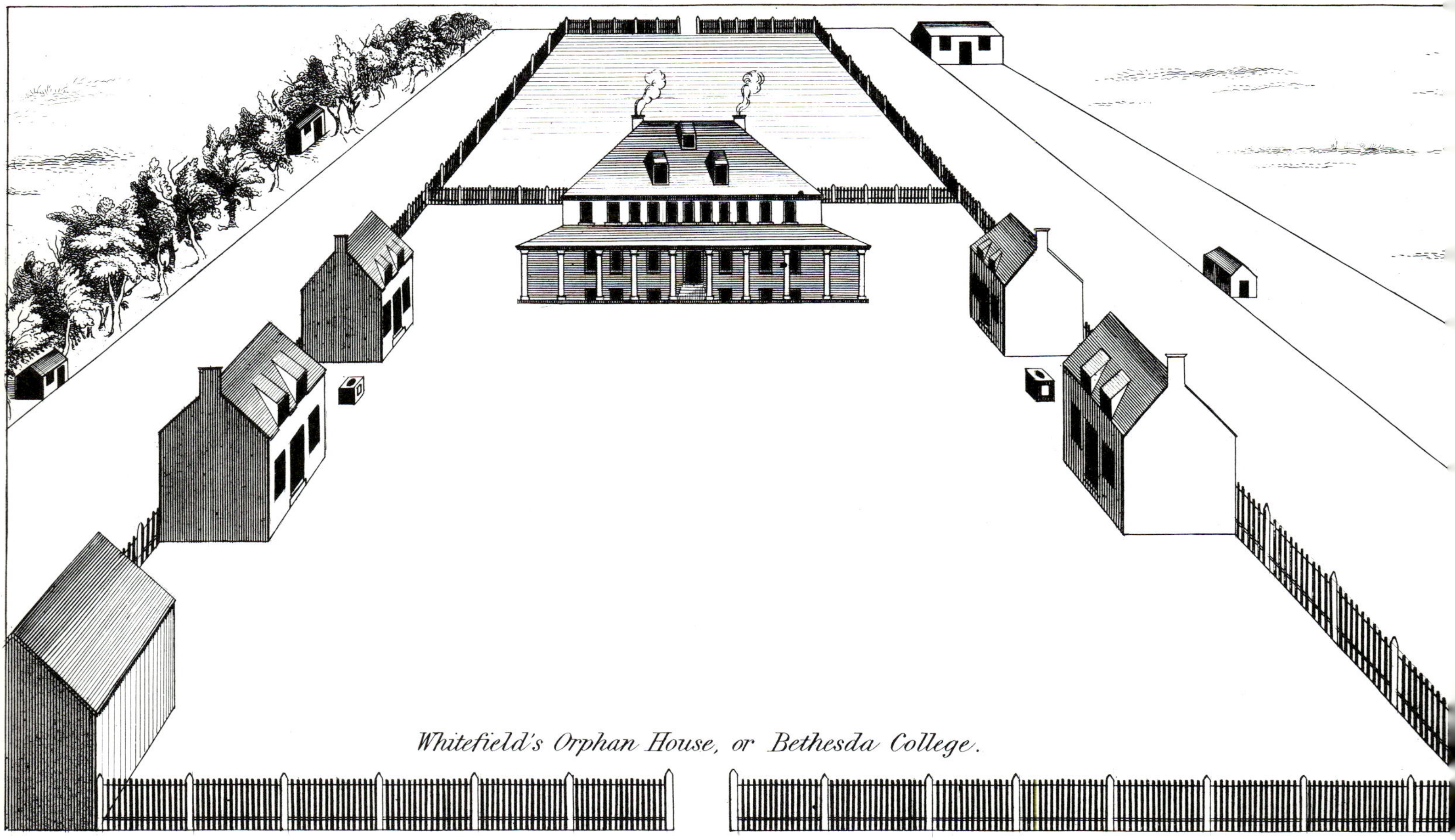

Whitefield's Orphan House, or Bethesda College.

so long delayed it finally took his life. Meanwhile, according to Wm. Stephens, "never was more the need, here is such distraction among us in religious matters as well as civil."[127]

To minister to those needs the Trustees now appointed young Mr. Christopher Orton,[128] who had been ordained only a few days before in London.[129] He "came ashore" in early December with his parish clerk, Mr. Thomas Bosomworth,[130] and seems immediately to have made a generally good impression. For his first sermon he "gave us an honest, plain, practical discourse, morning and afternoon, tending to the reformation of life, obedience to the will of God, revealed to us in the Gospel by His son, our Blessed Savior."[131]

We have no word from Mr. Orton indicating what he thought of his new home, but perhaps he was pleased when, after being in town only a few weeks, several prominent citizens called upon him for tea. At his door were Mr. James Habersham, Mr. Barber, the chaplain at Bethesda, and Mr. Patrick Hunter, the apothecary. The sequence of the afternoon led from tea to conversation to Orton's views on predestination, which his callers proceeded to attack with vigor. The assault shifted subtley, as such maneuvers often do, from Orton's views to Orton. In the verbal melee that followed they reportedly condemned him "for teaching false doctrine", being "no Christian", having "no call By the Holy Spirit", and having "no understanding of the Articles of Religion." The visitors further took trouble to express their assurance of his eternal "damnation!"[132] William Stephens, President of the colonial Council, described the three as part of a "parcel of wild enthusiasts," "Methodists" who may soon need restraint, having only "newly sprung up under the discipleship of their master, Whitefield."[133]

If we are to value Stephens' remarks properly, we must bear in mind two things. First his reaction grew from an account of the episode given him by Mr. Bosomworth, an "ear witness".[134] Second, the term "Methodist" is at this point still a new rather poorly defined label that refers more to a "suspicious" style of Anglican practice than to an organization.[135] Stephens recognized that style and felt it to be one of several things adversely affecting the life of the parish.

Mr. Orton seems to have survived the fray quite nicely, and three months later reported the congregation "much improved both in number and in their regard and zeal for the established Church." In his judgment the "late rude behavior of the chief dissenting part (i.e. the "methodists") has backfired, exposing their errors and the bad effects of their mistaken principles."[136]

Amid such distress within the established Church, it is heartening to see that among differing religious bodies there seems to have been amity at the time. Stephens records that the French, German, and other ministers frequently used the same buildings for services — balancing schedules so as not to interfere with each other.[137] It is also he who informs us, less happily, that

> about seven this morning it pleased God to take from us our worthy minister, the Reverend Mr. Christopher Orton, whose loss is very justly lamented . . . for his truly Christian deportment . . . [and] his labor to reconcile our unhappy jarrs . . . He was decently interred the same evening by torch light, when he was attended to his grave by almost everybody that was able, and I read the funeral service to a mournful assembly.[138]

The search for a new rector was short and simple this time. It was to be Thomas Bosomworth, who had served as parish clerk under Mr. Orton. Getting him here on the job was more difficult. Ordination meant a journey to England, and only after sixteen months away and many rumors did Mr. Bosomworth return to Savannah to take up his office.[139] President Stephens' journal smiles with the considerable satisfaction he felt when Mr. Bosomworth at last "performed the Divine Service of the Church" with usual sermons, catechism and lecture activities. Of special interest are Stephens' observations on that occasion about the population profile of the parish.

> Mr. Driesler, the German minister, returning from Ebenezer, preached to the Dutch in the forenoon and after, at proper hours not interfering with the English . . . The new settlers at Vernonburgh and Acton, having notice, flocking to town and joining with others who live among us, made the largest congregation that has been seen a long while past. The number of Dutch, computing three to each family, we judged to be at Vernonburgh 90, at Acton 60, and at Savannah 50 — in all 200 souls.[140]

The following weeks brought both satisfaction to his hearers and remarkably large congregations of over one hundred.[141] But Mr. Bosomworth, like so many of his predecessors, had to serve both Savannah and Frederica. Duties and other attractions then kept him in the southern outpost for some two months, during which time lay readers led the services and occasionally read one of the standard *Homilies* as well.[142] Just what had kept him so long became clearer when he ventured south again after only a few weeks in Savannah and word reached town that he had married Mary Musgrove Matthews[143] — well known translator, trader's wife, and woman-about-colony. The news brought amusement to some and incredulity to nearly all at first. But truth it was, and a few weeks later Bosomworth reappeared with his bride.[144] His clerical effectiveness diminished rapidly thereafter as he became increasingly involved in private business affairs, some of them controversial. After marrying he devoted himself heavily to prosecuting his wife's claims for "losses" and "services" to the colony, finally demanding Ossabaw, Sapelo, and St. Catherine's Islands as well as a large tract near Savannah as compensation!

The details of Mr. Bosomworth's progressive distraction are rather obscure and tell us little of parish life.[145] Perhaps it is sufficient to note that in little more than a year after his marriage, steps to prepare his replacement for service in Georgia were already well advanced. Ordained by the Bishop of London, Mr. Bartholomew Zouberbuhler was appointed to fill Bosomworth's position 1 November 1745,[146] and arrived in

COURTESY OF V. & J. DUNCAN, ANTIQUE MAPS AND PRINTS, SAVANNAH, GEORGIA.

This scene in 1744 is only conjectural, but despite a few anachronistic elements, it does effectively suggest some of the curiosity and eyebrows raised at Mr. Bosomworth's return.

Savannah a few months later. The Trustees were especially pleased with their choice of Zouberbuhler because of his linguistic versatility. A Swiss by birth, he agreed to minister not only to the English, but also "to the French and German inhabitants . . . in and near Savannah, according to the ceremonies of the Church of England."[147] His talents further pleased them in that they seemed to offer "a happy inducement to additional Protestant settlement in Georgia."[148]

Happily, Zouberbuhler's arrival marks a major turning point in the life of Christ Church. With him came stability in the rectorship and consistently effective work in the parish. Indeed, he served well enough that after three years the Trustees extended his appointment and simultaneously renewed their application to the SPG, something they had never before even had opportunity to do![149] There is a price to success, however, and in Zouberbuhler's case it meant that when work was extended to Augusta, it was contemplated that he should serve there also! Even though he was also serving Frederica at the time, the point had to be made rather strongly that duties in and around Savannah made it impossible to add Augusta.[150]

One of the many signs of the improving health of parish life is the increased regularity with which Zouberbuhler wrote the Trustees to inform them of the "state of the congregation" — reports so long desired but seldom received. Early in the series he notes the number of members and communicants "much increased."[151] This is a trend that appears to be documented as the series continued, but of even greater interest to us are some other aspects of the figures. For example, in 1748 he offered interesting details about the demography of the parish: of 613 inhabitants, 225 were professed believers of the Church of England and 388(!) were described as "Dissenters of all sorts," i.e. Presbyterians, Independents, etc.[152] Among the 225 Anglicans, slightly over one-fourth (63) were identified as active communicants.

Numerous questions arise from such a set of figures to tempt us. For instance, how does their active communicant ratio compare to modern ones? Another question that caused some dismay at the time was obviously in Governor Stephens' mind when he observed in his journal

> Mr. Zubly kept on his course in preaching to the Dutch who came from Vernonburgh, Acton and all the country within ten miles round to hear him so that his congregation was always very numerous — ordinarily from 150 to upwards of many more . . .[153]

Stephens seems to be wondering rather disgustedly, "does being the King's Church count for nothing?" He was not alone. For despite the improving condition of his own congregation and despite Mr. Zouberbuhler's commitment to serve the settlers of Vernonburgh and Acton, the Honorable Trustees seemed quite willing to by-pass the royal Church. Perhaps distance was the problem, but Zouberbuhler nevertheless was shocked and troubled when on petition from the inhabitants of those outlying villages the Trustees displayed unaccustomed generosity. They gave initial approval to a plan which would appoint Mr. Zubly as their minister, pay him £10/ a year, and give them lands for a "tabernacle" and money for necessaries for the building.[154] The "shock" came because Zubly was well known to be a Calvinist! — essentially Presbyterian in his views, and in no way committed to the doctrines or usage of the Church of England. He was "troubled" because there was still not a completed Church building in town yet the Trustees seemed willing to offer funds for a "tabernacle" in the country — for Dissenters! For personal reasons he was even more troubled because he felt his own salary and accommodations to be so inadequate. Indeed, he had just repaired the parsonage and built an outside kitchen for it at his own expense, in order to make it livable. The resulting debt was now such a great burden as to make it most difficult to show charity to others when he needed it so badly himself![155] No wonder that when Zouberbuhler's first three year term was nearly completed and his salary still unimproved, he begged removal to South Carolina.[156]

Happily, however, Mr. Zouberbuhler remained to see to completion another long-awaited change in the life of the "Church at Savannah." A house of worship for the congregation had been planned, attracted donations, and even accumulated building materials and cash since before the arrival of the *Anne*. No material results had arisen from the ground until Zouberbuhler's day, however, and "publick prayers" were held in the courthouse for almost twenty years. This long delay is all the more surprising considering the Trustees' interest in seeing the construction completed and their 1733 instructions to Mr. Oglethorpe to "lay out the site for the Church and order preparations for building it, as well as the minister's house."[157] Nor were the Trustees alone in their intent, for the records teem with "hopes of a new church being built speedily"[158] and with notes of practical steps in that direction.[159] By 1736 construction seemed imminent and so did the Spanish, making it important that the new church "be of brick and made strong so as to be capable of defense in case of sudden surprise . . . [and] that the Churchyard be enclosed and also be made defensible."[160]

Among the donations toward the new structure was one that will quicken the interest of every antique hunter: a large clock dial "for the Church at Savannah."[161] Others, that might perhaps do more to quicken the nostrils of auditors, make apparent both the Trustees' good intentions and the difficulty of effecting them. Early in Mr. Whitefield's tenure in Savannah (July 1739) they dispatched £150 to Mr. Oglethorpe to be used toward the building of a Church at Savannah, part of £300 previously allocated for the purpose. The General then forwarded the funds to Whitefield, giving to all the hope expressed by the minister "to see the Church built before my return to england."[162] In this situation with generous needs but scarce resources to meet them, apparently there was a marked tendency toward a Peter-to-Paul cash flow system. Thus, with the construction still not underway, Whitefield used some of the amount for other purposes and it was soon lost from sight in a sea of need. The Trustees were not unreasonable, just diligent, in asking Whitefield to account for the money. They were willing that "£5 be paid to Mr. Whitefield, being so much expended for candles for twelve months for public worship at Savannah,"[163] but they felt no compulsion to compensate him for other uses he made of the funds, regardless of their merit. Further delays in construction were the inevitable result, for the money was indeed spent and the Trustees were, as their financial secretary so discreetly put it, "not well possessed of cash."[164]

These delays were particularly frustrating since much of the building material was already on hand, having been ordered years earlier and piled up at the site.[164a] For us, however, the frustrations do have a good side. They tend to increase discussion of the construction, or at least of its problems, and thereby leave us more richly supplied with information in the surviving record. We know, for instance, that estimates had been requested by the Trustees as early as June 1737[165] and building material ordered in the spring of 1738. The order itself, which included Swedish and Siberian iron, and 90 tons of flintstones to be used in the foundation, gives us our first clue as to the look of the building that eventually resulted.[166] The plan to be used was developed by "Mr. Flitchcroft" and put into the hands of Capt. Thomas, an "ingenier" who had gone over with Gen. Oglethorpe, for execution in a manner "he judges most likely to answer the Trustees intention."[167] Planning even reached the point where decisions regarding the interior of the building were made. The Trustees, for example, had determined that

to save expense, discourage vanity, and pride of distinction, and make the Church more useful to the inhabitants . . . there [should] be no pews erected therin, but one for the minister, and one for the magistrate; and instead of pews that there be benches, as in the chapel at Tunbridge, and in some of the country churches in England, whereby there will be more room for the inhabitants who attend the public services.[168]

But plans and personnel were not enough, apparently. Even tears and vigils which may have been devoted to the cause[169] were ineffective, if we are to believe John Fallowfield. The correspondent complained of many things in his letter to the Trustees, but among his specific grievances listed that "the church had not yet got its foundation laid."[170] The reaction of the Trustees' to their latest plantiff is unclear. They may have seen some value in his comments although the recent delays could easily be attributed to Captain Thomas' untimely death in Charlestown.[171] It might have been more difficult, however, to explain what followed: nothing. The piled stones and stacked lumber merely accumulated dust and seniority.

Finally, after two more years the Trustees asked Mr. Stephens himself to oversee the matter personally. Agreeing to accept the burden,[172] Stephens' journal now becomes an informative source on the matter, and indirectly offers us what may be a very important insight for twentieth century observers. His efforts to secure a talent to fill the void left by Capt. Thomas' death led him to Peter Joubert as one skilled in engraving and drafting. Yet with all Stephens' esteem for the building project it nevertheless required a year and a day, literally, for him to transform good intentions into a plan. Perhaps, we must face it that in order to trade our modern cardio-threatening, neurosis-generating lives for what we suppose to be the "simplicity" and "earthy tranquility" of the colonial era, there would be costs not normally measured. We would also have to accept the painfully slow communication, lack of leisure time and energy to be spared from our primary labors, and frequent visits of untimely death that go with it. The differences of detail that distinguish 18th century life from that of the 20th sometimes lend a falsely attractive glow to one or the other, especially if we fail to count those hidden costs with care.

No wonder there was joy in what Stephens wrote in his journal regarding the plan for the Church

In 1758 Savannah's burial ground became the parish cemetery for Christ Church yet remained a public graveyard. In 1895 the city reacquired it and restored it to its present day beauty.

December 15 [1743]. Thursday morning [Mr. Joubert] brought it, to the satisfaction of divers who were with me . . . It may suffice to say, that Covent Garden Church happening to be well known to us both, I had recommended that to him as a model in his imagination to work by, as well for its being deemed a curious piece of Inico Jones, as because the work will come much the cheaper for being so very plain. Wherefore I apprehend the less we vary from it the better, except in the difference necessary to observe in relation to its extension, and that admired work, the roof, which surpasses (I believe) all our skill here to imitate. Having thus far attempted something that has long been wished for, by God's help I resolved now to proceed with such men as are capable of carrying on the whole to perfection with all convenient speed.[173]

Stephens was as good as his word, for while we have no date for the turning of the first shovel of earth, preparations appear to have begun very soon after this date. By February 7th, 1744, Shrove Tuesday, he recorded that a portion of "the day was spent in conference with the workmen how to hasten on the building of the Church . . ."[174] For a few weeks the *Journal* reads like a fast paced detective story as the materials are assembled, labor negotiations carried out and the actual construction begun. Indeed, the process, as well as the goal of the project, now takes on considerable interest.

February 25, [1744]. The several persons intended to be employed in building the Church, having sufficient time allowed 'em to make proposals on what terms and rates they would under-take that work, (viz.) carpenters per the square, masons per the perch, sawyers per the 100 ft., lime burners per bushel, delivered at the work . . . we had now a meeting with them, their several proposals given us; and after some reduction and abatement, as low as we could get it, we concluded on proceeding instantly . . .[175]

One week later,

The work, . . . now went on in good earnest; the carpenters and sawyers busy in providing scantlings, boards, etc. others burning lime and carters bringing home all materials; wherefore we should soon lay the foundation and begin with the masonry, designed in a wall about three feet high . . .[176]

Finally, the great day arrived when the first cornerstone was laid, March 28th, 1744. "A Psalm was sung suitable to the occasion, after which we all went to Church where (Mr. Bosomworth) read the ordinary service . . ." The occasion had been too long awaited to let it go at that, however! Somewhat sheepishly, and knowing the Trustees would eventually read what he wrote, Stephens confesses

This being done . . . I hoped it would not be thought unseasonable or extravagant in me to contribute towards the festivity at the expense of the Trustees for an hour or two in a small collation provided for the principal workmen, together with the Parson [and] Magistrates and avoiding all excess in either eatables or drink.[177]

Now that it was actually underway, construction progressed rapidly with visible changes evident daily. By April 20th, "our Church work [was] beginning to make some appearance above ground in the masonry, which is intended to be three feet above the surface, and upon which a timber frame is to rest. . . ."[178] Stephens became a devoted sidewalk superintendent, and enjoyed passing "a few hours there, . . . in conference with the workmen, delighting in seeing it go forward."[179] In another month the foundation work was complete[180] and Stephens could begin to see through his excitement to the problems ahead. By midsummer insight had turned into worry, for although the construction moved "forward with good success," money began to trouble him.

From the expense already past, and the computation from thence of what might be expected yet to come, 'tis too plain that it cannot be brought to perfection within the compass of £300 appropriated . . . When everything is done to bring it as near the estimate as possible 'tis hoped 'twill not be judged by the Honorable Trustees unpardonable in me to be found guilty of a little exceeding. . . .[181]

The structure itself, however, continued to show progress. By early September the frame was prepared[182] and a month later

the whole timberframe of the Church (sides and roof) being now compleatly put together, the next stop must be to get it covered; which we hoped would take us no long time, having prepared a sufficient quantity of shingles for the purpose, drawn out of cypress about 20 in. long, an inch thick at the lower end, and tapered upwards to the thickness of a knife blade, the Best I ever saw.[183]

With the workmen soon employed in "laying on the roof", which would unfortunately "bring us to an end of what fund we had" the next worry became clearer. Stephens pondered how to bring the incomplete structure to such a point as to avoid vulnerability to weather damage after work ceased altogether.[184]

Too soon, the exciting growth of spring and summer passed into the barren dormancy of winter. The Church stood weathering like a forgotten skeleton on its humble "acropolis", a foundation and frame beneath a roof that gave too little shelter. It is probably more than coincidence that for the moment the congregation seems to have lapsed into a similar state. Mr. Bosomworth's marriage took place during the summer and by autumn it was already apparent that his primary interests now lay elsewhere. For most of the year that followed both Bosomworth and progress on the building project were largely absent. Not until a year later, a few weeks after Mr. Zouber-

This informal view of Savannah, emphasizing the town's relationship to the fortifications surrounding it, was probably executed in preparation for the seige of 1779. The house of worship on the left could represent Christ Church but the artist's casual presentation of the town itself leaves much room for skepticism. If that is Christ Church then it is the only known picture of the congregation's first building. Try comparing the structure shown with the one described by Mr. Stephens.

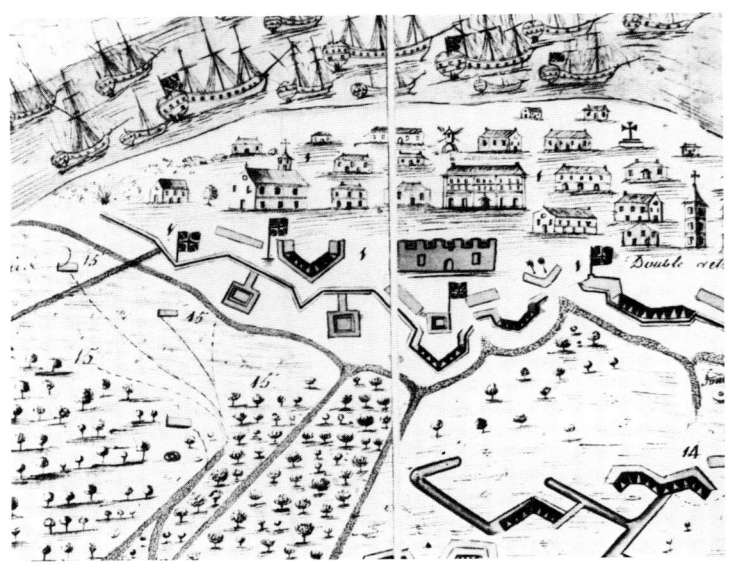

buhler's arrival do we see much change. By that time Stephens had nearly completed his longtime wish, "with the help of Capt. Noble Jones (whose qualifications are well known), to get the carpenters and masons works about the Church measured, that I might inform the Trustees what expense was created . . . paid . . . and in arrear!"[185] That task was understandably slow for it often involved negotiation of charges thought to be excessive, unforseen expenses, etc. The Trustees slowed it even further out of vexation. It troubled them that the building was still unfinished despite their investment, and despite the fact — as they understood — the sawmill at Ebenezer had already prepared the needed planking.[186] There is reason to believe some progress was made during Mr. Zouberbuhler's first year, however, for at that time (i.e., March 1747) along with their reproof the Trustees sent paint for the new structure.[187]

The ensuing discussion yields important insights into contemporary building techniques, and also into the frailty of their communication lines. Both merit closer scrutiny. First, the "original" 1741 plan called for plaster-finished walls inside and out, and the long-standing building frame was prepared accordingly. At last renewed support and instructions arrived in April from the Trustees with further instructions "that the inside walls should be lined with boards", much pleasing local officials. Then, the following August entirely new instructions directed that both interior and exterior walls should be "feather-boarded." After "consulting the workmen thereon and computing the different expenses betwixt plastering and boarding, we found the latter exceeded the former by at least one third." Pursuing the latest instructions would also have entailed the additional expense of redoing some of the work already accomplished to accommodate the boards.

These things being duly considered induced us to send for the workmen, when we contracted to finish the walls in the manner following Viz———
To be watled betwixt the studs with white oak watling, and filled up on each side with a strong plaster, that the studs should be wholly covered at least three quarters of an inch, so that the wall will be upwards of eight inches thick; the outside to be covered with a strong cement, and neatly set off in imitation of stone work; the inside when finished to be a clean plaistered white wall, which wall upon strict enquiry is found by proper judges to last five times longer than any weather boards that can be laid on; the carpenters allowing that no weather boards will last above ten years before the heats of the sun rends them.[188]

Regarding communications it need only be pointed out that all the instructional letters mentioned required 4½ to 5 months *en route*. Correspondence often crossed at sea or arrived much out of the order of writing . . . if it reached its destination at all. One of these last letters, for example, contained a note of relief to hear that certain items were in the intended hands "as it is hazardous to send by Merchantman since so many from South Carolina are taken." It was, therefore, ordered that important correspondence be sent only by Man-of-War, which normally sailed much less frequently, and even then it should be "wrapped in an oil skin and put in a box, filling all with sawdust, lest they be spoiled in passage."[189]

Until all of this could be completed, however, Mr. Zouberbuhler continued to officiate in the courthouse, "the new Church being in the same condition as she was some years agone . . . But since fresh orders concerning her came over, it is given out that within a little time we shall have the pleasure to perform divine service in her." Thinking ahead, he adds his hope that the Trustees will send a surplice, two large books of *Common Prayer,* and a cushion for the pulpit."[190]

With these latest developments, the end was in sight. "All we can add now is that it wants nothing to complete it but the seats, pulpit, and Communion Table, all which will be finished in a little time."[191] Then, of course, there was the normal

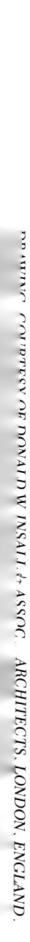

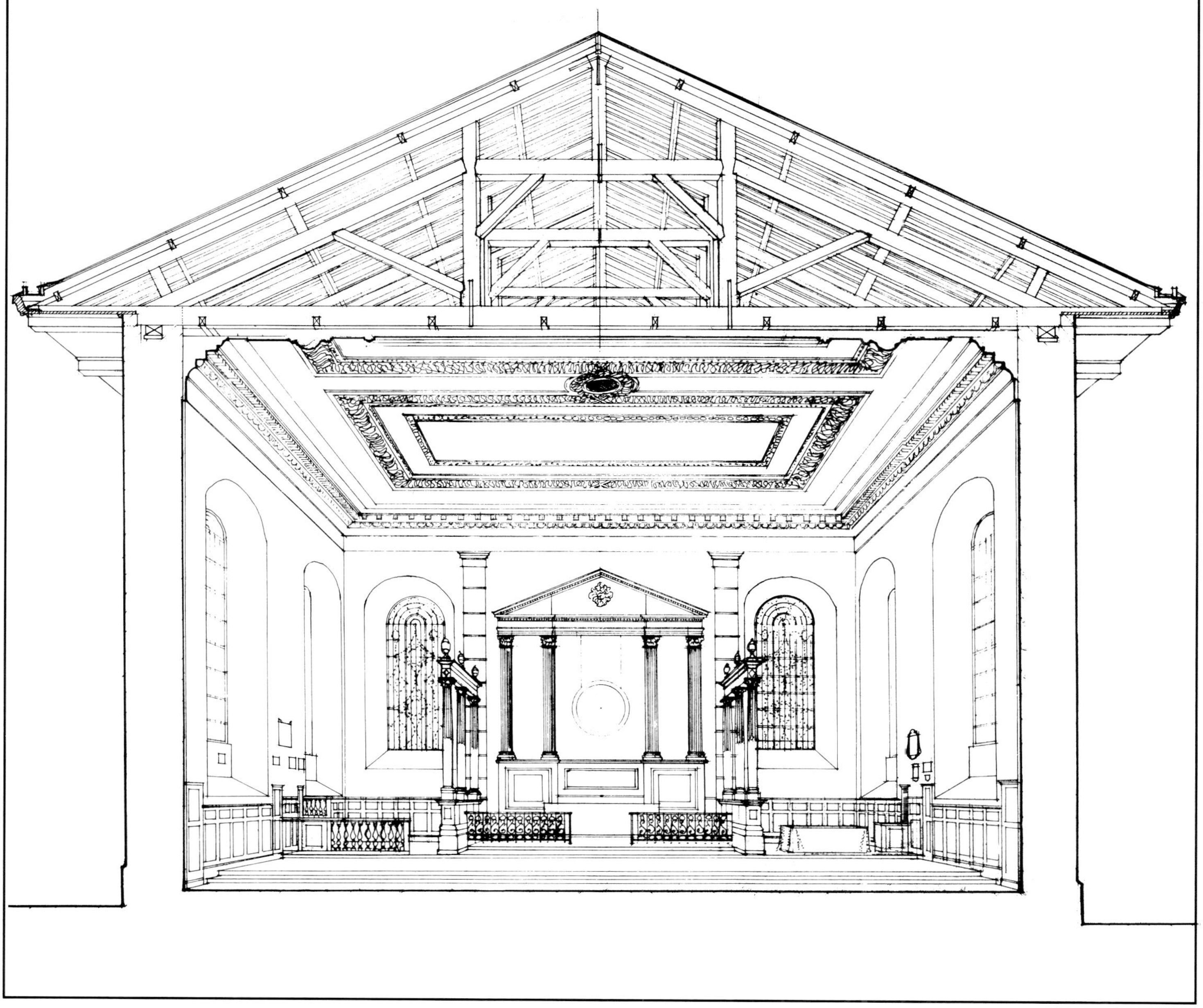

DRAWING COURTESY OF DONALD W. INSALL & ASSOC. ARCHITECTS, LONDON, ENGLAND.

problem of "how far the Church exceeds the Trustees' expectations and ours — due to the dearness of the materials and labor." In their explanation of the excessive cost officials in Savannah made response a bit difficult by pointing out how they thought it worthy to use the best material, "being a work of such consequence as required it standing to future ages."[192]

On 7th July 1750, however, all of the effort and patience had its reward as the day "was spent dedicating our new church to God's solemn worship and the offices of religion."[193] Mr. Zouberbuhler went on to describe the occasion in exuberant terms.

> *The building is large, beautiful, and comodious. My parishioners are constant in their attendance, and I have the pleasure to see many negroes decently join in our service.*

Indeed, in the same letter he reported the baptism of one negro woman during the past year.[193.1]

These drawings, prepared in 1981 for the restoration of St. Paul's Church, Covent Garden, may tell us a little at least of what Messrs. Stephens and Joubert had in mind as they talked over plans for Christ Church. Some imagination is required, however, for St. Paul's has been considerably altered by fire and renovation since the 1740's. Fortunately for us, the configuration of its walls and windows is basically unchanged, but the galleries once supported by the columns which now flank the altar were removed in 1871. The construction shown in the roof and ceiling is also "new," built to replace the burned original in 1795. Yet the whole, when scaled down a good bit, may still be reasonably suggestive of the mood created by the first Christ Church structure.

The Chapel altar.

II
Revolutionary Fever 1750-1785

The dedication of this first English ecclesiastical edifice in Georgia makes an ideal point at which to pause and catch our breath, and from which to preview the future. When we do, our attention is drawn immediately to developments during the two decades following 1750 that greatly affected the status of the colony and the life of the parish. The most obvious of these is suggested by Mr. Zouberbuhler's description of the dedication and the congregation that attended. Especially the large number of Blacks in the congregation was a change that had come rapidly since the 1749 removal of Georgia's prohibition of slavery. With that change the Church moved to reach this growing population spiritually by engaging Joseph Ottolenghe as a catechist.[193.2] Reaching slaves and indentured servants, of course, meant reaching their owners — first to persuade them to allow their slaves to be taught, and then to grant them the time and freedom to attend the catechist and the Church. Opinion among slave owners differed sharply as to the merits and risks in such activities.

Ottolenghe appears to have had some success convincing planters along the Savannah River to allow his work for he was able to report to the S.P.G. that "I have the slaves with me three times a week, in the evening . . . when their owners can best spare them."[193.3] Evidence suggests he may have done well with the slave population, perhaps because of his understanding and unthreatening style. In his charges he found "tis true that in general they are slow of apprehension . . . which might easily be accounted for by . . . their unhappy conditions, and different stations in life." As for himself, he took "hope in Christ who died for the salvation of all, both Black and White Sons of Adam. . . ."[193.4] Through his work as catechist, Ottolenghe developed some interesting and strong opinions about the art of teaching across the linguistic, social, and other cultural barriers that divided him from his charges. His work is worthy of separate investigation, but for our purposes the reports he returned to the sponsoring S.P.G. and to friends are perhaps the best indication of its relation to the Church. Within a year he could see results that gave him hope of permanent gain. "Most are gone through the Catechism and several begin to read tolerably well." "All repeat by heart prayers and answer questions. . . ."[193.5] To the same correspondent he also reported that "several [of his people] have really good voices, and having learned the words and tune [of the Psalms] at schole, join in the congregation at Church."[193.6] That theirs was a significant contribution is affirmed by Zouberbuhler's statement the same year that "above 60 Negroes decently join in the service."[193.7]

Mr. Ottolenghe eventually became involved in other matters in the colony. Twenty years later, however, thanks in part to Mr. Zouberbuhler's benefaction, the mission he began was still underway and in the capable hands of Mr. Cornelius Winter. James Habersham described him as one "possessed of an inoffensive manner," who "by that means removed some people's weak objections to having their poor ignorant servants instructed in the principles of the Christian religion."[193.8]

Significantly, although care for the souls of the slave and indentured populations seems to have influenced the pattern of evangelism — i.e., where it was allowed — it apparently had little affect on the pattern of ownership. The Rev. Messrs. Zouberbuhler and Frink both owned slaves, for example, as did their Presbyterian colleague, Mr. Zubly.[193.9] Before them, George Whitefield not only owned slaves, he staunchly advocated the institution by arguing to the Trustees that "Georgia never can or will be a flourishing province without negroes are allowed."[193.91] At least he practiced what he preached. In 1747 he bought a 640 acre plantation in South Carolina, slaves and all. His purpose was to use "Providence", as he named it, both to demonstrate the value of such operations to the Trustees, and to devote its profits to the support of his Orphan House at Bethesda.[193.92]

A second topic of special interest arises as we approach expiration of the Trustees' twenty year charter. The King's instructions to his new royal governor, John Reynolds, indicate an intention to continue much of what had been policy under the Trustees, e.g. "liberty of conscience to all except pap-

Entrance and interior view of the Chapel dedicated as a memorial to Raymond M. Demere. (See Chapter 9.)

ists."[194] Royal policy went beyond the Trustees license, however, in church matters. Whereas the Church of England had a "privileged" status in Georgia's first twenty years, the new charter now made it the "established church". In practice the "establishment" meant maintaining or building at public cost churches, ministers' houses, and glebes under the ecclesiastical jurisdiction of the Bishop of London.[195] By the time establishment was complete in 1758, eight parishes had been created. They had duties to look after the taxation (assessed of all residents) destined to support Church property, poor relief, and such other social services as the King might choose to effect through them. It was also a parish duty to function as the local bureau of vital statistics by keeping records of births, marriages, deaths, etc.[196]

Establishment brought many things. Among the obvious implications is the formation of defined parishes. Thus it was that what earlier documents had described as the "Church at Savannah," became officially known as Christ Church in 1758 — the boundaries corresponding approximately to those of modern Chatham County. Some of the less apparent implications involve even more profound change. Since the charter invests ecclesiastical bodies with civil functions, in effect it makes the parish vestry into something equivalent to a county commission or board of supervisors. Moreover, since in each parish only the priest will assuredly have sworn his loyalty directly to the King, his role as a "civil servant" becomes crucial. It is easy to understand, therefore, why written into the royal instructions to the governor is the clause (#79) that

> *every orthodox minister within your government be one of the vestry of his respective parish, and that no vestry [meeting] be held without him, except in the case of sickness, or that after notice of a vestry summoned, he omit to come.*

The extent to which civil functions and ecclesiastical become intermixed is well demonstrated by yet another element of the instructions. The King required the governor to "facilitate and encourage conversion of Negroes and Indians to the Christian religion." The mixture of civil office with religious assignments, and the question of evangelization are not really so surprising as they might first appear to moderns. The issue had been much argued before, whether conversion of slaves or Indians to Christianity should affect their social and legal status. Also, there is ample justification for mixture in the contemporary theories of the value of religion in maintaining civil order. It is, however, a bit startling to realize just *how* unembarrassed the King appears in so mixing his motives. Certainly something more than pure evangelical purpose showed when he required his new governor "to make provision . . . for . . . some ministers to inhabit amongst the Indians . . . to instruct them . . . also to prevent their being seduced from their allegiance to us by French priests and jesuits"![197] It adds a slight touch of pain to recall that now, after so long, the King had his own reasons for assigning the task John Wesley had so much wanted.

Attending the status of "established Church" were certain privileges such as greater visibility and access to the general public, especially in high places. Thus it was that Mr. Zouberbuhler, Christ Church's rector of sixteen years, came to preach to the provincial House of Assembly in November of 1761. The following day along with their thanks, the House expressed its desire that the rector, wardens and vestry erect a "commodious pew in the north aisle at public expense for the accomodation of strangers".[198] Privileges come with responsibilities attached normally, and one that came to Christ Church was the care of the burial ground.[199] A legislative committee further resolved in 1762 that it should be extended (to Abercorn Street), enclosed, and another plot 100 feet square added in line with it "for negroes and other slaves."[200] The resolution was then formally enacted by the legislature in April of 1763.[201]

As already noted, an important function in every parish was relief for the poor. Much in the way of contemporary attitudes and problems is visible in the memorial presented to the Assembly by the vestry in 1767. It seems that the task had indebted the parish some £100 in excess of what they were empowered to assess the inhabitants, and they begged some relief themselves

> *Lest they be under the lamentable necessity of being deaf to the cries of the distressed, and . . . obliged to dismiss them to perish in the streets.*[202]

Interestingly, this function continued to belong to the parish even after the Revolution, and disestablishment of the Church of England. Notices were frequently placed in the newspaper to inform the general public of the dates when special collections would be made for the purpose of poor relief.[203]

Some things have changed greatly since the colonial era for church wardens. Modern day wardens, for example, are no longer vested with the duty given them by legislation in 1770

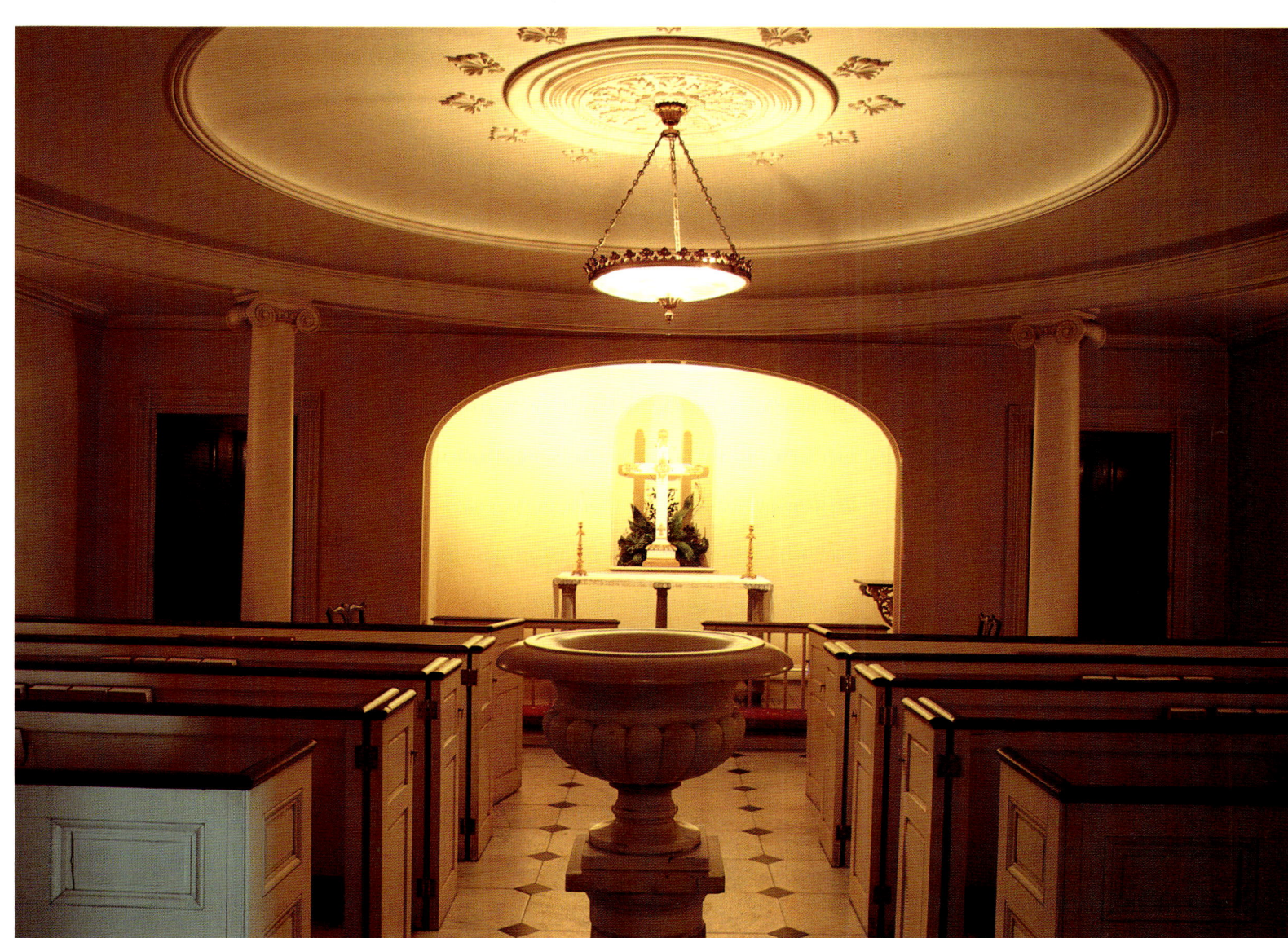

"for the better security of the inhabitants." The Assembly sought that security by "obliging [all] male white persons to carry firearms to all places of public worship". The small print further required "at least six charges of powder and ball — carrying all into the pew — on pain of 10 shillings fine."[204] The cunning legislators, perhaps because they knew them to be experienced in handling explosive issues, charged the wardens and vestry with responsiblity to inspect arms and enforce the law! The *Tax Act* of the same year carried the public function of vestrymen a step further. Was it a reflection on the preaching of the day that the new law required the wardens and vestry to see to the upkeep and repair of fire engines?[205]

For these examples, it is obvious enough that the duties of the wardens and vestry have undergone considerable change. There is still truth, however, in the common wisdom that "much as things change, nothing changes much." Pick up the *Georgia Gazette*, for example, without looking at the date, and read how

The Collectors of the publick tax for this parish, finding little notice taken of their repeated advertisements, give this their last notice, that they close their accounts the first day of July next, at which time those that are defaulters will be dealt with according to the law.
Signed:
John Smith
William Telfair
Robert Bolton

Were it not for the spelling and parish trimmings, there would be no way to date the notice in 1767,[206] The foot-dragging reluctance to pay taxes, regardless of their level, must be a sentiment precious to every generation.

Finally, there is the matter of the building itself — this first Christ Church. Although functioning only five years, the building already needed attention to its fabric. Mr. Zouberbuhler sent a memorial to provincial officials "setting forth that the condition of the church in Savannah . . . was so ruinous that unless . . . given repair, assembling therein for the solemn purposes intended would be dangerous."[207] Matters moved rather slowly, apparently, for in 1758 Henry Ellis was moved to underscore the rector's claim, declaring the safety of worshippers and "common decency" both demanded immediate repair.[208] Orders were given to survey and report on the condition of the structure which appears to have felt the ill-effects of many years of unclad exposure to the elements.[209] Indeed, the survey discovered the building's state to be so deteriorated that serious consideration was given to the possibility of replacing it. Designs for a new structure were prepared, which proposed relocating the Church,[210] but these were finally laid aside — probably for reasons of cost.[211] Instead, the old structure was renovated in 1763, eight years after Zouberbuhler's original memorial.[212]

Now, the matter of structures needing repair much sooner than expected, and the time required for us to adjust and deal with the need, would seem to fit nicely among "those things that do not change" much. The new ingredient in this formula, one modern building committees understandably might covet, was that the Provincial Assembly chose to raise funds for the renovation through a special tax on taverns, punch houses, and "skittle dens"![213]

About this same time the interior of the Church was altered, too. Precisely when is not clear, but by the early 1760's both pews and a west gallery were in place. The notice appeared in the *Georgia Gazette* which announced that:

The vestry having come to a resolution to sell the pews in the Church of Savannah, all who are desirous to purchase must give their names to the church wardens by Monday next, being the 4th day of July, at farthest.
Jas Read
Charles Watson Church Wardens[214]

The next week purchasers could call at the Church to receive their pew numbers.[215] Evidently the sale was a success for no further notices appeared until, two years later, another ad revealed "pews in the gallery will be sold at public vendue under the porch of the Church, Tuesday, 24 September, 10:00 forenoon."[216] Both the pews and the gallery may have been added when the repairs were carried out in 1763. In any case the gallery soon had to accommodate one especially large "pewholder" as

On Sunday, the 17th instant, an organ presented by Mr. Edward Barnard, Esq. (of Augusta), and placed in the new gallery of the Church in this town, was opened by Mr. John Stevens, jun., who is the appointed organist.[217]

The new instrument created a shortage of space once again in all probability. At least it wasn't long before changes were announced. The

Church wardens and vestry of Christ Church parish have come to a resolution to erect two new galleries in Christ Church, this is . . . to give notice . . . that any person willing to undertake the same may apply to
William Ewen
Phillip Box Church Wardens[218]

These notices, regarding the side galleries, are the last items observed which deal with the original structure of 1744-50 and its modifications. The church stood in essentially this form until the great fire of 1796 changed everything.

Two events of 1766 make it a convenient time for us once more to pause in our journey, and to reflect on the picture brought to mind by those first decades. Both events, one a death and the other a critique, invite retrospection; and this will be better done before than after the fires and tempers of Revolution have clouded all vision. When we turn to look back from our vantage point on the height, we can easily survey the entire scene through which we have just passed, as it stretches below us in a Claude-like landscape to the horizon.

The Georgia we see was to be a model society, a "child of philanthropy" Bishop Stevens called it.[219] Indeed, the enterprise so captured the mind of the age that more than a hundred clergy throughout Britain sought and received commission to collect money for its support. Yet the colony also inspired much criticism, so lavish at times as to leave one searching for some deeper cause than was stated. One critic, writing in the last year of Mr. Zouberbuhler's life (1766), was unhappy enough in his perception of the colony to shout his complaint that "the people of Georgia are greatly below those of South Carolina both in manners, morals, and wealth!" He leaves us little clue as to the shortcomings he saw, nothing but the spinose comfort that, bad as they are, "Georgians are far beyond and much superior in all respects to [the people] of North Carolina."[220] Ah, what consolation . . . to be so much better than the worst! Beyond revealing the intensity of his feelings, however, the author is not much help until we narrow our gaze to focus on the detail of the landscape before us.

When we do, the church is clearly visible even from our distance, there in the midst of the village that occupies the center of the scene. For more than twenty years that church was in the care of Mr. Bartholomew Zouberbuhler. Prior to his death in 1766, he could report much improvement in the spiritual life of the parish and in the productivity of its glebe lands.[221] What encouraged the rector, however, did not silence critics. Mr. Woodmason's diagnosis of local ills was that "men such as Wesley and Whitefield have thrown a damp on religious matters in this colony. They strained the cord till it broke — and it will require half an age to repair the damages they did . . ."[223]

Is our critic one of those timeless personalities who is much happier with problems than with solutions? Since we have no way to know for certain we should probably hear him out.[224] It may be that he can help us better appreciate an attitude we have detected already in others. It is also his judgment "the Church in Savannah town is but mean, as indeed is the town itself. . . The present incumbent, (Mr. Zouberbuhler,) is now retiring with a fortune accumulated."[225] Our realism will counsel us that his reviews of church and town, though unkind, are probably not unfair. His assessment of Mr. Zouberbuhler's fortune, however, is questionable at best.[226] Could such a mean town yield any fortunes? In any case, there is sign neither of fortune nor of resentment of it visible in local sources. To the contrary, when the ailing rector attempted to retire a few years earlier and young Mr. Duncanson was sent to relieve him, the vestry refused to receive the newcomer. It seems that a very negative reputation had preceded the young clergyman. Thus, in an exemplary bit of understatement, the Vestry told the SPG they thought him "not to answer the Society's pious intention . . ." Instead, they preferred to leave Mr. Zouberbuhler in charge despite his ill health, knowing this meant doing without clerical ministrations for a time.[227] Woodmason might have done better to press his critique of Whitefield and Wesley or point to the fairly common resentment of the Church of England in the colonies. Yet in his way, perhaps he does help us to sharpen our perception of the Church, the town, and the colony which are spread before us on our canvas. Although still a bit blurred by the haze of time, the Church in the center of our view has indeed, taken on a reasonable degree of clarity. We will not be overdoing it if we take that clarity to signify that it now has a secure grip on life, an ability to serve that more nearly balances the need to be served.

One sign of the slowly emerging prosperity of the parish in the 1760's was visible in the river a few hundred yards from the church. Weekly listings in the *Georgia Gazette* show a surprising number and variety of ships, goods, and ports of call. A typical issue, for example, notes the arrival of ships from London, South Carolina, and Rhode Island as others head down river for St. Kitts, Antigua, Jamaica, Cowes (Isle of Wight), London, Montserrat, and St. Croix.[228] Other issues during the period reinforce the point as they record ships trafficking to or from such places as Penzance, Whitby, Liverpool, Martinico, St. Christopher's, Nevis, the Bay of Honduras, Marblehead, Salem, Bristol, Lisbon, Grenada, Tobago, Curaçao, Barbadoes. Philadelphia, Boston, St. Augustine, Mobile, Bermudas, St. Thomas, Providence, Dominicoi, New York, Guadaloupe, and many more, including some bringing unhappy cargoes direct from Africa. All of this coming and going would appear to be due to sharp increases in the export trade in the 1760's, estimated by a contemporary report to be on the order of 50% to 80% annually![228a]

The strengthening pulse on the river can be detected also in the expectant mood of the vestry. Writing the SPG early in 1767 to report Mr. Zouberbuhler's death, they presented the case of German Protestants near town who were earnestly desirous of joining the Church of England. Especially needed was someone who was capable of performing divine service in the German tongue and of teaching their children English. Reporting that the "congregation" had already "fitted up a chapel" and proposed to procure "a commodious house and a salary of £50", the vestry entreated compliance. The benefits were obvious enough they thought, needing only the Society's support and a generous supply of Prayer Books to set up a "chapel of ease" with an assistant to the Rector at Christ Church.[229] Unfortunately, the plan never came to fruition despite the Society's resolution to send the missionary requested.[230]

The challenge of this new era fell to a series of short term rectors, the first being the Rev. Mr. Samuel Frink, of Augusta. Frink had come to St. Paul's, Augusta, in April 1765, arriving in Charlestown on the same ship that carried the news that Parliament had passed a Stamp Act for the American colonies.[231] Perhaps that was an omen he should have taken seriously, for Augusta was not to his liking. He visited Savannah as frequently as he could find excuses, and by the time of Bartholomew Zouberbuhler's death, had actually removed to Savannah for "reasons of health."[232] Either by good luck or good planning things worked very much to his liking this time. Gov. Wright officially collated him to Chirst Church as its rector in January of 1767, where he had voluntarily filled the vacancy for several weeks.[233]

Mr. Frink seems to have been well accepted in the community and done many of the right things. He preached to the courts on invitation[234] and to his Masonic brothers with regularity.[235] The "people of Savannah", he told the SPG, want him to preach morning and afternoon on Sunday which Mr. Zouberbuhler had not done for many years. They also desired him to revive customs of prayers on Wednesdays, Fridays, and Holy Days, which he reports he readily complied with. One gets the feeling, however, that he would never find contentment or happiness in any condition. At any rate, he took the trouble to inform the Society that these sundry duties rendered his "cure" a very laborious one, "especially in this suffocating climate", but he would not complain.[236]

All questions of attitude aside, however, Mr. Frink did, indeed, have a point. In addition to the duties already noted, it became his task to oversee the enlargment of the burial ground[237] and, far worse, to care for a "parish" that in practice covered the entire province! For sometime after his relocation to Savannah he remained Georgia's only clergyman of the established church. Thus he journeyed to Augusta during Easter week, 1767, to preach and baptize and when he returned had to set out almost immediately for St. George's to do the same.[238]

It may be that neither Frink nor Georgia were alone in this condition. At least he seemed to be thinking broadly when he wrote that the solution lay in the appointment of a bishop to support the establishment, and thereby "keep order and decency in religion."[239] If he seems to have had as little success in this cause as others before him, the reasons are clear enough. Colonists' fears appeared in the *Georgia Gazette* in 1764, where:

> *We are told there is not, nor ever was, any scheme proposed for appointing an archbishop, or for any more than four bishops in our Americn plantations . . . or for placing them elsewhere than in episcopal colonies, . . . or for giving them any authority in civil matters, . . . or over any dissenters from the Church of England, . . . or for levying any tax in any place [for] their support.*[240]

Since such powers were facts, not merely fears, in the mother country, it is easy to see why Mr. Frink and colleagues were doomed to disappointment. Given the make-up of Christ Church parish in this particular episcopal colony it becomes ever more obvious. For as reported to the SPG in the 1760's, only about 20% of the parish's 4000 inhabitants were of the Church of England persuasion, and only 6-7% of that minority active communicants![241]

Mr. Frink felt his mission had somewhat improved those figures and that his people were growing "more constant in their attendance upon Christian ordinances" than they had been, and less wavering in their resolve. These good effects he attributed to the double blessings of his own good health, which enabled him to carry out his mission, and Mr. Whitefield's longer than usual *absence* from Georgia![242]

Why Mr. Frink so resented his colleague's visits is not fully clear, although guessing is easy in such a matter. It seems likely that professional rivalry, fed by what he felt to be an overblown adulation of the noted preacher, was part of it—something he suspected Whitefield chose to encourage by never staying in one place too long. The *Georgia Gazette* certainly treated Whitefield very generously when they reported on his last visit in 1764. After noting his departure, this time for Long Island and Boston, the editor went on to describe the successes of his most recent seven weeks in Savannah. He preached twice weekly to "more general acceptance than ever," including several charity sermons. Then in most laudatory terms, the article celebrated his annual collection "for the benefit of Mr. Wheelock's Indian School at Lebanon" (later known as Dartmouth College), in which he collected £120, "notwithstanding the prejudices of many people against the Indians!"[243] Plainly there is in such treatment considerable matter for professional jealousy, especially of one who stays just long enough to pluck the glory, then departs to another vineyard . . . to pluck some more.

Regardless of the justice of Whitefield's reception locally, or the legitimacy of his intinerant style, Mr. Frink might have done well to learn at least a few things from him. Instead, he seems to have been a model of intolerance, even for an age that made it fashionable. When a child of the Rev. Mr. Zubly died, for example, even though he was the only other resident clergyman in town, Frink refused to speak at the funeral since Zubly was a Presbyterian.[244] Indeed, on several occasions he condemned Whitefield and his resident chaplain at Bethesda, the Rev. Mr. Edward Ellington, for just such instances of cooperation with dissenters.[245] It may be that he felt particularly strongly about dissenters, having been one himself during his Harvard days and by family heritage, yet obviously he does not limit his intolerance to them.

There is another plausible explanation for Mr. Frink's style, too. Perhaps he liked sounding harsh. For while incidents such as the Zubly funeral turn up with some regularity, it is often the case that his bark and bite don't match. When Whitefield prepared the celebration to lay the foundations of two new wings at Bethesda, for instance, it was Mr. Frink he asked to preach. Frink did so. The Governor, most of the Council, and a host of dignitaries and workmen gathered for the occasion.[246] Yet he continued to complain that on several occasions Whitefield had sought, without success, "to make disturbance in this parish, " and to rejoice that he is now "gone to a place (presumably New England) where he can be of as much service to religion as the man in the moon."[247]

Our closest approach to the true source of such irritation might have begun on the 20th of December, 1769, had we been able to join Mr. Frink at tea. That was a Wednesday, the day the *Gazette* was published each week, and we could have read his expressions as he read the editor's: that Mr. Whitefield "preached Sunday morning to universal acceptance to a crowded and attentive Christ Church."[248] His irritation probably grew visibly as the writer went on to observe that "Savannahians, appreciative of his unwearied labors on their

Window treatment in the Church as it now appears, following the extensive restoration in the 1970's. The northeast tower of the modern church houses the bell crafted in 1819 by Revere and Sons of Boston. (See Chapter 3.)

behalf, seem to outvie each other in showing him their grateful respects."

If there was an element of jealousy behind reactions such as Mr. Frink's or a touch of haughtiness in Mr. Whitefield's manner, it was most likely generated by the preacher's flair for showmanship. When the time came to show off Bethesda's two new wings, the buildings Mr Frink had helped found only a few months before, for instance, Mr. Whitefield threw a party that kept tongues busy for weeks! It is worth including here, not only for its intrinsic interest, but because it offers insight into the ceremonial taste of the period and possibly into the relationship between the rector of Christ Church and the widely acclaimed preacher. The festivities began with a service at the Chapel of the "Orphan House-Academy", to which the Governor and Council were invited, with prayers read by Mr. Ellington and a sermon by Mr. Whitefield. Afterward,

> *The company were, very genteely and politely entertained with a handsome and plentiful dinner, and were greatly pleased to see the useful improvements in the house, and the two additional buildings for apartments for students, of 150' each in length, and other lesser buildings.*[249]

Specifically, genteel and polite entertainment for the guests meant "tea, coffee, frontiniak, English hams, etc. in the Library Room" on arrival at Bethesda. This was followed by a procession to the chapel in which Mr. Ambrose Wright and Mr. John Crane preceded the Rev. Mr. Whitefield with white rods or staffs, in the habit of an M.A., and he was accompanied by the Rev. Mr. Ellington."[250]

> *After the service the company returned from Chapel in procession, Mr. Whitefield's family singing very melodiously as they walked. No Blacks attended at table, Mr. Whitefield and his friends waiting upon his guests himself. The whole entertainment was exceeding elegant and made a solemn and grand appearance. The company . . . re-*

turned in the evening highly satisfied, and great expectations are formed from this hopeful beginning.[251]

In the weeks that followed the affair continued to receive attention and even more elaborate description in the pages of the *Gazette*, some of it via London correspondence.[252] Indeed, the occasion was still a favorite topic of conversation when word reached Savannah of Whitefield's death in October. The end came, not surprisingly, while he was itinerating in New England. Yet the impact on Savannah was undiminished by the distance, apparently. An unknown local clergyman assured his colleague in England that

you can have no conception of the effect of Mr. Whitefield's death upon the inhabitants of . . . Georgia. All the black cloth in the stores was bought up. The pulpit and desks of the Church, the branches, the organ-loft, the pews of the Governor and Council were covered in black. The Governor and Council, in deep mourning, convened at the State House and went in procession to the Church, and were received by the organ playing a funeral dirge.[253]

He reports further that Messrs, Frink, Ellington, and Zubly all preached on the occasion, and that the Presbyterian Church was also draped.

Occasions such as the celebration at Bethesda and Whitefield's funeral give us some insight into the life of Christ Church in 1770, but they still leave many questions about Mr. Frink unanswered. Was it Whitefield's style that irked him so? Yes, but not solely that, apparently. He reported to the SPG that "since the death of Mr. Whitefield, Mr. Ellington has attempted to push himself into his parish, but without success. He is now preparing to send his baggage to South Carolina [exhibiting] a rambling inclination . . . peculiar to Methodism."[254] Itinerancy was viewed by the geographically structured established Church as a means to escape subjection to ecclesiastical authority, whatever else. This, added to Whitefield's ability to charm his way into the affections of other people's parishioners, may supply all the explanation we need. Had we peeked over the shoulder of James Habersham as he wrote to the Countess of Huntingdon, however, we might have glimpsed yet another aspect of the matter. Quite apart from any feelings attributed to Samuel Frink, it may be that some of the old infection of the Trusteeship still festered when Habersham observed

in this town. . . we have three places of public worship, a Church of England, a Swiss and English dissenting congregation, over which Mr. Zubly presides, and a Lutheran Church. The Minister of the Church of England has not yet taken the least notice of either Mr. Piercy, or Mr. Eccles . . . Mr. Piercy does not chose any connection with Mr. Zubly, for which I do not blame him.[255]

Such universal dissatisfaction of nearly everybody with nearly everybody was surely far broader than Mr. Frink's powers. He fit the pattern well enough, but did not create it.

Samuel Frink survived Whitefield only by a year. He must have been much more winsome in person that he appears through the lens of time, for when he died, 4 October 1771, he was "much lamented by the inhabitants which appeared in the countenances of great numbers of people who attended his funeral." Indeed, wrote the Wardens and Vestry in their official notice to the SPG, attendance "was so great that the Church was not sufficent to contain them"[257]

His successor is noteworthly both because he arrived in record time and because he marks the end of the parish's mission period. With a tenure so brief he could hardly have done more! Timothy Lowten had been rector at St. John's Sunbury,[258] for a short time before being called to Savannah, where he replaced Mr. Frink by December of 1771.[259] There were some doubts about his suitability, apparently, although he had made a very good impression on many at Christ Church while at Sunbury. James Habersham noted the delay in his collation without stating any reason except that "the parish is so very much divided in its opinion of him."[260] That was soon resolved, however, as by the end of March 1772, the same reporter felt that the "tongues of his opponents seem to be stopped."[261]

In securing Mr. Lowten's position, officials at Christ Church wrote to the SPG requesting the same salary as that given Mr. Frink and once again raised the idea of another missionary and "chapels of ease."[262] This time they appear to have been refused in both requests.[263] The parish's days as a mission had ended ready or not, and in a short while Christ Church was described as "a comfortable preferment, being worth upwards of £300 sterling a year."[264] Unfortunately Mr. Lowten died just two years later without leaving us much information on himself or his activities. We don't even know when he died, only that by July of 1774 his wife, Elizabeth, was settling his estate.[265]

The last of this group of short term rectors was also something of a landmark. Haddon Smith came from South Carolina, probably in September, 1773,[266] to fill the vacancy created by Mr. Lowten's death and to preside over the parish's final years as a part of the established Church. Since that establishment was nearing its end, this may be an appropriate context in which to reflect on its signficance for Christ Church. Actually, it would be nearly impossible to over-estimate the significance of establishment in the life of the parish, since it was probably *the* paramount factor in shaping its entire ecclesiology — its view of its purpose and function as a congregation — what now we would describe as its "self-image." As we do so, it will soon become apparent why Haddon Smith, and most of his predecessors too no doubt, would have found it so difficult to make the adjustment that was soon to be demanded of them. It will also explain why Christ Church itself had such difficulty in weathering the storms of revolution.

To begin our reflection we have only to recall that in the post-Reformation era, commonly accepted theory considered all social order to rest on three traditional pillars. These were the throne, the church, and the aristocracy or structure of social classes. Debate there would always be over the precise definition or implications of the three, but there was virtually universal assent to their necessity in some form, and to the principle that *they must be respected*. Certainly, such thinking was not new. What was new in the 17th and 18th centuries, however, was the intensity with which our ancestors believed. They had been taught by a century and a half of war — what the history books are pleased to call the "Wars of Religion" — to see cracks in any of the three pillars as threatening all social order, or even the edifice of civilization itself. The England of Olgethorpe and Haddon Smith had undergone two revolutions almost within living memory and seemed at times perilously close to realizing everyone's worst fears of social chaos.

When our reflection focuses specifically on the church, some very important ideas appear which we can safely presume to have been in the minds of parishioners in the 1770's. Their church they conceived to be, above all else, a major feature of the divine plan to hold society together. It is noteworthy for instance, that while the American colonies illustrate much disagreement over who should be "established," nearly all of the thirteen colonies had establishments.[267] Perhaps the clearest statement of the prevailing view came after the war in a religious establishment bill of 1785 which argued that because "a knowledge and practice of the Christian religion tended to make good men and citizens . . . the regular establishment and support of religion were among the most important objects of legislative action."[268] Thus, loyalty to church was also loyalty to king or country and to the existing social order. They were all but indistinguishable. What was true of the parishioners was particularly true of the rector, for he alone among their congregation would certainly have been required by law personally to swear loyalty to the king.

Among the consequences of this concept of the Church could be requests to alter the liturgy on special occasions. Thus, in 1772, clergy were directed by the king to modify the

> *Public service of the Church, where the Royal Family are particularly prayed for, and . . . also publickly notified that it is expected upon the present occasion of the Death of Her Royal Highness the Princess Dowager of Wales, all persons do put themselves in deep Mourning.*[269]

Even more indicative of the intimate relation of civil functions to ecclesiastical are the numerous cases brought before the courts by the parish sexton, to clarify his "right of franchise" in cases involving burial of the dead or tolling the Church bell. These were his tasks within the parish, and his suits claimed that he was entitled to his standard fee even if someone else rang the bell or dug the grave. The court agreed.[270] Finally, although it may sound quite unrelated, it was a consequence of the same principle that made it a task of wardens and vestry to set the rates and assess taxes for the poor of the parish.[271]

With such interwoven loyalties it is easy to see why the Revolution created serious problems for all Church of England congregations, including Christ Church. What was problematical for the congregations, however, was virtually insoluble for their rectors. That is, the idea of revolution no doubt raised a battery of questions for every colonist; for Anglican clergy, however, it offered an additional, personal, moral dilemma: whether to risk bearing false witness. Did the cause justify breaking the oath they had sworn?[272] Not for Haddon Smith. During the summer of 1774, with discussions of revolution beginning to simmer throughout the squares and taverns of the town, he decided to take a stand. Moving cautiously at first, he announced his lack of sympathy for colonial opposition to royal policy in a series of editorials. Published in the *Georgia Gazette* under the pseudonym "Mercurius," he defended what colonials were already calling "the intolerable acts."[273] When his identity was suspected, reprisals began immediately. In the *Gazette* there were rebuttals from another phantom calling himself "Libertus." In addition, Sexton John Neidlinger claimed that William Ewen, the junior warden, held the Church's "surplices, communion table, desk, and pulpit cloth in his own house" and even kept the key to the door of the Church! On two occasions "Mr. Smith was obliged to read evening prayers without surplice, there being nobody at the said Church-warden's house to deliver him one."[274]

The same issue of the *Georgia Gazette* that reported Neidlinger's accusation also revealed another sort of reaction to the Rector's views. William Gibbons, a prominent parishioner, not only refused to read Smith's pseudonymous editorials but saw no reason to listen to him either. Thus he advertised "to be let on very reasonable terms, a pew in the Church during the Reign of the Rector."[275] For his part, Major Ewen was not willing to let Neidlinger's accusation go unchallenged. However, his rebuttal tells us more of the escalating emotions than of anyone's culpability.

> *In order to prove that I locked the door the Grave Digger is brought forth, who is used to dig dirt, so that he might throw some at me . . . As to the man who calls himself sexton, when he was sober [he] acted as such, but that was not always the case. . .*[276]

Unfortunately for his cause, the sexton also reported seeing the ghost of the Rev. Mr. Zouberbuhler walk the streets of Savannah in a wig and white gloves. Apparently he assumed it would lend authority to his testimony. Instead, Mr. Ewen seized the opportunity it demean his accuser further and cast doubt upon his credibility by suggesting that he had "not yet recovered his senses from a great panick!"[277]

When at last the Rector entered the fray to defend Mr. Neidlinger,[278] the sexton's tormentors gained what they most desired: opportunity to attack Mr. Smith himself. He was, after all, the primary target of their animosity, especially since "Libertus" (probably Ewen himself) had grown confident

The interior of Christ Church as it appeared from 1964 until the early 1980's.

enough of "Mercurius'" identity to state as much publicly. The clue lay in the eloquence of the writer signing himself "Mercurius," whom "Libertus" wished

> *would follow the example of his worthy predecessor who never troubled himself with the intricacies of politicks, never appeared fond of paper skirmishes, or of displaying juvenile and puny witticisms in a newspaper.*[279]

In spite of the controversy, or perhaps to cool it, Georgia's colonial House of Assembly notified Mr. Smith that they would attend divine services early in February, 1775.[280] Whatever their reason, the legislature's presence may have had a calming effect (although paucity of modern parallels could invite some skepticism, admittedly . . .). Maybe it was only that events in the northern colonies began to overshadow local distresses. This was the spring of Paul Revere's ride, the battles at Lexington Green and Concord Bridge, Ft. Ticonderoga, and Bunker Hill. It was also the spring in which the Second Continental Congress gathered in Philadelphia. To better prepare the colonies for any future Lexingtons, the Congress gave George Washington the task of organizing a "Continental Army." It also encouraged formation of local "committees of safety" to maintain order in event colonial governments should falter. The Congress' suggestion stimulated a wave of action committees and provincial congresses up and down the seaboard.

In Christ Church Parish, those who shared this "rebellious spirit" would not be left behind. They saw their chance to show it at the official celebration of the King's Birthday in early June, 1775. To prepare for that annual English feast day, cannons for the salute had been set up along the bluff above the Savannah River. Then, on the eve of the holiday, enjoying the cover of darkness, a gang of local partisans spiked the cannons and pushed them off the bluff into the river mud below![281]

Locally, matters reached the flash point after July 4th, when another spontaneous committee calling itself the "Provincial Congress" began its session at Tondee's Tavern, just around the corner from the Church.[281a] There, on behalf of its better known parent, the Continental Congress, the Provincial group proclaimed July 20th to be "a day of fasting, humiliation, and prayer." They "requested" all congregations to participate and their clergy "to preach suitably to the occasion." Mr. Smith had complied happily with a nearly identical request for the previous day when Governor Wright called on the churches to pray that the unhappy differences between Colonies and King might be reconciled.[282] This time, however, he refused, "not thinking it proper to acknowledge an unlawful authority".[283] The Provincial Congress did not feel very unlawful. It responded by resolving

> *That the Rev. Haddon Smith, by . . . refusing to comply with the request of this Congress and to join on a day of fasting and prayer appointed by the Continental Congress to be observed throughout all America . . . has given too much reason to believe [he] ought to be considered unfriendly to America.*[284]

To make certain their view was "understood" a deputation which included Edward Telfair, George Walton, and Oliver Bowen from Savannah went to the rector to present the resolution personally, which also informed him that he would be "suffered no longer to officiate in this town."[285] The same day another committee, led by a Mr. Biddulph and Peter Tondee, called upon Sexton Neidlinger to inform him that he was not to ring the bell nor open the Church door without their permission "or abide by the consequences."[286] Just what they meant by "consequences" was made clear when the callers appeared at Mr. Smith's door in a few days to tar and feather him — a mischief they had already brought to another parishioner![287] "Happening Providentially to be out upon a visit," the Rector reported with a sigh of relief, he and his family "escaped their fury that night.[288]

Having begun late, "revolutionary fever" now rose rapidly in Georgia. The Rector viewed another sign of it from the comparative security of a rectory window a few days later, when he saw "two men with halberts" and a drummer who were recruiting about the town for men to serve in the South Carolina Service. They had already gathered six recruits, who were marching with them with blue and white ribbons in their hats, when he heard one of the recruiters read from a paper:

> *All Gentlemen Volunteers, that are willing to serve his Majesty King George . . . in order to pull down the high spirit of Lord North, who wants to put his foot on the neck of America, let him repair to our drum head . . . where they shall enter into present pay and good quarters; they shall be allowed £10 entrance Money, and £5 upon inlisting; they shall have One Shilling Sterling a Day, and good Cloaths, and Provisions Gratis; And when they have done gathering in laurels, They shall have plenty of good Rum punch to Drink. God Save the King."*[289]

Troubled though he was, the Rector was not alone in growing apprehensive over the rising hysteria. The tendency for the community's hotter heads to set the agenda for all was polarizing opinion as sharply as were Lord North's policies themselves. By mid-August the situation had reached the point where more than a hundred of the most respected citizens in Savannah, including many from Christ Church itself and a majority of the Vestry, were willing to put their names on the line in the cause of moderation, thinking it

> *necessary to exculpate ourselves from the misery brought on this Country by several unconstitutional bodies, called a Provincial Congress — a Council of Safety — and Parochial Committee, who have in a great measure subverted our civil and Religious Liberties . . .*

Among the specific complaints that followed was "silencing the Rector of Christ Church." Worse yet, in the petitioners' view, was their information that the Parochial Committee which did the silencing contained Jewish and Presbyterian members, one of them the chairman! The Committee had even appointed Edward Langworthy, a layman of "doubtful Religious Character," to perform divine services in place of the Rector.[290]

Considering the upheavals of July, 1775, it is not surprising that by early August Mr. Smith, no longer "thought himself safe in doing his duty as Rector."[291] Thus, fearing to press Providence too much further, he took his family to Tybee where he sought passage to England. No effort was made to prevent him, apparently, despite many days delay awaiting suitable passage. There was merely a routine notice in the *Gazette* to indicate that "yesterday sailed from Tybee, for Liverpool, the Brigantine *Joe*, Capt. Aiken, on which went passangers the Rev. Haddon Smith, Rector of Christ Church parish, with his wife and family."[292] Shortly thereafter, his tormentors were bidding over what he had left behind in this world — "furniture, 3 slaves, and a few horses, to be auctioned 7th November" at the customary place, on the courthouse steps.[293]

Through the autumn and winter that followed, tensions continued to increase. Indeed, they reached the point where moderation was no longer acceptable to either side, and in February 1776 editor James Johnston found it necessary to cease publication of the *Gazette*. Unfortunately, this denies us our most consistently useful source of information about affairs at Christ Church. For the war years, our records that do survive tend to be so fragmentary as to leave us in doubt about their full significance. Yet there is enough to give us at least a ragged picture of these difficult years during the Revolution.

The strong party sentiment that drove Haddon Smith into exile and forced the *Gazette* to cease publication climbed to a new level in August of 1776, when news of the "Declaration of Independence" reached Savannah. It was read several times around the town including the public square (probably in front of Christ Church) complete with punctuation by ceremonial cannons. "That night a great funeral procession carried through the streets of Savannah an effigy of George III and buried it with high mockery."[294]

Whether Edward Langworthy actually performed, as appointed by the Parochial Committee, is not known. We do know, however, that services of recognized clergymen were not totally lacking. Mr. Piercy, Anglican Chaplain at Bethesda, preached occasionally and performed other clerical duties at times. One such occasion came in January, 1776, at the opening of Georgia's first Provincial Congress,[295] and clearly indicates his acceptability to current local leadership. Another figure of particular interest appeared to help fill the gap in the person of Rev. Mr. John Rennie, who has a double connection with Christ Church. In his way, he too was a victim of the rising tension, one of its displaced persons, but like Mr. Piercy he was still marginally acceptable locally. Mr. Rennie had come to Georgia early in 1774 to be catechist to the slaves at Beth Abram, Mr. Zouberbuhler's plantation, which was now in the care of the trustees designated in his will. Shortly after his arrival Mr. Rennie was also elected Rector of St. Philip's Parish (Georgia). He continued in both functions until late in 1775 "when his loyalty [to the crown] rendered him obnixious to the people" of his parish. Subsequently, through the influence of Wardens James Powell and Josiah Tattnall he came to Christ Church.[295.1] As Rennie himself later stated, "it was at the request and invitation of the loyal part of the inhabitants of the parish of Christ Church," that Governor Wright appointed him to officiate "in the room of the Rev. Haddon Smith." He continued to hold services in the church with frequency, if not perfect regularity, until the summer of 1776 and the Declaration of Independence. Refusing to acknowledge the independent colonies "in any shape whatever by altering the Liturgy of the Church or renouncing . . . allegiance to the King of Great Britain," he was prohibited from reading prayers or preaching any more in Church. Yet he

> *was permitted to continue the discharge of his duties at Beth Abram and in occasional baptizing, marrying, and burying till. . . . September, 1777 when the Explusion Act . . . obliged [him] to relinquish his property and banish himself from America.*[295.2]

It is odd, in a way, that years which saw such momentous events for the Church and the birthing nation should leave us so short of witnesses. Nevertheless, the parish records as well as the public and journalistic sources, that can be so helpful under normal conditions, are cast in disarray by the very powers we seek to observe. Example: the Church of England was formally disestablished by the adoption of Georgia's new constitution in 1777. The implications for the Church are monumental yet little local record of the impact of the change has survived. We know only the obvious, such as the replacing of parishes and their saints' names with counties. The old parish names now survive only in the churches themselves. A less obvious feature of the new constitution was its grant of religious liberty to all (a moderate extension of the colonial charter) and its exclusion of clergy from membership in the House of Assembly.[296]

Locally, whatever else, it meant also that after Mr. Rennie's departure it was not until British troops occupied the city that Christ Church once again held regular services and enjoyed a real live Rector. To that post, the British commander appointed the Rev. Edward Jenkins in March of 1779.[298] According to Gov. Wright, who returned with the British occupation, Jenkins

> *did duly and regularly discharge the duty of Rector of Christ Church . . . to which he had been inducted by Lt. Colonel . . Cambell after the reduction of [the] province — from the first day of February 1779 to the 7th of February 1780. . . .*

Wright's statement goes on to assert that he did his work in an "examplary and proper manner" although he "received no pecuniary reward (save only a few trifling surplice fees.)"[299]

The ornamental detail seen here dates from the reconstruction which followed the fire of 1897. A radical change from what had been in place before the fire, the new design was the creation of William Gibbons Preston.

The upheaval which had deprived the Church of its Rector originally now led Mr. Jenkins to retire with the Army to Carolina where he had family and property to look after.[300]

It also provided a successor. Fortunately we have enough surviving bits and pieces regarding the Rev. Mr. James Brown to give us some idea of the impact of the war on the parish. Most obviously, it was the fortunes of war which determined who held power over the city, who was welcome and who was not, and which directions one might travel. With the British Army moving toward his home, for example, Jenkins saw an opportunity he might not soon have again. He took it. James Brown for another, was in Savannah as a stepping stone toward filling his post as SPG missionary to St. George's parish, South Carolina, but the war prevented his futher progress at the moment.

Writing in April of 1780 to his sponsors, the S.P.G., Brown comments "that there has been no clergyman of the Church of England in Savannah, nor indeed in any part of the province that is under His Majesty's government for some months past." So while awaiting an opportunity to complete his journey he thought to put his time to good use. With the approbation of Sir James Wright, he performed Divine Services every Sunday in Christ Church after his arrival, and also gave notice that he was ready to do any other duty that might be needed by the unattended flock such as baptisms, funerals, etc.[301] One year later, he was still serving in Savannah, waiting for war conditions to change! But, alas,

> on account of these continual alarms, Mr. Brown . . . has never yet been able to go thither. Gov. Wright has advised him to take charge of the parish of Savannah for the present, where his punctual performance of his duty recommends him to very general esteem . . .[302]

Oddly enough, this last glimpse of Mr. Brown in his patient frustration was given us by an observer in a similar situation. The Rev. Mr. James Seymour was under sponsorship of the

49

S.P.G., as missionary to St. Paul's (Augusta), and was forced to flee his parish when matters there became intolerable. Now, unable to return, he filled his days in Savannah by representing his parish in the Commons House of Assembly and occasionally assisting Brown.[303] Evidently, Seymour's situation in Savannah was something of an improvement, for he now had time to write the S.P.G. after a six year silence! Like so many correspondents, he began with an apology for his delinquency. In exploring it, however, he left us a most instructive view not only of his own experience, but that of Haddon Smith at Christ Church as well, and probably of Anglican clergy throughout the colonies. In the words of the S.P.G. journalist,

> *For about two years after the breaking out of the rebellion, he met with indulgence from some leading men of his parish of the rebel party, and was suffered to perform the duties of his function without interruption. Great respect was paid to his clerical character and though he was frequently threatened by the mob, yet he received no personal injury. The Liturgy, at last, however, became so offensive that they discontinued their attendance on the service. Many were afraid to go to Church for fear of being deemed what is called Tories and treated accordingly. Some Loyalists and the most respectable of his hearers now advised him to discontinue the public service entirely. He did so, [but remained] punctual in performance of such as are private.[304]*

Seymour's recollection of events in Augusta would have been recognized by numerous colonial clergy. Their own positions often experienced similar deterioration as rebellion became "the Revolution," and tolerable differences of opinion came to look like treason.

Despite the instability, Christ Church was well served by Brown and Seymour. That situation was about to change, however. Surprising though it may seem, Haddon Smith was still Rector, officially. Indeed, he had been drawing the part of his salary that came from the King throughout his exile, while Messrs. Jenkins, Brown, and Seymour etc. went with little to none. Thinking to do his duty better, Smith send a substitute, a curate, to take charge of the parish on his behalf. The curate's arrival changed everything. As James Brown tells us, writing the S.P.G. from Charleston,

> *He continued to do his duty at Savannah till lately, when superseded by a curate sent out by Rector Smith. "A Curate is a new thing in that part of America, and therefore the appointing one has given great offence to the People there, and more especially as it was done without consulting them, or even the Governor." Mr. (John) Stuart is the Curate . . . (Brown) remained for some time at Savannah, "but finding it helped to keep up the prejudice against Mr. Stuart," he departed.[305]*

Another factor contributing to his departure was the inflated price he had to pay for "the most indifferent accommodations" now that the rectory was occupied by Mr. Stuart.

James Seymour gives us our final first hand glimpse of the state of the parish during the latter part of the war. He was once again in Savannah as a refugee, because "rebels possess all Georgia except a few miles round the town." He, too, comments on the high price of provisions and "the dearness of house rent" under these nearly-seige conditions. He even set up a short-lived school to keep his family from absolute want, because though he "frequently assists at public service, visits the sick and performs other duties of his office, he receives not the smallest endowment." "The fees of the 'Living' in Savannah all devolve on Mr. Stuart via Mr. Smith (who now resides in Ireland)."[306]

What became of John Stuart is unknown, but it is not likely he remained in Savannah for long. In early July British forces evacuated the city. Shortly thereafter, on 13 July 1782, the members of the Georgia House of Assembly met in Christ Church, and thus reasserted their claim to jurisdiction over the city and its parish.[307]

The evacuation which swept away John Stuart opened the way for new leadership at the close of the Revolutionary era. We know nothing about his advent or achievement, but the Rev. Mr. John Holmes was identified as "the late rector of Christ Church, who for some time past officiated," when his obituary appeared in 1784.[308] The epitaph that was prepared gives us virtually all that we have about him. Even allowing for the hyperbole of tombstone rhetoric, it leaves us wishing we could know more.

THIS STONE
Is Sacred to the Memory
OF THE REVEREND JOHN HOLMES,
Late Rector of Christ Church Parish,
AND CHAPLAIN
Of the State Society of the Cincinnati.
He was
A NATIVE OF IRELAND:
AT
The Commencement of the late War
He stood forth a decided Advocate
OF AMERICAN FREEDOM:
in
The Course of that Contest
He suffered Captivity with Patience,
Remained stedfast in his Principles,
and saw the
GLORIOUS REVOLUTION ACCOMPLISHED.
As
A Gentleman of exalted Genius,
Extensive Erudition, and strict Integrity,
He lived in general Estimation;
AND DIED
March 30th, A.D. 1784, in Savannah
Aetatis Suae
XLI,
UNIVERSALLY LAMENTED.
He
Exhibited a happy instance

of
Political Zeal without Rancour;
of
Wisdom without Pendantry;
OF GENUINE WIT
With unbounded Philanthrophy;
and
Of acknowledged Eminence
Without a personal Enemy.
THIS CHARACTER
IS DRAWN BY A FRIEND,
To whom his many Virtues were known.
Reader, whene'er this solemn Turf you touch,
When o'er his honour'd Dust you chance to bend,
Let fall a Tear upon the sacred Couch;
If thou art honest-thou hast lost a Friend.[309]

Probably it was just prior to Mr. Holmes brief sojourn among us that, with the turmoil of revolution finally subsiding, the vestry gathered to take stock of the Church's condition. The *Minutes* of their May meeting, 1783, reveal both the fatigue of war and the dreary inventory of worries they recited to mark this fiftieth anniversary of the parish:

1 Double lot, on which is a Church. . . . . out of repair,
1 Double lot, on which is a Parsonage House . . . . out of repair,
1 Tract of land containing 300 acc., 3 miles from the town, being a glebe,
1 Set of Derelick Pews in the Church. . . .[310]

Yet even with several notes of indebtedness due also, they were not devoid of hope. For the *Minutes* go on to indicate that a search is underway for a permanent Rector to lead the only Anglican parish in Georgia that survived the Revolution intact.

The narthex of the Church as it appeared after being enlarged and redesigned in 1982. (See Chapter 9.)

Altar cross given c. 1884, and still in use, helped to inspire an outpouring of memorial gifts. (See chapter 6.)

III
Fire and Tempest
1785-1835

With everything so "out of repair" after the war, restoring parish life must have looked like a gigantic task. Nevertheless, efforts began almost immediately on several fronts to deal with the most pressing needs. During the spring of 1784, evidence suggests some repairs to the Church building were already underway. For along with the usual Easter Monday notice in the *Gazette* that new wardens and vestry would be elected for the coming year, there was the special note that Christ Church's "Divine Service will be performed in the Dutch Church on Sunday next."[308] Actually, there may have been several small projects undertaken about this time, because two years later pew holders were informed that they would be expected to pay for the repair of their own pews.[309] Although the magnitude of the work done is unknown, there may be some indication of it in a published notice of July 1786, informing the public that Divine Service would once again be held in Christ Church on the arrival of the new Rector, the Rev. Mr. William Nixon.[310]

Almost immediately Mr. Nixon set up an academy in the parsonage, offering to teach to the youth of the town "English, Latin, Greek, and such Sciences as are generally taught in European Colleges."[311] Real recovery from the war must have come slowly, however, for it was a weary Rector who wrote to his wardens and vestry a year later. He was no doubt describing much more than his own experience when he complained that although he began it to help out financially the school succeeded only in exhausting him physically. And now,

far from being able to support the dignity of my station, I have yet been under the disagreeable necessity of borrowing money to support a meaner and far more disagreeable and inconvenient manner of living than I ever before experienced. It is now almost four years since I arrived on the Continent, during which time I regularly attended to either your Church or some other . . . for which I have not yet . . . received above £17. . . . The parsonage house is in so ruinous a condition that I once would have been ashamed to live in it. I need not mention the state of the Church. These and the minister are worn threadbare. . . .

Some of Mr. Nixon's disappointment can perhaps be attributed to false expectations. Yet when he reports travelling 20, 30, or even 50 miles to funerals, marriages, and Christenings without the smallest fees offered it tends to evoke sympathy both for the Rector's condition and the parish's.[312] Before the year was out, however, he decided to seek a greener pasture,[313] and by November of 1787 the Rev. Mr. Benjamin Lindsay was already well established in his place.[314]

Mr. Lindsay was newly immigrated, apparently. His wife arrived in Savannah the following June aboard the sloop, *Jenny*, "after a tedious passage of 21 days,"[315] and he became a citizen the next October.[316] The new Rector quickly immersed himself in local affairs, becoming active in the Masons[317] and co-founding an academy during his first year in town,[318] as well as establishing connection with "Bethesda College."

Perhaps it was that same energy which also began to make things happen in the parish. Early in the new year, 1789, arrangements were underway to make needed repairs to the Church building. Top priority was a new roof.[319] Then in 1790 proposals were solicited for work on the steeple.[320] Some sort of steeple structure must already have existed by that time, as an open letter in the *Gazette* complained at the disquieting affects of the Church's bell. The critic, who obviously enjoyed his complaint, is also informative.

"I am a sojourner, as all my fathers were" and arrived a few weeks ago. The day which succeeded . . . my arrival it pleased God to afflict me with a dangerous, a most threatening malady . . . The bell tolled so mournfully solemn, that, if my apprehensions had not been governed by reason, and conviction that heaven is preferable to Georgia, I must, alas, have desponded. . . . Pray sir, in this enlightened age, why tinkle that knell, why continue that relick of the customs of a barbarous age?[321]

The thought of augmenting the steeple to embellish such a "barbarous relick", one he assures us "hath long been abandoned" in Jamaica, must surely have further distressed him. Not so the targets of his critique, however, for the bell stayed. It was used frequently to announce everything from pew sales to fires to liturgical occasions and funerals, just as when it was "rung muffled" in June 1802 as news of Mrs. Washington's death reached the city.³²²

Mr. Lindsay's presence also marks an interesting period of transition in the identity of the parish. It was a time when, concurrent with numerous survivals of the old "establishment," there is evidence of a new acceptance of the Church in the community — that the stigmata of the colonial church, although still visible, are no longer considered stains. For instance, in 1788, a notice in the newspaper reminded readers of the poverty around them, that frequent applications to the wardens showed the presence of great need "about this town." Since no system then existed to relieve such need, observed the notice, "it is intended that a Public Collection be made on Sunday next at Christ Church, when it is hoped all humane and charitable persons will contribute to alleviate the sufferings of their fellow creatures."³²³ The old pattern of "establishment" days seemed the obvious one to follow under the circumstances.

It seemed a useful pattern to Mordecai Sheftall, too, as chairman of the Savannah "Board of Wardens." In 1789 he wrote to the Rector, Wardens and Vestry requesting that they ring the Church's bell at eight and nine o'clock in the evening to mark the curfew hour when seaman were required to return to their vessels.³²⁴ The Board wanted to be certain both seaman and taverners knew the hour. Quite similar also to arrangements under the old establishment was the look of the fee schedule published by the wardens and vestry in 1790. It listed charges to be exacted for bans and marriages, funerals, baptismal certificates, tolling the bell, digging graves, etc.³²⁵ There was a difference, however. Unlike the days when Samuel Frink tried to collect for all such acts within the parish, regardless of who performed them, this schedule specified fees for services actually rendered by the rector or sexton and levied a fine on attempts to overcharge.

Despite similarities to its pre-Revolutionary role, it is clear that Christ Church had out lived any suspicion as a haven for royalists by this time. In July 1788 the *Gazette of the State of Georgia* proudly proclaimed the 13th year of American independence. Describing the festivities which had taken place six days earlier, the weekly paper recalled for its readers how

*early in the morning Capt. Lloyd's Company of Artillery ushered in the day with 13 discharges . . . In the forenoon the Hon. William Pierce, Esq., delivered an oration suited to the occasion . . . at Christ Church. . . . The Artillery Company fired a salute of 39 guns in honour of the Cincinnati on their coming out of Church.*³²⁶

Could there be better proof that old sins were now forgiven, old stains forgotten, than to have the Society of the Cincinnati observe the day in Christ Church? It simply underscores the point to notice that purely civil business was sometimes conducted in the Church as well, on occasions when crowds overflowed the courthouse.³²⁷

It must have aided this process considerably that during these same years Episcopal Churches up and down the new nation were publically working out the implications of independence. Christ Church joined in the new developments at least as early as January, 1789. The *Vestry Minutes* show

*That from and after next Easter Day, the Liturgy of the Church of England, as altered and amended by the American Episcopal Convention lately held in Philadelphia, be read invariably in Christ Church. That the Congregation of the said Church be requested to furnish new . . . Common Prayer Books as published under the direction of the said Convention.*³²⁸

Later that year, the congregation was chartered by the State of Georgia³²⁹ further establishing its legitimacy. But the most sensational sign of changing times occurred when General Washington visited the city in 1791, and "on Sunday morning the President attended Divine Service in Christ Church."³²⁹·¹ Such a visit surely did much to encourage the idea that Christ Church, like the newly organized "Protestant Episcopal Church," was now a legitimately American body. The process of adjustment was nearly complete in 1793 when the congregation reaffirmed its adoption of the now fully Americanized *BCP* "subject to such alterations as shall hereafter be agreed on by the minister of Christ Church and the vestry thereof."³³⁰

This last noted adjustment was carried through by the Rev. Mr. Edward Ellington who became Rector following Mr. Lindsay's departure, probably early in 1792.³³¹ Ellington came to Christ Church from Goose Creek, S.C., but he knew the Church well from twenty-five years of close association. After coming to Georgia as an SPG missionary to succeed Samuel Frink at St. Paul's in 1767,³³³ he accepted care of Bethesda in 1770 under Whitefield.³³⁴ Apart from earning the scorn of Samuel Frink, not a notable distinction, Mr. Ellington came to enjoy great esteem locally. Later he gained recognition as one of the most distinguished of the Church's early Rectors. It is disappointing that we know so little about him and his work, since he was probably the one who guided the congregation into its relationship with the newly organized Protestant Episcopal Church.³³⁵ But beyond that achievement, only a few fragments of his work are still evident in the records today, such as his preaching at a collection service for the poor.³³⁶ Yet when he died in 1795, of what was described as "violent peripneumonia," the tribute to him in the *Gazette* leaves us with the feeling that we have surely missed someone special.

*He often directed the delightful talent of wit against vice, but always with so judicious a delicacy as to spare personal feelings . . . We shall scare look upon his like again.*³³⁷

Mr. Ellington's death seems to have taken all by surprise for there was no immediate action to discover a replacement. William Nixon filled in by performing marriages and burials, and preaching occasionally,[338] as he probably did on the news of Samuel Seabury's death in April of 1796.[339]

Still no replacement for Ellington had been found when the town was stunned by a great fire in November. Word was that the conflagration began in a small bake house in Market Square. Before it was over, however, the flames had moved eastward and southward to consume some 60% of the city, including Christ Church.[340] While still dazed and disorganized, the city was visited by a second fire ten days later that left it in a nearly neurotic state.[341] We can sense a mixture of numbness and exhaustion still present when the Vestry was notified to gather for its annual elections "at the ruins of the old Church," Easter Monday 1797.[342] William Nixon continued to fill in, preaching frequently in the Franklin Square Courthouse,[343] while the other tasks of rebuilding were faced one by one.

Not until the summer of 1799 can we see any solid signs of rebuilding the Church. At that time the *Georgia Gazette* carried the first of a great new wave of solicitations for proposals on the "intended Church."[344]

Matters still moved slowly, however, and it was another year and a half before proposals for building a structure "80 feet long and 60 feet wide of brick and stone" were invited.[345] The problem seems clear enough: money. Several possibilities for raising additional funds were considered, such as leasing the Church lots, selling off the old glebe lands, and a campaign to collect outstanding debts.[346] Eventually all were attempted, but it was not until the glebe lands were sold in March of 1801 that matters visibly began to move ahead.[347]

Bills of lading extant in the parish archives show that by May of 1803 sizable shipments of building materials intended for the new church at last began to reach Savannah. The construction that followed used some 35,000 "Philadelphia brick" and 75,000 "common brick," plus "rustick stone" from New York.[348] The success of the effort was joyfully commemorated with an oval plaque which reminded all who would read it of the structural history of the site.

> Christ's Church
> first erected 1744
> and
> By the Great Fire of 1796
> Reduced to Ashes,
> with
> A Principal Part of Savannah.
> In the Year 1803
> The Foundation of this Building
> was laid, reviving the Episcopal
> Church in this City.[348]

During the construction the congregation accepted the offer of refuge in the Lutheran Church, and pews were sold at auction with one Sunday per month reserved to the Lutherans.[349] The Rev. Dr. William Best, from Charleston, became Rector just in time to oversee the transition — beginning with Divine Service "at the German Church in the Episcopal form."[350] With a new Church rising and a new Rector on the job, after more than eight years without, all was poised for the challenge of the new century already upon us.

The winds of change blew fresher than anyone knew, however, and on September 8th a great storm struck. The water rose continuously for hours until "all of our lands under cultivation were covered . . . and the sea [had] covered the shallows of the chain of islands along our coast which before had impeded its passage." The storm was devastating:

> *Crops of cotton, potatoes, and corn destroyed, every panel of fence swept away, lime kilns . . . leveled, the foundations on which they stood, which was made land, destroyed; schooners, sloops, and shell boats driven ashore — into fields — the injury done and the losses sustained on the shore can only be repaired by time and great industry.*[351]

The walls of the Episcopal Church were "blown down" as was the steeple of the Presbyterian Meeting House.[352]

Time and great industry were indeed required as it turned out. Two years after the storm the vestry was still searching for some means to get the reconstruction underway, and worship was still at the Lutheran Church "where divine services agreeably to the ordinances of our church . . . have been (performed) for upwards of 18 months by the Rev. Mr. Best."[353] When the rector moved to St. Simon's, probably about Easter, 1807,[354] progress slowed even more. The only hopeful sign was an action by the Georgia Assembly which enabled the congregation to hold a lottery.[355] Detailed plans were worked out for the affair, which promised to raise $10,000 toward the rebuilding goal if successful.[356] Despite the great popularity of fund-raising lotteries at the time and the very reasonable hope of their success, the vestry hestitated to make use of such a resource "unless compelled by absolute necessity."[357]

The ruins of the Church remained essentially as the great tempest had left them in 1804. Oddly, almost no news of the Church appears in the newspapers of the next two years, and other usually reliable sources become mute as well. There is not even the annual ad reminding parishioners of the Easter Monday pewholders' meeting to elect the wardens and vestry. While negatives prove little, they can suggest much. This lapse in the vital signs of the parish suggests that spirits may have reached an all time low. Surely it was a time for discouragement — after the Church had been totally destroyed twice in eight years, and most of those years had been rectorless. Now, after four years, again there was no rector, and all "proposals so far exceed our means" that rebuilding the Church seemed beyond hope. A letter to the editor of the *Republican and Savannah Evening Ledger* in 1810 suggests that by that time many members had taken to attending different churches while others, scrupling to attend elsewhere, went without.[358] The same correspondent offered the judgment

What a gloomy representation of the state of public spirit, and indeed of religion, does our town present to a stranger who beholds the Episcopal Church! At a time when three or four thousand are collected for the establishment of a Theatre; three or four thousand dollars more for the prosecution of agricultural experiments, the Episcopal Church lies neglected and its half-finished walls totter to the earth!

It was a strong and timely rebuke, and there was something prophetic in its tone. But as a good prophet, the writer spoke not merely rebuke, but hope also. Thus, in the same letter attention was called to the Easter Monday meeting set for later the same month, requesting Episcopalians "particularly to attend as business important to the affairs of the church will be laid before them." Minutes for that meeting have not been discovered, but the "important business" was revealed in an "address" to the newspaper-reading public by the wardens a few days later. They shared

their anxiety for rebuilding of this Church, whose ruins have served so long to offend the sight of this community, and of the strangers who visit it, and to the uncharitable have afforded cause of reproach for . . . this congregation.[359]

Then, recounting in detail the calamities which had made it necessary, they appealed directly "to the liberality of this community . . . and to that of. . .Episcopal Brethren in other places."

Miraculously, within days, word came to the building committee that 75,000 bricks were on their way.[360] The appeal, the unnoticed work of the committee, and the years of anxious waiting had begun to work! By the end of 1810, materials for the roof were on hand.[361] Also on hand was the Rev. Mr. John V. Bartow to "perform Divine Service at the Lutheran Church" early in 1811.[362] The following month they were able to raise the roof on a building the *Columbian Museum* predicted would prove ornamental to the city and an object of pride and pleasure to the citizens. "We regret to learn that the funds raised are expended," however, and hope that by their liberality the citizens will not allow construction "to come to a stand."[363] They did not. Indeed, the wardens and vestry were so encouraged by the sale of pews in the "new" church that they moved immediately toward finishing the building.[364] This success came in spite of the faithful having concurrently to buy their pews in the Lutheran Church. When sale time came again early in 1813 purchases were made for six month terms "at the expiration of which time, it is expected that Christ Church will be completed."[365]

By the autumn of 1813 things seemed finally to be returning to "normal" at Christ Church, although the finishing touches which gave the new building its distinctive look required several more years.[367] Normal meant opportunity to show concern for others; not just preoccupation with survival. In particular it meant occasional charity sermons preached in the Church to raise funds for worthy local causes. Typically the churches of the city coordinated their efforts with a special sermon in the Presbyterian Church Sunday morning, at the Baptist Church in the afternoon, and in the Episcopal Church the following Sunday morning. Funds collected were then given to such enterprises as the Savannah Female Asylum or the Savannah Free School to sustain their operation.[368]

Normal also meant having a Rector and regular services. Yet for nearly twenty years since the great fire Christ Church had gone without both of these more often than not. Once the building project was well in hand, in November of 1813, Mr. Bartow gave notice he did not intend to renew as Rector, but agreed to carry on until a successor was arranged.[369] The search for his replacement led to the Rev. Mr. Walter Cranston of Rhode Island, and to this inviting promise:

> *In no place in America are the clergy of respectability treated with more attention and respect than they are in Savannah — but in return they require a clergyman to be a clergyman in all respects.*

The letter also went on to state the challenge he would face. "Christ Church must have a Clergyman of talent — as the Independent Church has the Rev. Dr. Kollock as preacher, a gentlemen of distinguished eloquence . . . [and] many of the old Church members attend his Church while we are without a pastor."[370]

Mr. Cranston arrived to accept the challenge in May of 1815, and even from this distance it is safe to claim that the search was profoundly successful. Certainly his first major act with the congregation was a joyful one, when the long struggle to rebuild finally was put behind and the parishioners gathered to consecrate the new structure. The Rt. Rev. Theodore Dehon, Bishop of South Carolina, led the celebration, accompanied by the Rev. Mr. Christopher Gadsden, Rector of St. Philips, Charleston. Along with Christ Church's newly arrived Rector, they "were received at the Church door by the wardens and vestry and conducted into the body of the Church where the usual form of consecration was performed in the presence of a numerous and respectable audience."[370a] Then, after the morning service was read by Mr. Cranston, the Bishop delivered a "most impressive and edifying discourse" to the congregation and confirmed more than sixty.[370b]

Mr. Cranston was from Rhode Island, of the family for whom the city is named. Prior to accepting the position as Rector he had been for several years a professor of languages at Harvard College.[371] According to a New England colleague, he was knowledgeable in French, German, Latin, Greek, and Hebrew . . . among other things, and a scholar of real significance.[372] Locally, he quickly won admirers in both the parish and the city, being often asked to speak at occasions such as the 67th anniversary gathering of the Union Society,[373] and his Church was frequently selected as the preferred site of musical performances. Typical of such occasions was the Oratorio given for the benefit of the Female Orphan Asylum in May of 1818. For the concert "Mrs. French . . . benevolently offered her services, assisted by the young ladies of this city, the Appollon-

Left, Children's chapel in the parish house during the 1950's. Below, The very simplicity of the wooden cross that is the focal point for Christ Church (Demere) Chapel does much to induce a mood of serenity.

The brass pulpit in use now was added in 1890. A survivor of the 1897 fire, it is one of several pieces which helped to establish the use of brass in the Church's interior. (See chapter 7.)

Processional cross in use since the early 20th century when it was given as a memorial to "Sarah Nuttman Mills, beloved wife of Charles Lucian Jones."

ian Society, and Mr. Brasch, organist." Together they presented a dozen or more selections, chiefly by Handel, Haydn, and Martin Luther,[374] to the great satisfaction of the beneficiaries and the audience.

The year 1819 was a headliner: with the visit of President Monroe and the sailing of the steamship *Savannah* for Liverpool. But for Christ Church parishioners, one of the most exciting events of the year was mentioned in a letter from warden J. B. Read to Mr. Cranston. Beside the news that a Mr. Adam of Bedford, Massachusetts, had agreed to put the organ "in the best repair," the letter also noted correspondence from Messrs. Hale and Revere "who promised our bell (a very good one from 1600-2000 lbs.) shall be shipped early in October."[375] Apparently all went according to plan for the vestry records note receipt of the "bell and tongs from Boston" in December, just before Christmas, 1819.

The bell may not even have been in place yet when, only three weeks later, fire once again swept through the city. Hundreds of buildings were destroyed, some of them much more substantial than the victims of the 1796 fire. Mr. Cranston recorded in this diary that

> *On the morning of January 3rd, at two o'clock, we were roused from our beds by the cry of fire. I reached it soon after its commencement. . . . . It was soon perceived that we were threatened with general destruction. No human effort could arrest the progress of the flames. . . .*
> *January 7th. I finished my services of the day in my Church. . . . which I expected never to have entered again. The Church was on fire frequently, and was once on the point of being abandoned. It now stands alone in the midst of a desert! Last Sunday I preached the Funeral Sermon for Dr. Kollock — today I preached the Funeral Sermon of Savannah.*[375a]

"Only Christ Church, the State and Planters' Bank, and Washington Hall survived" in the burned area from Bay to

59

The second church as it was depicted by Fermin Cerveau in 1837. In 1875 this commemorative plaque from the second Church was set in the exterior east wall of the present Church.

COURTESY OF THE GEORGIA HISTORICAL SOCIETY, SAVANNAH, GEORGIA.

Broughton and Jefferson to Abercorn. "Alas! Never did the sun set on a gloomier day for Savannah, or on so many aching hearts."[376]

This time, however, relief funds came to the city from all directions — from Georgetown, S.C.; from Augusta, where the Society of Amateurs held a benefit performance; from Annapolis, where "Mrs. French" offered a solo recital; from a benefit performance by the Philadelphia Theatre; from St. Simon's for needy victims of the fire, and many, many more.[377]

Damage to the Church seemed relatively light, and was apparently repaired by November 1820 when pews were sold again. It was not an ordinary pew sale, however. This time places were sold to the highest bidder, instead of using traditional pre-set rates. But just as in the days before the fires, the Church bell was rung to mark the hour the sale commenced.[378] Despite the fire, and even the yellow fever influx that followed it the next summer, signs of prosperity remained abundant — both in the city and the Church. Mr. Cranston set about building a handsome new house for himself the very next year,[379] and the Church did, apparently, have a preacher who could uphold its place with the likes of Dr. Kollock.[380]

Unfortunately, that situation was short-lived. In August, 1822, word reached Savannah that on July 25th Mr. Cranston had died while vacationing and visiting family in Middletown, Connecticut. The newspaper's obituary called attention to the loss all had "sustained by the death of this estimable man." The writer lauded his steadfastness as Rector of Christ Church for seven years, citing especially how "in seasons of calamity he did not desert them," either in fire or plague. His reference was to the severe epidemic of yellow fever which closely followed the fire. During those awful seasons, while most fled who were able, Cranston stayed behind to minister to those who were not. Thus the writer continues, "in the chamber of sickness or the abode of poverty and distress, none could have been more assiduous in administering the consolation of religion or the sympathy of a feeling heart." Cranston's

This 1802 design and pew plan probably gives us our best peek inside the second structure built by the congregation. The original plan shows many names which have been scratched through as the pews were rented to others, and several where even the second pewholders suffered the same — eloquent testimony to the many difficulties and doubts which so long delayed rebuilding of the Church.

religion was "characterized by meekness and toleration, he sought to win by persuasion not terror, and condemned none for differing belief." His mind was "highly cultivated and enriched by extensive reading in both dead and living languages." In life, "he was pious without bigotry; learned without pedantry; benevolent without ostentation." Now, at 32, he was at rest.[381]

Mr. Cranston's body was returned to Savannah a few weeks later, aboard the ship *Howard*, which also carried such local notables as Oliver Sturges and Amos Scudder back from their visits in the north. The new Rector was aboard the *Howard*, too.[382] The Rev. Mr. Abiel Carter, as his predecessor, was a New Englander, born in Concord, New Hampshire (1791). He was educated at Dartmouth, and had already begun the study of law in New York City when drawn to holy orders. After his ordinations by Bps. Hobart and White, he served several years in posts in the mid-Atlantic states, including Trenton, where he married Maria Beach, daughter of a prominent New Jersey clergyman.[383] During that period he also labored as a missionary in western Pennsylvania. Now, after a brief period as Rector of Trinity Church in the frontier town of Pittsburg, he accepted his call to Savannah.[384]

Services began immediately on Mr. Carter's arrival,[385] and so did his absorption into local society. Within a few months he had replaced Walter Cranston as Grand Chaplain of the Masons, been invited by the Hibernian Society, the Georgia Bible Society, the Union Society, the Savannah Female Asylum, Chatham Academy, and the Georgia Militia, among others, to join, serve, lead, or otherwise support their cause![386] No wonder the rector felt the need to return to his family home in upstate New York for several weeks each summer "to restore his health."[387] When in 1825 the Carters decided to take in 4-6 young ladies "who may wish to complete their course of literary education" and a "few day scholars,"[388] the need for times of restoration surely grew even more pressing.

By far the greatest event of Mr. Carter's years at Christ Church occurred when General Lafayette visited to help the

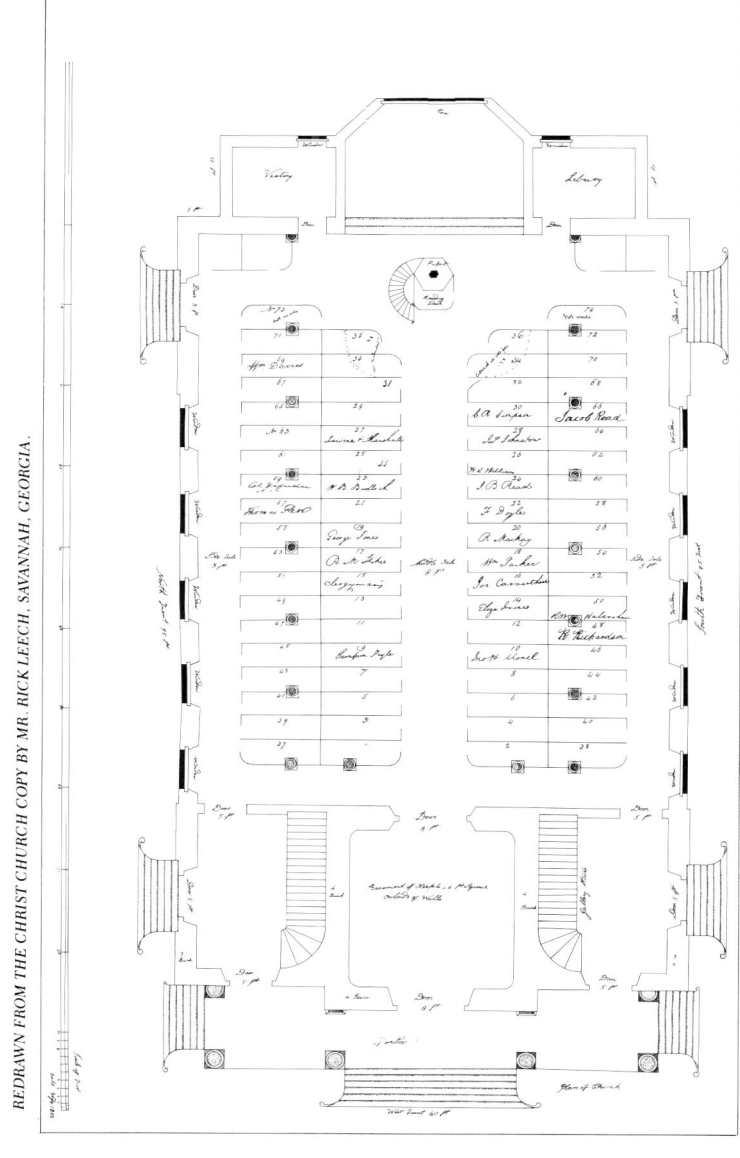

REDRAWN FROM THE CHRIST CHURCH COPY BY MR. RICK LEECH, SAVANNAH, GEORGIA.

61

nation celebrate as it approached its fiftieth year of independence. Locally, July 4th had long been a major feature of the annual calendar by that time. Typically, as in Mr. Carter's first summer in Savannah, the schedule would include a full day of ceremony, speeches, and cannon firings. The highlight was a ceremonial procession from the City Exchange down Bull Street and across Johnson Square into Christ Church under escort by the Savannah Volunteer Guards.[389] Usually the bells of both the Church and the exchange would be rung as the signal to form the military escort and the procession. The Church itself would be "crowded almost to suffocation, by an audience in a great part of our fair country women, who . . . have arrayed themselves in all their charms for the grateful occasion."[390] While there the celebrants would be treated to an address "suitable to the occasion" delivered by a local dignitary — perhaps the rector. None of the previous observances, however, compared to the grand celebration of 1825! It began March 19th when Lafayette arrived in the city and Mr. Carter was chosen to welcome him for the clergy of Savannah with a brief address. On this occasion he began by recalling that

> *among those blessings procured for us by that national independence which you, sir, so essentially and generously aided our fathers to achieve, by no means the least . . . is that religious liberty which is here universally enjoyed.*

The Rector then went on to assure the General that he and his brethren make good use of that victory, dwelling in mutual charity and harmony . . . that despite differences of theology they unite in supplicating on his behalf for his welfare and prosperity in this world, and especially for his eternal felicity in the next.[391]

The Hibernian Society "suggested" at the time that Lafayette had actually planned his arrival in March in order to celebrate St. Patrick's Day with them! But his days in Savannah were quite filled enough with such greetings as Carter's, and with parades, dedications, corner-stone layings, and speeches of his own. The monuments he dedicated still stand and the balconies hallowed by his having spoken from them, have become articles of faith in Savannah history. Christ Church has its place in such memories, for not only did the General dedicate the Nathanael Greene monument that stands before the Church in Johnson Square at this time, but he also attended the Church to hear a sermon delivered by Mr. Carter.[392] Perhaps the greatest significance in all the happy clamor, at least for the history of Christ Church, is that it leaves little doubt that virtually all vestiges of the old "Church of England stigma" had disappeared.

Not all of Mr. Carter's sermons were fortunate enough to discover such receptive and decorous congregations, however. One particularly flavorful occasion has been saved for us by a scion of one of the parish's oldest families. The incident involved an impish young "R.W.H." and also a "Mrs. E." whose pew was immediately behind the "H" family's. This substantial lady was reputed to be a descendant of one of the first colonists, but she was even more widely famed for her pronounced German accent, extreme garrulity and a nearly psychotic horror of dogs. Finally, the cast included an old gentleman "of the highest respectability," who when his own pew was filled often took a seat with the H's. beside the young R.W.H. and the pillar that also shared the pew.

> *He never appeared unaccompanied by a poodle, sheared, as was the fashion, to resemble a lion in mane and tail. In entering the pew, the old gentleman would stand up for a moment, look over the church, clear his throat, and, deliberately parting his swallow-tail coat, turn once more around then slowly take his seat. In the same way, his little dog would walk in after him, look under the foot board and seat, give a little sniffle, turn around . . . and then lie down to await the conclusion of the service. I very often felt tempted to disturb his response, but dared not for several reasons easily guessed at. . . . One Sunday our friend and his poodle did not appear at the door of the pew till the moment the minister . . . arose to commence the service. [He] paused on seeing many not yet in their seats — young men mostly who have remained on the porch or come late, as was even in those "good old times" too much the case, I have heard. From some like cause, the poodle did not immediately follow his master, and the devil — I suppose it was — took the opportunity to whisper into my ear the question "will the old lady ever stop talking . . . if she once begins?" The intrusions of genius often come like a flash, and seeing that her pew door was open, I closed ours, while the old gentleman was busy dividing his coat-tail, so that he did not observe the act. At length the service began, but the minister had just got to "Dearly beloved brethren, the Scripture moveth us in sundry places" when it became too evident that something else was moving the congregation in our part of the church . . . The poodle finding the door shut in its face was too proud or well bred to knock or whine for admittance, and naturally, seeing the next door open, turned into it. The apparition of the hated canine in her pew was more than Mrs. E. could stand, and she, commencing her protests against the intrusion in a whisper, . . . rose in volume and distinctness as their effect . . . appeared to be null.*

According to R.W.H.'s recollection, as her distress, underscored by her heavy accent, became obvious to many, excitement spread until "an audible titter was heard, and the parson stopped in amazement." Soon "the cause of the uproar became evident to the poodle's master; he stretched across me" to open the door, "called the dog in and then closed it behind him."

> *Mrs. E., with her head sunk in her coal-skuttle bonnet, . . . was breathing hard and fanning herself violently, while my father and mother were threatened with apoplexy from their efforts to suppress their laughter. The only two imperturbable persons present in that church were the dog's master and my innocent self.*

As R.W.H. recalls, "I was never punished, for there was no proof of malice . . . Two people only seemed to guess the truth — my old nurse, and the Rev. Mr. Carter, who was not a little bit of a wag himself, in spite of his cloth . . . He suspected that . . . my goodness was not of grace." Eventually, when he was at tea at our house, we compromised the matter, he implying he would keep his suspicions to himself "on condition that I would never look at him from behind the pillar while he was preaching."[392.a]

Most encouraging during Mr. Carter's years were the growing symptoms that the parish was no longer on the defensive — trying to salvage the fragments of fabric and respectability that had survived fires, windstorm, and the Revolution. Instead, it began reaching out beyond the old limits to carry its message and make its impact. In a most significant act Christ Church joined St. Paul's (Augusta) and Christ Church (Frederica) to create the Diocese of Georgia. Abiel Carter published, at the request of the wardens and vestry, notice of the convention to gather at St. Paul's in Feburary 1823.[393] As one of the key motivating powers in the creation of diocese, Mr. Carter was elected president of its first convention.[394]

When the diocese was founded Georgia lagged well behind most other seaboard states in parish development,[395] and until it was so organized, its parishes could not participate fully in the work of the national Episcopal Church.[396] But in 1823 the first steps were taken toward formal union with PECUSA and the foundations laid for missions in interior Georgia. The crucial step was taken by that first convention when it founded the "Protestant Episcopal Society for the General Advancement of Christianity in the State of Georgia."[397.a]

It was during this same era that Christ Church began to open its doors to "persons desirous of seats . . . who cannot afford to pay for them." A long series of ads in the *Savannah Georgian* repeated the assurance that "there are seats reserved for their use," and the invitation to make application to the Wardens.[398] Contemporary with this outreach was a rising concern for the observance of Sunday as a day set apart. Evidence of this concern appeared at least as early as 1820, when Walter Cranston was Rector. He and more than 250 fellow citizens signed a petition drawn up by Dr. Kollock of the Independent Church which complained against "public violation of the Holy Sabbath." The complaint focussed especially upon the open shops and routine market place transactions which they said openly violated the laws of the land, the authority of God, public morality, and the reputation of the city.[399] By 1828, the cause had reached the point where its advocates organized a meeting "held at the Episcopal Church . . . for the purpose of forming an association for promotion of better observance of the Sabbath."[400] Christ Church names figured prominently in the new group created at the meeting, from president William Bulloch (frequently a warden or vestryman) on down.[401]

During the following decade activities directed toward various needs grew more diverse. They involved such things as new Sunday School classes formed "to teach elementary principles of religious knowledge and right understanding of

Top, this commemorative plaque honoring Mr. Carter and his work in Georgia is now affixed to the wall at the head of the north aisle of the Church. Bottom, another of the striking brass pieces which so greatly enhance the worship and appearance of the Church. Baptismal ewer given in honor of Maria Campbell Kollock, Feb. 3, 1901.

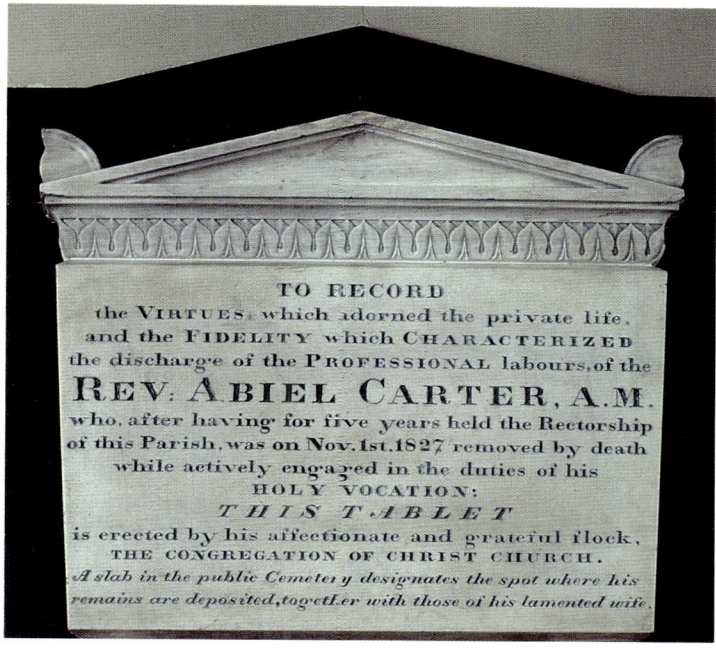

Scripture." These were well attended, including "in the colored school," 35 children.[401a] They also involved playing host to the Union Society's annual meetings, in which a number of parishioners were usually involved, and which occasionally drew notable personalities. The 84th anniversary meeting in 1834, for instance, gathered in the Church to hear an address by Col. Howell Cobb, a well known political figure of the day.[401a2] Other major projects which drew support from the parish were the Savannah Free School, whose "Subscribers and Friends" frequently met in the Church Sunday School Room,[401b] and the Female Orphan Society, which always had one of the vestry appointed as its manager.[401c]

At times the Church's outreach extended far beyond Savannah and Georgia. One fairly common cause for appeals from afar was disaster from fire or storm. In 1831, for example, St. John's Church in Fayetteville, N. C., was devastated by fire, as was most of the town. In such cases, usually a well-advertised charity sermon was preached and the offering sent to the stricken.[401d] The next call was from closer to home when St. Philip's, Charleston, was destroyed by fire in February of 1835.[401e] Not yet satisfied, however, disaster again struck Charleston in the great fire of 1838, which produced charity sermons and donations from a number of local sources, including Christ Church.[401f]

Georgia Missions also had been a concern since the founding of the diocese, and now the first new Episcopal congregation in Georgia since the Revolution was founded in Macon (Christ Church) in 1825.[403] But the struggle of the new church in Macon to establish itself reinforced the importance of an effective instrument of diocesan support. Renewed emphasis was given the Society organized in 1823 and the Rector of Christ Church, Savannah, was now its president.[404] Christ Church furnished not only the leadership for the Missionary Society but the greatest share of its financial support,[405] as well, during its crucial early days. Often the money was raised by activities which will have a very familiar ring, such as a spring concert of sacred music or a New Year's "bazaar." New Year's Eve, 1829, for instance, the "Episcopal Society for the Advancement of Christianity in Georgia" planned on having an Exhibition in the Exchange "for the sale of an extensive variety of beautiful and useful articles, many of them not to be procured in the Southern Country." The notices in the *Daily Georgian* appealed to "the ladies of Savannah who are disposed to aid the Society . . . with the ladies of the Episcopal Church particularly requested" to help.[406]

Even the untimely death of Abiel Carter in November of 1827 slowed the pace of activity only momentarily. It was thought they had escaped the yellow fever ravage of 1827, but in "the last week of October Maria Carter caught it and died in a few hours." Her husband "followed her to the same grave . . . after a separation of but 82 hours." "From the time that it became known that the malady had seized him, the most intense anxiety was manifested . . . by all classes of people, and by all religious denominations, not excepting Jews and Roman Catholics." "His funeral brought together an immense concourse; and all without distinction of creed, colour, or

A close-up view of the bell which hangs in the tower above St. Julian and Drayton Streets. This plaque, which reminds congregants and visitors of the bell's location, is on the west porch of the Church.

station, lamented his death, as if it had been a personal bereavement."[407]

After a few weeks' interval, during which services were handled by the Rev. Mr. Lot Jones, fresh from the mission at Macon,[409] a new Rector was on hand to take up the work of his predecessor. The Rev. Mr. Edward Neufville began at Christ Church on 1 December 1827. Even though only 25 years old at the time, he seemed already to possess many of the same qualities Mr. Carter did, and soon showed himself to be a worthy successor. Neufville had taken his degree at Columbia College, New York, and entered the General Theological Seminary, probably in 1822. The next year he was ordained deacon by Bp. Bowen of South Carolina, after which he served Prince William Parish (the ruins still stand near Sheldon, S.C.), and received priests orders in 1827.[410] A few months later Mr. Carter's death created the vacancy which brought him to Christ Church and introduced him to his life's work. It also introduced him to Mary Bulloch, whom he married the following June in the Church.[411]

The next decade witnessed a surge in missionary activity by the Society under auspices of the Diocese of Georgia and the "Domestic Committee" of the national Episcopal Church. Of special interest here is the activity of Edward Neufville, whose powerful voice in diocesan affairs sounded with peculiar eloquence on the subject of missions. While chairing the Diocese's Standing Committee in the 1830's, he spent several months scouting newly opened lands in northern and western Georgia.[411a] In his travels he noted many places suited to concentrated missionary effort, such as Clarkesville and Milledgeville. Work was soon carried on there and elsewhere around the State with a vigor which produced results. The new Church in Macon had ended a 75 year drought in new foundations, and in the fifteen years following its establishment the Diocese of Georgia grew to six established parishes plus half-a-dozen missions.[411b]

In addition to maintaining the momentum of the Church's outreach program, an immediate concern of the Rector had to be repair of the Church building itself. Nothing of any note had been done to its fabric since the 1820 fire, and there was some evidence of deterioration. The newspaper carried the announcement to pewholders early in 1829 requesting they "remove goods, cushions, books, carpets *this day*, as the Church is to undergo repair immediately."[412] Nothing too major was done, apparently, for only six weeks later the same medium carried the notice that regular services would be resumed in the Church two weeks before Easter.[413]

There is a hint of more significant renovation a year and a half later when pewholders were requested to meet and express their "views on removal and alteration of the pulpit."[414] Almost everything we know about what was done at that time we learn from the next report to the diocese. It was a bequest from the late Miss Wilkins that enabled them to "liquidate the remaining debt and to improve the appearance of the building as well as to add a number of pews by altering the arrangement of the Pulpit and Reading Desk."[414a]

Unfortunately, no further documentary evidence on this particular renovation has survived, except for one final matter which drew considerable attention. The ladies of the Church did their part through sewing projects — presenting "the Georgia Hussars with an elegant new standard in order to raise money for a new organ."[415] Undoubtedly that was not their first effort though, because the organ soon "arrived . . . in the Ship *Tybee* from New York." The builder, Mr. Erben, accompanied it to superintend erection of the $2000 instrument.[416] It must have been a colorful scene with the new organ being moved into the Church for installation by Mr. Erben, while Samuel Philbrick attempted to sell the "materials of the old organ in front of Christ Church" for cash![417] But all must have gone smoothly, for in only six days the Church was opened to try the power of the new instrument with "musicians, amateurs, and citizens generally invited to attend."[418] The new organ was certainly prominent in traditional celebrations such as that on Christmas Eve, 1833, which took place at seven o'clock in the evening.[419]

The altered interior also set the scene for ceremonies which had not been common in the Christ Church of old. In fact, when the Rev. Mr. Neufville presented Theodore B. Bartow, a son of this parish, to be ordained deacon by Bp. Nathaniel Bowen of South Carolina in 1830,[420] the act may have been the first ever seen in Savannah. Whereas in colonial days ordination had required a voyage to Britain, after the Revolution it was typical to journey to the north, or to Charleston. This was still the dominant pattern in 1836 when the Rev. Mr. George White was ordained to the priesthood by this same Bp. Bowen in St. Michael's, Charleston.[421]

In the decade of the 1830's, however, things began to change in this regard. The years that followed saw many events of special significance take place in Christ Church. Some of the change should probably be credited to the organization of the Diocese and the success of its missions, and perhaps to a generally rising prosperity. Without a doubt, however, much was also due to the leadership exhibited by the parish and the driving power of Mr. Neufville, the Rector. Despite his perpetually fragile health, he was constantly presenting the parish to the Diocese of Georgia and to the National Church in prominent fashion by his ceaseless labors in its behalf and through the conventions.[422] It seemed only natural then that the Diocesan Convention of 1836 would nominate him "as a suitable person to be Bishop of the Diocese under the canon of 1835." Notably, the nomination was made despite his having resigned temporarily due to illness in his family, and his devoting himself exclusively to missionary labor in interior Georgia in the interim.[423] Even though Mr. Neufville declined that offer, he continued to fill the leadership role which had accrued to him and to Christ Church. It was this leadership which Bp. Elliott recognized years later in remarking that "his labors had brought the diocese to a condition which called for a bishop of its own, and he might well have claimed the post as his by right of creation."[424]

IV

The Mid-19th Century: Progress, Prosperity, and Puseyism 1835-1851

Amid the vigorous activity of the 1830's, the Church structure itself claimed a share of the attention. At first the problems appeared simple enough. Since the west stairways were noisy underfoot, and frequently allowed cold winter drafts to chill the fervor of worshipers,[425] they were enclosed. Next, in December of 1833, the Church had a near miss with fire — close enough to make anyone nervous. The *Daily Georgian* reported the flames had moved from Whitaker Street eastward along Bryan Street and Bay Lane, and that the Church's steeple was briefly set afire.[426]

Concern deepened greatly, however, when it was noticed that the south wall of the building was cracked. The Vestry named a committee to call upon competent craftsmen to examine the condition of the wall and report on its safety. Within a few days the report was made to a relieved vestry that both foundations and the walls were "perfectly safe." The inspectors

> *assigned as the cause for the irregular appearance of the wall its condition at the period of its rebuilding, produced by the injuries sustained during the storm of 1804, but that since that period it has always been deemed perfectly secure.*[427]

But relief was short lived. Serious decay was noted in the main girders of the belfry,[428] and a second look at the cracked south wall of the Church brought a different assessment only a year and a half later. In the autumn of 1835, two of the city's most prominent building men, Amos Scudder and Matthew Luffburrow, judged the wall to be "in some danger of giving-way." Their recommendation was to dismantle the wall partially and rebuild it, but they offered this faint comfort: "we think that Building may be safely used for four or five months to come.."[429] Now urgency was added to gravity, and to help meet the crisis Mr. Neufville offered to have his salary reduced by $1000 "in consideration of the heavy expense to which you may be subjected."[430] Although the Vestry "respectfully declined" the offer, they must have wondered just a bit when six months later a third assessment considered that "no repairs would give it any lasting security." Therefore, it was recommended "that the Church be carefully taken down, and a new one constructed" using the old materials as far as they go.[431]

Considering the progressive nature of these reports the two year period over which they were made may have seen the building visibly deteriorating. In any case, enthusiasm for replacing it began to grow stronger. After a period of soul searching and doubt during the winter of 1836[432] the Wardens and Vestry concluded, on the basis of subscription amounts, that it was practicable to rebuild the church. They, therefore, resolved to proceed with procuring plans and estimates, and building as soon as possible.[433] Not all doubts were resolved yet, however, as one of the vestry felt compelled to "dissent and protest against the pulling down or destruction of the present building."[434] Even four years later, after the old church was gone and the new one rapidly rising, the question still may have smarted a bit. At least it was worth making the *Minutes* read that the Vestry had been wise to seek several opinions and to act as they did. For its condition, they found when they dismantled it, "imposed upon them the obligation to take down the Church to avoid the greater calamity of its tumbling down."[435]

Once the decision was made, matters moved quickly forward. By November, 1836, several designs were under consideration, and on this question there was unanimity. Without dissent the Wardens and Vestry adopted the plan submitted by Mr. James Couper and agreed to solicit specific proposals.[436] Advertisements were published within a few days in terms that will be recognizable to modern readers. In addition to taking down the old Church, builders were invited to bid on erecting the new one according to the plan now in possession of the committee. Specifically, this called for

The Ascension window in the morning sun, Easter 1983

The Ionic order to be used in a building
100 ft. × 60 ft.,
brick-stuccoed to imitate white marble, with
exterior walls at least three feet thick,
side walls 50 ft. high, plus
two towers or belfrys on the east end, to rise 15 ft.
   (One of which is to be properly finished for the bell.)
The portico 60 ft. × 16 ft. 9 inches, with six columns, above
   (32 ft. 6 inches high, with white marble capitals.)
Steps, granite or marble, 11 ft. high across the whole front, and
Three doors and two rows of side windows (six each row).
Basement 10 ft. high to be fitted up as a Sunday School Room,
Pews of the most approved modern form, and
galleries supported by ten Ionic columns.

The advertisements went on to state that "all bricks, slate, woodwork, etc., of the present building were susceptible to use in the reconstruction", and to assure bidders that "the bricks of the tower and walls of the present building will . . . be amply sufficient to construct those of the new." Finally, it was specified that construction was to be complete one year from the date of the contract.[437]

It must have brought considerable relief to have reached this stage, for it had not been an easy year in Christ Church parish. Adding to the pain that accompanies honest doubt and division had been the Rector's extended absence. Then, late in the summer, word reached Savannah of the death of the Church's Presiding Bishop, the Rt. Rev. Mr. William White. The death of one of the Eipscopal Church's "original" bishops is noteworthy in itself, but it has a particular value here. For the Vestry's response to the event reveals a quality of character, a sense of perspective and priority, that may also account for its ability to lead the parish in good order through this season of stress. They resolved simply that

While we sympathize with the Church in general . . . and more especially with the family, and the congregations among whom he . . . ministered, we feel that we have greater cause for gratitude to Almighty God, that such a man was so long spared to the Church on Earth, and for the firm hope that this "Valiant Soldier of the Cross — when taken full of years and honour, and Ripe for Heaven — has but gone to his station in the Ranks of the Church Triumphant."[438]

Surely the Rector himself is also the source of much of that admirable character. The picture we are left vividly catches

his slight figure, his quick elastic step, his twinkling eye, his finely chiseled face, and his expressive gesticulation, giving emphasis to his earnest words. . . . He was a charming man — a loving, tender Pastor, . . . respected by the whole community. . . . Never have I heard our Liturgy read with more unction and effectiveness than by him; while his readings of the Bible were like an illuminated exposition of it.[438a]

Yet whatever one might say of its leadership, the parish was ready for the challenge, too. At a general meeting late in January, 1837, with proposals in hand, the congregation gave the go ahead, commiting themselves as a body to raise the $30-$40,000 needed to build. They also acted to establish subscription committees intended to involve the entire membership.[439] Best of all, this represented no mere flash of enthusiasm. In fact for several years they had demonstrated a determination to improve facilities at the Church. One of the favorite goals was a new Sunday School Room — a project which had stimulated book fairs and special collections as far back as 1832.[440] An especially charming encounter, reported anonymously in the *Daily Georgian* during the spring of 1836, gives us a good idea of the spirit behind the movement. It was in the "Lyceum Hall" (at Bull and Broughton Sts.) that the writer discovered

a most busy and animated circle of young girls surrounding a worktable . . . strewed over with . . . . shreds and fragments of muslin, crape, silk, etc. . . . under the plastic fingers of . . . ingenious juvenile workwomen.

I inquired to what object they intended . . . the beautiful results of all this industry? They replied that they intended giving a fair on the 29th of April, . . . that they were a voluntary association of the female Sunday School Scholars of Christ Church, that they had frequently heard their teachers lamenting the want of a suitable school room, and had at length devised the plan . . . amongst themselves, in order to raise a fund to assist in building [a] room, which might induce more scholars to attend.[441]

Now at last laborers could envision their reward, for the plan called for space in the basement of the new strtucture to be "fitted up as a Sunday School Room."

By year-end, 1837, action was imminent. Terms for the annual pew rental, which always took place in early December, this year included a special proviso

with the understanding that when the Church shall be taken down for the purpose of erecting a new one, the officers of the church will provide another place for the service . . . and the accommodation of the congregation.[442]

Excitement began to mount early the next year when the *Daily Georgian* reported

the services of Christ Church will be performed on and after Sunday next (i.e., January 28th) in the building on the north side of courthouse square, formerly known as Messrs. Blodgett and Williams school house. The congregation will be accommodated with seats corresponding with the numbers and situations of their [present] pews . . .

Pewholders are requested to have their books and cushions removed from the present building and taken home this morning.[443]

Offers to share space were received from several congregations, notably the Unitarians and the Independent Presbyterians, but these were appreciatively declined. The Wardens and Vestry apparently felt that the time involved for demolition and subsequent reconstruction was simply too great to make such arrangements suitable. Apparently they did question whether to erect a temporary structure or to lease space for the congregation while construction was underway.[444] Since pew advertisements in 1838 referred to "the temporary building" some doubt remains as to what actually was done. The best guess, however, would seem to be that visitors could have found the congregation gathered at the former school house of Messrs. Blodgett and Williams.[445]

No such doubt shrouds the next major mile marker, however. Generous records virtually make us part of the crowd that gathered when

the interesting ceremony of laying the cornerstone of the new edifice to be erected for the congregation of Christ Church was performed yesterday at 12 M. A very numerous assemblage walked in procession from the "temporary building" in Court House square to the site of the Church. . . .[446]

There Mr. Neufville, presiding over "the proper ceremonies for the occasion", listed the several items to be placed "in a glass vessel within the stone": A copy of the *Holy Bible*, a *Book of Common Prayer*, the *Journal* of the Diocese of Georgia's 1837 convention, a copy of the Churchman's *Almanac* of 1838, the newspapers of the day, and sundry coins. Concluding the list was a roll of parchment with a lengthy dedicatory inscription of considerable interest, which read:

IHS
Glory to God
Christ Church
Founded in 1743
Destroyed by Fire, 1796
Re-founded on an enlarged plan 1803
Partially destroyed in the Hurricane of 1804.
Rebuilt in 1810. Taken down in 1838.
This cornerstone laid
February 26th, 1838
of a new edifice to be erected
(according to a plan furnished by James Hamilton Couper,
Esq., of Georgia.) by Amos Scudder, mason, and
Gilbert Butler, carpenter, under the direction of
William Scarborough, William Thorne Williams,
Robert Habersham,
William P. Hunter, and Dr. T. Bartow, building committee.
Rev. Edward Neufville, rector.
George James, M.D., and William B. Bulloch, wardens

T. Bartow, M.D., William Thorne Williams, Robert Habersham, William Scarborough, R.R. Cuyler, William P. Hunter, and P.M. Kollock, M.D., vestrymen[447]

Continuing its description of the ceremony, the *Daily Georgian* noted that "the books were placed in the glass vessel by two of the Sunday Scholars, Masters George Jones and William H. Turner." Finally, with the stone in place, there was "prayer, the singing of the last two verses of the 90th Psalm, and a short address, [after which] the assembly was dismissed."[448]

Just over a year later the basement of the still unfinished structure was ready for the congregation when "on the 31st of March, being Easter Sunday, Divine Service was first performed in the New Church By the Rector, the Reverend Edward Neufville." Construction continued to make visible progress during the spring and summer of 1839, while the usual second thoughts about the plans required minor negotiations with the builders. Chiefly these involved only decorative trim or an occasional needed door or stairway that had been overlooked.[450]

Meanwhile, health problems once again moved Mr. Neufville to request leave during the summer and take his family to the north. This the Vestry cheerfully granted although regretting the cause that rendered it necessary.[451] Regret became embarrassment, however. Because of a minor flaw in timing both Vestry and Rector took steps to procure substitutes for the five months Mr. Neufville would be absent, and thus one of those nightmarish fears that attend responsibility came to pass. When the Rev. Messrs. George White (of Springfield) and T.B. Bartow (of St. Simon's) both accepted, and arrived in town to take charge a sea of faces blushed — a sea that was restored to order by the gracious withdrawal of Mr. White.[452]

Happily, the incident had no apparent effect on the construction timetable, which was well advanced when Mr. Neufville returned in November.[453] Indeed, planning for the building's completion and dedication must have begun by that time, for it was only a matter of weeks until

the impressive rites of Consecration were celebrated in the new and beautiful edifice recently erected by the Episcopal Church of this city. The day was inclement, but the audience was large, composed not only of those who usually worship with the congregation, but also from every other Church in the city.[454]

The day of consecration was the third Sunday in Lent, March 22nd, 1840; but the usual solemnity of the season and the weather seem not to have dampened excitement one bit. Bishops Ives of North Carolina and Chase of Illinois led the celebration along with numerous clergy in addition to the Rector: William Spear of Charleston, Stephen Elliott of Columbia, Seneca Bragg of Macon, Theodosius Bartow of St. Simon's, and George White of nearby Springfield. The service, with its impressive ritual and "learned . . . eloquent discourse" by Bishop Ives, "riveted the attention of the whole assembly," according to the *Daily Georgian*. What the journal-

Were the Maison Carrée (top) and the Virginia State Capital (middle) influential in the design of the new Christ Church?

ist reporting the occasion found equally noteworthy, however, was the edifice itself. On entering through the west doors, he wrote,

> *We are struck at once with the rich appearance of the chancel; its chastely stuccoed arch; the elegant and expressive carving of the reading desk and pulpit; the splendid marble communion table, and baptismal font; all enclosed within the altar . . .*

The only feature of the interior viewed negatively was the "highly decorated" ceiling, the "point of objection being its massiveness." Generally, however the reviewer used such terms as "eminently beautiful, judicious, and tasteful," and described the whole as "a building which reflects great honor and credit, both on those who planned and those who executed it."[455]

Most significantly, the collective effort to create the new building seems also to have helped generate new energy in the congregation generally. The quickened spirit was especially visible when the Wardens and Vestry gathered on the day following the consecration. They met to pass formal resolutions of thanks to the bishops who led the service and to Mr. Couper for his building plan, as we might expect. The outpouring of gratitude also reached specific donors such as "Mrs. Mary Marshall for her liberal contributions, but more particularly for the marble communion table now erected within the chancel," and the numerous others whose contributions allowed purchase of the marble baptismal font and the material and decoration for the pulpit and altar.[456]

In their enthusiasm the Wardens and Vestry also acted to raise Mr. Neufville's salary from $1500 to $2000 per annum, and to propose even more far reaching changes. Essentially, these involved commiting funds toward the support of a bishop for the diocese "since we now have enough churches with regularly established ministry to (so) entitle us" and since it is "of the utmost importance to the spread of the light of the truth and the future prosperity of the Church . . ."[457]

The new Church made an imposing addition to Johnson Square. Note the original configuration of the steps leading up to the west portico and the handsome iron fence, traces of which can still be seen in a few places.

The interior of the new Church (1840) as it appeared through its first three decades.

Sentiment favoring election of a bishop had been building for at least two years, ever since a grant from Christ Church in 1838 had assured a solid foundation for Grace Church, Clarkesville.[458] Now, with six parishes, the diocese had reached the canonical minimum required to elect its own bishop. In the same year a memorial from the Diocese of Florida proposed joining together with Georgia and Alabama to elect a bishop in common.[459] While viewed with appreciaiton, the obvious weakness in such a plan added a note of urgency to the question already on the minds of many churchmen in Georgia, especially in Christ Church. The death of South Carolina's Bishop Bowen the following summer brought the matter to the top of the agenda since his loss would be so keenly felt. A frequent visitor to Christ Church,

> *for many years he has been our only Bishop, and though struggling with diseases and burdened with the care of his own large Diocese, he was ever ready to perform Episcopal offices for this Church and to guide its clergy by his paternal counsels.*[460]

Thus, with the need now more pressing and enthusiasm higher than ever, the Vestry further developed its proposal for a bishop. In order to encourage a "new bishop" to settle in Savannah, and to help in his support if one should be elected,

> *"it is in the opinion of this Vestry expedient and proper that a new parish under the name of St. John's Church should be formed, the Rectorship thereof to be tendered to the bishop-elect."*

Moreover, the offer of rectorship was to be made with the expressed understanding that the bishop and the Rector of Christ Church should alternate in the respective churches and "thus the interests of both be united." It was a bold gesture, but a bit frightening, too. This is why the idea was so carefully couched in words of caution, to assure that "there should be no division in this congregation, but that the parish thus formed should be connected with this Church, thereby extending, but not dividing the Church."[461]

When the May, 1840, convention of the diocese in fact did elect a bishop, the Vestry acted again. A committee was directed to proceed with organizing the congregation, locating a place for its worship, and gathering such material support as benches and the small organ from the basement of the Church for its use.[462]

The city granted several lots, and in December, 1840, newspapers spread the word that

> *Members of the Episcopal Church and all others who are disposed to unite in organizing the new parish of St. John's are requested to meet in the basement room of Christ Church tomorrow . . . for the purpose of electing wardens and vestrymen.*[463]

The new parish was off and running and the new bishop soon was running, too. The proposal presented to the convention in May had "worked perfectly,"[464] Elected was the Rev. Mr. Stephen Elliott, originally from Beaufort, South Carolina, who had participated in consecrating the new church in the spring, and whom the *Charleston Mercury* called "one of the brightest luminaries of the American Church."[465] In July he wrote to the Wardens and Vestry of Christ Church that

> *having examined the solemn question submitted to me in every point of view, I have been brought very clearly to the conclusion that it is my duty to cast my lot among you, and with your hearty cooperation, upon which I count, and the peace of God preventing, to labor for the furtherance of the Gospel and the Church in the State of Georgia.*[466]

Dr. Elliott went on to express his "decided opinion" that the bishop should be free to move about the diocese "pioneering the way for the local missionary and the settled pastor." Nevertheless, he agreed to the rectorship, and the alternating plan involving Christ Church and St. John's "for a limited time."[467]

Through the medium of the *Daily Georgian* we are made virtual participants in the Bishop's consecration. It took place on Sunday morning, the 28th of February, 1841, in Christ Church[468]

> *on a day which was exceedingly unfavorable; heavy showers, thunder and lightening. The usual condition of our submerged streets on such occasions prevented many from attending this solemn ceremony. The church was, however, nearly filled. Morning prayers were read by the Rev'd Paul Trapier and the lessons by the Rev. William H. Barnwell. The sermon was preached by Bishop Meade of Virginia from I Tim., chapter 3, 15th verse . . . Dr. Elliott was then presented by Bishops Ives of North Carolina and Gadsden of South Carolina to the presiding Bishop . . . The Service was throughout solemn and affecting — particularly when the Bishop-elect was invested by Rev. E. Neufville, assisted by Rev. T.B. Bartow, with the robes of his official station, and during the imposition of hands and the presentation of the Bible, which the Bishop-elect was exhorted to give heed unto in all things. The celebration of the Lord's Supper closed the interesting scene by which one of the ablest sons of the church was introduced into the Episcopate of Georgia.*[469]

The *Georgian*'s columnist went on to point out the special significance of the occasion. "This is the first time that a Bishop has been consecrated in any of the Southern States." In the matter of credit he noted that "it is to the zeal and executions of the Rector of Christ Church that we are indebted for witnessing the imposing ceremonial."[469a]

The writer's very positive feelings extended beyond the ceremony to the young Bishop himself. Although fearing to embarrass him with overripe praise, for "we know his mind too well to fume before him the nauseous incense of adulation," the journalist had obvious difficulty in restraining himself.

> *Of him who has thus come amongst us . . . we will only say that not his diocese merely, but all christians, of whatever name, rejoice in the coming of such a faithful and zealous champion of the truth to labour in our borders.*[470]

If the Vestry's concept of tying election of a bishop to creation of a new parish "worked perfectly," the new building was somewhat less willing to conform to their vision. Only months after its consecration some repair to the belfry was needed.[471] Then a much more serious situation developed in 1846, when "various defects" required considerable roof, gutter, cornice, and plaster work on the portico.[472] The bad news side of the problem may have a familiar ring: proper repair demanded much more work and expense than first suspected. Further, because of a shortage of good workmen long delays were encountered, and some work even had to be performed twice — once for immediate measures to preserve the building, then again to restore it properly.[473] The good news side is only a memory, however, for when the job was finally completed after nearly two years of worry and frustration, the entire exterior of the Church was repainted . . . for $550![474]

Matters of routine upkeep occurred with the same unreasonable insistence they do now. For example, during the same month a Mr. Penfield rehung the bell to improve its sound (for $25), and a workman of Mr. Erben's, also in town, tuned the organ for $30, just as the city was insisting on the Church paving the south side of its lot.[475]

Other changes, in the interior fabric of the Church, including some of considerable magnitude, may be worth specific attention. In 1846, for instance, while the portico work was underway, congregational complaint moved the Rector to raise the issue of heating the Church. Fear of another fire was still very real, however, and "the general feeling of the Vestry (appeared) to be decidedly against the introduction of stoves into the building." Only after much assurance as to the safety of the modern device proposed did the Vestry solicit a bid from architect John Norris to furnish and install one of "Fox's Patent Air Heaters," complete for $300.[476] Four years later, in 1850, gas lighting was installed in the Church,[477] after which the Vestry resolved "that the glass chandelier lately removed . . . be presented to Grace Church, Clarkesville, in this state."[478]

Most important of all, contemplated changes in the east end of the Church suggest some alteration in the congregation's thinking during this period. Probably we should not attach great significance to the initial adjustments made in 1846, although they are worth noting. At that time the Rector requested that the pulpit be lowered some eighteen inches, and the reading desk moved a bit to facilitate movement within the area of the chancel.[479] Mr. Neufville reminded the vestry that the pulpit had been raised by the same distance shortly after construction of the new Church, but that the purpose of the changes had not been served. This was only the beginning of an extended process, however, and by 1851 parish leaders were discussing extensive changes with architect Charles Scholl. This time attention was focused on the chancel area as a whole where any alteration involves so much more than just moving the furniture. The *Vestry Minutes* relate with guarded simplicity that "plans (were) explained by Mr. Scholl and much discussion ensued, but no definite result was obtained and the subject was indefinitely postponed."[480]

Alas, just what was being discussed is nowhere recorded at length, nor are Mr. Scholl's "detailed plans" anywhere to be found. It is quite probable, however, that the contemplated changes were linked in many minds to the "Puseyism" which so excited the church, nationally and locally, during the preceding decade. Puseyism was the label popular at the time for the liturgical, devotional, or "Catholic" revival within the Anglican communion which we now call the Oxford Movement. It attracted attention at the convention of the diocese as early as 1841, and word of it was frequently spread across the pages of the local papers as they relayed reports of the stir from northern correspondents.[481] The locals even became involved at times, as when one reader complained that the *Savannah Republican* too summarily dismissed "the other side" and begged the *Georgian* to let the Puseyites speak.[482] Neutrality on the matter, apparently, ceased to be a realistic possiblity. Few churchmen lacked strong opinions about it, and fewer still left them unexpressed! What was to some a glorious revival, in which they were spiritually quickened by discovering anew the richness of ancient traditions, was to the opposition a pernicious theological kudzu which threatened to suffocate everything beneath a pall of "Oxford tracts" and "Romish trim."[483]

Regardless of their opinions on the topic, Christ Church folk were not to escape direct impact. The controversy remained an active one, and while they were yet postponing the question of rearranging the chancel in 1852, shocking news came. Bishop Ives, of North Carolina, resigned his see and submitted to the Pope in Rome! The *Daily Morning News* reported that he handed his episcopal ring and seal to the Pope with the words, "Holy Father, these are the signs of my rebellion."[484] This is the same Bishop Ives who had entered Christ Church in 1840 to join in consecrating it, and again the following year to help consecrate Georgia's first bishop. He was a familiar figure locally. We should probably assume, therefore, that parishioners felt deeply the gravity of this particular controversy. It was not just another verbal tournament among unknown voices in the distance. Almost certainly that made it more difficult to decide, or even discuss, any change in the chancel.[484a]

With or without the alterations accomplished, the carpets were replaced in the aisles of the Church and on the stairs leading to the galleries. As was typical, the old carpets from the ground floor were moved to the galleries.[485] Happily, amid all of this attention to the interior furnishings of the Church and the details of their arrangements, there were moments of relief. Perhaps it was only coincidence, but a local newspaper chose this time to pass along a tip on etiquette, by advising that

> *chewers of tobacco are earnestly requested to avoid the use of this article in the Church, or else to spit in their hats.*[486]

With all of these developments in mind, it is especially interesting to note that during the same years, the record tends to become much more generous with information about music in the Church. Whereas, prior the 1830's we were left only the barest fragments from which we might make inference about musical activity, in the 1840's and 1850's we regularly discover names of organists and singers, programs for special occasions, etc. It is interesting to speculate on the reason for the change: increased emphasis on music? . . . greater prosperity in the parish? . . . the city? . . . better records?

Whatever else, surely some of the increase can be attributed to the survival of nearly complete vestry minutes after 1839. It is these which give us our first clear sign of the existence of a regular choir in 1844, and which reveal the name of a certain Mr. Fisher who was retained as a singer at $100 per annum.[487] Apparently the employment of such a lead singer as he was not yet followed consistently, for two years later a rather distressed rector wrote to his vestry pleading for the engagement of a "professional singer." Complaining that "our former dependence upon voluntary assistance in the musical department of our public service has proved so precarious", Mr. Neufville had hired a singer at his own expense four months earlier. The experiment had given such "entire relief from the embarrassment occasioned by the want of a singer in the organ gallery" as to induce him to suppose the wardens and vestry would now be inclined to make the arrangement permanent . . . at their expense.[488]

To the Rector's satisfaction the vestry was so inclined. They went even further, hiring a new organist and a "leader of the choir" as well, each at a salary of $200 per annum. The new organist, Moses Coburn, who became such a fixture in the Church through the rest of the decade, was filling a position of long standing. The post of choirmaster, however, seems to have been new, for one of the duties assigned was to "take all possible measures to form and instruct a choir." In addition, both contracts specified that their incumbents were (1) to be present whenever the Church was open for service (Sunday or weekday) including all festival days and fasts, (2) to substitute for one another if either had been excused by the vestry, and (3) since the Church was closed at night on Sunday, "the congregation uniting with St. John's," they were subject to service there.[489] Mr. Neufville's original wish, as expressed in 1846, seems to have been generally fulfilled, and at times enjoyed great success. For example, the work of one lead singer was applauded for having "elicited universal commendation, as well from other persons skilled in music as from the Rector and the whole congregation."[490]

Evidence suggests that this pattern, using professionals in the positions of organist, lead singer, and choir leader, remained typical through the 1840's and 1850's. Only occasional exceptions occurred when the "lead singer" doubled as "choir leader",[491] or when there may have been more than one singer on the payroll or none at all.[492] Less typical was an interesting device the vestry introduced, presumably as a cost control measure. When it raised the organist's salary by fifty dollars per year in 1851, it was done with the understanding "that he is to make all repairs [which are] now needed or may hereafter be required to keep the instrument in tune, cleaned etc., without further expense to the Church."[493] Whether there is any connection between that innovation and Mr. Coburn's resignation a year later is not disclosed, but at any rate the clause does not reappear. The contract of his successor, Mr. Gnospelius, was sealed on the old terms and at the old salary level.[494]

With this foundation in place, music flourished during the 1850's to the point that it became a form of outreach. A key step in this development began when the old 1831 Erben organ was recognized to be in such a state of dilapidation as to leave few alternatives to replacing it. The "organ committee" found the instrument's "resources very limited" and becoming "more and more unmanageable." To begin with the organ was a small one having only seventeen stops, and only one of these had any power. That was a trumpet stop which "from its peculiar formation is constantly out of order." Worst of all, the committee discovered the keys did not return, "throwing the music into inevitable discord, and the swell [organ could] not be used at all."[495] The Vestrymen were convinced by the report, or perhaps by having heard the organ themslves! In either case, their *Minutes* record that nearly two-thirds of the cost of the new instrument recommended by the organ committee had been raised already by subscription, that more was expected, and more still could be derived from sale of the old organ. The relacement they envisioned was a $3500 marvel by Mr. H. Knauff of Philadelphia, similar to the one by the same builder then in the Lutheran Church. The one proposed for Christ Church would have 34 to 36 stops, "the largest size capable at being placed in the Church, i.e. next to the largest . . . ever made."[496]

Anticipation reached the painful stage the next summer, when the *Daily Morning News* reported that the organ had been completed and tested at the factory by Mr. Knauff with the help of "many of the most prominent organists of that city." The trial of the "large, first class organ [is] said to have given perfect satisfaction . . . and reflected the highest credit on . . . the builder." The *Philadelphia Inquirer*, from which the *Morning News* took its information, described the organ as "comprising some thirty-six registers, three keyboards and pedals, and also an array of composition pedals." Further, it comprehends "a great variety of tone", especially in the solo stops: "trumpet, night horn, clarinet, hollow flute, hautboy, [and] viol di amour."[497]

By late August, at last, the local papers could report that the organ "will be tried this evening" in the Church.[498] It must have been almost immediately that preparations began for the fall season and for the first of what were to become fairly frequent benefit concerts. This initial effort was a program of oratorio music given by the choir for the benefit of the new Episcopal Orphan Assylum.[499] So pleased was the congregation with its new purchase after a few months of getting acquainted with it, the Vestry wrote to Mr. Knauff reporting that the organ "has given general satisfaction to judges of music" and deserved their commendation and thanks to its builder.[500] An even more telling sign of satisfaction with the instrument came two years later when the Independent Presbyterian Church decided to purchase an organ from Knauff as well.[501]

Before we conclude our exploration of these extremely rich mid-century decades, it will be worth our time to take notice of the great variety in parish activity even beyond what we have already seen. Some of the congregation, including the Rector, were involved in the "Savannah Bible Society" which was active during the 1840's;[511] and others, again including Mr. Neufville, supported the "Friends of Seamen."[512] Often the Rector himself faced special tasks, because of the high trust placed in him by the community. Thus, when an epistolary controversy arose in the *Daily Georgian* between "S" and "J.F.O'N." over Masonry, Mr. Neufville was one of the five community leaders suggested to arbitrate the matter.[512a] Still others in Christ Church felt deeply about the matter of alcohol use. As early as 1831 Christ Church had presented, through its Vestry, a memorial to the Diocesan Convention asking that,

> *feeling a deep interest in the honour of the church and in the safety of her members, [it] recommend to the respective communicants of the Churches in this diocese to observe that sobriety and seriousness of deportment which should ever distinguish the followers of Christ from the lovers of pleasure.*[513]

A "Temperance Society" was still active locally twenty years later. The newspaper noted, however, with a hint of complaint, that of twelve ministers attending a temperance speech requesting them to preach on the topic, only six complied.[514] Whether the response indicates weakness in the temperance movement, in the speaker, or in the editor's confidence that twelve clergy will agree on anything is a point for speculation.

Education was also an area of concern, especially when Mr. Neufville was made a trustee of the General Theological Seminary in 1841.[514a] An educational enterprise that caught the interest of many locally was the "Georgia Episcopal Institute and Montpelier College." Incorporated by the legislature in 1840,[515] the Institute at Montpelier Springs (near Macon) attracted a number of young ladies from Christ Church as students. Despite its unique "endowment" of slaves, financial problems forced the sale of the Institute in 1856.[516] Throughout its brief life the school's driving spirit was Bishop Elliott, who often served it in person when episcopal responsibilities would allow. Its closure brought him great disappointment which was only somewhat eased when a new project arose. Conceiving a university and theological seminary for the southern region as the joint enterprise of several dioceses, the new idea was presented to Christ Church hearers in 1857.[517] The concept was different and, happily, so was the fate of the new "University of the South."

Closer to home, Christ Church people were involved in some manner in many charitable enterprises. For example, a very important institution came into being on 3 March 1853 when "a number of ladies belonging to Christ Church met at the home of Mrs. Francis S. Bartow and perfected an organization . . . to found an Episcopal Orphans' Home."[517a] In later years, long after it ceased to be primarily a parish organization, the Orphans' Home continued to include many ladies of the Church among its Board of Managers.[518] In addition, in 1854 the Diocese asked the Wardens and Vestry of Christ Church to act as trustees of a fund for the support of "Widows and Orphans of Deceased Clergymen" — a function they carried already for the "Bishops Fund" and the Savannah Female Assylum.[519]

Among the congregation's varied activities, however, one concern appeared with greater consistency than any other: missions. It showed in a wide variety of ways through the mid-century years, but the essential core remained constant. We have already noted the prominent role Christ Church played in the 1820's and 1830's. In the decades that followed, mission-minded efforts of this sort continued and they also broadened considerably. There were the usual fairs to support missions, such as the one in December, 1840.

> *Held in the basement of the Chatham Academy Proceeds to be appropriated to Missionary objects connected with the Protestant Episcopal Church in this state — Admission 12½¢, children half price.*[520]

An article about the coming fair contained some intriguing features. After appealing for generosity, despite hard times, it cautioned the unwary to "leave your Central Bank money at home," but "go well provided with cash if you expect the ladies to be gracious."[521] Although puzzling in a way, the advice reminds us that the good old days were not trouble free either, and that raising money entailed currency problems we no longer face.

Special mission efforts involving Christ Church reached from Blacks working the Savannah River plantations[522] to China.[523] The congregation also was instrumental in founding new parishes in Savannah during the 1850's. One of these was St. Stephen's, which was established in 1855-56 under the Rev. Mr. S. W. Kennerly, who also served the Savannah River Mission.[524] As the River Mission was largely taken over by the Diocese of South Carolina in the mid-1850's, Mr. Kennerly increasingly gave his energy toward developing St. Stephen's as a mission to free Blacks in town. The success of the new mission was due in part, Kennerly recalled, to the "praiseworthy zeal, energy, and industry of several ladies of Christ Church and St. John's." Further support came from afar when, "through the kindness of Mr. [Abram Beach] Carter of this diocese, now in New York, I received a donation of 100 prayer books."[524a] Cited for special praise as a friend of the new

This plaque commemorating the life and work of Mr. Neufville is mounted in the wall at the head of the Church's south aisle. Below, this engraving of Mr. Neufville probably dates from the 1840's, when he was at the peak of his career and influence in the community.

congregation was Mrs. [P.M.] Kollock, wife of a vestryman of Christ Church. From St. Stephen's founding, and for many years thereafter, she acted as its treasurer.[524b] Thanks to such support the new parish took shape rapidly. The cornerstone for its Troup Ward building was laid in 1860,[525] and the Church was in full operation about a year later when its advertisement notified readers "that free seats have been reserved for visitors, both white and colored."[526] At that point Mrs. Kollock again lent her aid by helping to eliminate the debt on the new building, which cleared the way for its consecration in 1863.[526a]

It seems fairly clear that the new parish was created to serve a segment of the society that previously had gone without. This is suggested not only by the style of the congregation itself, but also by the absence of any visible impact on the Black population within Christ Church. For example, in 1855 Christ Church reported 100 Black children in its Sunday School,[526a2] yet no significant change in that figure is noted after the organization of St. Stephens. Likewise, there is no significant change in the number of Black baptisms, confirmations, marriages, etc., reported by the parish each year to the diocese.[526a3]

Shortly after St. Stephen's, another new and noteworthy parish was organized through the aid of Christ Church and St. John's, plus support from a generous legacy.[526b] The special feature of St. Paul's "Free Chapel" was that its *pews* were to be free. There was little precedent for the idea[527] since virtually all churches at the time drew their income from rental or sale of pews, rather than pledged contributions. The rental system obviously tended to discourage visitors, especially the poor, from attendance. To avoid some of that negative effect, Christ Church had set aside a few free pews for visitors as early as 1828. Then a bequest from Archibald Wilkins in 1844 assured the permanency of the idea by instructing the Wardens and Vestry "to set aside two good pews for such poor females as are not able (but willing) to pay for seats."[528] Subsequently, a free chapel or "City Mission" emerged in Savannah about 1852. The idea finally achieved solid form c. 1857 with the organization of St. Paul's.[529]

78

Top left, old Chalices dating back to 1816. Bottom left, this communion silver, given by the "Women of Christ Church" soon after the second structure was consecrated, is still in use.

Below, intricate silver medallion in the center of the alms basin.

The original 1840 communion table is now in Demere Chapel. Can you recognize it in the interior view of the new Church?

Right, old silver, dated 1816.

It is little wonder that amid such a rising swirl of activity the Rector had found increasing need to retreat occasionally to his family home in upper New York State. Summer leaves of several months became more frequent during the 1840's as his deteriorating health further emphasized that need. At times the journey north could serve a double purpose. This was the case in 1844 when he was a delegate to the General Convention in Philadelphia. In his absence of four months, Bishop Elliott and a young candidate for ordination, James Jackson, filled in for him.[530] A similar leave in 1847 was also timed so as to allow him to attend the General Convention.[531] Two years after that a rather ominous tone sounded in Mr. Neufville's next request for leave. "Duties pressed so heavily upon me during the last season as to convince me that a change of climate is almost indispensable to the continuance of my ministry"[532]

The same "press of duties" had earlier prompted him in 1846, to request that the Vestry consider securing the services of an assistant.[533] Unfortunately, the plan was momentarily frustrated when the young man he intended to propose accepted a call to Macon. Now by 1850, the combination of increasing duties and failing health once again forced the issue and it was decided to invite the Bishop to become associate Rector.[534] This proposal, too, was doomed to failure. Bishop Elliott had one week earlier accepted a call to Columbus,[535] and since he was deeply committed at the Montpelier Institute it would be some time before he could make "change of any sort." All such plans and proposals became irrelevant when Mr. Neufville died on the first day of the new year, 1851.[536]

The Rector's rather unexpected death at only 48 seemed to command the immediate attention of everyone in any way connected to the Church. Commendations and memorials of every sort appeared,[537] and many stories of the final hours circulated as his countless admirers attempted to cope with their shock. One account recalls how "as soon as the Bishop was allowed to see him. [Mr. Neufville] opened his eyes and turned towards him; then put his arms around him and drew him down on his breast and held him there a long time and kissed him. The bishop seemed very much affected."[537.a] When he suddenly turned worse some time later, the Bishop returned to celebrate Holy Communion for him.

> *All supposed him too unstrung to participate intelligently, but he seemed to rally for the occasion. When the Bishop prepared to administer the elements, he asked, "do you understand what I am doing?" "Perfectly." It was a gleam of light in the midst of surrounding darkness. Once again he joined in prayer with those around his bedside, and then sunk . . ."*[537.b]

The funeral itself was delayed to allow time for those who must journey far to reach Savannah. St. John's was closed to enable the congregation to attend.[538] On Sunday morning, January 5th, at 11:00 A.M., "the tolling of the Bell announced to the citizens . . . that the funeral procession had commenced toward the Church." Relatives, wardens and vestrymen accompanied the body (those of both Christ Church and St. John's acting as pall bearers.) They were "met at the Church porch by Bishop Elliott and others, and proceeded up the center aisle repeating the opening lines of the Burial Service." The Bishop then read from Psalms 39 and 90 with the congregation responding. After the lesson was read by the Rev. Rufus White, Rector of St. John's, and the 124th Psalm was sung, Bishop Elliott then spoke personally of this beloved friend and colleague with the "frame unusually slight."[539] In his eulogy, he noted especially how

> *few ministers have ever read our liturgy with more . . . beauty . . . Gifted by nature with a sweet and flexible voice, he used it in excellent taste, and passed not the bounds of strict devotional propriety, while yet he gave full power and meaning to the magnificent anthems and litanies*

which have come down to us embalmed in the devotion of centuries. But it was as a pastor that Dr. Neufville was most decidedly eminent.[540]

Rufus White reveals a different side of Mr. Neufville, describing his death as

a loss which extends itself to many others besides his congregation. I have lost in him a Christian brother most beloved, and an honored elder in the ministry; . . . one to whose wise and Christian counsels I have often stood indebted; one whose kind fraternal sympathies have cheered and strengthened me . . . in more than one time of trial and suffering.[541]

At its next convention, the diocese added its own commendation, feeling especially the loss of "one who long presided over its deliberations, before it had a Bishop of its own."[542]

Meanwhile, the congregation and Vestry acted in very practical ways to ease some of the pain felt by the Neufville family. They resolved to continue paying the Rector's salary to his widow and three surviving children for three months, and they assumed all responsibility for funeral arrangements. Finally, they took action toward placing a permanent memorial tablet in the church.[543]

The Ascension window was created by Redding, Baird & Co. of Boston for reconstruction of the Church after the disastrous fire of 1897. (See Chapter 7.)

V
Crisis in Church and Nation 1851-1867

While others mourned, the Vestry had to look ahead, toward filling the vacancy left by Mr. Neufville's death.[544] For the moment the problem was addressed when the Bishop and Rufus White agreed to serve Christ Church on alternate Sundays.[545] For the long term, however, their hope was to persuade Bishop Elliott to accept the position of Rector. When a second invitation was also declined, the Bishop citing his many other commitments,[546] the call went to the Rev. Abram Beach Carter of New York state.[547] Mr. Carter had grown up in Christ Church while his father was Rector (1822-1827).

Hopes were high that Mr. Carter would accept. Local newspapers advertised him enthusiastically as eloquent, a fine reader, possessed of a fine, deep voice, and affirmed that "as a pulpit orator Mr. Carter occupies a place of high rank."[548] When he accepted the rectorship all were delighted, including Mr. Carter,[549] who arrived to begin his new ministry the first Sunday in November, 1851.[550]

That was not soon enough, however, to enable him to join his new congregation in observing a most notable anniversary which had occurred during the summer of 1851. While Mr. Carter was preparing to relocate his family to Savannah, the Society for the Propagation of the Gospel in Foreign Parts (S.P.G.), which had been so instrumental in the founding of Christ Church, celebrated its sesquincentennial anniversary with special services throughout the Anglican Communion. In Christ Church, Bishop Elliott preached a sermon in honor of this "third jubilee" of the Society.[551] The months that followed were filled with the double excitement of a new ministry and a homecoming. Yet it seemed the Carters had hardly settled in when their family physician, Dr. P.M. Kollock, urged the Rector to remove his wife from this climate "at once" if he hoped to save her! Accordingly, they embarked the next day for the north, Mr. Carter promising to keep the Vestry informed.[552]

Within a few weeks the unwanted letter came which contained Mr. Carter's resignation and "the fervent prayer that God will soon send you a Pastor, who though he cannot love you more, may yet prove more faithful to you than I have done . . . ."[553] The Vestry's response was equally touching.

Welcoming back an old friend, [we] had hoped to prolong for many years the connection so happily begun, when the son returned to minister at the same altar which had been . . . faithfully served a quarter part of a century since by his lamented father.[554]

Local newspapers recalled how "many feared when Mr. Carter recently went north with his family that his connection with this Church would soon cease . . . ." Now that the worst was known, they expressed the regret of the broader public that a ministry of only "8 or 9 months" must be cut short "in consequence of the continued illness" in the family for which "residence in a northern climate is deemed essential."[555]

With the rectorship vacant, once again the Bishop was called! This time, to the great delight of the parish, and of Savannahians generally, he accepted. There were limitations, however. Episcopal duties would require his being away frequently, so it was agreed in the beginning that there must be regular assistance in parish duties. Moreover, cautioned Bishop Elliott, "as many young ladies have been sent to Montpelier with the understanding that I would be at the Institute during the present term" he could not take charge until December (1852). Until then, he offered to continue the current every other week arrangement "if you can do no better."[556] The Vestry was so pleased to have gained at last Bishop's acceptance that they readily agreed to all terms, and purchased for him a $50 annual ticket on the Central of Georgia Railroad for good measure.[557]

As usual, matters returned to "normal" only briefly. Early in 1854 the city began to sense the presence of an old enemy. By summer yellow fever had reached epidemic proportions, creating one of the worst seasons in Savannah's entire history, and sweeping away hundreds of its citizens. Among the victims was the Rector of St. John's Church, and so once again the two parishes combined their efforts. Bishop Elliott provided pastoral services to both congregations and evening worship was suspended at Christ Church, freeing him to celebrate at St. John's Sunday afternoons.[558] Fortunately, reinforcements came in the person of a transient clergyman, the Rev. Mr. Dalzell, who was "desirous of remaining to aid the bishop during the present epidemic." When he was invited to act as assistant to the Rector, he chose to do so without compensation. That did not free him from the danger involved, however, as the Vestry recognized when it resolved that the clergy "be requested under the present circumstances to perform all funeral services at the houses of the deceased, and thus avoid the fatigue and exposure [of] going to the cemetery."[559]

From what we have seen already, the 1840's and 1850's appear to have been incredibly full decades. Yet no review of those years would be complete without some notice of two interesting questions of law and organization, and even more, of the rising intersectional tensions within the nation. The legal questions may appear unimportant at first, but when some unknown organizational purist noticed that Christ Church apparently had no by-laws, it did bring some interesting points to light. To many such a lack might seem to deserve something less than alarm; nevertheless, the Vestry did the likely thing — it appointed a committee. In their investigation the committee discovered that, indeed, there were no by-laws. A commitee created in 1794 showed that work toward that end had begun, according to the *Vestry Minutes* of that day, but it had never reported, or at least had "left no trace upon the record."[560] The ancient oversight was then corrected and by-laws adopted in 1856.[561] Even more important for the history of the parish, however, is the information that the Vestry's search had "examined the Books of Minutes of this body from 14 January 1786 down to the present." The pre-1839 Minutes, now missing, are generally assumed to have perished in one of the Church's early calamaties, but obviously in 1856 they still survived.

A second and much more involved question arose the same year relative to ownership and jurisdiction over the "old cemetery", alias, the "old brick cemetery", now commonly called Colonial Park. The Vestry felt that the city's establishment of a new cemetry at Laurel Grove and "abandonment for purposes of burial the Old Brick Cemetery afforded a proper occasion for putting on record their claim." Specifically, the claim involved a 380′ x 210′ segment which they feared might be sought for some secular use if title were not clearly established. The anxiety of the Vestry did prompt a search of old colonial, parish, and city records that was well worth the effort even though when all was done, they decided to take no action "for the present."[562]

The Bishop's years as Rector continued the lively tradition of his predecessors. He was much desired as a speaker and preacher for occasions of many sorts, and often drew response from the public. The words of a Trinity Sunday sermon, for example, provoked a letter to the editor of the *Morning News* from a Unitarian minister which invited him to public controversy.[563] By invitation, he also delivered the opening address for the new Savannah Medical College;[564] and two years later, as the College president, he conferred degrees on the first graduates.[565] In addition he offered his own lectures or courses in the Church on occasions,[566] and even exchanged places with Bishop Potter of Pennsylvania for a few weeks during the winter of 1856.[567] To fill in the gaps, he held positions on countless boards of directors and trustees during these years, too. Usually he was an officer of the Georgia Historical Society, and trustee of the Chatham Academy and the Savannah, Albany, and Gulf Railroad, among other things.[568] There were always many others, in addition, although most tended to be less enduring positions.

Understandably, Bishop Elliott also travelled frequently throughout the diocese and beyond. Then when his schedule afforded, or illness demanded, he loved to escape to his favorite vacation spot in Cuba.[569] Despite this seemingly endless list of responsibilities and activities he perferred to carry on without an assistant. The question had been raised when he accepted the rectorship, but the only real assistance sought was for the Sundays he must be absent. Toward the end of the decade, however, the diocese began to press the case[570] and the Bishop reluctantly agreed.

It was a case of no sooner said than undone, however, for within weeks the Bishop was appointed to a position with the embryonic University of the South. The chance to share directly in an enterprise so dear to him was irresistable, even though it required his resignation from Christ Church.[571] This came in the autumn of 1859. His decision was accepted "with heartfelt regret" and the knowledge that any action to the contrary "would not only be . . . fruitless, but painful to the Bishop."

The search for Bishop Elliott's replacement began immediately, and soon led to the Rev. Mr. L.P. Balch, late of Christ Church, Baltimore. After many weeks of correspondence Balch declined the offer, citing his poor health as the reason. But things looked different when the Bishop was persuaded to withdraw *his* resignation and become "honorary rector" with an associate of his choosing. Bishop Elliott then invited Mr. Balch himself, and Balch accepted.[572] He served from March, 1860, through May, when he headed north for the summer in deference to his health.

At this point the Vestry had once again to reckon with one of the great paradoxes of life: that although things seldom become easier, especially for committees, they often become more difficult! The first sign of trouble appeared when Bishop Elliott resigned again, recognizing that he could not possibly do justice to the demands of his several offices. This required new negotiations between Mr. Balch and the Vestry. In the course of their correspondence during the summer, however, it became apparent that the two parties understood their agreeement quite differently. Thus, having resigned in May, and re-accepted the rectorship in June, Balch then resigned again in August never to return.[572]

The Church was kept open during the summer of 1860 by engaging available clergy on a weekly basis. Failing that, "Mr.

George A. Gordon . . . kept the church open by layreading, whenever a clergyman was lacking."[574] But now, opportunity for attracting a new rector was fast slipping away. The next candidate would have come happily but for the "increasing gloom and uncertainty . . . of the times."[575] For this reason the Vestry once more turned to Bishop Elliott, and once more he accepted the rectorship. For his assistant he chose the Rev. Mr. Charles H. Coley, who was to prove a faithful leader through the trying years ahead.[576]

The gloom and uncertainty which was gripping the nation had been drawing public attention in Savannah for at least twenty years. As early as 1841 a visitor to Savannah complained at how, in his view, the clergy (especially Episcopalians) advocated slavery and yet deprecated public discussion and agitation on the matter. On this occasion the *Daily Georgian* took up the defense of local honor. Quarrelling with the visitor's judgements, and his violation of the hospitality he had received, the editors nevertheless "agreed" with him on one point. To their credit, Episcopal clergy "preach Christ and Him Crucified," and avoid the wrangling and unproductive disputation which reduce clergy "to unhallowed passions, sending schism into the Church, and division into our republic."[577] By the mid-1850's tension had increased to the point, according to local news reports, that slavery quarrels were now threatening to divide this Church, too.[578]

Matters reached the militant stage after the elections of November, 1860. That very month, in response to an open invitation by the Georgia legislature, the citizens of Chatham County, "ignoring all past party names and issues," cordially united in resolving:

> *That the election of Abraham Lincoln and Hannibal Hamlin to the Presidency and Vice Presidency of the United States, ought not to be, and will not be submitted to . . . .*
> *That we respectfully suggest to the Legislature to take immediate steps to arm and organize the forces of the State.*[579]

For weeks little circles of men standing in Johnson Square or in front of the news offices on Bay Street had tested the sound of words like "secession". Now, these resolutions presented to the legislature made it sound like more than talk. The very idea raised such profound questions about the status of the National Church and the relationship of dioceses in seceded areas that no one could see clearly through the thicket. The questions were obvious; the answers were not.

Throughout the entire trauma and the war that followed, the Rector of Christ Church, Bishop Stephen Elliott, gave vigorous leadership with a moderating touch that proved crucial to the course of events. One of his least moderate moves came after South Carolina seceded in December, 1860. When it seemed likely that other states would soon follow, the Bishop suggested that, if secession were enacted here, clergy should acknowledge the change liturgically by shifting the focus of the "prayer for the President" to "Thy Servant, the Governor of the State of Georgia."[580] More typically, however, his voice could be heard attempting to subdue the unprofitable zeal of others who would have made changes merely for the sake of change. Even after secession, and with war only a few days away, there was still widespread hope to prevent schism in the Episcopal Church.[581] It was in this spirit that Bishop Elliott used his influence to assure that when division finally became inevitable, it was effected gradually and without an ecclessiastical Ft. Sumter that might require generations to repair. Throughout the series of councils among the confederate dioceses that began in 1861, his approach largely prevailed to the end that nothing was done which would permanently alienate northern and southern churches. Basically, this meant that any changes were relatively minor and limited to organizational matters. Doctrinal novelty was deliberately avoided. Elliott-style moderation became even more influential after Bishop Meade (Virginia) died in March of 1862. This left the Rector of Christ Church as the senior active and, therefore, "presiding bishop" in the Protestant Episcopal Church, Confederate States of America.[582]

If Bishop Elliott was moderate in matters of churchmanship, in his support of the Confederacy, once the key decisions were made, he was a zealot! He preached "Our Cause in Harmony with the Purposes of Christ Jesus."[582s] While the war was still in its first summer he made a public appeal to Georgians, and especially Georgia Episcopalians, to organize their efforts to the maximum benefit of the Southern cause and those who serve it. "Georgia expects every man to do his duty," regardless of age, sex, or physical state! Specifically, he called upon parishes and their rectors to collect goods, money, and labor which could supply clothing, food, and nursing care when and where they were most needed.[583] His appeal drew considerable response and in a short while the "Christ Church Association" was making regular donations of bandage rolls, clothing, bed linen, etc., for use in field hospitals. The bishop often led the way with donations of his own.[584] A statewide version of the Association, the Georgia Relief and Hospital Association, continued to receive and distribute similar donations throughout the War, which the Central of Georgia Railroad patriotically shipped "free of charge on the afternoon train to Atlanta," and thence to wherever they were needed.[585]

In addition to supporting relief efforts, the Bishop found many occasions to preach to military congregations and on topics directly related to the war. For instance, in June, 1861, he preached to Savannah's Pulaski Guards in Christ Church just prior to their departure for Virginia.[586] Later that summer, after the victory, he preached on "God's Presence with Our Army at Manassas." Many such sermons, including these two, were published on the initiative of the Vestry or sold on subscription by printer George Nichols from his shop just across the square.[587] Another of Bishop Elliott's sermons, on "Women's Heroism in War," gained him an audience far larger than the congregation that heard it originally in Christ Church, after it appeared in print.[588]

For the general public special days were appointed with some frequency by proclamation of the President, CSA, to be

Close-up views of portions of the Elliott Memorial window.

devoted to "fasting, humiliation, and prayer," or to "prayer and thanksgiving." At such times businesses closed and the churches opened. "It was Sabbath in our land."[589] Those were the occasions when worshippers in Christ Church were likely to hear sermons on "Gideon's Water-lappers," "Ezra's Dilemma," or "Samson's Riddle" from their Bishop.[589a] The Bishop would usually direct his clergy to use a service created especially for the day, in which he specified the Psalms, lessons, litanies or hymns to be used along with a prayer of his own composition. Imagine the impact of opening the *Morning News* to read the entire order of service, along with the prayer for the day, as you breakfast. The prayer that would have met your eye on November 12th (1861) reveals much. In it we can sense the power of the Bishop's words and something of what Savannahians must have felt on reading them, even as the final elements of the Union naval blockade were being fitted into place along the Georgia-Carolina coast —

O Lord God that dwellest in the Heavens and Who reignest overall the kingdoms of men, we praise and bless Thy name, that in our troubles and perils Thou has stood on our side and pleaded for us . . . Thou, O Lord, didst blast the design of our enemies with the breath of Thy displeasure, and to Thee we ascribe the praise and honor of our present safety. Perpetuate Thy mercies to us; let a guard of Holy Angels stand round about us and about all Thy people, like the hills, for our defense and safety, that we may be inaccessible to all the attempts of our enemies . . .[590]

While the conflict often shaped the prayers of the day and disarranged the lives and plans of many, some things would not be turned from their courses even by war. Bishop Elliott remained the tireless missionary he had always been. On one occasion, in June 1863, he confirmed General Braxton Bragg along with several other officers and a large number of troops in the Army of Tennessee while visiting them.[591] The sons and daughters of the parish continued to think of marriage too.

Thus, the following October he joined Edward F. Neufville, son of the late rector and now a Lt. in the C.S. Marines, and Miss Mary Drayton Tattnall in Christ Church.[592] A few days later, amid a flutter that seemed little subdued by the war, Jefferson Davis visited the city. His Saturday in town was filled with speeches, fort visits, troop reviews, and receptions. The next morning, from his lodging at Pulaski House, he walked across the square to worship at Christ Church as so many before him had done, and to gather his strength for the day and the larger ordeal that lay ahead.[593]

It brings a certain comfort to recognize that neither missionary zeal nor love and marriage, nor even politics would be daunted by the war. Yet there was another, perhaps less comforting power, that was even more unyielding.

Amid the convulsions of a nation struggling for liberty, Death . . . snatched a moment to desolate a peaceful home and rob the Church of one of its most devoted worshippers, a devout Christian, an unselfish patriot, an honest man, James Potter, for many years a vestryman of the Church, and an earnest promoter of her every interest . . .[594]

In addition to reminding us of the distress we feel at the end of a life, even a long and productive one, Mr. Potter's death highlights for us one consequence of the war we might easily overlook. He left $5000 to the Church, which he specified should be used to build a rectory.[595] While arrangements were being made, however, the money had to be invested . . . but where? Temporarily placed in the locally popular Central Rail Road Bank stock, the funds seemed more secure when moved to the stock of the Great Southern Insurance Co.[596] Then "objectionable features" discovered the Great Southern's charter caused the Vestry to re-invest the entire legacy in 8% Confederate Government Bonds.[597] For several months their investment strategy worked so well that the Wardens and Vestry were confronted by a rare problem — what to do with a

Top, close-up of stained glass window after the 1890 renovation. Bottom, showing the floor of the Church as it was from 1925-1964, this view also will remind many of how the narthex appeared prior to renovation in the 1980's. Far left, this first Elliott Memorial window was seen by parishioners from 1869 until it was lost in the great fire of 1897.

treasury surplus.[598] The "problem" proved ephemeral, however, for as soon as the money had been committed it evaporated in a 33 1/3% currency devaluation carried out, early in 1864.[599]

As the fiscal news suggests, the war overall had taken several turns for the worse in recent months and some of its long-term costs were now being felt. The last year had been filled with stories from Chancellorsville, Gettysburg, Chickamauga, Lookout Mountain, Missionary Ridge and Spotsylvania. Although some of these actions were claimed as victories and others acknowledged as defeats, the deeper truth that all were tragedies was becoming too painfully clear. Lengthening casualty lists tended to bleed such words as "victory" and "defeat" of meaningful distinction. By late in the summer of 1864, a few days after the fall of Atlanta, Bishop Elliott was moved to remind his congregation, and himself, how "Vain is the Hope of Man."[600]

The gravity of their situation was not a complete surprise to the congregation. More than a year before, the Vestry conceived a plan of action to be followed in case of attack, instructing the treasurer to remove Church papers and valuables to Macon and to leave them with the rector or in some safe vault there.[601] Now, in early December, with General Sherman's irresistible force bearing down on Savannah, the plan was put into action. When the Vestry met on the 11th the senior warden, William P. Hunter, stated that treasurer George A. Cuyler "had been ordered a week since to Macon with the assets of the Central Railroad and Banking Co., and had taken with him sundry [records] for safe keeping." Also, the communion plate was "placed at the joint disposal" of the rector and acting treasurer, Edward C. Hough, to be hidden away.[602] Bishop Elliott departed with General Hardee's forces, then made his way to Augusta, not knowing how long he might be restricted from travel in the diocese if he remained. Union forces reached Savannah a few days later, and a whole city held its breath — not knowing what to expect.

Six weeks later the Vestry again convened, "in consequence of the changes . . . since their last meeting, the city having been occupied by the Federal Army since the 21st day of December last, and the affairs of the parish necessarily totally deranged."[603] Their actions give us at least a glimpse of the insecurity that accompanies "occupation," even one without major destruction. The minutes of the former meetings were "annulled" so far as pew rents and salaries were concerned, and they resolved that, since the salaries of the Rector and Assistant were paid to April 1st: (1) the Rector's salary thereafter "be fixed dependent upon the condition of the funds of the Church and the state of the currency, whenever he may resume charge of the parish," and (2) "that the salary of the Assistant Minister be at the rate of $1500 per annum . . . payable in the present currency."[604]

Amid the confusion and disappointment of those days, it must have lessened the privation, and perhaps even a little of the pain, to see the *Rebecca Clyde* sail up the Savannah River with a cargo of bread stuffs and other necessaries "as a good will offering from their fellow countrymen in the city of New York."[604a] Within days similar ships of mercy also arrived from Boston and Philadelphia. Perhaps the letter brought from Boston, resolved by a mass gathering at Faneuil Hall the week before, spoke for all when it reminded recipients that

The History of former days is not forgotten. It has rather been deepened by the late trials of our nation. We remember the earlier kindness and liberality of the citizens of Savannah towards the people of Boston in the dark colonial days . . .

We remember that Nathanael Greene, the noble son of Rhode Island, sleeps in your beautiful cemetery. We recall the scenes on the banks of the Savannah River when the military and the municipality met the mournful procession at the landing in your city, the whole body of citizens joining with one accord in this last demonstration of respect to him . . .

The memory of past days of common danger and the common suffering of an united people, struggling to be

free, stands before us. The annals of the South and the North, engraved together upon the tablets of memory, still live, and we believe that neither the South nor the North will permit them to die.[604b]

Despite such gestures, there were still problems enough to go around. "From the fact that all practicable communication with the interior of the state is at present cut off, it is determined to make no appointments of delegates to the Diocesan Convention."[605] Another was discovered by the Assistant Rector, Charles H. Coley, when

returning to his house on Saturday night (i,e, April 22nd) about ten o'clock, he found an officer waiting for him with an order from the Provost Marshall to read . . . the following Sunday the prayer for the President of the United States, and for all in civil authority.

The Provost Marshall's sudden concern for the prayer life of the city was almost certainly provoked by the news of the President's assassination. Mr. Lincoln was shot on the 14th, and although he died early the next day, the news reached most Savannahians only when it filled the columns of the *Daily Herald* on the 19th of April. To prevent any spread of violence was the army's first priority, which is why the order to Mr. Coley took the trouble to specify in advance the consequences of disobedience. He would be sent as a prisoner to Ft. Pulaski or the Church would be closed. Since the order further demanded "that his answer be given forth with," and he was unable to consult the Vestry, he chose to yield passively on the closing of the Church and to take his chances on imprisonment. The Church was indeed closed the next day, the Sunday after Easter, but instead of to Ft. Pulaski Mr. Coley was ordered to leave the city.[606] A few tense hours later, when he had opportunity to speak with the Vestry, they agreed that if allowed to officiate he would "offer the prayer for the President of the United States, as contained in the Prayer Book." A deputation was then sent to Gen. Groover, Commander of the post and district of Savannah, to ask that the expulsion order be revoked.[607] Although unsuccessful there, appeal to his superior, Gen. Gilmore, found a more willing ear and the order was set aside.[608]

The derangement of affairs brought by the war and the occupation did not cease even with the meeting at Appomattox Courthouse. This was especially true in financial matters. For example, by November of 1865, when war news was a fading memory, it was realized that the money paid the Bishop toward his annual salary was no longer of any value!

It having come to the knowledge of the Vestry that the Bishop had incurred a heavy cost in the quota from Christ Church for the present year paid in Confederate currency, [it was] Resolved to pay him $250.00 in present currency in addition.[609]

The assistant minister was forced to live week by week, entirely dependent on the collections for income at times, as were "pensioners" supported by the Church. Regarding the latter, the Vestry urged Mr. Coley to exercise "sound judgement" in paying them, and certainly to add no new names to those "already on the list."[610]

The Church, too, faced losses. Several *Minute Books* were misplaced along with some *Account Books*, including those of the Female Episcopal Society, and those with the scrip of the Central Rail Road and Planters' Banks. These may well be the very volumes taken to Macon "for safekeeping."[611] Despite the treasurer's lingering hope that they could be located, they were never found. A year after the end of the war, he had to face his Vestry colleagues and admit that with the books "lost during the troubles, they were unable to give any account." Things do seem to work out, however. By that time it had also become less important, "as the only receipts were for dividends in Confederate notes and therefore valueless."[612]

Missing account books were, however, not the only problem. In each of the special funds over which the Vestry had charge — Widows and Orphans, Parsonage, etc. — a deeper reality presented itself and repeatedly forced the same disappointed conclusion: "this entire amount, excepting the City of Savannah Bonds . . . is in Confederate Notes and Bonds and is consequently of no value whatever and will not again be referred to."[613] The books were officially wiped clean and a new accounting was begun.

Despite an epidemic of smallpox in the city, by September of 1865 Bishop Elliott returned and agreed to resume his duties at a reduced salary. In his words, "he had been with us in prosperity, and was now willing to be with us in adversity."[614] Fortunately for all, real adversity seems to have been short-lived. Martial governance was lifted November first, ending the city's second experience with military occupation,[614a] and things could begin their return to normal. The month after the Bishop again took up his duties, new gas burners were installed in the Church.[615] Even though not an expensive matter, the act would seem to be symptomatic of renewed hope. Even clearer signs occurred the following summer when a "competent person" was sought to repair and tune the organ, and Mr. Coley was granted a much deserved leave with "a $200 check in addition to his salary."[616] Finally, at summer's end, a new rectory was rented for the Bishop at a cost of $200 for the year.[617]

With the parish so visibly recovering its health and vigor financially [618] Bishop Elliott was free to devote his energy to the great question of Church reunion. Leadership in the matter now fell entirely upon him, since neither of his senior colleagues in the Southern episcopate had survived the war. To his great joy, the gate of reconciliation was opened fully when the 1865 General Convention gathered the northern bishops at Philadelphia in October.

Instead of anathemas, there were warm greetings of renewed friendship and tears of reconciled love — instead of excommunications, there was hearty welcome and assurances of rejoicing hearts over the healing of the wounds . . .[619]

The Bishop's own extensive correspondence with fellow churchmen — northern and southern — had done much to encourage such an attitude. Now that it had been given formal expression in Philadelphia, his energy and skillful guidance led his parish, his diocese, and the Confederate Church generally back into full communion with PECUSA. After all, the action which had separated them originally was not taken for the "formation of a new church . . . [God forbid,] but [was] merely an organization for legislative purposes."[620]

Bishop Elliott's direct communication and high repute had another value, too. They helped avoid the pitfalls dug by those whose hostility war had not exhausted — the sort who find problems more satisfying than solutions. Pen and ink skirmishes filled the pages of many of the nation's newspapers in the months following Appomattox, but the Bishop would not be distracted.[621] He pressed the issue of reunion, publishing formal notice of his intention early in 1866.

In pursuance of the fifth resolution passed at the second Council of the Protestant Episcopal Church of the late Confederate States of America, which convened at Augusta, November 1865, I hereby give you official notice under my hand and seal of the Episcopate, of my withdrawal from [that] Ecclesiastical Federation, and of the reunion of the Diocese of Georgia with the Protestant Episcopal Church of the United State of America.
Most sincerely do I trust that all the Dioceses may be very soon battling, side by side, for the cause of Christ in the world.[622]

For Georgia, the work of reunion was virtually completed at what would be Bishop Elliott's last diocesan convention, in May, 1866.

During the same season we get an intriguing insight into the mind of the parish — the way they sought the security of familiar things, even while recognizing that nothing they had known would ever be the same again. That the "unholy war" was finally over brought relief. It also brought time for grief. Yet it was a grief unconsoled by victory, made deeper by the aching awareness that the hopes and the very society which so recently had given meaning to their lives were, as their loved ones, casualties of the war.

We can imagine the burdens carried when, "yesterday, being Ash Wednesday, commenced the holy season of Lent . . . in the Catholic and Episcopal Churches of the City." The "Services in Christ Church, Monday, Tuesday, Thursday, and Saturday each week at 7:00 AM and on Wednesday and Friday of each week at 11:00 AM,"[623] must surely have been more than usually intense times of searching. In due course, however, even in 1866, Lent's agony was infused with Easter's hope. Fortunately, we are able to share the congregation's struggle toward joy through the journal of a visitor "going off to church to hear Bishop Elliott." He

preached one of the most beautiful sermons I ever heard, on Resurrection, the one thought that can bring hope and

Bishop Elliott in his clerical garb, probably about 1865.

PHOTOGRAPH BY J.N. WILSON FROM THE COLLECTIONS OF THE GEORGIA HISTORICAL SOCIETY.

comfort to these poor broken-hearted people. There was hardly anyone at Church out of deep mourning, and it was piteous to see so many mere girls' faces, shaded by deep crape veils and widows' caps.[624]

In such words we sense the strange intermingling of sorrow and hope that they felt, when the pain of war and the joy of peace both were still so fresh. It must have felt the same when some talked of economic recovery or Church reunion even before they had begun the awful task of learning to live with the vacancies gouged in their lives by the war. This was the confusion toward which Bishop Elliott directed his final counsel to his people. He wanted them to recognize that this epilogue they were all living, to the old way of life, was more than just "the end of something." It was also a beginning; and he saw more clearly than most that the strength of the old could become the foundation of the new. Even though slavery was destroyed, for example, and the old ways proven "unsound and unsatisfactory," their legacy of intimate personal contact could become the basis of a new relationship between the races. Freed from the "fearful responsibility" that accompanied slaveholding, he called on Georgia Episcopalians to be up and working, to move "boldly and fearlessly" into the new age by capitalizing on their ancient tradition of Negro instruction. They must press on with the task of educating the Freedmen.[625] While the Bishop retained much of the traditional racial paternalism of the times, and grew more apprehensive of the trend toward what he saw as "foreign" meddling in the southern country, he also led the way in encouraging his Diocese to look to the future with positive eyes.

The Bishop spoke forcefully that the Church should lead the way in reorienting the spirits of men and the institutions of society. Whether his own "benevolent paternalism" toward Blacks could have been made to serve that cause is a matter for speculation. His words were moving. Yet, as always, it is after the speeches are over and the crowds returned home that the work begins. What the new society should be, or would become, would remain unclear until defined by time and experience. That social arrangements were already changed to some degree, however, and in a direction that foreshadowed the century to come, was demonstrated one Sunday

just before the morning services commenced at Christ Church . . . The members who had assembled were very much astonished and naturally indignant at seeing two negro girls, neatly dressed, walk up the middle aisle and take seat in the pew of one of our most prominent citizens, the owner being therein seated. After looking vainly around for the sexton, the owner of the pew put them out of it and out of the church.

The anonymous journalist apparently felt less mystified than the witnesses he reports. His editorial conclusion was that "some negro worshipper, doubtless, sent them in in order to see what would be the effect, and if possible to make capital of it."[626] Significantly, the Bishop's wise counsel and esteemed leadership were no longer available to lend perspective to such incidents through the difficult years of adjustment. For Stephen Elliott died very suddenly, after returning from a journey through his diocese, on the 21st day of December, 1866.

In the death of this distinguished prelate, the Episcopal Church has lost one of its brightest ornaments, and the country one of its most cultivated and brilliant intellects. In due time abler pens will record the talents and virtues which adorned a character that has few parallels among the distinguished men of our day.[627]

Perhaps the most telling sign of the universal admiration he enjoyed was the way so many joined in his funeral rites on Christmas Day. Clergy from throughout the diocese had joined in Holy Communion at 7 AM with sorrowing communicants of the parish. Then

at 11 AM the beloved remains were born to the hearse from the Episcopal residence by ten colored communicants of St. Stephen's Church, Savannah, attended by the appointed pall-bearers consisting of two clerical members of the Standing Committee in the surplice and stole, wardens and vestry of Christ Church, the wardens of St. John's and St. Paul's, Savannah, preceded by four surpliced priests . . . followed by relatives . . .

The bell tolled at the usual hour inviting mourners into the Church, which was decorated with black crepe entwined in Christmas wreathing.

The body was met at the entrance gate of Christ Church by six priests, who preceded it into the Church, the Rev. Mr. C. H. Coley saying the opening lines of the burial service . . . A funeral anthem was sung by the [voices of several choirs] . . . and the hymn "I Would Not Live Always" — sung by a congregation bathed in tears — concluded the services in the Church . . .
The procession then moved to Laurel Grove Cemetery, the bells of all the Churches tolling — the clergy attending either side of the hearse, followed by the pall-bearers and relatives, the members of the Georgia Historical Society, and . . . an immense concourse of citizens.
At the grave [after] the liturgy . . . a choir of male voices sang "Man that is Born of Woman . . ."[628]

Nationally, too, and from throughout the state of Georgia, the Bishop's death drew condolences and commendations of a high order, which gave at least some comfort in "so irreparable a loss." Yet as is so often the case, the most persuasive testimony came from those who knew him best — his own parish. Speaking for the whole, the Vestry proclaimed that although we

do bow in humility and resignation, . . . acutely realizing that we have lost a beloved Father in the Church . . . be it RESOLVED

That while, together with the whole country we mourn the death of our sainted Rector and Bishop, it is yet an inexpressable comfort that we can render unto almighty God "hearty thanks for the good example of this his servant," who, "having fought the good fight and finished his course," has in the evening of his life calmly laid down the armour of his Divine Office, untarnished, to receive the crown of life promised to those who are faithful unto death.[629]

Another survivor of the fire, the great brass lectern has served in strength and beauty for nearly a century.

VI
Reconstruction, Reproach, and Recovery
1867-1889

It must have seemed like beginning all over again, taking those first steps into the post war, post-Elliott world. At the first Vestry meeting of the new year, January of 1867, Mr. Coley was invited to stay, taking all clerical duties until, December 1, 1867. These were not prosperous times, however, and "under the existing state of our finances" he was also requested to take up no collections except on communion Sundays and those especially appointed by the diocese. The Vestry further resolved that the house rented for Bishop Elliott and still occupied by his family, "should continue in their possession free of rent for the present year." The treasurer was directed to pay to the family the balance of his salary for the quarter, and the following week a pension fund was begun for Mrs. Elliott.[630]

The next few months witnessed many adjustments. For one thing, the Bishop's death forced Mr. Coley to curtail special activities. In its annual report to the Diocese, for example, St. Stephen's Church noted that

The Rev. C.H. Coley, by appointment of our late lamented Bishop, exercised partial Pastoral Care *over us, ministering in Holy things, until his duties to his own flock compelled him to leave us. During his . . . sojourn, he performed many kindly offices for us, which has greatly endeared him to our people.*[630a]

Other adjustments were revealed in Christ Church's own report to the convention when Mr. Coley spoke of a significant drop in the number of communicants. He attributed some of the reduction to "several families residing temporarily in Europe." Nearly twenty additional communicants removed to St. Paul's Free Church. He offered no explanation for the latter; perhaps the stresses of war and reconstruction seemed reasons enough. Hardships clearly made maintenance of pew rentals difficult for many, but it could also have been simply that the Bishop's death now made a contemplated change of parishes seem timely.[630.b]

By summer time, however, matters had begun to resume a more normal state. Mr. Coley was granted six weeks leave in September and October to be married,[631] and even before he departed the Vestry invited him to remain as Rector-in-Charge for the following year.[632] Step were taken also "for forming a choir", giving the carpet from the basement of the Church to the Episcopal Orphans' Home,[633] and holding a fair. The last was held in the "Armory Hall" for the benefit of orphan relief. At this festive December affair, sponsored by the Episcopal ladies of the city, "a novel feature [was] a cake modelled after Christ Church to the raffled off."[634] Mr. Coley was even authorized to purchase a new surplice.[635]

Perhaps the surest signs of a return to normal occurred the following spring when the *Daily News and Herald* announced that

A picnic will be given for the Sunday School children of Christ Church at "Rockingham" on the Atlantic and Gulf R.R., nine miles from the city. The school and their guests, the children of St. John's, will assemble at the depot at 9 1/2 o'clock . . . their lunches with them. The occasion will doubtless be most pleasant.[636]

A few days later the same medium made news of a vastly more ambitious plan in the city: the founding of the St. Patrick's Total Abstinence Society "for the noble purpose of discouraging the use of ardent spirits".[637] The picnic, at least, appears to have been quite successful.

This was also the season in which the diocese and the city welcomed their new bishop, John W. Beckwith, from New Orleans. By the time of his consecration in April he was already a well known figure here, in a way. For the newspapers had made great sport of the mystery which surrounded his response to Georgia's invitation. While Savannah journals were reporting his probable acceptance, the New Orleans *Picayune* claimed "there is no reason to believe . . . Beckwith has accepted . . . the Bishopric of Georgia . . . twice rendered him and twice declined."[640] Accept he did, however, and both the consecration and his first diocesan convention took place in Savannah during that busy spring of 1868. Christ Church was offered as the site for the consecration,[641] but the ceremony actually took place at St. John's where it attracted considerable attention. Involving the best singers in town, some of whom were even members of the Mozart Club, "the choral service was sung on this occasion for the first time in Savannah, and was intoned antiphonally."[642] Christ Church had its hands full enough perhaps, welcoming the new Bishop on Easter Day, when he celebrated and confirmed 41, and hosting the convention of the diocese one month later.[643] In his address to the convention Bishop Beckwith spoke appreciatively of "this noble old parish . . . to whose generosity the Diocese is largely indebted, under God, for its present prosperity." He seemed sensitive as well to the condition of the congregation as he spoke, noting that

> *while she mourns, as none others can, the loss of one who was . . . both Bishop and Rector, has not permitted her grief to settle into despair. Under the faithful activity of the Rector-in-charge, she is putting forth her energies, and in her present zeal I see the pledge that her future . . . shall fulfill the promise of the past.*[644]

During the spring Mr. Coley took ill, which forced him to spend much of the summer away from the city. In August he wrote to the vestry from the north that he had decided to remain another month. His "health not yet recovered," his physician recommended the "more bracing climate."[645] That proved to be but the first sign of a more profound change, however, for shortly after his return to Savannah the newspapers disclosed that Mr. Coley was about to depart. Having received a call to Shelbyville, Tennessee, he "will preach his farewell sermon tomorrow morning."[646]

The search for a new rector led to the Rev. Mr. John M. Mitchell of Montgomery, Alabama. Commencing his duties on the second Sunday in Advent, 1868, Mr. Mitchell confessed the great diffidence he felt in attempting to follow in Bishop Elliott's footsteps.[647] Diffident or not, it was only a month after he arrived that a movement arose to alter and renovate the Church the Bishop had known. A group of prominent parishioners, including two vestrymen, proposed "improvements" to the church building and procurement of a parsonage, and the vestry's response was explosive. Not only did they endorse the idea, but they immediately moved to lead the way by subscribing 50 shares of Central Railroad stock (worth about $5000) plus another $5000 in city of Savannah Bonds.[648] Whatever else, the vestry's action would seem to be a clear sign of renewed prosperity in the parish, and perhaps of long-frustrated desire for some changes as well.

Designs were developed by John F. Miller of New York with local assistance by Augustus Schwaab.[649] Once their architectural plans were approved, by early summer of 1869, the building committee was directed to have them carried out.[650]

Graciously, St. Johns offered shelter to the homeless congregation while its own church was closed for the renovation.[651] By November, the work was sufficiently advanced that worship could take place and allow the congregation its first inside view of the "new" church.[652] One notable change greeted them even as they approached the Building. For the front steps had been modified from the imposing "bold flight" of the original design to their present arrangement, one the 1869 reviewer described as a "twist and turn" style. Obviously disliking the change, the reviewer wrote "we honestly think it detracts from the architectural appearance of the building."[653] One suspects, however, that even his contemporaries had already begun to think the original steps more intimidating than bold. Certainly the vestry observed with satisfaction that "the steps have been made easier of ascent and furnished with suitable iron railings and gates."[654] Once inside, the first thing to attract the attention of parishioners would surely have been the new Bishop Elliott Memorial Window directly before them in the east end of the Church. The window had been paid for by numerous Sunday School projects, ranging from Lenten and Easter offerings to an "Episcopal Fair" held in the hall of Prof. Semon's Dancing Academy on Broughton St."[655] Viewed for the first time on Christmas Day, 1869, the new window was dedicated "in memory of their beloved Father in God, the Rt. Rev. Stephen Elliott, D.D., by the Children of Christ Church . . ."[656]

Equally striking was the totally new appearance of the entire east end of the Church. The rounded classical apse had been squared off to accommodate the new window and to suit current taste. With the old apse, of course, the inscription that stretched around its semi-circular wall — "Hark the Herald Angels Sing, Glory to the New Born King" — was also destroyed. In its stead, the simple plastered surface of the new chancel arch was painted with Scriptural motifs which were set within a banner and a trefoil — centered directly over the arch. Many of the furnishings within the chancel were replaced also, but unfortunately the changes are not specified.

Nearly as obvious would have been the reconstructed galleries. They were lowered several feet so as to render the pulpit visible from pews that had formerly been all but useless, or at least unsalable. Coupled with the sixteen pews that were added to the ground floor it was estimated that 250 additional worshippers could now be comfortably seated.[657]

Elsewhere in the interior there were other notable changes and repairs, although surely none so startling to viewers as the alterations to the chancel arch and the apse. For instance, the old ceiling, which was found to be dangerous, was "taken down and replaced with new plastering and cornices." Down also had come the large old chandelier which used to illuminate the Church. An increased number of gas jets were mounted along the sides to make up for the loss. The new fixtures known as "church fixtures," had pipes of ultra-marine blue and gilt branches ornamented with gilt leaves.[658] It goes, almost without saying, that those two most tireless competitors for church funds also staked their claims at this time: the roof was repaired and the organ repaired and somewhat rear-

Christ Church viewed from across the square, in front of Pulaski House, as the new street railway is being laid in the 1870's.

ranged. Finishing touches included repainting the pews and other woodwork in the galleries and recarpeting the aisles and chancel.[659]

With so much involved it was fortunate that the good folks of St. John's Church had offered to provide seats, to divide services, and to alternate parochial duties during the upheaval.[660] Enthusiastic thanks for the hospitality were given solid form with the gift of the former chancel furniture and railing for use in St. John's chapel,[661] and by inviting the faithful of that congregation to attend Christ Church while their own building was closed for repairs the following Spring (1870).[662] In reviewing for parishioners its rationale for undertaking so large a task, the Vestry acknowledged that "our action has not met with the approval of all." Yet they were clearly pleased with what had been accomplished thus far — and accomplished without debt at that. In challenging the parish to complete the work they made their own position quite clear.

> *It certainly seems to [us] that the oldest congregation in the state, a congregation with 450 communicants, a number equalled in only a very few parishes in the United States, should be willing to keep their House of Worship in a condition worthy of the cause they espouse and the Master they serve.*[663]

Apparently the challenge was at least partially successful. For the game of musical pews continued the next summer when final touches were given to the interior of the Church, once more necessitating its closing. Again St. John's offered shelter to the homeless.[664]

While all the renovation work was going on, Mr. Mitchell also successfully established himself as a figure to be respected in the community and the diocese. During the first closure of the Church, for instance, in the summer and autumn of 1869, he used the opportunity to travel northward. On his return, bound for Savannah out of New York aboard the steamer *San Jacinto*, the ship ran aground near Body Island, N.C. The captain managed to charter two sloops and see his passengers safely ashore at Norfolk by way of Elizabeth City and Dismal Swamp. From that point, however, they were on their own. It seems Mr. Mitchell was "honored" with the duty to make all arrangements for their return to Savannah. Back home at last, the comrades in shipwreck then celebrated their adventure, survival, and Mr. Mitchell's leadership with a special Saturday afternoon get together at the Marshall House.[665]

Among Georgia churchmen, too, he seems quickly to have made his mark. He was even made the first Dean of the Savannah "Convocation" when the Diocese established these, primarily as missionary districts, in 1870.[666] His first report to the Diocese as Dean emphasized the need of a full time missionary-priest for the area, and happily reported that considerable money had already been pledged toward a salary. Interestingly, one of the first respondents to his leadership in this cause was the congregation of the "Ogeechee Mission", the same congregation which had been so attentively nurtured by Bishop Elliott in prior decades, and "originally" established in the area by Bartholomew Zouberbuhler in the 1760's.[667]

Adding to the general excitement which accompanied new bishop, new rector and refurbished church building was the latest rumor that Bishop Beckwith might choose to reside in Savannah. Having heard this, the vestry promised full cooperation, and offered to pay half the rent for a suitable house, providing St. John's would pay the other half.[668] Beyond these things, however, by 1870-71 parish affairs had resumed a rather normal pattern. The character of the times is most effectively sketched simply by noting the prominent questions and events of the day. What to do with the Wilkins property was one topic under discussion.[669] Another arose with the death of Robert E. Lee in the fall of 1870. Since the Rector

The Bishop Elliott window in the east end of the Church had a completely new setting after the 1883 renovation.

was out of town at the time Bishop Beckwith was requested to hold a memorial service on the day of the burial.[670] Closer to home was the funeral of Commodore Josiah Tattnall late the following spring. The service for the celebrated war hero was impressive in many ways, but it was especially so when, "as the Body entered the Church, the choir sang a requiem."[671]

Other matters of concern were community service and missions. With an eye to the former, Christ Church Guild was founded early in 1870. Its purpose was "to find employment for those in need, and charity for those unable to work."[672] The Savannah Port Society, too, was still active after some fifty years of service to visiting seamen. "One of the largest congregations ever seen in Savannah" gathered at Christ Church for the Society's anniversary celebration, and to hear Bishop Beckwith preach. "Hundreds went away because they could not gain admittance."[673]

Locals took special interest also in the ordination of the Rev. Mr. R.W.B. Elliott, son of the late bishop.[674] The ceremony was held on Easter Day when the chancel was filled with spring color. According to journalists, "the cross at Christ Church was decorated and wreaths of brilliant and fragrant roses hung around in beautiful festoons."[675] At such seasons, as now, the services of the Church drew special attention. For the summer months, however, things seemed different. The Vestry voted "that evening services be omitted — at the discretion of the Rector."[676] Then on rare occasions truly extraordinary things were done, as on the last Sunday before Lent, 1872.

The 9:55 a.m. train which left the city . . . on the Savannah, Skidaway and Seaboard Railroad, took a number of persons to the Isle of Hope, where the distinguished pulpit orator, Bishop Beckwith . . . administered the rite of confirmation and delivered an eloquent sermon appropriate to the day and solemn ceremony. The service attracted a goodly congregation and the choir was assisted by a lady organist and others from this city.[677]

Doctrinal questions also claimed a share of the conversation in the early 1870's. There was some anxiety over rumors of change in the Book of Common Prayer, for example. With regard to these the Vestry

Resolved – that the delegates to the approaching dioceasan convention be and are hereby requested not to cast their votes for any deputies, either clerical or lay, in the next General Convention who will countenance any attempt to alter the *Book of Common Prayer* in any particular whatever, excepting only in the Nicene Creed.[678]

Without a doubt, however, the most sensational question of the day grew from the new pronouncement out of Rome and the Vatican Council on papal infallibility. Not only did this one create excited discussion in the churches, but it reached far beyond the circles that normally discussed ecclesiastical topics. The issue surfaced in countless streetcorner discussions, political speeches, and special lectures from Bismark to Bay St. to St. John the Baptist Cathedral.[679]

The focus of conversation soon shifted, however, from the churches in the world and services at the Isle of Hope to activities in Johnson Square. One early sign of what was to come emerged in a special meeting of the Vestry called in the spring of 1872, at the Rector's request. Action was needed regarding "certain reports, which were current throughout the city, of immoral conduct on the part of the Rector, and which were injurious to the welfare of the Church."[680] Actually, this was not the first time Dr. Mitchell had been accused in such a way. For nearly two years there had been some suspicion. "A gentleman who resided in the vicinity of Christ Church learned from his family that they were subjected, on account of their promxinity to the Church, their windows being on a direct line with the upper floor, to disgusting exhibitions by Dr. Mitchell, the character of which it is unnecessary to state." Since he was unwilling to involve his family in prosecution he relocated them. The next dweller

The steps to the west porch of the Church were changed in 1869 to what one unhappy reviewer described as a "twist and turn" style. The marble cross in the pediment was added later in 1884.

had the same experience, however, and he wrote the Bishop. Subsequent inquiry reassured Bishop Beckwith that the charges were unfounded. But at that point damaging rumors began to circulate and in their own way to demand this further investigation.[681]

The following day Dr. Mitchell appeared in person before the Vestry to defend his cause, and his denial was so persuasive that he convinced all present of his innocence. On the advice of counsel, and to restore confidence, a character endorsement, signed by every man on the Vestry, was printed. The next Sunday it was circulated throughout the congregation and copies were sent to the Bishop, other clergy, vestries, etc.[682] Rumors persisted, however, virtually forcing a meeting of the Bishop, Vestry, and counsel to the conclusion "that the Rector owed it to the church and himself to demand a regular Ecclesiastical trial."[683]

Wheels began to turn, and as the trial approached, Mr. Mitchell requested the Vestry "to intermit his services" pending disposition of his case.[684] Two weeks later he resigned, despite the restraint of friends, for fear it appear he was clinging to the position for protection. "May God guide us all in . . . this perplexing matter, and overrule it in all His own good time and way to his glory and the good of His Church."[685] That letter was tabled until the Bishop advised the Vestry to accept it for "the good of the Church."[686]

Three days later there was yet another special meeting, this time at the request of the Bishop. As soon as the Wardens and Vestry had arrived, along with three visiting clergy, Bishop Beckwith requested all to unite with him in prayer and litany. He then proceeded to his "very painful duty" to depose the Rev. Dr. John M. Mitchell from the priesthood. Presenting his statement from the chancel, he pointed out that his action was based on canon law, on Dr. Mitchell's written renunciation of his ministry, and on his confession before clerical and lay witnesses that he was guilty of "gross immorality". For its part, the Vestry asked the Bishop to repeat the sentence of deposition tomorrow (Sunday) in the presence of the congregation, and resolved to write to Dr. Royall, Dr. Mitchell's accuser.[687] Secretary and Treasurer W.W. Lincoln was given the difficult task of expressing their appreciation of Dr. Royall's action, "which helped the Vestry relieve themselves of errors into which they had been led by a dissimulation . . . too skillful for easy detection and too abhorrent even for denunication."[688]

After his confession to the Bishop, Dr. Mitchell left town with his family the same day. They did not hear the sentence of deposition, nor have to read the *Morning News'* scornful description of "the unfortunate man" who in the opinion of the writer, was "entitled to but little commiseration."[689] Neither did they suffer to observe the people of the congregation as they struggled to cope with the rebuke they inevitably shared, and with their own indignation. For better or worse they also missed the parish's climactic attempt to put that struggle behind and "to set the record straight:"

We, the Wardens and Vestry of Christ Church, do hearby declare our unalterable abhorrence of the "gross immoralities" confessed by . . . John M. Mitchell, and of other . . . immoralities and criminal practices charged against him and undisproved — and of the dissimulation, falsehood, and constructive perjury, by which he betrayed the confidence of his Bishop, his Brethren, his Congregation, and the members of this Body — all to the injury of the ministry, to the humiliation of the Church, and to the unmingled grief and indignation of her children.[690]

For leadership during this time of trial and shock the parish turned to an old old friend, the Rev. C.H. Coley. He had been with them through more profoundly shaken times than this while he was assistant Rector to Bishop Elliott, during the war. Making the move from Brunswick sometime during the summer of 1872, Mr. Coley was in charge as Rector by

Detail of the brass lectern, given as a memorial in c. 1881.

October.[691] His comforting presence was the parish's good fortune, for as things turned out, the Mitchell scandal proved to be but the first episode in a most trying year.

Matters were still far from normal in the Church when Sr. Warden Jacob Waldburg died late in the summer, about the time Mr. Coley was relocating his family to Savannah.[692] Then he was followed to the grave by his junior colleague, Dr. Phineas M. Kollock, only three months later, in December.[693] Added to the impact of losing two such faithful and long-serving churchmen was their survivors' growing recognition of the appalling state of parish finances. In hope of taking firmer grip on the situation the Vestry for the first time organized itself into a set of standing committees — on finance, music, and church property. The newly organized Finance Committee then faced the disagreeable duty to report that with one large (improperly contracted) note overdue and other creditors not punctually paid, the overall debt of the parish unreduced from last year, and the budget for the current year in deficit, "the credit of the Church is at a low ebb."[694]

In the Vestry actions, one senses more than normal fiscal anxiety. There is almost a sense of alarm — albeit undefined. It could have been merely that the scars left by last spring's "gross immoralities" were not yet fully hardened. It could have been, . . . but it was more. In February (1873) the parish treasurer of many years, who also served as treasurer for the Diocese, was abruptly "retired" and a review of financial records begun.[695] Among other things it was discovered that the diocesan "Fund for the Relief of Widows and Orphans of Deceased Clergyman" was missing! Further inquiry learned from the treasurer himself "that he had used the funds, and pledged the Bonds as collateral for money borrowed for his own private uses."[696] Since the "Wardens and Vestry of Christ Church" served as trustees for these and other funds belonging to the Diocese, new trustees were appointed, but not without great embarrassment.[697] That was the easy part, however. Resolving questions of culpability, restitution, and correction of the situation became incredibly tangled and resulted in prolonged litigation.[698]

Meanwhile, when other duties required Mr. Coley to leave Christ Church early in 1873,[699] Bishop Beckwith agreed to take charge of the parish as Rector with the Rev. Mr. R.C. Foute as his assistant.[700] Even with an assistant, however, and the understanding that the Bishop would need several months each year to visit the middle and upper parts of his Diocese, many feared he could not possibly satisfy both parochial and episcopal demands.[701] To this he replied

> *There were two causes which induced me to accept this position. First: the condition of the Parish — depressed, disheartened, almost paralyzed . . . [Second:] Good Christian men . . . bade me hope that, under God, I might aid the Parish to cast aside its despondency and renew its vigor."*

He then went on to express his expectation that "the Parish will . . . soon be independent of me."[702]

There was, indeed, some reason for hope. Not everything had collapsed. The choir, for example, showed enough vitality under the leadership of Mr. H.L. Schreiner to stage an opera. Taking advantage of a vocal windfall, it "was reinforced by several members of the operatic troupe now in our city."[703] The Sunday School, too, kept things going by joining the children of St. John's to hold a Christmas party at the Episcopal Orphan's Home. Together they set up "a large Christmas tree loaded with presents of every description . . . affording happiness to those unfortunate children."[704]

Yet there is no doubt the Bishop was accurate in describing the state of the parish. The injury it suffered in these twin diasters was plain to all. Bishop Beckwith saw it in the dispirited, "almost paralyzed," condition of the people. We can see it in the normally lifeless statistics submitted in the annual report to the Diocese. During the tragic year of 1872 there were probably fewer confirmations than in any year since 1856, when the parish numbered less than half as many communicants.[705] Significantly, the Sunday School also showed its lowest degree of participation since the disturbed years of the late war. The Bishop had his work cut out for him and knew it. Parishioners knew it, too, and welcomed him warmly.[706]

Almost immediately a parish school was begun which soon reported 19 students — probably the first since colonial days.[707] Sunday School and confirmation activity and statistics show similarly heartening revival.[708] Despite a lapse in Mr. Beckwith's health which forced his resignation during the summer 1873[709] he appears to have continued much of his work with good effect.[710]

Regardless of the state of the Bishop's health, it was soon enough apparent that two jobs were indeed too much. It was time for the parish to become "independent of him." The search for a permanent Rector began early in 1874,[711] and progressed normally until it turned up an interesting problem in communication. In issuing a call to its first candidate, no one on the Vestry thought to inform Mr. Foute, the Assistant Rector, of his status. He assumed, therefore, that his services were no longer desired and accepted another call, apparently without telling the Vestry. No wonder when the first candidate declined and a call was then given to Mr. Foute, both he and the Vestry were astonished at their situation![712] Ultimately, the search identified the Rev. Mr. George D.E. Mortimer, of New Orleans, who assumed his duties as Rector early in the summer of 1874.[713]

Health returned slowly, but after a year or more of Mr. Mortimer's leadership signs of real recovery were abundant. The Sunday School amazingly doubled its enrollment in that time.[714] Its vitality was especially evident in the seasonal festivals which became program fixtures during the 1870's. Occasionally, there was a May Festival, perhaps including a bazaar, which would have been located in the nearby "Mozart Hall" because of the need for space.[715] Typical was the Great Easter Festival of 1876, which received a generous write-up in the *Morning News*. The program was described as joyful throughout — from the processional "Brightly Gleams Our Banner," through the offering at which more than $300 in Lenten savings was presented by the children, and the singing of "Christ is Risen" and "The Day of Resurrection." Even the sermon, "We Bring No Glistening Treasurers" was attentively heard by the young congregation.[716] Each year, as well, there were Christmas Festivals, which seem to have enjoyed equal popularity.[717]

Beyond the Sunday School, other aspects of parish service once again received attention in the news. There were the poor, of whom we have heard no mention for several years. But during Christmastide, 1874, the Church gave "its annual dinner to the pensioners of the parish and to other indigent persons." "Lavishly supplied with all good things," the ladies of the Church served, and everyone "had enough to spare."[718] The congregation also "provided for the expenses of one of the candidates" for the priesthood in the Diocese.[719] The "Bible and Prayer Book Society" was now actively carrying out its mission, and the Bishop Elliott Society" distributed over $1250 in communion alms and funds it had raised for the needy. The latter group also reported that it had made well over a thousand "benevolent visits" to widows, orphans, and others, and given out some 900 garments to the needy in the parish.[720]

The same sort of vitality is visible in their active liturgical calendar. For example, during Lent in 1875, beyond the usual Sunday schedule, there were daily services each week at 4 PM, Litany each Saturday at 11 AM, and special lectures every Monday, Wednesday, and Friday evening.[721]

Of course, its not likely that everything will go so well, is it? That the choir needed some combination of improvement, encouragement, and money was apparent in the reports of the Music Committee.[722] From our distance, however, it is less clear just where the problem lay when Mr. Penfield, the organist, complained that "the blower was inefficient." The "blower," in 1874, was the Sexton, James Anderson! Indignant when told of Mr. Penfield's complaint, he yelped that the organist "required a blower at the time he was engaged in ringing the Bell." To avoid further problem Mr. Penfield thoughtfully pointed out that new fangled water-powered equipment could be installed for $250, but the Vestry thought better of that. Instead, "the Sexton was generally overhauled in his duties."[723]

With the "mother church" of the Diocese once again in a spiritually prosperous state, Bishop Beckwith gave greater attention to several matters which were beginning to trouble him deeply. His concerns are most instructive, for whatever we might think today of his opinions they do help us recover the context of parish life in the 1870's. Troubling him most were the divergent forces he perceived which seemed to be bent on diverting the Episcopal Church aside from its traditional course. On the one hand he saw an exaggerated emphasis on what some liked to call "heart religion," which gave great stress to emotion and too little appreciated the heritage of an apostolic tradition. He would not undervalue heart religion, "God forbid!" But if unchecked he feared it would transform the Church into just another 19th century sect.[724] Equally distressing in his view, however, was the opposite deviation of the "Catholic Party" to create a medieval one.[725] His annual diatribes against the "Romish teaching," which he felt was growing ever more virulent and anti-Protestant in its "novel doctrines," became almost routine.[726]

In speaking thus, whatever else, the Bishop does accurately represent to us the mood of the day. There is no question that the years following Vatican I witnessed a general deterioration in ecumenical relations. It is reasonably safe, therefore, for us to presume that what weighed so heavily on the Bishop's mind also pressed to some degree upon the thinking of his many congregations. No doubt it was likewise perceptible in their devotional styles, although somewhat more difficult to detect in historical records. The party lines in this ecclesiastical warfare became most sharply defined in the periodic controversy over whether to drop the term "Protestant" from the official name of the denomination[727] — a question which, at the time, could not be disassociated from the "high" and "low" church extremes that so vexed Bishop Beckwith.

Considering the spirited combat triggered by questions of churchmanship, whether centering on "heart religion", papal claims, or the official name of the denomination, it is to the Bishop's credit that he recognized it would not be sufficient merely to deplore "deviations." The middle-way itself would have to be strengthened. To that end he urged certain refinements in church music, liturgy, the manner of reading scripture, voicing responses, etc. Especially bothersome to him was the treatment given the rubric at the end of the Communion Service which required *"If any of the consecrated Bread, and Wine remain after the Communion, . . . the Minister and other Communicants shall . . . reverently eat and drink the same."* "This rubric," he lamented, "is neglected by many of our congregations," where instead of reverence, he has himself found "communicants standing at the chancel rail consuming the bread and wine, and talking of the weather and the health of their families!"[729] Leaving much to be desired also were some common musical practices. To rectify these he urged increasing use of congregational hymns, now greatly facilitated by joint resolution of the last General Convention, but still not well established in the parishes of the Diocese.

I believe it would greatly add to congregational singing if Parishes would take advantage of this permission . . . in place of the elaborate voluntaries and extraordinary singings which sometimes disturb our public worship . . . The congregations will soon become familiar with the hymn and music, and . . . will be singing the Lord's praises, instead of leaving this important part of our worship to the skill of paid choirs, who so often praise them with their lips while their hearts are far from Him.[730]

Bishop Beckwith's concerns aside, prospects were beginning to look securely bright for Christ Church when a national depression began to make serious impact during 1875. That was why, when the Rector took his vacation two months late in the summer, instead of following the normal course to obtain a substitute, the Church was simply closed and the choir disbanded for the duration.[731] A year later, the situation still unimproved, "in view of the empty treasury . . . it is inexpedient" to maintain any longer a paid choir. The four paid singers, who made up the usual choir, were notified "that their services will not be required after February 1st next," and a movement was initiated to organize a voluntary choir.[732] Subsequently, the financial crisis deepened to the point were even more drastic measures had to be considered. "Whereas the recent calamities which have befallen the people of Christ Church have deprived them of their usual material resources," it was decided to give up the effort to provide housing for the Rector, and to consider reducing his salary in the face of almost certain budgetary deficit. They even decided to hold no public pew sale in 1876, but simply to continue all on the same terms and rely on their good faith to make up the rental deficit of $3000.[733]

Adding to the distress that accompanied fiscal collapse in the parish and the nation was the "sickness, sorrow, and death" which struck the city in a severe yellow fever epidemic during the summer and autumn of 1876. Through the peak weeks, in August-September-October, between twenty and forty per day died of the plague in Savannah. So fearsome was the threat that the children in the Episcopal Orphanage were hustled out of town for several months.[734] Mr. Mortimer was out of town, too, through July and August on vacation in Virginia. But in September, when he was due to return, he did not. In fact, he did not reappear until mid-November so that the Church had to remain closed through most of the autumn. There was obviously some muttering, even suspicion, over his prolonged absence, for he appeared in person before the Vestry after his return — a sure sign of trouble. He explained that he had been abed all of that time with an aggravated form of the same ailment that had sent him away originally for rest. The Vestry expressed "their entire confidence in his fidelity to his flock [and] in his inability to be

The old York Street Rectory was given in 1884, the bequest of Miss Jane Young.

present during any part of the late epidemic."⁷³⁵ Someone's confidence must have dissolved rapidly, however. Within two weeks Mr. Mortimer had resigned, offended that the Vestry had asked for verification justifying his recent absence. For its part the Vestry refused to consider his action "under so thorough a misunderstanding of our purposes and opinions."⁷³⁶ At this the Rector withdrew his resignation and the breach appeared to be healed, but for so brief a span we cannot help but wonder.

As the affair ripened, early in 1877, accurate diagnosis is complicated by the fact that this crisis in trust was overtaken by and confounded with the enduring economic one. All we can say for certain is that it must have been a bad season! In January the Vestry made some difficult decisions: to reduce the Rector's salary, to try reducing others as well (such as the Sexton), to look into mortgaging the church building, and to approach the congregation with the bad news.⁷³⁷ Then in mid-March both Mr. Mortimer and the entire body of wardens and vestry resigned!⁷³⁸ It all caused quite a stir around the town.⁷³⁹

Helping us to sort through this wreckage, or rather denying us any easy interpretation of its causes, are two puzzling statements. One is the Rector's comment that, under present circumstances, he would have been willing to accept a salary cut.⁷⁴⁰ The other is the resolution of the Wardens and Vestrymen that "the habit of re-electing gentlemen already in office has . . . long prevailed."⁷⁴¹ Their clear implication was that it had prevailed much too long, and that a matter of such importance in the life of the parish should be the result of conscious choice, not mere habit. On reflection, the evidence seems to suggest the possibility that what we have witnessed was not really a specific quarrel or case of injured professional honor at all. Rather it may have been a kind of general emotional overload which caused the system to short-circuit altogether — a situation in which the multiple distresses of the previous year raised too many doubts in the minds of too many people that their work was appreciated or was accomplishing anything.

Whatever the explanation, the great flare-up seems to have cleared the air a bit. All nine Wardens and Vestrymen were given a vote of confidence and re-elected.⁷⁴² As for Mr. Mortimer, expressions of appreciation evoked by his imminent departure seemed notably genuine, generous and general. A spokesman for St. Stephen's Church called him "a true and untiring friend and brother," thanking him for his "heartily rendered ministerial services" with the good wishes of the congregation.⁷⁴³ Within Christ Church the Mortimers were honored with a gift of silver from the children of the Sunday School, "The garden of his love."⁷⁴⁴ At the time of the resignation the *Morning News* described Mr. Mortimer as "universally esteemed by the entire community."⁷⁴⁵ Significantly, the newpaper continued to follow his progress with interest. They noted the family's departure on the Central Railroad's evening train "to take charge of the most flourishing Episcopal Church in the west,"⁷⁴⁶ and kept track of them for many years thereafter.⁷⁴⁷ All of this was in addition to the Vestry's own "wish it could have been otherwise," as they bid him "take . . . to your new field of labor our earnest wishes and prayers for your success and happiness in all things, both temporal and spiritual."⁷⁴⁸

The summer of 1877 was a quiet one, and the Church even closed on some Sundays.⁷⁴⁸ Hope was not far off, however, for early in August the *Morning News* advised "that the Rev. Thomas Boone, now of Athens, . . . has accepted rectorship of Christ Church." Noting that he was expected by the first week of October, the newspaper happily advertised that "Mr. Boone has the reputation of being one of the most able and eloquent ministers in the state."⁷⁴⁹ Although the *Minutes* of the Vestry have no entry until several days later, they confirm the accuracy of the journal's earlier revelation. What the news release did not reveal, however, was the note of encouragement which filled Mr. Boone's letters of acceptance. Commencing with the Vestry's nostalgic reference to the "bright days of the past," he urged them to believe they could come again. Then in thanking them for their trust, which he "will try never to abuse,"⁷⁵⁰ he reminded the congregation that his own "ancestors and relations for five generations have been connected with . . . old Christ Church," and promised "she shall have my best efforts in behalf of her prosperity."⁷⁵¹ To the faithful who had weathered the recent storms, both national and parochial, his words seemed to bring special comfort. One parishioner wrote

*I sincerely hope and pray it is the dawn of brighter days for our poor, sticken old Christ Church, and that she will rise from the dust and once more take her place as the Mother Church of the Diocese.*⁷⁵²

Rather unexpectedly, Mr. Boone was called to attend the General Convention as a delegate. So to accommodate the congregation he arrived to take charge two weeks early, on the 23rd of September, prior to leaving for Boston.⁷⁵³ In November he returned to stay, determined to bring new life to the parish that was still, rather surprisingly, the second largest in the Diocese . . . on paper.⁷⁵⁴ He was still making his first acquaintance with much of the parish when the Vestry made a most significant decision. It involved a question which had apparently been simmering for several years, ever since an impetuous young clergyman had given them a large piece of his mind. His name was R.C. Foute and he had been assistant briefly during the Rectorship of Bishop Beckwith. He was disappointed and offended at the way he had been by-passed and left totally uninformed in the early stages of the search that called Mr. Mortimer. Thus, at his departure, he took the trouble to point out that he would not have accepted a call in any case "since he would be prohibited *by law* from exercise of one of the most important prerogatives pertaining to such an office — by being excluded from the meetings of the Vestry." He had a point, so he made it again. Such a custom "fosters a spirit of dissatisfaction and indifference by erecting a barrier between Rector, Vestry, and people, which is fatal to the harmony of feeling and unity of action."⁷⁵⁵ At the time, some saw merit amid the heat in that message and

*Resolved: that any bye law, rule, or regulation of this Body which . . . pretends to constitute the Wardens the Spiritual advisor of the Rector . . . be and the same is hereby abolished.*⁷⁵⁶

But now, after three more years of hard experience and difficult communication, the fuller meaning of Mr. Foute's parting salvo had become much clearer. That is why they chose

*cordially and unanimously [to] invite the Rev. Thomas Boone, the Rector of the Parish, to be present at the meetings of the Vestry as often as his convenience will permit, assuring him that it will not only be agreeable to them personally but that they sincerely wish for his advice and assistance in their deliberations for the good of the parish.*⁷⁵⁷

Mr. Boone willingly assented "for the good of the parish", but retained some misgivings, expressed in his hope for a "fully satisfactory settlement" at some point in the future.⁷⁵⁸ He appears unclear himself about just what would constitute a "fully satisfactory" one, but certainly the immediate problem of communication was addressed by the new arrangement. It helped greatly that from 1878 onward Mr. Boone and his successors in office were almost unfailing in their attendance at meetings of the Vestry. Yet through the decades that followed, only slowly did it dawn on everyone that what they were developing, what Mr. Boone had found himself unable to put into words, was an entirely new "corporate style," legally speaking. In other words, what was emerging was an organizational concept that made the Rector, Wardens, and Vestry together — not just the Wardens and Vestry — responsible for the governance of the parish. It was an idea that transformed the rector from a spectator, albeit now a welcome one, to a participant. More than that, when the concept finally achieved fruition in 1918, with the revision of the original 1789 charter of the parish, the rector became "*ex-officio the chairman of the Vestry,*"⁷⁵⁹ as he remains to the present.

After agreeing to attend meetings of the Wardens and Vestry Mr. Boone's next act was to resign! No need for alarm, however, for he resigned many times during his eleven year rectorship. While presumably he did not so conceive it, with Mr. Boone resigning was more an administrative technique than a terminal act. Harsh? Not really. To see the point we need only recall what has just been said regarding the administrative weakness inherent in the Rector's position. Holders of that offce had literally no constituted power in the governance of this parish, only the power of moral suasion. Therefore, the Rector's best leverage for change was through the Vestry's desire to retain him — perhaps his only real leverage. Mr. Boone used it to advantage, this time in making the point that he was "unwilling to hold the Rectorship and have the work either *not done*, or *half done.*"⁷⁶⁰ Inquiry made clear that his health and the need for an assistant had

The alabaster baptismal font, given in 1884, attracted a good bit of attention even outside the congregation

prompted the resignation, and that if an assistant were available he would withdraw it. He had not asked for one, however, because of the still fragile financial condition of the parish.[761] With this information in hand a parish meeting quickly raised the needed amount, the issue was settled and the resignation withdrawn.[762]

This was the second noteworthy change in operating style Christ Church made during Mr. Boone's first year. From that day to the present the typical pattern has been for Rectors to have an assistant of some sort, although there have been some exceptional periods. By November of 1878 Mr. Boone's first assistant, George H. Chadwell, was on the job to preach at "both services," his first Sunday.[763] He was succeeded the next year by R.H. Barnwell, confirming what was to become an important tradition in parish life.[764]

Several additional new touches achieved noteworthy prominence during Mr. Boone's rectorship. Among these was the increasing attention given to liturgy and music. Second, we see a greater assortment of social service activities and groups than was characteristic in the past. Finally, and most apparent of all, was a much heightened emphasis on missions. This is not to say that such interests were lacking earlier, certainly. But for nearly two decades now the energies of the congregation had been often diverted elsewhere, surviving weakness within and demands from without made by war and reconstruction. During Mr. Boone's time such things were at last put behind. Although his years were not ones of sensational spiritual or economic prosperity, they were nevertheless years which exhibited a strong trend toward real recovery of purpose and forward motion.

The new attention given liturgy and music is most obviously demonstrated by the foundation of a Sacristan Society, in December of 1878, under the presidency of Mrs. L. Habersham.[765] That occurred little more than a year after Boone's arrival. The dozen or so ladies of the society quickly set about doing their work with admirable thoroughness. Among their earliest records, posted inside the cover of the first *Minute*

Book, is a series of measurements which includes the span of the chancel arch, the organ loft, and the numerous others they might require in decorating the Church for various occasions.[766] They made a difference, too, and the Rector made public note of it in thanking them "for their constant devotion to our Church Edifice, and in particular for their attention to the . . . Chancel at Easter."[767]

That Mr. Boone made an impact on the liturgical style and emphasis of the parish is further supported by the unprecedented outpouring of worship related gifts that his work elicited. True enough, there had been notable gifts made at the time the 1838 Church was completed, but nothing of similar magnitude had occurred since then. What began in Boone's time, however, became an important memorial tradition. Many items which are still important elements in the decor of the Church today were donated, usually as memorials, during his time. One of the first of these was the brass eagle lectern presented by the Cuyler family.[768] Another gift still to be seen today was the baptismal font — depicting an angel kneeling and holding a twenty inch sea shell. Executed in "spotless white Italian marble", contemporaries were said to regard it as "one of the most beautiful works of art in the country."[769] Given by W. Grayson Mann as a memorial to his wife, Susie, and executed by "one of the best Italian sculptors," it was said that there was "only one other of similar design, and that one . . . in front of the altar of the famous Cathedral at Cologne."[770] About this same time, Christ Church installed its first recorded hymn boards, designed to display the days, Sundays, hymns, etc.[771] Equally visible was the new altar cross of "burnished brass," given by Miss Henriette Tattnall as a memorial to the "late Flag Officer, Josiah Tattnall, and his wife."[772]

These gifts mark only the beginning, however, and only list benefactions which were visible inside the Church. A very important gift of a different sort came in 1884 when Miss Jane Young bequeathed her home and furniture on York St., thus satisfying the Church's long felt need for a rectory.[773] Actually, the Young legacy was so generous that it also allowed painting of the Church, the discharge of several outstanding debts, and placement of a "handsome marble cross over the front entrance . . . during the past year."[774]

Fortunately, in addition to the material evidence of heightened liturgical concern, we are able to infer a good bit about what took place in the services from what we know went on behind them. No sooner had Mr. Boone arrived in the autumn of 1877 than the choir was reorganized. The Savannah papers wrote with delight about some of the developments. "We are glad to learn," they crowed, that Mrs. Annie T. Cleveland has been permanently engaged in the Christ Church choir "thus insuring her talents to our city, and giving a brilliant star to the musical world of Savannah." Apparently well known locally, the writer added: "no recommendation is needed to . . . the Savannah public."[775] Musically, some interesting things happened during Mrs. Cleveland's tenure. Obviously, she brought a style to Christ Church that drew attention both from congregants and the general public. For instance, she set to music a hymn of the "Blessed Virgin" which she and the combined choirs of Christ Church and St. John's sang for the Knights Templar Lodge at a special service in St. Johns Church.[776] On another occasion a trio of the choir sang an "Ave Maria" composed by another local musician who was organist at the Cathedral Church of St. John the Baptist.[777]

Mrs. Cleveland's personal style must have made equally good copy, for within a few days of her arrival at Christ Church, the choir conductor, the organist, and one of the soloists all resigned.[778] Throughout her years in the Church she kept the Music Committee busy unruffling feathers and bandaging injured dignities. Often at odds with her vocal colleagues, she was always at war with the organ, which she complained needed weekly repair. This, she argued, was best carried out each Sunday morning between 9 and 11 AM to make certain it would last through the service![779] Finally, after four years, she resigned, then unresigned and instead "offered" to release the Wardens and Vestry from "their obligations." When that didn't work she pleaded for them to release her. When even that failed, she left for vacation one summer and disappeared.[780]

Fascinating as undoubtedly she was, her importance here is in the way she illustrates the lengths to which the Rector and Vestry were willing to go to strenghten the worship of the Church with the best musical talent they could find. When she did not return, the Rector employed a talent of equal magnitude to replace her. This brought Madame Margaret Bouligny to Savannah from New York, where her talents as a singer and teacher were highly regarded.[781] It also brought Professor Mehrtens to be organist and choirmaster. Together they formed the core of what proved to be a productive, if short-lived, musical team.[782] In the spring of 1883 they even presented an operetta at the Savannah Theatre, "Little Red Riding Hood," which involved many of the children of the Church. Their object was to raise money toward purchase of a new water motor to operate the organ bellows — and thus solve at least one of the instrument's now infamous problems.[783]

This happy situation did not long endure, however, as either personalities, costs, new ideas, or some combination of them soon provoked another change. One certain motivation was the wish expressed by "many ladies, members of the congregation," to begin a boys choir[784] as soon as existing contracts should expire. Madame Bouligny — out but not down — finished up with a flourish, which the *Morning News* celebrated at length in a most informative review.

All the world knows that Christ Church enjoys a reputation for fine music, but within the past year its reputation has been enhanced by the services and conscientious labors of that estimable lady and painstaking teacher of the voice, Madame Bouligny. To her efforts yesterday we were indebted for one of the finest treats in the offertory solo, rendered by Mr. Otto Vogel., a young German of pluck and talent, and for whom a brilliant future is predicted. Both teacher and pupil are to be heartily congratulated.[785]

Just in time to hear Madame Bouligny's final triumph, "Prof. William Atkinson of New York, the newly appointed organist of Christ Church," arrived in the city to begin work organizing a boys choir. "Not only a talented organist, but a skillful leader, . . . the choir of Christ Church is to be congratulated in securing the services of such a talented and gifted musician."[786] The Rector seems to have been quite pleased with the work of the choir, for in his annual report to the Diocese he voiced his "hopes that heartier services will result from the change, to a more devotional style of music."[787] The ladies, on the other hand, abruptly changed their minds and came to oppose the boys choir. It was a perplexed Vestry that wondered "whereas, . . . in response to a petition signed by about seventy-five Ladies of the Congregation, [we] established the Boy Choir *One Year Ago*," how could it be that "there seems . . . *now* an equally decided opposition thereto?!" With poorly disguised impatience they wrote every pewholder in the Church, even enclosing a return postal card, to ask for an expression of opinion. As a further precaution, they also gave fair notice that any not responding "would be deemed satisfied with the present Boy Choir."[788]

Whatever else, this extended saga of music and musicians in the Church would seem to establish firmly that the Rector cared very much about the role of music in worship. He was determined that, at all costs, it should enrich this central activity of the congregation even at early morning services each Sunday.[789] With all of the attention he gave to discovering the right musical formula, however, it is a bit disappointing that we know so little about the parish's liturgical style during the early Boone years. Oh, we are left a few nuggets, such as that among the favored funeral hymns were "Just As I Am Without One Plea" and "There Is A Fountain Filled With Blood,"[790] or that by the early 1880's "for many years past it has been the custom of this parish to have an early service on Christmas and Easter."[791] We know, too, that on such occasions we might have seen over the Communion Table "the stained-glass window . . . ornamented with evergreen, and a large medallion centerpiece in the form of a star composed of white camellias and other flowers."[792] Certainly it is interesting to discover that in those days Thanksgiving Services were held in the late days of summer, in the tradition of the English harvest festival.[793] But as to what went on "between the rubrics" we are told little beyond what may be inferred from the Bishop's annual declamations. That was the case, at least, until a visitor from Philadelphia complained he found "too much form and popish mummery" in Christ Church! After describing the services as "highly ritualistic," filled with genuflections and worse, and calling the minister a "priest", the visitor's indictment became more specific. The "priest goes inside the chancel and kneels bolt upright before the altar with his back to the congregation, [then] commences reading the service, responses to which are sung by the choir, the congregation kneeling but not saying a word." The final straws in this critic's view were added when the "priest" held the offering above his head before the altar "for several seconds," the organist never ceasing to perform "in a most operatic style."[794]

Finally in the mid-1880's, we gain a clearer and somewhat more balanced picture of the services because the Easter programs for 1884 and 1885 have survived.[794.1] At that time it appears that most if not all of the communion service was done chorally — at least the creed and perhaps the Lord's Prayer and Collects as well. Could this be one of the things Bishop Beckwith had in mind when he delivered a lengthy complaint to the clergy of the Diocese against "diversity in the use of the prayer Book?" Possibly, but not certainly, for all he specified was his distaste for the use of "lights on the altar," a matter not even mentioned in the Philadelphian's inappreciative critique of services at Christ Church.[794.2] The whole trend of the times he considered to be part of a

deliberate, well-digested plan to bring about a union between our Church and the Church of Rome, and . . . an important part of that plan is familiarizing our people with the Ritual of "the West" — i.e., of Rome![795]

Obviously, the Bishop represented a rather extreme position in his diocese, or at least represented it in an extreme fashion. The fact that he felt compelled to do so, however, gives us one of our best clues regarding the flavor of the times and the probable mind of the parish.

Despite all of the care Mr. Boone gave to the services of the Church, there were occasions on which matters did not go according to plan. For instance, one morning

during the service at Christ Church, the congregation was considerably startled by the sudden appearance of a strange woman, who entered the Church and immediately proceeded up the middle aisle to the chancel where she knelt down with bowed head for nearly five minutes, as the Rector was conducting the service. No one in the congregation knew or could tell of her whereabouts.[796]

More frustrating, no doubt, was the situation of the organist when the pressure of the city water was so reduced as to render the newly installed water motor useless.[797] He might even, for one fleeting moment, have longed for the old sexton back on the job!

Worship was the central activity of the church; but emanating from it were countless others of great variety — intellectual, charitable, social, and community-directed ones. Several of these seem particularly worthy of mention, such as a mission to deaf mutes which was long a recipient of benefactions from the parish. On Sunday night, the Rev. Dr. Gallaudet, of St. Ann's Church (New York City) accompanied a normal reading of Evening prayer with a reading in sign language for the deaf. He then delivered an address on sign language education of deaf mutes and the progress of the Church's work in the American sector of that field.[798] Another project of special interest was the "fruit and flower" mission, which took up the task of distributing fruit and flowers among the sick and poor. Membership was not confined to any denomination, but the group received hearty support from the ladies of the parish and made its headquarters in the Church basement. It was here, at the St. Julian Street door, that contributors dropped off their gifts early each Tuesday morning, and here that the ladies sorted and arranged them before beginning their delivery to hospitals and homes throughout the city.[799] The Bishop Elliott Society, one of the most durable groups in the history of the parish was especially active during the Boone years. Such was the reputation it gained through many years of distributing food, money, and garments to the poor of the parish that the *Morning News* claimed "few charitable associations in the country of the same number of members — have done as much good in a quiet way."[800]

Occasionally charity flowed the other way, too, as when the children of the Episcopal Orphan's Home were out looking at holiday displays one December 23rd. "Mr. Altmayer invited them into his store, and presented to each of the little girls a fine doll."[801] But no matter in which direction it moved, the children of the Church were usually somewhere near the center of the action. It was with their help, for example, that the Church Aid Society staged a "Children's Carnival" at Armory Hall.

The "Pinafore Quadrille" was the feature of the evening, and passed off in an eminently successful manner. Such a cunning "Josephine" as little Miss Gordon and such a winsome "Little Buttercup" as Miss Reitze have never been seen in Savannah, while young Masters May, Waller, Douglas, and Morrison presented a "Rackstraw", "Captain Corcoran," "Sir Joseph," and "Dick Deadeye" which would have made Ford's Juvenile Opera Troupe jealous. . . . Several characters besides those of the Pinafore heroes were assumed by other children present. Of these, Master Edward Demere as a page, and others, whose names we failed to obtain, shone conspicuously. . . .[802]

As we might expect, the Rector and other individuals were involved in many activities beyond the limits of the parish. The Union Society, the WCTU, the White Cross Society,[803] and the still flourishing Savannah Port Society often showed prominently among their interests. The last organization listed celebrated its 41st anniversary in Christ Church, "crowding [it] from the chancel to the doors" to hear Mr. Boone preach. Other congregations cancelled services for the evening so that all could unite to recognize this venerable mission to seamen "as one of the most efficient and worthy branches of religious work in the city."[804]

Often, the concerns presented were more far reaching, such as when Bishop Robert W. B. Elliott appeared at Christ Church in support of theological education at the University of the South.[805] In January of 1884, another visitor caused considerable curiosity and interest. This was an exotic figure known as Pere Hyacinthe, of the Old Gallican Church, who preached in Christ Church to a large congregation of both Catholics and Protestants. After Mr. Boone explained the nature of the Old Gallican Church, the visitor presented his discourse entirely in French, which the congregation "listened to throughout with the closest attention."[806]

"Reaching out" sometimes meant encouraging people to come in. This was precisely the goal of several churchwomen who petitioned the Vestry to make pews free for evening services. After due deliberation this was accomplished although the old rental system remained in place for Sunday morning services.[807] Outreach also took Mr. Boone to preach at the consecration of the new Christ Church, St. Simons Island, temporarily made him "nominal Rector" of St. Stephen's Church in Savannah, and also called upon him to fill in at St. Augustine's when there was no priest-in-charge.[808] In this same vein he frequently aided Bishop Beckwith in special ways. This might mean anything from accompanying him as he visited various missions in this end of the diocese–from St. Mark's Ogeechee, to Sylvania — to supervising the Episcopal Orphans' Home.[809]

One of the most direct ways to sense the spirit of the Church in those years is simply to examine how the congregation spent its money. A typical budget during Mr. Boone's rectorship devoted by far the largest sums to missions and to charity within the parish, then to the Bishop's salary and the Episcopal Orphans' Home. Significant contributions were also made toward special missions within the Convocation, the Sunday School Library, the University of the South, and to the funds for aged and infirm clergy and for the widows and orphans of deceased clergy.[810] Characteristically, through these years we find also donations to such causes as the Appleton Church Home (Macon), St. Matthew's Mission (Savannah), Pere Hyacinthe's work, the Savannah Port Society, toward building new churches at Mt. Airy, Valdosta, etc., or rebuilding the one at Frederica, to support students studying for orders, and to provide blankets and fuel for the poor during the extremely cold weather of January, 1886. Expenditures outside the immediate parish, typically, were just about equal to what was spent in maintaining it. Exceptions occurred in the years when major work was done on the building. All in all, to present day eyes most of the budgets would appear fairly normal in their profile. Only occasional jolts, such as the Rector's thanks for one parishioner's "generosity . . . in providing him with the use of a horse and buggy," would remind us of the lapse of a century.[811]

As we have seen, in many ways it was Mr. Boone's rectorship that laid the foundation of the modern parish. It was his leadership that helped the congregation overcome a decade of uncertainty after the war — the decade of Reconstruction. Further, it was his leadership that inspired it to regain confidence and a sense of direction when these had been shaken so profoundly by moral disasters within. It was also through his leadership that the parish began to develop its own distinctive style with which to move ahead toward another new century. Yet without doubt the most distinctive feature of his rectorship was not in any of these things, but in its extraordinary emphasis on missions. Missions there had always been. Yet somehow, after Mr. Boone's arrival, virtually every act became in some sense an act of mission. There were parish missions, missions within the Convocation, and Diocesan missions, plus the usual domestic and foreign missions, and all became prominent in the life of the parish.

A case in point appeared during Mr. Boone's first weeks as Rector when a local mission church, St. Matthew's, reached a particularly difficult point in its long struggle for survival. An "evening of drama" was staged for the benefit of the chapel by the children of the Sunday School.[812] From that point onward no appeal went without positive response of some kind whether it came from the Convocation on behalf of the Ogeechee and Satilla River missions, the Diocese to support a missionary evangelist, or St. John's Church in support of its parish mission.[813] Such calls for aid were, of course, in addition to the regular support given to domestic and foreign missions causes of the National Church, and to the support Christ Church began giving St. Matthew's after taking it on as a parish mission in 1884.[814]

Frequently, guests in the parish were mission-oriented as well. The first visitor discovered is the example that gives us our best clue to the whole. He was the Rev. Mr. William J. Boone, brother of the Rector, who came to preach on China and the work being done there, where he had been a missionary for nine years.[815] The brothers were themselves sons of the first Missionary Bishop of Shanghai, and indeed William succeeded his father in that post only a short while after this visit to Christ Church. Missions were almost literally in their blood. Given such a background, it was hardly surprising when Thomas Boone, too, was called to a post in China only two years later. At that early point in his ministry here, however, he felt that "this wounded Mother Church still bowed . . . to the earth, . . . still mourning for her children," needed him more. "The distrust crime and indiscretion had inspired" was not yet fully in the past; in the "work of harmonizing and strengthening the dear old Mother Church of our Diocese" there was still much to be done.[816]

When a deputation from the national Board of Foreign and Domestic Missions visited in 1883, the Rev. Mr. Joshua Kimber spoke to the congregation on the Church's missions, and in the process offered additional detail in the Boone family saga. Among other things, he reminded his audience of how difficult things used to be in the "old days" — such as when the elder Bishop Boone first went to China some 47 years ago, he was not allowed to enter the country but forced to work from a base in Java.[817] As the grown-ups listened with fascination to Mr. Kimber, the children attended a missionary meeting of their own at St. John's. Joining with that Sunday School, as they often did for special occasions,[818] and others from the missions, the children filled the Church "nearly to the doors" to hear the Rev. Mr. Tiffany preach on the text " Is There Any Taste in the White of An Egg?"[819]

It was like that almost every year as visitors from distant fields would come to recount their experiences and encourage support for missions throughout the world. One gets the feeling that this was the Episcopal counterpart of the revival staged in other churches by the likes of Moody and Sankey.[819.1] In 1887 William Boone, himself a Missionary Bishop in China now, returned to speak at Christ Church once more.[820] The following year it was Miss Sybil Carter who stirred a large congregation at Christ Church, St. John's joining. The children especially were delighted to hear her stories.[821]

With so much going on inside the Church and emanating from it, one could get the idea that the usual problems of buildings, routine maintenance and other concomitants of physical existence, were suspended for the decade. Not too likely, is it? Actually, everything that we have noted about the liturgical, musical, community service, and missions activity of the 1880's took place in spite of severe assaults on the physical and fiscal fabric of the Church. The destructive forces included a hurricane, an earthquake, and a major national depression. The last of these was made all the more threatening because it was accompanied by tempting offers to buy the Church which would have led either to its demolition or conversion into a post office!

Even before the disastrous hurricane of August, 1881, visited the city, there had been a growing consciousness of the pressing need for repair of the Church structure and other parish properties. Finally, in February of 1881, the Vestry approached the congregation with the bad news. The roof was the chief problem. It suffered from "defective slopes," and "decay of the slating with which it [was] covered," all of which have left "runious stains" on the interior ceiling. As if that weren't enough, the gutters were so shallow and small that they frequently emptied their surplus on the cornices and walls.[822] Then, as if to greet the water cascading down the walls, more arose from below, since drainage around the Church was also poor.[823] Facing a repair bill of such magnitude, one which would require the doubling of a standing debt the parish had been unable to eliminate in several years of trying, the idea arose that it might be better to build a brand new Church. But since no site, and more importantly, no money were offered, it remained just another "interesting idea."[824]

Preparation was made to carry out the badly needed repairs during the summer of 1881. Even the choregraphy for the season was rather neat — the congregation being invited to St. John's for worship while Christ Church was closed and the Rector on leave.[825] Unfortunately, the storm knew its part well, too. It entered on the 27th of August with devastating fury just as the repairs were in mid-course and the building in a particularly vulnerable state. Several hundred were drowned in or near the city; and hundreds of buildings were unroofed or had walls sheared off, with the result that they were "sluiced from garret to cellar" by the torrential rains. From the harbor ships, or parts of them, were strewn for miles. In the river itself, at Ft. Pulaski, the tide "rose a foot above the floor of the officers quarters," destroyed every house, and swept away every head of cattle on the island.[826]

As for Christ Church, the storm left the edifice in such a condition "that there can be no services held in it."[827] Closer examination proved "the damage . . by the late storm . . . far greater than at first supposed." "The walls and ceiling [were] badly damaged" and the fine organ "stained with water and

110

greatly injured."[828] Understandably, the roof now took priority. By early October workmen were ready for "between 8000 and 9000 pounds of galvanized iron [to] arrive, which will be used to make a handsome new roof for christ church."[829]

New roof or no, the question of the availability of the church's site was again broached during the autumn.[830] A few weeks later the U.S. government formally requested a price for the property, to be used for a new post office and courthouse. This time the Vestry's response was concrete: it would accept $100,000, or $50,000 plus suitable property in exchange.[831] Actually, we get the impression that no one truly expected an offer to be made on those terms, and indeed none was. Conversation soon shifted to redoing the ceiling of the Church, now that the roof was fixed. That impression is reinforced by the elaborate nature of the plan adopted for the job, which called for a decorated ceiling of oiled and varnished woodwork, even though it meant incurring additional debt of about $3500.[832]

Work began during the summer of 1882, and was far enough advanced that services could be held "in the body of the Church by the last Sunday of October."[833] Adding excitement to the project was an offer by the Brush Electric Light and Power Co. to illuminate the Church, "both the interior and front exterior for $200 per annum." Since these would have been the first electric lights in the Church, response was postponed to gain more time to think it over and to await "further experiments."[834] Even so the job was already making headlines; the contractor was using electric lights which, for the first time locally, allowed work to be done at night![835]

When the new ceiling was at last made visible to the public, "it was considered to be one of the most elaborate and beautiful works of its character in modern architecture," and "superior to the famous ceilings of the old world." Wrought in native Georgia pine finished in oil "in the modern Gothic Style," the ceiling was designed by Mr. John Nevitt, architect. Key to the design was Nevitt's use of the structure's main girders as the principle elements dividing the ceiling into panels. The main girders and two "cross girders" cut the whole into twenty-one major panels. These were each sub-divided, the center row into five minor panels and the side rows into four — making ninety panels in all. Setting off the panels were elaborate carvings, chamferings, mouldings, cornices, rosettes, and pendants, producing a composition "worthy of the closest study." In the decorating and finishing "the architect followed the same rule adopted in the construction", and has highlighted the main features "in gold and colors, enhancing the beauty and showing the details of the work which would otherwise have been wholly lost. The principle colors are earmine, maroon, ebony, orange, and lemon gold." Some idea of the extent of the decoration may be gathered from the claim that "nearly two thousand books of gold leaf, manufactured expressly for this work, were used." Before any gold or color was applied, however, "the entire woodwork of ceiling and cornice underwent a very elaborate treatment of oiling, sand papering, filling, japannying hard oil finish and varnishing according to the modern style of car finish."[836] On Sexagesima, 1883, the congregation had its first chance to view the finished ceiling. Surely that was exciting enough, but there was more. The day also brought opportunity to see the work in an entirely new light since, as the Sunday paper announced, "Three lamps have been erected and will be lighted for the first time at the service tonight."[837]

The only problem with the renovated interior of the Church was that it stimulated growing dissatisfaction with the state of the exterior. By the following summer that feeling had so taken charge that it was decided "the whole exterior will be plastered with Georgia cement and painted with silicate paint of a dark gray color. The blinds will be finished in a light chocolate."[838]

Although the Building itself was now in excellent condition, a major national depression through the middle of the decade made the resulting debt more tenacious than had been anticipated. The gravity of the situation was brought home by a special plea of the Vestry. "In view of the necessities of the Church in many ways, and the great need of cooperation on the part of all interested in her welfare, the children of the Sunday School are requested to apply their offerings to the repair of the Church edifice."[839] That was not to be the limit of the problem, however, for one of the rules of the human condition seems to be "if it's not one thing, it's two . . . at least." Number two in this case was Mr. Boone's forthcoming marriage. Happy as the occasion would be, it compelled the Vestry to put the rectory in order, "borrowing as necessary" to make it habitable.[840] The York St. house was quickly "refitted and beautified" in time for the return of the newlyweds from the north in February, 1886.[841] Although poorer because of it, in a way, the parish was also enriched by the marriage, for Mrs. Boone soon became immersed in its affairs. She was especially active in support of the Episcopal Orphans' Home during a period of significant growth.[842]

Things were hardly back to normal and the Boones settled into place when the countryside for miles around was shaken as never before in memory. The major tremor came on the last day of August, 1886, but Savannah felt aftershocks every day of the following week,[843] and intermittently for at least the next two months.[844] The earthquake was centered near Charleston, but was felt sharply and caused considerable damage in Savannah. The city immediately began to assess the damage done to buildings.[845] Others assessed the shock differently and the spectrum of reactions was colorful indeed! While some interpreted the quake as divine retribution, assuredly brought upon Savannah and Charleston for their sinfulness,[846] from those less didactically inclined it evoked genuine expressions of sympathy.[847] Christ Church sent a small contribution "to the Churches in Charleston . . . injured by the earthquake,"[848] but the damage at home was too great and too obvious to allow much.

The magnitude of the injury to Christ Church was revealed when architect Nevitt met the Vestry early in November. At their request he had thoroughly inspected every nook and cranny of the Church structure and now, after several weeks of searching, his report was ready. He discovered that the

quake had caused damage from one end of the building to the other, but the chief areas of concern were:

> a crack in the "rear gable" running from the peak to the upper portion of the chancel window frame. Extending below the window were several more cracks which had recently been filled with cement, but now were much increased and widened.
> Other cracks were discovered at the frieze-level on each corner of the west portico, in the chimney (running from top to bottom), and at the bases of the towers.
> Both gables (i.e. pediments) had been tilted considerably out of vertical.
> Most fearful, however, were the many instances of pulverized mortar. One of these was in the chimney where the mortar was so damaged as to allow "free passage of sparks to the dry pine of the roof and ceiling." For the same reason, bricks in the arch which supports the portico appeared loose enough to drop out. Equally threatening was the problem with one of the trusses which supported the organ loft. At the point where it entered the wall crumbled mortar had loosened it dangerously.[849]

With such information in hand, there was little debate about what to do. The Vestry quickly agreed to go ahead with all the needed repairs. One suspects there may have been more doubts about the justice of it all, for Mr. Nevitt's report came just three weeks after the final settlement of the Young legacy had put the parish in the black for the first time in years.[850]

The transient nature of prosperity was powerfully demonstrated through 1887. As the repair bills piled up alarm grew that the parish now faced a serious financial deficit for the year, and most probably for the year following as well. For this reason the Vestry resolved to inform Mr. Boone they would probably have to reduce his salary from $2500 to $2000. Similarly, choir singers were to be told "their services will not be required for next year except new arrangements be made with different members."[851] A few days later Mr. Boone submitted his resignation. Fearing that the act was prompted by misunderstanding of their budget resolution, the Vestry returned the Rector's letter of resignation for reconsideration with emphatic assurances of their appreciation for his "fidelity and faithfulness." Their action, they stressed, had been intended solely "to inform him of the condition of the Church."[852] The Vestry's affirmation seems to have been sincerely intended yet relations obviously became very fragile at that point. Reiterating his original intention of departing "for another field of labor by the first of January," Mr. Boone acknowledged that, since no call had yet come, he was willing to "stay a while longer . . . trying as that position is under

The remodelled interior of the Church as it appeared in Mr. Mitchell's time. The new memorial window honoring Bishop Elliott was described in detail by a contemporary news article. (See note 656.)

these circumstances."⁸⁵³ The "circumstances" are never fully disclosed, but it is fairly clear that at last some of the "trial" must have been taking place in Thomas Boone's own mind. On several occasions in his correspondence with the Vestry, Boone rather pointedly confided "I am deeply conscious of my own short comings." The shortcomings are not specified either, and we might suppose the statement to represent no more than an attempt to ease an awkward situation were it not for his deliberate repetition of it. Whatever the causes, however, their effect was to weaken the bond of confidence between Rector and Vestry that helped to make the last eleven years in the parish so productive.

It may actually have been something of a relief when an old familiar question reappeared suddenly to demand everyone's attention. First, cautious feelers, then an official offer to purchase the Church came from the government early in January of 1888. The old offer of $49,500, said the government, would be good only for three or four more days!⁸⁵⁴ But when the Vestry refused to be stampeded, pointing out that they would not act in such a matter without consulting the congregation, somehow more time was found. Not only did negotiations continue, they spread as the next week a story on the sale appeared in the *Morning News* and the whole city became party to them.⁸⁵⁵ Indeed, it was the *News* that noted Col. Mercer's resolution, expressing the logic of those favoring the sale:

> *Whereas* the members of the congregation have removed from the neighborhood of the Church . . . and *Whereas* the interest and welfare of the Church require a more appropriate location . . . it is desirable that the Wardens and Vestry take, without delay, the necessary steps . . . . for sale to the government.⁸⁵⁶

It was the newspaper, too, that recorded the predictable differences of opinion precipitated by the Colonel's resolution. At a congregational meeting called especially to discuss the matter, we can almost hear the speakers' tones as they iterate their points. "We should ask at least $100,000," said one, which caused his respondent to "wish" we could get $500,000 — a price he deemed no less likely! While they discussed whether the price was high enough, others feared "we may never get so good a chance again." Similarly, those citing the special value of the Church remaining on "the original site" were countered by others who argued that "our affection should be for the Church as an organization, not as an edifice." One line of thinking, which seemed especially persuasive to many of the vestrymen, found no ready counterpoint at the meeting. This one suggested that dislocation would bring so great an inconvenience to the congregation that it would cause it to dwindle through the months, or even years, that we would be without a building. In the end "instead of being a congregation without a Church, we would be a Church without a congregation!" Nevertheless the meeting overwhelmingly adopted the resolution favoring sale.⁸⁵⁷

At its own meeting, however, the Vestry stood its ground. An opening motion in favor of selling to the government was sidetracked by one which placed the burden of proving feasibility on the advocates of the sale. It read "that the Vestry were unwilling to consider sale unless $25,000 first be pledged as a further and additional sum for construction of a new Church."⁸⁵⁸ One week later, another congregational meeting accepted the challenge and created a committee to commence fund raising.⁸⁵⁹

Unfortunately, what became of their efforts remains a mystery, for our sources — *Vestry Minutes*, newspapers, etc. — all are mute, as though unwilling to discuss the matter any further. Did the government withdraw its offer? Was the ambitious fund raising design unsuccessful? At these questions the past merely purses its lips, refusing to give up any more secrets. Only the survival of the building testifies to us that at some point the plan failed.⁸⁶⁰

Mr. Boone's final resignation soon displaced other topics of conversation in any case. Even though he had no firm plans for the future the Rector notified the Vestry he would take his wife north to reside, in December. Mrs. Boone's ill health, he said, now forced the move they had contemplated for some time.⁸⁶¹

During the final months of his rectorship activity in the parish did not cease by any means. In 1888, for example, there emerged considerable sentiment in favor of making further improvements to the Church, now that prosperity had returned to the land. Specific plans were presented by Mr. J.J. Nevitt, the architect who had presided over the renovation of 1883 and who three years later had supervised the repairs needed following the earthquake. At the time, the plans were "laid by for future reference,"⁸⁶² but only a month later Mr. Nevitt was instructed to go ahead with "working drawings and estimates".⁸⁶³

The brass pulpit was installed as a part of a general renovation in 1890.

VII
Flamboyant Preparation for the 20th Century 1889-1914

By the time detailed plans for renovation were prepared, early in 1889, Mr. Boone was already gone. The search for a new Rector then began in earnest and the parish was placed in the care of temporary and visiting clergy. Chief among these were the Rev. Mr. Edward Huntington Coley, who officiated through the winter and spring of 1889,[864] and the Rev. Mr. William Graham of Nashville, who carried on through the summer and autumn that year.[865] There were others, however, who filled in one Sunday at a time. One of these was the Rev. Canon Leigh, from England. He had come to this country frequently during the 1880's to work along the coast. This time he interrupted his usual activities in Darien to preside at Christ Church.[866]

Despite the lack of permanent clerical leadership the renovation plan was vigorously pressed. Work was expected to include major redecoration in the chancel area (such as plastering, installation of columns, a reredos, and a new rail), as well as entirely new pews and considerable repair to the organ. No signs of second thoughts show in the record even after estimates announced the cost would be nearly $9,000.[867] Work did not begin immediately, however, for just as final preparation was being made disaster struck one of the parish's oldest neighbors. The Independent Presbyterian Church was offered the use of Christ Church "on account of the destruction of their church edifice by fire on Saturday night," the 6th of April.[868]

Although renovation was at a standstill for the time being, the search, for a permanent Rector was not. At its June meeting the Vestry called the Rev. Mr. Robb White, Assistant Rector at Charlottesville, VA, to take charge of Christ Church.[869] A Virginian, and a graduate of the University of Virginia and the Seminary at Alexandria, the 40 year old Rector brought with him his wife, several small children and a very promising reputation.[869.1] Mr. White accepted and arrived in time to lead the memorial service for Jefferson Davis the following December.[870]

During the months that followed the parish showed renewed vitality. The Savannah Port Society held its annual service in Christ Church with Mr. White delivering the anniversary sermon and President Joseph D. Weed (of Christ Church) recounting "an interesting history of the Bethel and the Port Society."[871] Also the Christ Church Club, an early men's organization in the parish, offered to see that notice of services was posted in the city's leading hotels and other prominent places. As a result Christ Church was soon listed in the "Church Directories" that were beginning to appear in such local hotels as the DeSoto, Pulaski, Screven, Marshall, etc.[872] Another sign of new life was the growing number of communicants in the parish. After ten years of hovering just over 400, the communicant list grew to 475 in Mr. White's first six months here, and continued to increase at a similar rate over the next several years.[873]

The mood in the parish had already become one of rejoicing in the spring of 1890, Mr. White's first as Rector. Reflecting the new exuberance, the *Morning News* announced that very soon "almost a complete reconstruction will take place in the interior of Christ Church."[874] The whole congregation seems to have felt it, especially the Wardens and Vestry, "ever since his coming among us." That is why when Mr. White was offered a European trip they "unanimously and heartily [urged] him to take advantage of this offer, not likely to occur again so opportunely," The fact that the trip would coincide with the worst of the construction disarray during the summer made it a special bonus.[875]

This pervasive joy may also have added extra sparkle to one of the season's most spectacular events, the marriage of Mr. Robert M. Hull, and Miss Minnie McLeod. Weddings in the Church were, of course, as common as ever, but few are so intricately described in surviving records or so neatly reflective of the mood of the day as this one. Although the ceremony was to begin at 6:30 p.m., guests began arriving before 6:00 o'clock and soon filled the Church. The march from Lohengrin was played by Prof. Steward as four ushers (including Charles Ellis, Jr., J.D. Carswell, and R.E.L. Daniel) led the procession. They were followed by "two little maids of honor" — the

Misses Albert and Elise Hull — who opened the floral bars admitting the party to the chancel. Following them were the bridesmaids, Miss Ruthie Stewart and Miss Axson, plus seven other attendants and the maid of honor. Finally came the bride, leaning upon the arm of her brother, Mr. Richard McLeod, all passing under an arch of ferns, evergreens, and roses. The Chancel was filled with potted plants, the rail entwined with vines, and the font covered with "exotics". After the ceremony the familiar Mendelsohn march accompanied the party's exit from the Church, but certainly it did not signal the end of the celebration! The guests were received at the home of the bride's mother on Liberty St. in her double parlors, decorated with festoons of orange blossoms, lilies-of-the-valley, and roses. Adding to the general festivity was a cake containing a bridesmaids ring, won by Miss Stewart. Not until 9:00 o'clock did things begin to break up when the party accompanied the bride and groom "to the S.F. and W. Railway Depot where they departed for Chicago, Niagara, New York, and Boston for three weeks."[876]

Actual renovation work began soon after the wedding and before the Rector's departure for Europe, probably in late spring. At least it was about that time the congregation sought space in the Chatham Academy which could be used for services while the Church was closed for repairs.[877] For their part the ladies of the Church took on the task of raising $4000 for a new organ.[878] Presumably, that was why "they gave another one of their pleasant entertainments at Col. W. W. Gordon's residence last night." The parlors were crowded and an interesting programme was excellently rendered. Those taking part in the entertainment were: Miss Brigham, Miss Cosens, Mrs. Finnie, and Messrs. Walker, McKenzie, and Charlton.[879]

The work carried out in 1890 included several noteworthy modifications or additions to the Church. For example, this was when the remarkable brass pulpit was introduced,[880] and also the credence table.[881] Most striking of the changes, however, was probably the addition of four columns of Tennessee marble to the east end of the Church. They were placed just outside (i.e. West) of the new rail, two on each side, to form the foundations of the chancel arch. In addition, new pews "in the latest style of antique oak" were placed on the main floor of the Church. This made it possible to use some of the older pews in the refurbished galleries, "but so improved as to make them equal to the new ones." Finishing touches added new dashes of gold and color to the ceiling, walls, and cornices, and placed "fine colored glass transoms over all windows."[882]

Despite all the detail we have about the work that was done, and only a little uncertainty about when it was done, great doubt surrounds the question of who designed it. Mr. Nevitt submitted plans which were approved by the Vestry, and there is no record of his design having been set aside or of another being approved in its place. Yet there is clear record of payment made to William Gibbons Preston of Boston "on account of services." Mr. Preston's invoice specifies that his services included "altering, remodeling, decorating, designing glass, reredos, and organ, . . . rearranging the pews, etc." with all work accomplished under the local supervision of Henry Urban, a well-known Savannah architect.[883] It is well established that Preston was in the city frequently and would have been available, for he was deeply involved with the reconstruction of the Independent Presbyterian Church. The question that remains unanswered is how much of the design was his and how much was actually Nevitt's.

None of this bothered anyone in 1891, however. What fascinated them was the new organ being erected in the gallery. It was reported to "be the most powerful and sweetest toned instrument of its kind in Savannah."[884] To test that reputation Frederick Archer, "the great English organist, now in New York," gave two recitals in the Church, crowded to the galleries to hear the organ for the first time.[885]

In the congregation spirits were high, and the debt incurred as a result of the $18,000 renovation does not seem to have depressed them one bit. On the contrary, it was decided to raise the Rector's salary by 20%, the first real raise for the position in many decades.[886] Protracted negotiations over what the City described as "encroachment" by the Church did not dampen spirits either. For several years the mayor and alderman had contended that the iron railing which surrounded the Church took up the sidewalks on Drayton and Congress Streets "unnecessarily", and that it "greatly interfered with their use." The city repeatedly requested their removal and the Vestry, with equal regularity, chose "respectfully [to] decline to accede to the request."[887] Even when agreement was finally worked out and the railings removed, in 1893, there was no sign of hard feelings or of reduced enthusiasm.[888] Indeed, it was at this very time, that a proposal was made to form a guild of volunteers "to create a stimulus in the congregation for systematic financial work."[889] The idea seems to have remained rather nebulous until a major financial panic struck the whole nation late in 1893. In the face of that crisis the guild idea took more solid form and a "Parochial Aid Society" was begun. Membership was open to all willing to lend aid, but its officers were to be "the Ladies of the Congregation."[890]

Clearly, the Rev. Mr. White was bringing a new energy to the parish.[891] Adding to this was the stimulating presence of the new diocesan, the Rt. Rev. Cleland Kinloch Nelson. After his consecreation in Feb. 1892,[892] the new Bishop visited Christ Church, joined the Wardens and Vestry at their April Meeting. From the beginning it was apparent that his vitality would be a force in the life of the parish. For one thing, he had a way of stating his wishes and opinions which gave them more than ordinary weight. He also had a way of making people feel that he took special interest in them. To the Wardens and Vestry he pledged "to do all in his power — ecclesiastical and personal — for Christ Church, and he expressed the hope that every relation between himself and this parish would be mutually agreeable and beneficial." In response, "the general expression of the Vestry was that this body and Church would always support and back the Bishop by all means in their power."[893]

It is easy to believe that when Bishop Nelson commented on the issues of the day people took him seriously. But whether they did or not, his remarks tell us much about what was on the minds of parishioners in the 1890's. Unlike Bishop Beckwith, he seemed generally pleased with the changes being incorporated into the new *Book of Common Prayer* (1892). "What has been done is in the main wisely done."[894] Yet he remained dissatisfied with some aspects of the Prayer Book's final version. He was disappointed, for instance, that the last rubric of the Communion Office had not been reconstructed so as to prevent absolutely "the bottling of the consecrated wine for future use . . . or the desecrating and immoral effects of distributing large quantities of wine to a small number of people." If these things were beyond the Bishop's control, others were not. After his first visitation through the Diocese, including Christ Church, he had some strong words, for his flock. He felt compelled to instruct them regarding the proper function of "amen" and to point out that "kneeling does not mean sitting." Furthermore, he knew "no authority or proper custom for reading the psalms or sentences toward the congregation". Finally, he ordered that in the Diocese of Georgia there would be no marriages during Advent or from Septuagesima to Easter, no burials on Sundays, and no evening communions.[895]

Unfortunately, we have no way to tell whether any of Bishop Nelson's pronouncements were directed at practices in Christ Church, but it is certainly a possibility since he found them so general as to deserve attention at a convention of the Diocese. Among the many practices he thought in need of correction, one in particular seemed to irk him. This was the custom of playing "a grand march on the organ" after communion but before the Benediction. Its intent was to "cover" the departure of congregants who left directly after communion but its effect was to encourage their mass exodus most prematurely. He ordered it abandoned throughout the Diocese on the grounds that it was, as the exode was in some ancient drama, "a farce, a travesty, grotesquely out of place."[895.1]

In the matter of revivals, on the other hand, Bishop Nelson saw eye to eye with his predecessors and the tradition of the Diocese. At his second convention, in 1893, he pointed out to the delegates that the Diocese had grown by 21% during his first 15 months "without revivals, missions or any other facetious aids."[896] Equally positive was his reaction to the growing role of women in the Church. He recalled how when Miss Emery had visited Christ Church and other Savannah parishes the year before, she "instilled enthusiasm into the women."

Men have not failed out of sight, but they have been eclipsed. The women of the Church have risen up in a body, not to secure rights, to control elections, to turn towns topsy-turvy, but to labour for Christ and His Church. They have hushed the old slander of their ability to talk by their capacity to work.[897]

The "Women's Auxilliary" became a fixture in Christ Church at that time, and in some form or other it has remained a vital force in the parish ever since.[898] To a certain extent the founding of the Women's Auxiliary represented a trend of the times. Not only were similar chapters rapidly appearing in Episcopal parishes throughout the country, but the number of special societies within *this* parish began to grow noticeably during the 1890's. Taking places beside the Women's Auxilliary and the established Altar Society and Bishop Elliott Society, were other groups with special functions such as the Bible and Prayer Book Society, the Orphan Home Society, the Bishop Beckwith Society, and the Missionary Society. Significantly, the Church also experienced rapid growth its corps of Lay Readers reported — from only one in 1888 to half a dozen by the middle 90's. Completing the list of active groups as it stood in 1895, was the Brotherhood of St. Andrew, which actively led the congregation's growing involvement in parish missions.

Local missions were certainly not new to Christ Church,[900] but never before had the congregation as a body set out with such deliberation to found its own missions in newer or unserved areas of the city. The idea of building a chapel in the expanding southeastern part of the city began to take concrete form early in 1891.[901] Plans called for St. Michael's Chapel to be built at Henry and Habersham Streets, and for the Church to call an assistant to take charge of it.[902] As matters turned out, building it was the easy part;[903] procuring a suitable assistant proved to be much more difficult.[904] This left responsibility for both Christ Church and St. Michael's on the Rector's shoulders. Understandably, he found it impossible to do both jobs to his satisfaction,[905] but continued the attempt until his health broke two years later.[906] St. Michael's continued as a mission chapel of Christ Church until 1920. It became an independent parish at that time and relocated to Anderson and Harmon Sts., where it remained until 1942.[907]

Almost contemporary with the founding of St. Michael's was another mission chapel begun in an oyster factory on the "Thunderbolt River." When the factory closed some months later, in 1894, the mission was moved to Yamacraw where space was found on Margaret St.[908] This mission was the work of the Brotherhood of St. Andrew, and thus soon became known as St. Andrew's Chapel. Members of The Brotherhood "visited all in the district continually," gave numerous "entertainments," Christmas parties, etc., and included chapel attendants in Christ Church's annual summer picnic. In addition, the Brotherhood held a regular Sunday School in the morning and Sunday services at night. They also dealt with the daily needs of the neighborhood by distributing wood during winter cold spells, running a night school, and by setting up a gym and a free clinic. To do all this the men of the Brotherhood obviously needed help from others, which usually came from the Bishop Beckwith Society or from a junior chapter of the Brotherhood itself. Such aid proved invaluable. Together they did everything from furnishing rooms and providing a new organ for the chapel to initiating "mothers meetings" and opening a manual training school. In 1905 the expanding enterprise moved nearby to a three-story brick house at 527 Zubly St.[909] (at Ann St.) where space was more

The credence table, given as a memorial in 1890.

adequate. There were over 70 in the Sunday School by that time, and another 50 in the "Sewing School." A year later, someone asked "Has it been a success?".

> *It is never fair to judge God's work by the results one can see, for he will often not permit a view of the harvest "lest any man should boast." But . . . every Easter we bring a class to the Mother Church for the Holy Rite of Confirmation. Over forty have been brought into the Church, many baptized, and many buried with the Church's benediction. It that all? No . . . a judge of one of our courts, unasked and unexpected [said] "that the Mission of Margaret St. had done and was doing more good for the city than all the other charities combined."*[910]

The mission continued to operate successfully in the Zubly St. building for many years until its closure in 1920.

Other missions in the city, for some of which Christ Church was not directly responsible, also received assistance — sometimes in very practical ways. For instance, shortly after renovation was begun in 1890 the old gas fixtures were given to St. Augustine's and St. Michael's. Also given to St. Augustine's were the pews and cushions which had recently been removed from the Church.[911]

From what we have seen the 1890's were busy years — what with the renewed spirit of the parish and the renovated building, the activities of the various societies and missions, and a rector and a bishop who seemed to keep everyone hopping. But this decade was far from over! For one thing, a surprising windfall came after years of controversy over the fate and condition of the "Old Cemetery." The burial ground had become a point of public discussion during the 1850's when its closure, and the development of Laurel Grove, raised concern that it might be used for other than its original purpose. To reduce this possibility, the Vestry of the Church memorialized the City Council in 1856 to establish its claim to the property. Citing the royal decree of 1758, which established the parish and formalized its title to the "burying ground," the Vestry asked merely that its petition be "spread upon the minutes" of the Council.[912]

Actually, special attention to the cemetery goes back even further, at least to 1846, when the City Council ordered trees planted around it "to protect . . . citizens from the posionous effluvia arising therefrom."[913] But it was in the following decades that rumors of development, demolishing the cemetery walls and widening the adjacent portion of Abercorn St. made the question of title an important one. Indeed, for thirty years rumors and litigation kept the "Old Cemetery" in the news until, by 1888, nearly everyone seemed to have opinions on the matter.[914] Such general interest is attributable to the rapidly deteriorating condition of "graves exposing their ghastly contents to passersby," and their "ghostly exhibitions for frightening children." Comments in this vain, frequently appearing in letters to the editor columns, became almost competitive in their search for suitably abhorrent and colorful language. A few writers were satisfied to describe the scene

Detail of pulpit brass.

simply as "repulsive" or "disgraceful." But others were more creative and accused those responsible of "generating nightmares" and composing "lullabies for vermin."⁹²⁰

After a sequence that led from an injunction through appeals to decisions and reversals, at last the matter reached Georgia's Supreme Court. There it stayed for six years.⁹²¹

Finally, a settlement was achieved in 1895 which laid the old questions to rest once and for all. For its part the Church yielded to the City all "right, title, interest, claim, or demand" relative to the burial ground. In return, the City agreed to pay the Church $6500 and to accept responsibility for care of the cemetery, along with a number of other conditions — all designed to insure it's preservation for the public as "Colonial Park."⁹²²

Perhaps the euphoria which followed the passing of this forty-year headache was the reason no one noticed the unusual light glimmering far into the night one Saturday. The choir had held its regular practice in the evening, but when they left around 9:30 everything seemed to be in good order. A passing couple who spotted the strange glow through a window in the southwest corner of the Church, thought it was a gas jet. But only ten minutes later that flame, probably from a candle which the organ blower had left flickering in the interior of the organ, had spread so far that the entire Church was engulfed in flames. The night clerk at Screven House, across the street, turned in an alarm, but it was already too late for the fire department to help much.

> *Messrs. T. Lloyd Owens and B.F. Finney, well-known members of the congregation, worked like Trojans, . . . They made their way to the chancel, vainly hoping to save ornaments, and went into several of the basement rooms. From these they succeeded in saving a large portion of the Church records, and some silver. . . . W.G. Charlton (who had been in the Oglethorpe Club) rushed in to save old books and records, especially old Bibles, including two old, rare volumes from 1700's.*

The interior of the Church as it appeared from the time of the 1890 renovation until the great fire of 1897. The new columns of Tennessee marble and the new pews on the main floor are watched over by some of the original 1840 pews, now refinished and placed in the gallery, and by the first Elliott memorial window (behind the curtain.) Some of the furnishings visible here, such as the pulpit, lectern, and baptismal font, along with a few of the newer pews are still in use.

Robb White wanted to go in, too, but was prevented when the ceiling fell in at 2:05 A.M. The next morning, headlines read: "Church in Ruins", "Only the Wall of the Historic Edifice Left." An accompanying photograph, taken "at the moment when total destruction was imminent, seemed to corroborate that assessment."[922.1] Happily, closer inspection gave a slightly brighter picture. The roof had not totally fallen in, nor had the galleries collapsed. In fact, much of the structure was still sound, even though it had been thoroughly gutted.[923]

By the time the Vestry gathered, the morning after the fire (Sunday), notes of sympathy and offers of space were already pouring in. They came from fellow Episcopalians and also from Presbyterians, Methodists, Lutherans, Baptists, and a dozen or more other groups.[924] Gratitutde was expressed for all such offers, of course, but it was the one from the Independent Presbyterian Church which was accepted, perhaps because the situation had so recently been the other way around in their case.[925] Other arrangements were made with St. John's (and possibly St. Paul's) during July and August, but then the Christ Church flock returned to their original hosts for several more months.[926]

Still in shock after the fire, the Vestry turned again to William Gibbons Preston of Boston for help. He arrived late in June to "get over the ground" and determine what must be done.[927] A month later, he was still assessing the damage and estimating costs,[928] and only beginning to make suggestions toward restoration. In part this slow pace was due to the frequent discovery of problems from damage previously undetected. Preston suggested, for example, that iron ties be added in the east wall to prevent re-opening of the 1886 earthquake cracks, and that a temporary roof must be put in place before any serious work toward restoring the building could begin.[929] But far too much delay was due, in the mind of the Building Committee at least, to Preston's dilatoriness. They felt that the architect was simply not giving their favorite project the attention it deserved. By September, with three or four months elapsed since the fire, there was still no visible repair underway. "Our people are getting very impatient and are daily desiring to know when the repairs will be commenced; the delay in getting roof plans is very annoying . . . ."[930] Feeling itself wedged between the anxiety of the congregation and the procrastination of the architect, the building Committee pressed its point. Their impatience is our blessing, however, for each letter brought a rejoinder from Mr. Preston containing decorative detail which might otherwise have gone unrecorded.

In one exchange, the Building Committee demanded that "we should have at once separate details for . . . plumbing, gas, water, heat, electrical wiring, . . . also colors, pew arrangement, window, organ case, chandeliers. . . ." The wounded architect fired back his crisp responses: accent touches should be in brass, the organ case gold and gray, and the chandeliers silver. Woodwork, such as the gallery faces and pews, should be painted for the most part. "This will save much of the wood work, which would otherwise be too badly damaged to use again."[931] Most significantly, correspondence about the style of the ceiling to be put up makes it clear that the one we now see overhead is the work of William Gibbons Preston.[932]

Finally, after seven months of talk and correspondence, the contract to begin restoration was signed[933] and attention could be directed to the other tasks at hand, such as refurnishing the interior of the Church. St. Michael's offered to return the font and communion table that had been loaned to them; meanwhile, the Altar Society set about obtaining a new communion table for the Church.[934] A new organ was ordered, and also a memorial stained-glass window.

It no doubt added considerably to the anxiety felt by all concerned with the rebuilding of the Church that, in the midst of this well publicized effort, Savannah's third disastrous church fire in less than a decade destroyed the Roman Catholic

On preceding pages, at the focal point of parish life is the devotional artistry of the Flower Guild.

Amid the debris it is surprising just how much is still clearly visible. Note the marble columns, the pulpit and lectern which somehow survived. Needless to say, the organ was not so fortunate!

Cathedral.⁹³⁵ Work on Christ Church pressed ahead, nevertheless, and by April plans were in the making for the re-opening services.⁹³⁶

A few days before the first services in the rebuilt Church, an enterprising *Morning News* reporter provided the public with a tantalizing preview of what it would see: "an entirely new building." Viewed from the interior, there is not a great deal of resemblance" to the old Christ Church.⁹³⁷ His claim was reinforced when a full review article appeared. Among other things the writer pointed out that the

> *wainscotting and the ceiling of the old Church were of natural wood, giving a dark color to the interior, while the wainscotting, gallery fronts, and columns, as well as the ceiling, of the new Church are made to represent ivory. . . . The ceiling, which is a magnificent piece of work, is plastered on laths made of wire.*⁹³⁸

Another significant feature of the rebuilt Church was a new 31 rank, 3 manual organ.⁹³⁹ Even better, it was powered by a "Ross Water Engine." This eliminated the ever-troublesome necessity of manual blowing, and therefore greatly reduced the likelihood of future bellows operators leaving candles burning inside the instrument!

Finally, on Sunday, the 22nd of May, 1898, a year to the day after the fire, the Church was reopened. The united parishioners of St. Paul's, St. John's, and Christ Church were greeted by a choir of thirteen voices singing Gounod's "Unfold Ye Portals," along with a Gregorian "Venite" and "Glorias." Then in the afternoon, the Sunday Schools of St. Michael's and St. Andrew's joined the children of Christ Church for a belated Easter service.⁹⁴¹ Giving a special boost to the mood of celebration that day was the presence of Bishop Nelson and four other visiting clergy.⁹⁴²

One major feature still was incomplete at the time of reopening. This was the memorial window being prepared for the east wall of the Church. A new window was seriously contemplated before the fire struck, but the disaster settled once and for all the question of replacing the old glass.⁹⁴³ Precisely what the new one should represent, however, was more difficult to decide. The subject was vigorously discussed until it was agreed that the new glass would depict the risen Christ, styled after Hoffman.⁹⁴⁴ Even with that problem solved, however, others had still to be dealt with. At one time, for instance, a Latin inscription of one of Bishop Elliott's favorite texts was planned for the window.⁹⁴⁵ That idea was dropped and an English inscription adopted instead, but when the window arrived the new one was found faulty both in spelling and size.⁹⁴⁶ This experience would seem to justify the conclusion that history, which often reveals our human frailty, shows it most colorfully through the medium of stained glass. . . .

In any case, the last odds and ends of the work were completed during the summer of 1898, allowing the Building Committee to make its report at year end. Total expenditure came to just over $34,000.⁹⁴⁷ No wonder that fund raising was a common topic for conversation. It probably also explains why wine donated for the Easter services by William Neyle Habersham was auctioned in the congregation for $50.00, and the proceeds given to the Building Fund.⁹⁴⁸

Whether it acted as a stimulus or was merely the result of new attitudes in the congregation, the great attention given to the interior of the Church since 1890 had at least one very happy result. It revived the benevolent tradition which had begun back in Mr. Boone's time. Mr. Preston himself donated grills to protect the new chancel window.⁹⁴⁹ Mrs. J.J. McCoy gave the mosaic floor now in the chancel as a memorial,⁹⁵⁰ and there were others.⁹⁵¹

One idea, which would radically have altered the entire impression created by the Church, did not find a donor. This was a "scheme of windows for Christ Church" that was dated June, 1901. The concept envisioned stained glass along each side of the Church, both main and gallery levels, as well as another window downstairs in what was then the Sunday School room. As finishing touches the plan would have placed statues of Wesley and Oglethorpe on the portico among the columns.⁹⁵²

If Robb White's first years as Rector were filled with renovation, fire, and rebuilding, his last ones were spent quite differently. Many of the larger issues of the day began to burn with special intensity around the turn of the century. One question that greatly exercised some congregations, for example, was whether to drop the adjective "Protestant" from the offical name of the denomination — a topic familiar to Episcopalians in every generation since 1789, it seems!⁹⁵³ About the same time Georgia congregations especially agonized over the proposal to divide the Diocese. When this issue arose seriously in the 1890's Christ Church officially opposed division. More precisely, the Vestry's response to the Bishop described the idea as acceptable, but "inadvisable."⁹⁵⁴ But as the Diocese continued to grow, sentiment favoring division strengthened. By 1906 it was apparent that division soon would be a reality, and Christ Church became personally involved. H.C. Cunningham, a long-time vestryman and warden, was one of three in the old Diocese chosen to define the boundaries of the new ones.⁹⁵⁵

Another question which was certainly on the minds of parishioners during these years was that of race. What to do in the face of deepening segregation and racial distrust? Nationally, this trend was manifest in the rapid growth of Jim Crow laws in the decades surrounding 1900. Although surviving Christ Church records tell us little, others close to the parish scene leave scant room for doubt that the matter must have troubled our predecessors considerably. In 1904, the Archdeacon of Savannah, charged with care of missions in the coastal portion of the Diocese, reflected on the changing situation:

> *In the old days (were they better?) the minister who was deemed fit to have charge of a Southern parish might preach to, baptize, give the Holy Communion to, and pray with negroes, and it was a matter of course. In a small degree a Southern priest may still preach to them; but let even him whose whole life proves him to be a loyal son of*

Right, view of the Church's west gallery after the renovation of 1890 and the installation of the new Hutchings organ.

the South beware how he offers them the real consolations of Christianity in the hour of suffering and sorrow.

Asking why that is the case,

the only reason given is that, because of race prejudice, work among the colored people would ruin the influence among white people of any clergyman, and . . . do much more harm than good . . . Those who make such a claim admit that it ought not to be; that Gospel ought to be preached to all alike. . . .[956]

Finally, he addressed an appeal to his colleagues at the annual meeting of the Diocese:

Surely this Convention ought to rise above every petty feeling of our common human nature, recognize its supreme responsibility, take up the burdens belonging to it as a body and as individuals, and meet promptly and cheerfully the full measure of its duty to itself, to its members, to the negroes of Georgia, to the whites of Georgia, and to the Master who has done more for us than we can possibly do for Him and His.[957]

His tone hints that he knew already neither logic nor eloquence would carry this particular day. In that he was correct. The following year the Diocese moved to form a "Council of Colored Churchmen" and designated a special archdeacon to take charge of "Colored Work."[958] The Council and the archdeacon were to meet and operate separately, and report to the Diocesan Convention. In addition to its immense social and political impact, this denial of direct voice by Blacks in the Diocesan Council renders most of our traditional historical sources all but mute on what had, for 170 years, been a significant part of the work of Christ Church.[959]

The solution adopted may have silenced most of our sources, but it did not remove the problem. Ten years later both the diocese and the National Church were still struggling with it

and debating whether to consecrate Black suffragans in affected dioceses, create a separate "Racial Missionary District" nationally, or to leave matters as they were. Here again we know very little — only that the Vestry of Christ Church preferred the latter, and declined comment on the other options presented.[960] In a matter as complex as this one, with so many shades of opinion expressed, and so many possible reasons for favoring a particular option, the Vestry's choice only teases us. We don't even know for certain whether their endorsement represented broadly based congregational sentiment or was simply their own opinion.

Burdensome as these problems were, at least they were shared by fellow churchmen throughout the region and the nation. There was another, however, which belonged to the Rector and congregation alone: the Rector's health. It had always been fragile. "He never knew what it was to be without pain", but in recent years his condition had become especially trying. Only with great effort was he able to take leave early in 1904 to witness the ordination of his son,[961] Robb White, Jr. Yet it was a joy he would not be denied. "His life was one of constant physical suffering," but he carried on with "kindly dignity" and determination "to serve his people, the Church, and Christ to the utmost of his ability." Late in 1904 his health seems to have deteriorated further.[962] Then, in February, "as he was about to leave his carriage at the rectory," he suffered an "apoplectic stroke" which hospitalized him. After four weeks he was moved to St. Luke's Hospital in Richmond, at which time his physician thought "his complete recovery was . . . a matter of a few months." Suddenly, on the 26th of March, he took an unexpected turn for the worse before a third stroke ended his life on the 27th.[963]

Word reached Savannah by telegram the same evening and set off a shock wave of grief. "No church was ever more devoted to a pastor than was . . . Christ Church to Mr. White"[964] and this outcome was wholly unexpected. The Vestry met the next morning and requested Mr. White's admired colleague, the Rev. C.H. Strong of St. John's, to take charge of a memorial service in Christ Church. This was set

Detail of the chancel rail brass.

for the 29th at noon, the hour of the Rector's funeral in Warrenton, Va. We can imagine with reasonable accuracy what was said at that service, for comments about Mr. White seldom failed to include reference to three rather distinct features of his personal style. First, they typically noted his vivacity and vigor, using such terms as "manly", "strong", "energetic", "quick of mind" — traits which came across despite his "great physical disabilities." Then they would always point to his straight forward approach to things through words such "honesty", and "candor", often describing him as "outspoken" and "eloquent." Usually, they also returned to softer points of personality, noting his "courtesy" and "sympathy."⁹⁶⁵ Clearly he was a rector to remember.⁹⁶⁶

After a painful spring and then a summer of fill-in clergy, the new Rector, Francis Alan Brown, arrived from Washington, Georgia, to take charge in October.⁹⁶⁷ With him he brought many "modern" ideas that rather soon began to change the look and sound of the parish and its ministry. For example, at his request, the new Rector was authorized to place a sign outside the Church which listed the hours of services, etc. Similar notices were placed in local hotels and also printed on cards along with a brief history of the parish. The Vestry also acceded to his wish to have the Church kept open on week days at certain hours.⁹⁶⁸

Within the congregation itself the most apparent change came in the mail. It arrived during the Christmas season in the form of an eight-page newsletter, *The Parish Helper*, which was simply packed with news of interest to parishioners . . . . and to us!⁹⁶⁹ Articles on "New Work", Missionary Meetings, St. Andrew's, various groups in the parish and the Sunday School were included along with memorials of the late Rector. There was also the 1905 financial statement of the parish and an extensive register of services, missions, organizations, Sunday School classes and personnel, and a list of nine lay readers.

Another of the Rev. Mr. Brown's innovations was to introduce a boy's choir. The innovation was not in the choir itself;

remember Mr. Boone had done that twenty years before. The real novelty lay in the fact that they were to be vested and seated in view of the congregation, in the east end of the Church near the chancel. Preparation for the change was made during Mr. Brown's first year as Rector, and by early autumn of 1906 the boys and their vestments were ready. Only the new choir stalls were now lacking — having not yet arrived from the carpenter's shop. The weeks of waiting were tedious, but Mr. Brown used them to good advantage as a time publicly "to impress the congregation that the choir being in front is to lead the congregation in the worship, not do it all for them, either in singing or in responses." The music will remain simple, there being "no desire for show or effect."⁹⁷⁰

After weeks of waiting, at last the new stalls arrived.

*It is now assured that the vested choir will be heard at Christ Church next Sunday. The necessary changes are now being made in the chancel. The stalls which were delayed in transmission have arrived and will be installed early this week . . . . A double choir will be a novelty in Savannah, though it has been heard in a number of other cities.*⁹⁷¹

The boys, plus eight men, were formally "admitted" at the regular 5:00 p.m. evensong on Sunday, 11 Nov. 1906. After that date plans were that they would take part in morning services, too. In announcing the boys' debut the *Morning News* encouraged its readers that "Director W.T. Hill has trained the little fellows so they should be able to give a good account of themselves."⁹⁷²

Music in the Church was obviously a subject of great importance to Mr. Brown and he was seldom satisfied with things as they were.⁹⁷³ Whether his impatience should be attributed to the quality of the music produced or to Mr. Brown himself is difficult to judge in retrospect. It could also have been that the congregation had better taste than it was willing to pay for, as the Rector seems to suggest in his 1911 report to the Vestry.

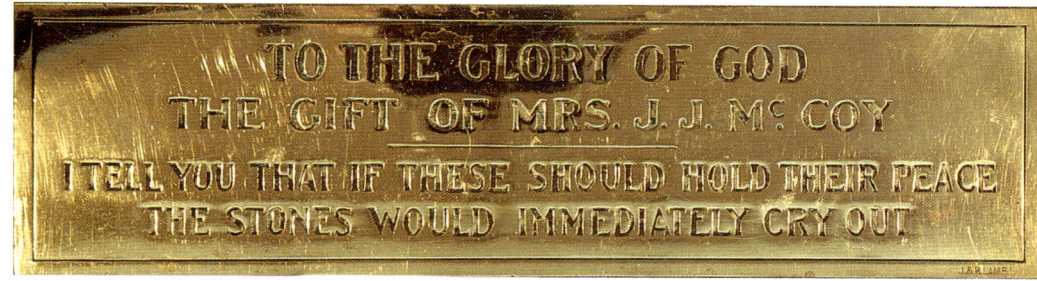

Central motif of the chancel's mosaic floor, given in 1900. The floor's memorial plaque.

Left, the Church as a whole had a very different look after it was rebuilt. Gone were the illuminated "modern gothic" ceiling and most of the dark interior trim that had dominated since 1883.

The Girl Guides, as the Girl Scouts were originally called, were organized in 1912 by Juliette Gordon Low, a daughter of the parish. Although not directly related to Christ Church they were nonetheless closely associated with it through their founder, and exemplify the impact the Church was having on the life of the community. Here a truckload of Guides is set to begin the trek to the very first summer camp, 1913.

Savannah stands alone in its musical difficulties. Nothing but experience would ever have persuaded him of the difficulties in keeping up a volunteer choir. As a matter of fact he is convinced that in our parish one cannot be maintained that will satisfy the congregation.

Most probably it was a combination of factors that sparked his dissatisfaction. Neither choir attendance nor the condition of the organ were all they should be. Indeed, he observed, the latter "at times does make exceeding obnoxious sounds or fails to make any at all." In his struggles with the instrument the organist "deserves sympathy and not criticism." The Rector was not alone in his feelings, and by the time his report was actually submitted steps had already been taken to improve the situation. Once again a paid quartet had been employed, this time with $500 raised by the Choir! By that time, too, the Rector had begun to hint that his next crusade would be for improvement to the organ.[974] In this effort Mr. Brown was again successful, as a 36-rank, 3-manual, Austin Organ was installed the next year.[975]

Since we have taken note of Mr. Brown's special interest in music as a means to enrich worship, we should also note the considerable evidence that the parish as a whole increasingly shared his view. Budgets, expenditures, and general visibility of questions relating to church music in the records of parish life all point in this direction.[976] Some of this change is perhaps attributable to the trend of the times, and some was certainly due to the influence of Francis Brown. It is also likely, however, that some of the new support for enrichment of worship was the result of the Church's heightened importance in its diocese. When the old diocese was finally divided in 1907 it left Savannah as the major population center of the new Diocese of Georgia, and Christ Church one of its leading congregations. It has always been so to some extent, of course. But now Christ Church came again to serve, at least in spirit and function, as the cathedral of the new diocese — just as it had 60 years earlier in the days of Bishop Elliott. We can sense through the records a certain expectation that this parish must become exemplary in worship, as it has long been in support of the diocese and missions. Thus, it was the Rector of this parish who, with one layman from Augusta, was appointed to wait upon the Bishop-elect and to receive his response to election.[977] It was also at Christ Church that the new bishop, the Rev. F.F. Reese of Nashville, chose to be consecrated.[978]

Surely that was a day worth remembering! With every seat taken and the Church decorated in white roses, a choir of 34 singers led the procession to the words of "O Sion Haste . . ." In all, six bishops were present in addition to the bishop-elect, including the Rt. Rev. Beverly Dandridge Tucker (then bishop coadjutor of Southern Virginia), father of the later rector. It is instructive that the Master of Ceremonies appointed to orchestrate the consecration service was Christ Church's own Francis Brown.[979]

After his consecration, Bishop Reese maintained an office at the Church, which was accessible "through the St. Julian St. door," and kept regular hours there whenever he was in town.[980] While the frequent presence of the bishop and the special music no doubt added luster, there were other activities, too, which made these first years of the new century busy and fruitful ones in the life of the parish. Its missions flourished so that a third one was begun. "On Sunday, May 1, 1910, the Junior Auxiliary of St. Michael's Chapel, under Miss Georgina B. Sack, founded the House of Prayer Mission in the southwestern part of the city." Some years later, on its twenty-first birthday, the name was changed to St. Andrew's "in honor of the mission that was held so successfully and for so many years by the Brotherhood of St. Andrew of Christ Church."[981] Located at Kline and Burroughs Sts., the mission continued to function, in varying degrees of prosperity, well into the 1930's.[981a] The Sunday Schools remained active also. The year House of Prayer was founded, for example, the total enrollment in missions' Sunday Schools nearly equalled that of the mother church in size (222 pupils in the missions and 250 at the Church.) Together the schools kept some 45-50 teachers busy each Sunday.[982] In the next year the Rector reported figures on the "Sunday School for colored children," which counted another 75 pupils,[983] and in 1912 a parish day school with 40 more was begun.[984]

Only vigorous lay support and a series of effective curates made such a program possible. Certainly it is obvious that no rector, working alone, could have done it all. Fortunately the lay groups have left records of reasonable clarity behind them. The curates, on the other hand, have not. Many seem to slip through cracks in the records, leaving only their names . . . . or less . . . . to tease us. One of those was the Rev. Mr. Charles S. Frazer, who served from May, 1908, through December, 1909. All we know for certain is that he assisted Mr. Brown by taking charge of St. Michael's during his year and half in town, and that he stands out because the Vestry was so sorry to see him go when he accepted a call to Cuba.[985] One of his successors is equally distinctive, although for a very different reason — one that might not leave him totally satisfied. His name was J. Hoffer Gibboney, and he became a curate a year or so after Frazer departed. The dissatisfaction would likely stem from the fact that the only surving document which gives us any personal touch with him is a note he wrote to the Rector from Emporia, Virginia, prior to his coming. In it he gave expression to two points which caused him some anxiety. One centered on his doubts about having or affording, the correct vestments, and the other concerned basic living accommodations. Not wishing to ask too much, yet hoping to convey to his new boss that there were limits, he wrote: "all I insist on is a bathtub."[986] This simple request tells us so little about Mr. Gibboney, it hardly seems fair that it should constitute our only memory of him. Yet it does, and thereby reminds us of an important truth that in matters historical, images are often shaped as much by the accidents of survival as by the actions of the players.

Gaps or no, surviving records make it clear that the last few had been years of abundance in the life of the parish. The war, nearly fifty years before, the stress of Reconstruction, and the scandals had afterall given way to recovery and rebuilding under Thomas Boone. Happily this was followed by a full flowering of parish activity and outreach under Robb White and Francis Brown. Significantly, the occasional setbacks and disasters of the recovery years did not abort the trend, rather they underscored it. Then came the summer of 1914, when everything seemed to change. The world was plunged into a war that nearly everyone found surprising and many had thought impossible. While some welcomed the exhilaration of war, "as swimmers into cleanness leaping," Americans commonly viewed the affair with distaste, as yet another sign of the old world's political bankruptcy. Few, if any, got what they expected.

At Christ Church the Vestry was surprised to receive Mr. Brown's resignation, written with very mixed feelings from his summer vacation spot in upstate New York. The Rector described his new situation as being in a poor neighborhood at a salary little more than half what he now received. The "possibilities were great," however, and the problems "most suited" to his talents. Cited as one factor in the change was his wife's health, but at bottom he appears to have felt that he had done what he could for Christ Church. It was now time for another to bring fresh strength and talents to the task here. At the end of October, 1914, he would leave for his new charge as Rector of St. Mary's, Lawrence St., New York.[987] On his last Sunday, the congregation of St. Michael's Mission attended service at the mother church to join in bidding a last farewell to their Rector of nine years.[988]

The main aisle and east end of the Church as they appeared after 1964.

VIII
War, Prosperity, Depression, & War
1914-1945

It was the Rev. H. Percival Spence, the Assistant, who kept things going between rectors by personally leading five or six services and classes at the Church and Chapels each Sunday. As minister-in-charge his Sundays typically began with an 8 A.M. Communion service at St. Michaels. This was often followed by the Sunday School at St. Andrew's (10:15 A.M.) before the main service began at the Church at 11:30 A.M. The Evening Prayer at the Church would begin at 5:00 P.M. followed by another, with sermon, in St. Andrew's at 8:30 P.M. Fortunately, lay readers led some of these functions, especially when they occurred simultaneously at the Church and its Chapels. Without them the entire system would have become unworkable.[989] On the other hand, it was Bishop Reese who got much of the attention — chiefly by barring women from the noonday Lenten services over which he presided. The congregation was notably upset at his plan. The Vestry both wrote and visited the Bishop to express their view that "we have no right to keep ladies out of Church at any of the services." There is no evidence that the Bishop relented, however, nor any specific information as to why he held such a view.[990]

One suspects that parishioners were still buzzing about the Bishop's attitude when early in the Easter season, the Rev. John Durham Wing accepted the call to become Rector. Coming from Grace Church in Anniston, Alabama, he arrived amid great excitement early in July, 1915.[991] In the beginning he dealt with the normal items of parish affairs, as so many before him had done. For example, he revived the Boys Choir,[992] and in time he even extended his predecessor's musical theme by a few measures. Specifically, there is evidence of a Sunday School orchestra in 1916,[993] and in 1920 the organ was virtually rebuilt. At that time, the console and many of the pipes were removed to join the choir in the east end of the Church.[994]

It wasn't long before forces began to manifest themselves which would make Mr. Wing's rectorate a milestone in the history of the parish. For one thing, by 1917 the noises of "tin-lizzies" clattering through Johnson Square had risen to such a level that it disturbed worshippers in the Church. Declaring war on the clatter, the Vestry dispatched Senior Warden J. Randolph Anderson to see the mayor about the problem.[995] That same day, in Washington, D.C., a Senate resolution opened the way to another declaration of war — one destined to bring disturbances vastly more threatening to the peace of the congregation and of the world. Each, in its own way, was to play a major role in redefining everything from the nature and function of parish life to the structure of the nation and the values of civilization itself.

Actually, the "Great War" had been a presence in the minds of most Americans for several years. During the first weeks of the upheaval President Wilson requested that "prayers for the termination of the European war" be said in all the churches of the land. In accordance with the President's proclamation, there was a special observance of "Peace Day" at Christ Church the next Sunday with a sermon by the Bishop.[996] Since that time the war had been in the news virtually every day. The latest Bulletins from the "Russian" and "Western" fronts competed for space with the alarming stories of U-boats sinking neutral or non-military shipping. But when war was actually declared, on the 6th of April, 1917, the news reports suddenly took on a different quality. The sons of the parish began enlisting; their absence each Sunday morning gave a new presence to the war. The conflict was no longer confined to distant headlines. Once again war had come to church!

Just one month after the nation's entry into the war, Bishop Reese addressed the annual convention of his diocese. The points he raised on that occasion were no doubt heard in Christ Church, too, more than once during the next year and a half. First he counseled hearers to disdain all forms of shirking, hoarding, of profiteering.

Let no man or woman seek to escape his share of the common burden and thereby lay it upon somebody less able to bear it... Every man's private gain must await his

One of Mrs. Waring's Thanksgiving pageants. This one could date from as early as 1917, but certainly no later than 1924. As leader of the Sunday School, Mrs. Pinckney Waring (seated on left, wearing white hat) seemed to love a good "cast of thousands" pageant. Her elaborately costumed productions might involve children from Christ Church and the mission Sunday Schools along with the junior choir, any of whom might carry placards or symbols and speak lines especially written for the occasion.

public service. On the firing line men give their lives for their country and for humanity. Behind, . . . men can at least give their physical comfort and their profit.

Looking beyond these immediate duties of responsible citizenship he also held before them some of President Wilson's high hope.

Let us fight without hatred and without malicious passion, . . . but save ourselves the degradation of hate, [and] do our bit to save our country and the world from an inheritance of hatred. This war is too solemn a business to be degraded into a mere contest for national supremacy, or . . . for the mere selfish satisfaction of destroying our enemies.

Finally, to guidance and hopeful idealism he added a note of prophetic judgment. Pointing out that while we are not, as a nation, responsible for the war, it was nevertheless as a result of our materialized civilization, heated competition, false standards of value, ambition, lusts, and passions that it came about. "Of these sins we, too, are partakers . . . and in so far as that is true, this war is a consequence . . . of our sin."[997]

The next year was one of all out effort. As the sons of the parish were inducted into the armed forces, their elders also served in many ways. Treasurer H. M. Johnson left the city in June of 1917 to serve with the Red Cross.[998] Col. George A. Gordon left for France, also to engage in work for the Red Cross.[999] Beyond these highly visible actions countless Sunday School and group projects within the Church were directed toward war-related ministry.[1000] For a time there was also thought of investing funds "accruing for the purpose of a Sunday School Building" in Liberty Bonds instead of a savings bank.[1001] Even the space used as a "parish house" and the rectory were rented out for a time to personnel of the Marine Hospital Service.[1002] Added to everything else were shortages, rationing, and, or course, inflation to exact their special demands from all. In fact, late in 1918, "in view of the great increase in the cost of living caused by the war over the last two years," the Vestry felt compelled to make special financial provision for the Rector.[1003]

After a year of direct involvement in the "Great War" most Americans were much shaken by the magnitude of its horrors. Certainly, Bishop Reese was as he delivered his annual message to the Diocese in May of 1918. Recounting the awful history of the year just passed, he called for a Christianity that was "more outgoing, less judgmental, more charitable, and more expressive than in the past."[1004] It seems reasonable to suppose that the Bishop was not alone in his reaction.

At first it may appear a bit odd that in the midst of war two long-simmering issues of ecclesiastical policy began to bubble anew. Yet actually we should probably expect such phenomena, for the fires of combat cast their eerie light upon everything — nothing looked as it had before 1914. Whatever the cause, these were the very years that some of the most ancient customs regarding the governance and financing of the parish were once again called in question. In both cases, after much soul-searching, the old ways at last were done away and new ones, fundamentally different, set in place. Together with the war, these matters came to dominate Mr. Wing's years as Rector, and clearly to identify them as crucial in the transition from 19th to 20th century style in parish affairs. Collectively, the changes they brought to Christ Church were as profound and as sweeping as any that accompanied the other great wars which had, even more literally, invaded the life of the congregation. In fact, on one of the points at issue, that of parish governance, the last significant changes had been brought by the Revolution. The other, the custom of rented pews, was even more ancient. The war of 1861-65, for all its upheaval, changed neither of these things, although it radically restructured the society to which the congregation would minister.

A closer look reveals that in the matter of parish governance there were two important changes at this time. One involved the function of the rector, who since 1789 had been officially

The Tennessee marble columns now grace the portico of 15 Gordon Street, east, on Monterey Square.

barred from Vestry meetings![1005] During Mr. Boone's rectorate that rule was "overlooked" in practice and he became the first Rector in a century to attend the meetings regularly. The pattern continued to evolve through the following decades although the old tradition was still strong enough in 1892 that Bishop Nelson went out of his way to condemn

> *that remnant of New England Congregationalism which debarrs the rector from his proper position as head of the vestry. The status of a vestry holding its meetings without the rector, or with him by courtesy and sufferance, is wholly anomalous.*[1006]

Robb White became increasingly involved in the doings of the Vestry; and in the time of his successor, Francis Brown, their meetings were often chaired by the Rector despite the offical prohibition of his presence. It was during Mr. Wing's rectorate, however, that the old order was formally overturned through amendment of the parish's charter of incorporation. The new version made the Rector *ex officio* chairman of the Vestry.[1007]

A second significant change in governance had to do with the number of vestrymen and the manner of their election. Under the Established Church of colonial days the offices of warden and vestryman were more civil than ecclesiastical — more or less equivalent to elective county offices in post-Revolutionary times. Such an arrangement opened those offices to virtually any free property holder in the colony, regardless of churchmanship (or lack), and usually resulted in new wardens each year.[1008] The Revolution changed all of that, of course, eliminating the church establishment and thereby transforming wardens and vestrymen into officers of the congregation only. The charter of 1789 made this a matter of law and specified that the congregation would elect two wardens and eight vestrymen each year. Gradually, through the 19th century the tendency grew for members of the vestry to serve for extended periods and actually reached the point at which seats were practically held for life. In one brief period soon after the Civil War, for instance, as one generation gave way to the next, three long-serving vestrymen died who between them had held office for 135 years![1009] Their records were exceptional, but tenures of 20 or more years were the rule and almost all served until health, relocation, or death cast the deciding vote. Looking at such figures, it is easy to suppose that those in office tended to treat the Vestry as an exclusive club. William P. Hunter, one of the three long-servers, gave us reason for caution, however, when he lamented the attitude of the congregation who "generally" take but little interest in these elections."[1010]

Whether due to lack of interest or some other cause, many seemed to agree with Mr. Hunter that things should be different. For while the system was not changed formally, such lengthy tenure ceased to be the rule in the later 19th century and proposals "to raise up a body of laymen who will understand the business end of the Parish's work" became rather commonplace. Still under discussion forty years later, a 1908 plan proposed that at each monthly meeting preceeding the annual election "the oldest member in point of service shall resign, and the vestry shall there upon elect a new member from the congregation to fill his place."[1011] None of these ideas were formally adopted, however, until the charter amendments of 1918 specified that a warden who had served five years must retire for at least a year before he could become eligible for re-election, either as warden or vestryman.[1012] One further change, prepared during Mr. Wing's final year at Christ Church, carried the idea of systematic retirement to its logical conclusion. By increasing the number of vestrymen to twelve, plus the two wardens, and informally agreeing that two of the fourteen would retire each year, this 1923 modification established seven years as the normal term of service on the Vestry.[1013] While the make-up of the body and the details of the retirement cycle have been altered from time to time,[1013.1] the general design and spirit of the 1923 model are still in place today, sixty years later.

Far older than any particular feature of vestry structure or power was the custom of raising parish funds through rental of pews. Indeed, it antedated the Georgia colony itself. It is easy to appreciate how difficult it must have been for our predecessors to conceive of practical alternatives, or to see much reason to change the rental system. It simply was . . . and ever had been. The desirability of having space available for those who were in no position to rent anything had been obvious for a very long time, but there was no problem. Such needs could easily be accommodated within the system. That was after all what motivated the colonial legislature to take action toward "erecting a commodious Pew in the North Isle of the . . . Church at the Publik Expence for Accommodation of Strangers."[1014] With similar intention, Archibald Wilkins, in 1844, endowed two pews for the use of poor females in the parish who were "willing but unable" to pay for their own.[1015] "Free pews" obviously had their value, but was it sensible to try to run a "free church" — one in which all of the pews were free? The idea had an appealing simplicity, and "free" parishes became fairly common in the later 1800's. Yet the system was replete with unmeasured risks which were pointedly cited by skeptics and traditionalists. Would it encourage irresponsible churchmanship? Would alms alone produce adequate revenue to support parish work? What if contracted obligations could not be met? It was after all, said the doubters, the poorer missions and parishes that had chosen the "free pew" system; in fact, they probably had little choice. Would it work for Christ Church? Then there was the social side of the question. If there were no rentals, presumably there would be no reserved pews. Would respectable people attend under such conditions? Or could just anyone attend with or without contributing? Is that appealing simplicity nothing more than shirking and sloth, very cleverly disguised?

Little wonder is it that the question of abandoning the rental system was discussed again and again before the first cautious steps were taken in 1893. At that time it was decided to have free pews for evening services, "with collections taken up," beginning on the first Sunday of the new year, 1894.[1016] This meant that roughly one third of the Church's services each year had free rather than rental pews.[1017] After that innovation, active debate continued over the advisability of broadening the system to include all Church services, but although there were reports and proposals from time to time,[1018] no further action was taken until 1917. Then, with the World War in full swing, things looked different. Pehaps it was the unprecedentedly large transient population now moving through the city, so difficult to accommodate within a system of reserved pews, that now moved the parish toward decisive action.[1019] Even then there was considerable anxiety since, from a business point of view, it was crucial to assure that the new system would produce no less revenue than the present one. That same anxiety also explains why, at least as early as 1917 and with the final decision not yet made, the Church tested the idea of an "every member canvass."[1020] Apparently this experiment supplied the needed assurance, or perhaps the times strengthened the conviction that the day had come, because at its 1919 annual meeting the congregation voted to go ahead with the plan "*provided*" amounts presently paid in pews be continued as contributions."[1020.1] The final OK was then given by the Vestry in Decmeber of that year.[1021] Thus it was that on the last day of 1919 the age-old system of rented pews was laid aside, and on the first Sunday of 1920 all pews became free.[1022]

Interestingly, the same day the congregation voted to go ahead with preparations for free pews, the Rector laid before them another major question. He asked that they consider the "desirability of Christ Church being the Cathedral Church of the Diocese." Although the issue is not reflected in any later minutes or reports it would be difficult to suppose it was not widely discussed![1022.1]

By the time Mr. Wing announced his intention to leave Christ Church, late in 1922, both of these major changes — the restructuring of the Vestry and the new fiscal style — were well in place, and so were many others. His compulsive drive toward organizational neatness had done much to bring the parish to a recognizably modern form. Not only was his leadership effective in guiding the Church through the sweeping changes in governance and finance just noted, it also helped to resolve some less ancient but none the less difficult issues. Soon after the war was over and thoughts could be turned to other matters, for example, adjustments were made which totally revamped the parish missions. St. Michael's became a self-supporting parish.[1023] St. Andrew's was closed after many years of slow decline,[1024] and House of Prayer finally gained a home it could count on after occupying 13 buildings in its 12 years of existence![1025]

Mr. Wing actually departed in January of 1923 to become Rector of St. Paul's, Chattanooga, and eventually Bishop of South Florida.[1026] Since his successor, the Rev. David Cady Wright did not arrive until the next January, 1923 became literally "a year without a rector."[1027] What a welcome sight the Wrights must have been! The new Rector was here in time to take charge for the first Sunday of 1924. He came to the parish from St. Paul's Church, Louisville, Kentucky, having remained there since his first call to Christ Church nine years

ABSTINENCE
PRAYER
GOOD WORK
COMPASSION
SELF DENIAL
SUNDAY
WORSHIP
LENT
ASH WEDNESDAY
FAITH
HOPE
LOVE

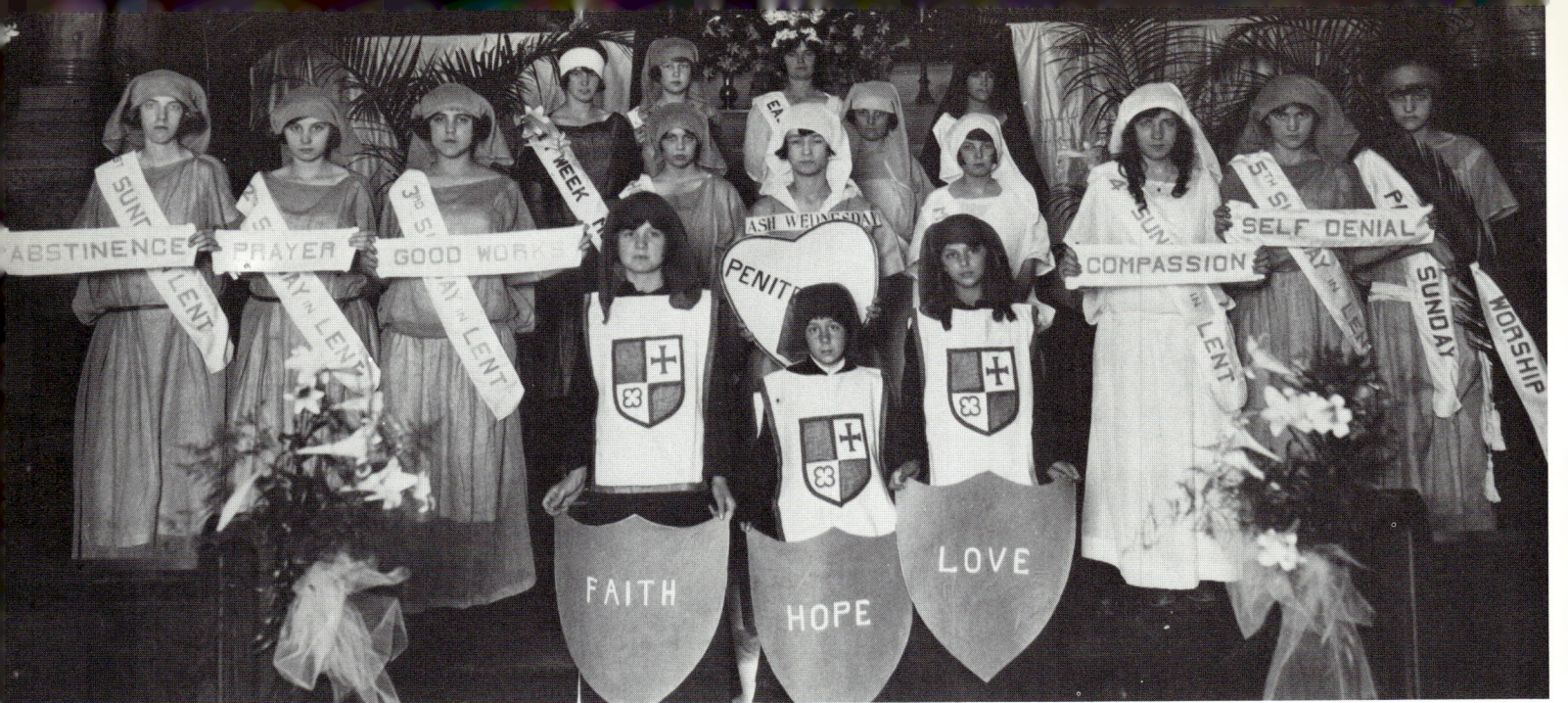

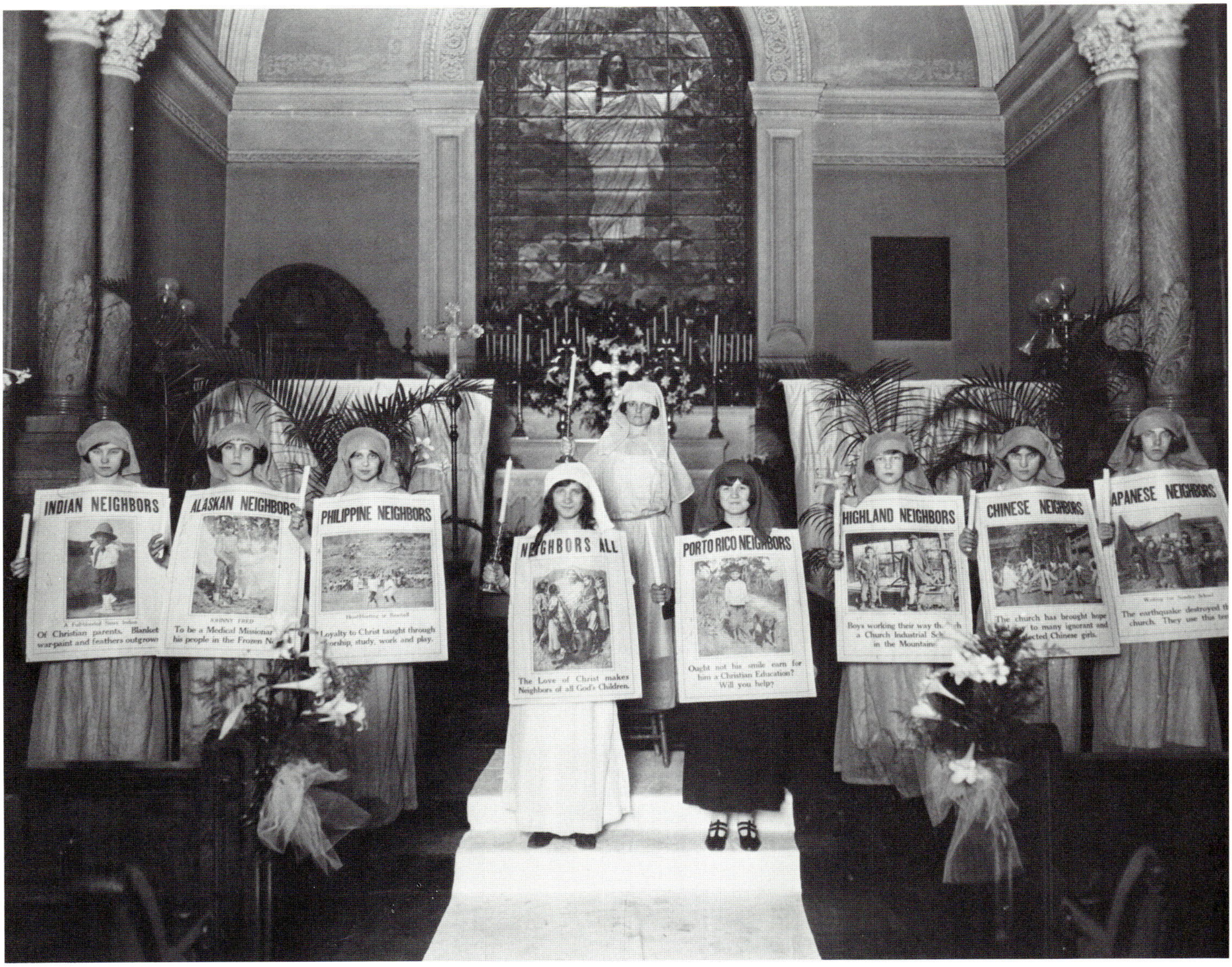
INDIAN NEIGHBORS
Of Christian parents. Blanket war-paint and feathers outgrow
ALASKAN NEIGHBORS
To be a Medical Missionar
his people in the Frozen N
PHILIPPINE NEIGHBORS
Loyalty to Christ taught through
worship, study, work and play.
NEIGHBORS ALL
The Love of Christ makes Neighbors of all God's Children.
PORTO RICO NEIGHBORS
Ought not his smile earn for him a Christian Education? Will you help?
HIGHLAND NEIGHBORS
Boys working their way th
a Church Industrial Sch
in the Mountains
CHINESE NEIGHBORS
The church has brought hope
to many ignorant and
Chinese girls.
APANESE NEIGHBORS
The earthquake destroyed th
church. They use this

Typical of Mrs. Waring's pageants were those which treated brotherhood, and the virtues especially cultivated through Lenten discipline. Among the participants are Lillian Sturtevant, Margaret Seabrook, Margaret Rockwell, Violet Nash, Pinckney Waring, Dorothy Williams, Betty Peeples, Sally Thesmar, Harriet Aldrich, Ann Gibson, Edith Hunter, and Alice Mae Brown. Can you recognize others? (Thanks to Betty Peeples Brannen for the identifications.)

before. A graduate of St. Stephen's College and the General Theological Seminary, he had been a priest since 1896.[1028] Thus, he brought 30 years practical experience with him to Savannah along with great energy and a host of new ideas.

Plans for another renovation of the Church building may already have been in the making when Mr. Wright arrived, but priority had to be given to providing adequate housing for his family. In preparation for its new inhabitants the rectory was thoroughly refurbished and given some of the latest modern touches, such as electric floor plugs![1029] Then reinforcing the welcome the Wrights must already have felt, a brand new automobile was purchased for the Rector's use at a cost of $869.25.[1030] Once Mr. Wright had settled in a bit, work on the Church Building became a major point of conversation and plans were ready for bidding by the summer of 1925.[1031] Without doubt it was time for the structure to receive some attention. Relocation of the choir stalls (1906) and the organ console (1920) to the east end of the Church were highly visible, but there had been no systematic work on the fabric of the building for nearly thirty years.[1032] Architecturally, the 1925 work is especially important since like the previous renovation in 1897, it moved in the direction of restoration. That is, there was conscious effort made to return the interior of the church more closely to the spirit of the 1838 design and away from the victorian "modernizations" of 1869, 1883, and 1890.

Work on the building actually began in August, 1925; the weekly notices on the newspaper's religious page read simply that the "Church is closed until further notice . . . on account of repairing the interior of the building.[1033] The plan was for the work to be accomplished while the Rector was away on two months vacation, but it may surprise no one that things did not work out exactly as planned. When the Rector returned the public was told that "owing to delays in the work . . . it is impossible to hold any service except Holy Communion in the [ground floor] Chapel." Therefore, the notice in the paper urged "Christ Church people to unite . . . in a union service at St. Paul's at 11:30 A.M. when . . . the Rev. Mr. Wright will preach."[1034]

Not until All Saints' Day was the Church, resored "to the form of a century ago, . . . formally reopened and rededicated." Bishop Reese was there to lead the large congregation in its grand celebration at the 11:30 service when "the usual custom . . . for All Saints' Day of calling the Bede Roll of the Departed for the past year" was observed.[1035] As a part of the rededication service, Mr. Wright presented a brief historical sketch of the history of the parish.[1036] In his sermon the Rector was true to his calling. He "dwelt on the spiritual rededication and revitalization that should accompany [renovation] of the building."[1037]

To describe the new interior, the *Morning News* headlined the work "Dignity," adding that "a beautiful simplicity is the keynote."

The walls have been painted light buff that shades into a soft cream color while the ceiling and wood work are white, the whole tending to emphasize the carving on the massive ceiling, around the windows, over the altar, and on the pillars supporting the balconies. The floor has been laid with tiles and the pews refinished in ecclesiastical oak and remodelled to conform to the rest of the Church. The chancel has been deepened to four feet (sic), and the arched doorways leading into the sacristies rebuilt.[1038]

In the journalist's opinion all "superfluous details" had been removed. Old chandeliers, for example, were taken down and new indirect lighting installed. "The interior of the Church", he wrote, was "now thoroughly in keeping with its historic traditions."

Restoring more of the neo-classical, or Greek-revival, spirit of the original architecture did not signify any wish to turn the clock back, however. This was also the decade when the first acousticon system was installed,[1039] and when Christ Church first seriously considered "hooking up" on the "Savannah radio broadcasting station" to disseminate its message.[1040]

After a decade of change, few things remained in their pre-war condition. One that did not undergo great change at this time, however, was the liturgical style of the Church. Lenten services, for example, exhibited a pattern in the 1920's that was almost unchanged from that of 1890 and 1905. Indeed, that same pattern carried well into the 1940's, until after World War II. The only points that show much variation, development, or doubt have to do with the treatment of Maundy Thursday and Good Friday. In 1919, for instance, a Thursday evening celebration of the Lord's Supper was added. Perhaps not unprecedented, it had certainly not been customary previously, and it was not repeated in 1920.[1041] A similar vacillation in the schedules for Good Friday was centered on the increasingly popular noon to 3 o'clock service. In 1919, Christ Church observed this vigil of the crucifixion, omitted it the following year, but continued to observe it sporadically thereafter. One especially interesting liturgical innovation, which appeared in 1922, was the celebration of a festival Evensong on Holy Saturday, in anticipation of Easter. Christmas Eve was treated in the same manner, with a festival Evensong at 6 P.M., one or more of the chapels often joining in the joyful service.[1042] This had been the custom of the parish since the early part of the century and it remained so until Mr. Wright's successor introduced the midnight Christmas Communion Service in 1945.[1043]

Although great changes in the pattern of services were not frequent, Mr. Wright was not above tinkering with anything that he thought could be made to work better. He seemed to have a flair for reforming, revising, or reviving practices and groups, usually to good effect. Parishioners soon learned to trust his intuition in such matters. Indeed, the first lessons began only weeks after his taking charge of the parish when Mr. Wright took aim at the practice of using a paid crucifer on Sunday morning. In place of the mercenary he proposed to encourage the boys of the parish to volunteer in matters of this kind.[1044]

About the same time Mr. Wright initiated a Men's club in the parish with a very successful "smoker" at the Colonial Lunch Room.[1045] Since the lunch room was operated by the ladies of the parish, the only cost of the venture was the $7.00 for cigars — a small investment considering that 110 attended the affair to initiate the club.[1046] After an auspicious beginning, however, and a period of productive work, the club withered, as groups tend to do. Undaunted, the Rector re-formed it three years later. This time it worked according to plan and the "Men of Christ Church" continued to operate successfully for many years. Perhaps it was the new foundation's clear sense of purpose that made the difference; they promised to assist the Rector in any way he "desires or thinks best."[1047] Beyond that they undertook sponsorship of Troop 11, Boy Scouts of America, which had begun in the parish about 1914.[1048]

Likewise, after several poor seasons, Mr. Wright revived the noonday Lenten Services in 1927.[1049] They did well, and the following year he invited Dean Fosbroke of the General Theological Seminary to lead them, in the hope that they might do even better.[1050] Apparently it worked, because the series of special services in 1928 reportedly drew some 10,000 worshippers to the Church! In 1929 attendance was greater still.[1051]

During these years, crowds were not confined to the special seasons. Indeed, they had presented something of a "problem" ever since Mr. Wright's arrival. Now, however, in the midst of a very successful "Church attendance campaign," two hundred new hymnals were purchased to aid in accommodating the large congregations. But that was only the beginning. Ushers had problems even finding seats for the numbers that attended, and especially had "their troubles giving people the seats which they had been accustomed to." Festival days, such as Palm Sunday, with a Procession of the Palms and the congregation from House of Prayer Mission in attendance, almost defied orderly management.[1052] Even the introduction of a new *Prayer Book* in 1928, in sharp contrast to the anxiety associated with the previous edition in 1892, does not appear to have caused any disturbance in the parish. One thousand of the new books were purchased and placed in the pews in 1929 without any sign of the controversy heard elsewhere around the Episcopal Church.[1053]

Like the liturgical style in the Church, the operation of the Sunday School had remained quite constant through the early decades of the century. The only really notable trend was steady increase in the size and strength of the Christian Education program as a whole. In fact, during the successive rectorates of Robb White, Francis Brown, J.D. Wing and D.C. Wright the Sunday School came to enjoy the largest enrollments in its history.[1054] Steady growth in the Sunday School was reinforced by one very notable change in its manner of operation, which was introduced by Mr. Wright. Professional supervision was added to the traditional lay superintendancy. The big change came quite naturally when Mrs. T.P. Waring resigned after five years as "principal," or "superintendant," in May of 1924. The hope at the time was that Rita Griffeth (Mrs. James W.) would agree to take her place, but apparently the job had become too demanding for such a simple solution. Acceptance would have forced her to give up her position with the public schools. When the Rector learned that Mrs. Griffeth felt she could not afford to give up that income, he agreed to pay her an equal salary if she would devote full time to parish work.[1055] Agreement was no sooner reached than lost, however, as Mrs. Griffeth and her husband relocated to Asheville during the summer.[1056] Nevertheless, the idea was a good one, and when the Griffeths returned to Savannah the next year she was made "supervisor of the Sunday School" under Mrs. Waring.[1057]

When Mrs. Griffeth took charge of the Sunday School it was already in a healthy state — efficiently run and well attended. Classes were alive with lessons and projects which had been thoughtfully cast into terms the children could appreciate. That was one of the reasons the new parish church in Moultrie, Georgia, got its roof![1057.1] Classes were closely graded, also,

Details of altar lace.

which created a notable press for space.[1057.2] Perhaps that was why one of the boys classes found itself relegated (or banished?) to the "tower room," despite its dilapidated condition.[1057.3] One of Mrs. Griffeth's first major projects, after she began her full-time work, was to bring a "Passion Play" on film to the Savannah Theatre. This she did during the Lent of 1926, with the joint sponsorship of Christ Church and St. John's.[1057.4]

Little wonder is it that crowding in the Sunday School had been a matter of concern for years, at least since 1920, when the question of acquiring property near the Church was brought before the Vestry.[1057.5] The situation was improved a little when the ladies of the Parochial Aid Society decided to close their Colonial Lunch Room, at 9 Bay Street, West, for the season.[1057.6] A deal was struck with the Society for use of both space and the equipment since the ladies did not expect to reopen until the next tourist season would begin in October.[1057.7] Forced to search for space once more a year later, a lease was taken on property at 121½ Congress Street, East, (for $60 per month!) to serve as a Parish House and Community Center.[1057.8] It was there that the Rector was able to create a children's theatre on the ground floor, "fully equipped and properly appointed," through the gift of a friend, "not a member of the parish."[1057.9] Before long, however, Mr. Wright was looking forward to even greater things. To the congregational meeting in January of 1929, he predicted "that by 1933 we shall have at least a $100,000 Parish House, as we have outgrown our present facilities." This, he thought, would make the perfect gift for the parish's 200th anniversary.[1057.91]

The energy which gave the spark of life to the "Men of Christ Church" and the Sunday School proved equally invigorating to existing organizations in the parish. Under Mr. Wright's leadership, old and established groups dreamed new dreams and younger ones saw visions of new fields of service. Even defunct groups were occasionally blessed with capacity to serve anew. At least, so it was in 1924 when the inactive Ladies Missionary Society[1057.92] gave its remaining funds toward earthquake relief in Japan. True to their missionary cause the money was devoted to rebuilding St. Luke's Hospital, the cathedral, and various local churches damaged or destroyed by the disaster.[1058] More commonly, however, it is the high level of vitality among the active groups that strikes one as their minutes and reports are read. The choir, for example prospered under its new organist and choirmistress, Mrs. Addie May Jackson.[1059] The Church's only remaining mission, House of Prayer, also flourished, maintaining an active "industrial work school" and classes for adults in "home nursing," "canning and preservation," "domestic science," and the "sewing and remodeling" of garments.[1060] In addition there were 43 enrolled in the Tuesday sewing circle, and 40 at the kindergarten which met simultaneously. Another ten, 14-16 year old girls calling themselves the "Rinkie Dinks," met once a week for activities, as did the "Merry Makers," their older counterparts (16 and up), who staged a minstrel show in 1928.[1061]

The Women's Guild provides another example of how things worked under Dr. Wright.[1061.1] The Guild which was established at the same time as the refounded men's club in 1927, quickly organized itself into fourteen committees. They were devoted to assisting the Rector as requested, but especially to the housekeeping of the Church and Parish Home, Social Service, visitation, and fellowship.[1062] Meanwhile, the revitalized Women's Auxiliary busied itself sending bundles of clothing, "some made and some bought," to needy families in the Virginia mountains, and to making weekly visits to the Detention Home to mend worn clothing for the boys there. During Lent in 1927, for instance, they made 65 sets of underwear for them out of cloth furnished by the Chatham County Commissioners. As the Auxiliary's report points out, "This was no small achievement." (One can't help but speculate whether it was the success of their sewing or their politicking which pleased the ladies most.) When not mending or manufacturing garments for the boys, the Auxiliary was gathering a United Thank Offering and preparing for its annual December sale of "Kimonas, cakes, fancies, etc." or was occupied with collecting books and periodicals for the Marine Hospital, Seamen's Bethel, and ships in the harbor.[1063]

Youth work was another area which showed considerable vitality during the 1920's and '30's. The Young People's Service League had an impressive list of activities for 1927 which ranged from their work in the Junior Choir and as crucifiers to their participation in the Easter Pageant, the Feast of Lights, and a community play at Christmas. In addition to substituting as needed in the Church School and helping at the Vacation Bible School, they sought to provide any other services needed by the parish, "at the call of the Rector." Perhaps they were most active in the area of social service: making monthly visits to the Detention Home, distributing Thanksgiving baskets, providing milk to a poor family, candy and presents to "colored children at St. Simon's Island," Books to the DuBose School, and presents to children at the Dunlop School, in addition to the flowers and bathrobe they provided for an elderly man in the parish. With all this, there was still time to prepare their own weekly programs, lend a helping hand to a struggling YPSL in Waycross, send delegates to the "Joint Convention" in Augusta, and enjoy a boatride, a marshmallow roast, and a session at camp![1064]

Although the YPSL organization dates from c. 1924,[1065] youth groups of some description began in the parish at least a decade earlier when the "Girls Friendly Society," and the church sponsored Boy Scout Troop 11 first appeared in the records.[1066] Both groups are shown consistently in the annual reports of the parish through the 1920's and '30's, but at no period during their existence do they appear more successful than during Dr. Wright's first years as Rector. Those were the days in which the Scouts of Troop 11 performed such tasks as cutting the fronds used on Palm Sunday, working on projects to benefit the Community Chest, helping out at the State Fair and serving as the guard of honor for the celebration of Confederate Veterans. There were some tough assignments, too, as when the boys were asked to usher for the Benedictine vs. Savannah High football game in 1927. The true test of

The Church's exterior in the 1920's (2 photos) and the 1930's. (1 photo)

their character came the next year, however, when in addiiton to that traditional meeting of local rivals, they were conscripted to usher the Georgia-Florida game! To their credit, the 36 members of BSA Troop 11 handled the ordeal bravely; at least there is not a single surviving record of whining or complaining about their assignment. Meetings were often given some special point of interest for the boys, which must certainly have boosted attendance as it raised enthusiasm. For instance, one meeting in January of 1927 began when B.H. Levy, acting as standard-bearer, and guards Leo Wachtel and Jerry Eckstein took their places for the opening ceremonies. The Scoutmaster then gave a father-to-sons talk to the boys, after which they all marched to the *Morning News* building where "Mr. Jenkins explained how the papers were made!" Many of the boys had their names linotyped. At the end "Mr. Jenkins was given a class 'A' for showing us such a fine time."[1067] Under imaginative leadership, by scoutmaster Francis Dasher and assistants A.H. Stoddard and Hugh Stephens, and with strong support from other groups, the troop clearly had a winning combination. The boys seemed to realize it, too, which was why it really meant something when the top scout was awarded a $5 gold piece at the annual banquet, thanks to the "Men of Christ Church."[1068]

Another secret of their success was that there was always something in sight for the boys to anticipate with pleasure or to celebrate. In the summer of 1929, the big event was that three of the troop sailed for Birkenhead, England, to the Scouts' World Jamboree. Then in the autumn all of the boys enjoyed a trip to Jacksonville in an open truck for a visit to Troop 19 there. That was also the year brothers Ralph and Fenwick Jones both made Eagle Scout! No wonder that a Mothers' Auxiliary was needed to help look after all the details.[1068.1]

The girls had their turn, too, especially under the pioneering leadrship of Mrs. Juliette Gordon Low. Although a loyal member of the parish,[1069] the Girls Guides (Girl Scouts) group she founded, almost contemporaneously with the Girl's Friendly

Society in the Church, was centered around her home and not directly Church connected.[1070] Quickly enough, the girls grew into the women whose reports give such an impressive account of parish activities during the prosperous 1920's and the difficult 1930's. One of the more striking features of that story is the frequency with which new organizations sprang to life as a need was perceived. The Business Women's League (formed in 1921), the Crittenden Home Circle (1922), and the St. Barnabas Guild for Nurses (1928), along with many others, exemplify this vitality.[1071] Yet perhaps it requires still greater vigor and vision to do the apparent opposite — to continue in loyal service to one's cause long after the novelty has faded. In this category none could outshine the luster years had given to the Altar Guild and the Bishop Elliott Society. Both more than 50 years old by 1930, the latter group still faithfully carried on its task to "look after the poor of Christ church each month, helping the sick, giving wood, clothes, shoes . . . and many other things." The Society also supplied food baskets filled with "chicken, tea, coffee, sugar, grits, meal, and canned goods" where needed.[1072]

Such good works were even more in need as the great depression of the 1930's spread its paralysis into more and more homes. The effects were felt gradually, and as late as 1931 it was reported that Christ Church had about fifty of its younger members in colleges from Athens and Atlanta to Boston and New Haven, including Charlottesville, Chapel Hill, Nashville (Vanderbilt), Williamsburg (William and Mary), West Point, and at schools such as Ashley Hall in Charleston.[1073] By 1932, however, depression began to strangle the parish budget to the point that costs had to be cut wherever possible. The choir budget and the Rector's salary were cut along with dozens of other items.[1074] Significantly, only two items rose in the budget projected for 1933: interest on notes due the bank and insurance premiums![1075]

Despite this involuntary fiscal fast, Mr. Wright determined to interrupt the depression long enough to celebrate the parish's 200th anniversary properly. A bicentennial committee was appointed[1076] which for a year sifted, sorted, and refined ideas about how the occasion should be observed, and corresponded with prospective participants. Finally, plans were complete for this day which had been more than 73,000 days in the making. On Sunday, the 12th February, after holding early services in their own churches, all parishes were invited to unite at Christ Church in the celebration. Leading the way were Dr. Wright, Bishop Reese, senior Bishop Boyd Vincent (standing in for the Presiding Bishop), former rector John D. Wing (now Bishop of South Florida), and Bishop Mikell (of Atlanta), who delivered an historical sermon. An exuberant congregation sang of "The Church's One Foundation" to accompany the processional of six bishops, some twenty other clergy (five of whom were Black), and a numerous choir.[1077]

Crowds on that day of celebration were such that visitors could not be admitted. Even at the 5:00 P.M. commemorative service led by the Colonial Dames admission was by ticket

Details of needlepoint kneelers.

only. That service included the Rev. Gerrassimos (of St. Paul's Greek Orthodox Church), the Most Rev. M.J. Keyes (Bishop of the Roman Catholic Diocese of Savannah), and Rabbi George Solomon (of Mickve Israel),[1078] and heard the combined choirs of Christ Church and St. John's perform special music for the occasion. Then at the 8:15 P.M. evensong Bishop Vincent preached to the opening service of the diocesan convention. For this gathering special music was provided by the combined choirs of Christ, St. Paul's and St. Michael's Churches, but adding to the sense of celebration at all of the services was the cover of more than a dozen national and society flags hanging from the galleries and carried in procession.[1079]

The celebration was grand indeed, but alas not quite grand enough to dispel the clouds of depression all around it. Never had there been greater need for the charitable work of the Bishop Elliott Society than during this time. Their Thanksgiving baskets and "Christmas Feast" were more welcome than ever.[1080] Fortunately, other groups were on the job as well. The Daughters of the King did much the same kind of charitable work, albeit on a different circuit. Their work in 1934 concentrated on entertaining, sewing, or otherwise serving needs at the Seamen's Bethel, the Children's Home, the Abrahams Home, Hampstead Home, and helping out numerous individual families.[1081] The Daughters also worked with the Women's Guild to build "Wright Cottage" at Camp Reese on St. Simon's Island. The Guild itself was also active in charitable work, supplying needed food and medications through Savannah Family Welfare and working with such groups as the Chatham TB Association. Especially creative at raising money to carry on its work — and in 1933-34 fund raising for any cause required extraordinary inventiveness — the Guild tried everything from card parties to magazine subscriptions for the sake of its causes. Not surprisingly, its most successful money-raiser was a November oyster roast at Turner's Rock.[1082]

In these determined efforts to deal with the immediate problems of the day we can detect a new strength developing within the parish during 1934. It is manifest also in attempts to reach beyond the parish, for example to build Wright Cottage, but even more importantly in the creation of a new umbrella organization called the Women's Auxiliary. With the chairs of all women's organizations meeting together under one name, their intent was to broaden the vision of the Church's program and to generate interest and zeal in its causes through cooperation. But almost immediately the Auxiliary began to consider undertaking some entirely new projects, such as a "Tour of Homes, Old and New."[1083]

About the same period there was a new attempt to create a parish newspaper. How long it continued is unknown, but because it was expected to publish reports of various Church organizations from time to time they were not read, "as had been the custom", at the annual congregational meeting in 1934.[1084] The medium used made little difference in any case, for the news was universally bad. Dr. Wright worried aloud over the falling attendance and generally weak spirit in his congregation, the diocese, and the nation.[1085] Perhaps his own spirits were down, too, for even the few bright spots somehow served more to highlight the gloom than to provide hope. For example, although the Altar Guild could report 1935 to be "another splendid year, inspite of the depression," it did so because of "friends who have gardens supplying us with flowers for the altar when we had no memorials or money to buy . . . from the florist." Thank goodness, the Scouts stood by their tradition and presented "two Christmas trees to put on each side of the altar." One might have found cause for hope in the news that even though "some had to give up their memorials on account of the depression, others have taken [some] of the dates given up;"[1086] or in the other signs of life which were present, such as the founding of the Neighborhood Woman's Club (1934) and Christian Social Service (1935). But such little victories were no match for the pervasive mood of depression or the large deficit foreseen by the Rector in 1936. That was why he offered a plan to reduce his salary for the year ahead. The congregation rejected that idea on the spot; while they recognized the need for cost cutting *somewhere* they "resolved there should be no reduction" as he proposed.[1087]

Actually, there was more to worry about for the year ahead than their numbing fiscal paralysis. The Women's Auxiliary must have perceived some of that when it observed Armistice Day, 1935, with a special "Day of Prayer for Peace." The vigil took place shortly after Adolph Hitler instituted a program of universal military training, and preceded by only three months his marching troops into the Rhineland.[1088] Yet it was difficult to be world-minded when everything was so out of joint at home. Everywhere in the records we sense the general mood of gloom, approaching despair at times, which after so many years had spread far beyond merely economic categories. The situation became so worrisome during 1936 that the Vestry held a special session, without the Rector, at the office of Senior Warden J. Randolph Anderson. After taking note of Dr. Wright's profound discouragement at the state of the parish Mr. Anderson confessed his fear that unless the confidence and affection the congregation feels for the Rector were given some more tangible expression "we might lose him." All concurred and vowed to do anything needed to keep him, including approaching the congregation directly with a strong plea for better attendance.[1089]

Bishop Reese's death the next month, although not unexpected, further deepened their darkness. Yet just when things looked worst it was reported that the 1937 budget had been over-subscribed! Better still, the list included many *new* subscribers, and "several gentlemen had paid off the Church debt."[1090] It is amazing how quickly the outlook improved. The change was confirmed a few weeks later when Senior Warden J. Randolph Anderson offered a landmark resolution for his colleagues to consider. His plan was to combine several existing parish funds — one of the "Widows and Orphans of Deceased Clergy," the remainder of the Jane Young legacy, and a special reserve account — into a single parish endowment fund. This he felt was absolutely essential to the healthy survival of a downtown parish. The vestry agreed and adopted the plan unanimously, rewarding a decade or more of thinking, planning, hoping, and working toward that goal.[1091] Once

Top Left, Mrs. Waring recruiting a Sunday School class for the cause — a new roof for St. John's, Moultrie. Bottom left, could this have been part of the Sunday School children's effort to raise money for earthquake relief in Japan? Participants are, in the back row: unknown, Alice Mae Brown, Meredith Butler, and Constance Blun. In the second row: Barrett LeHardy, Mary Altstaetter, and Virginia Lawrence. In the front row are: Margaret Dasher, David Barrow, the next two unknown and Eunice Foss. (Thanks to Betty Peeples Brannen for the identifications.) Top right, these Wednesday afternoon "workshops" in the Church basement helped to prepare the children of the parish for work in the "five fields of service." That is Mrs. Griffeth with the girls' class. Bottom right, on Wednesday evenings the boys' workshop was held in the old Sunday School area beneath the Church.

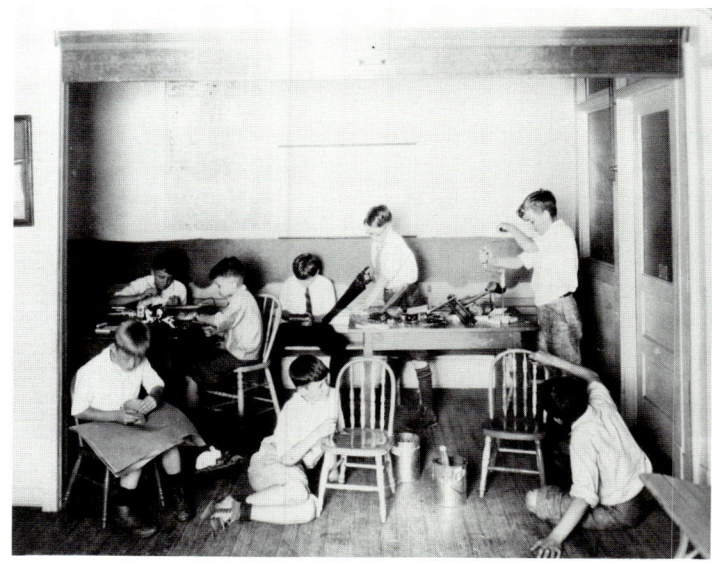

created the fund began to grow immediately, but it achieved its most sensational growth in 1942 with the addition of the Lynah legacy.[1092]

Economic recovery was dissappointingly short-lived, as the very next year the Every Member Canvass was *undersubscribed* by 35-40%![1093] This new and very sharp, downturn in the national economy brought some of the worst conditions of the entire depression. In the parish it forced major cuts in expenses which completely eliminanted paid choir members and summer fill-in clergy.[1094] Volunteers took up the slack, and when Dr. Wright returned from his vacation, in the autumn, he applauded the example and the "splendid work . . . done by Mr. Thomas Hilton, Jr., and Mr. Irvin Hulbert, Jr., as lay readers, and Miss Lucy Harms, as musician, for three months during the summer."[1095]

That year brought another shock, too, Mrs. Wright, the wife of the Rector, "in good health in the morning," died at home during the afternoon of 30 May 1938.[1096] Painful and unexpected as were her loss and the "second depression," the outlook of the parish remained positive and hopeful. The dour and beaten spirits of the earlier 1930's did not return. While nothing could repair Dr. Wright's personal loss, his spirits were lifted by the rapid fiscal recovery, which greatly brightened the outlook for the coming year, and having the largest confirmation class in his entire ministry.[1097]

It helped also that the men of the Church responded so well to his "earnest desire to organize in this parish a branch of the Laymen's League." Part of a broad national movement, the Christ Church chapter, in effect, was simply a reborn Men's Club. Under the leadership of Walter Nelson, Joseph Harrison, and Gawin Corbin, the 64 charter members set out to enlist "every man in the church a worker for the Church."[1098] It elated Dr. Wright that after such a low ebb only one year earlier, "both financially and in the work of the Church," an entirely different spirit had now appeared. Parish groups had become more active and productive, communicants topped 900 for the first time in the history of the parish, and attendance at Church had reached the highest level in his memory.[1099]

During 1939-40, before the joy of recovery was suffocated by the horror of a new war, good things continued to happen. Professional voices were once again insured for the choir,[1100] the Mary Lebey Cottage at the Episcopal Orphan's Home was dedicated by Bishop Barnwell,[1101] and the congregation celebrated Miss Phoebe Elliott's 50 years as a teacher in the Sunday School.[1102]

One of the most exciting topics of the day had to do with the prospects for acquiring a parish house. The excitement stemmed both from the fact that the idea had been contemplated for so long,[1103] and because the need was so great. In 1939 the search for a permanent location led to the Lucas Building (then under lease from Mr. Lucas) and to the Southern Bell property at Congress and Drayton Sts.[1104] But it was the structure commonly known as the "Cortez Cigar Co. Building," across Reynolds Square from the others, which was finally purchased in the autumn of 1940.[1105]

If the immediacy with which the building was put to use, and the zeal with which renovation activity was carried on are any indication, then the new acquisition was welcome indeed! Within days after purchase, Church meetings began to populate it. For one, the Laymen's League, held their first meeting in the new hall on the 10th of October. There they heard talks by their president, J.N. Glover, and the Rector verbally exploring the property and explaining the uses envisioned for the "commodious buildings." The four-story structure on Bryan Street was to be devoted mainly to classroom, office, and assembly spaces with the fourth floor remaining unused for the present, since the building lacked a passenger elevator. Its two-story mate on Bay Lane contained an ideal sewing room for the women of the parish and the neighborhood to carry on their "very necessary work," then led by a WPA instructress. In the tin building which connected the main structures, "the men decided to use their effort to equip a gymnasium." There was also room in it for a workshop where neighborhood boys and WPA instructors could continue their weekly lessons for apprentices.[1106]

By Thanksgiving, renovation work was well along, and the following March (1941), Lent or not, the new Parish House was dedicated. Bishop Barnwell joined all of the congregation for dinner in the "great room" on the second floor to celebrate the occasion. As toastmaster, Dr. Wright recalled how some had described the whole parish house project as "his baby." It went so far that one day he found a carton wrapped in silver paper waiting for him on his office desk. Opening it he found a doll, which he now displayed with a full explanation, amid much laughter. Always unable to pass up a good text, however, he pointed out that the "real parents" were the wardens, workers, and groups who had helped to bring the facility to this point, and those who were already working from it: the Altar Society, Bishop Elliott Society, Girl Scouts, Boy Scouts, Boys' Club, Missions Chapter, Sunday School, Laymen's League, etc. To top off the evening a grand tour was conducted through the entire building.[1107]

Revelling in this long-awaited victory Dr. Wright took time to enjoy three weeks of spiritual refreshment in study that summer at the Union Theological Seminary in New York.[1108] The time was well chosen, for events would not soon afford him such luxury again. The previous year had been replete with unmistakable signs of what was to come. Denmark, Norway, the Netherlands, and Belgium all were engulfed by Hitler's advancing tide, and headlines were filled with news of Dunkirk, the fall of France, and the Battle of Britain. News from eastern Europe and the Pacific was no better, as the great powers jockeyed for position and attitudes grew more brittle. It was during the very months that the deal on the Parish House was being closed and plans laid for its use, for example, that Britain was fighting for its life in the skies over London, Southampton, and the industrial cities of the Midlands.

Now, by the summer of 1941, darkness was closing rapidly when events in the parish took again a personal turn. Serious *angina pectoris* began to afflict the Rector, and his doctor advised that he "should not attempt to hold a service or preach

again."[1109] He was given one alternative to resignation, however; he might safely continue in his position with the help of an assistant "to relieve the nervous strain." Obviously, the choice would not be easy for anyone but Dr. Wright thought it best to place the question before the Vestry.[1110] That body overwhelmingly favored the assistant plan, yet a few days later the Rector resigned anyway — having concluded, or been persuaded, that he should do so.[1111] Two months later, however, he was still right there on the job presiding over the Vestry and planning for the annual meeting the following week.[1112] The next May (1942), when the Rev. Charles M. Snowden was called as assistant, Dr. Wright was *still* working, with no apparent plans to do otherwise.[1113]

By the time Mr. Snowden arrived, in July, the war had come to dominate every conversation. True, it was not really a new topic — the atmosphere and activity of war had been evident for some time. Even while the air over Britain was filled with Hitler's *Luftwaffe* each night, a year and a half before, the Men's Club had set up a hospitality committee to contact and welcome to Church the many soldiers around Savannah who were Episcopalians, and the ladies of the parish served supper to them.[1114] Then, at a convention of the Diocese, early in 1941, Bishop Barnwell prophetically lamented the "selfish nationalism" expressed in "Germany over all," "Britannia rules the waves," and "America first," which condemned us all to be "born in hatred and baptized in blood."[1115] And five weeks after Pearl Harbor, when the congregation gathered for its annual meeting in 1942, it was Dr. Wright who raised a prophetic finger to declare "the Church is asleep!" Ardently, he urged the parish not to repeat the mistakes of World War I, "when men who fought felt let down," as the nation rushed into prosperity after the war. Reminding his hearers of the sixty sons of Christ Church already serving in the military, Dr. Wright called not for emotionalism but for discipline — discipline now, "to keep the doctrine of Christ alive," and preparation of a plan for Church action after the war. Only in that way can we pay "on our debt to these boys for their sacrifice." Then, describing military training exercises, he called on parishioners to practice "spiritual setting up exercises" — blessing at meals, daily prayer, devotional reading, Sunday worship, and service through one of the groups of the Church.[1116] In effect, the Rector was urging his hearers to create an order in their lives, through self-discipline, which would help them maintain their bearings through this time when world events threatened to destroy all customary spiritual landmarks.

In addition to personal involvement through loved ones, glaring headlines, and occasional "brown outs," the war was felt most sharply at home in the scarcity of key commodities. Rationing of sugar, meat, gasoline and other essentials soon forced changes in ordinary life-style. Indeed, it was to lessen the impact of "the present situation in regard to gasoline and tires" that the parish inaugurated a "share the ride" policy. Then to implement it, the young people's division organized itself into the "Junior Commandos" and "volunteered to do the necessary telephoning and clerical work." The city and surrounding areas were divided zones so that they could efficiently arrange the needed rides and thereby facilitate "effective ministry and fellowship."[1117] Apparently the effort brought results. With the work of the "Commandos," and the streetcars and buses which carried others, the shortage of gas and tires caused no resignations of Sunday School teachers during the first year of all out war.[1118]

In the Social Service Department, several sewing groups carried on Red Cross work in Jane Wright House — one group alone doing between 300 and 400 garments. Another made garments and quilts from scraps furnished by the Red Cross. Despite the loss of the WPA cooks who ran the cooking school for mothers and furnished nutritional lunches for children in the summer, the Daughters of the King and other groups served himalayan mounds of "sandwiches, cakes, and candy to the men in service, at the parish house." They also made a speciality of preparing "embarkation kit bags" for men sailing out of the port of Savannah into war zones.[1119]

Juliette Gordon Low, Founder of the Girl Scouts, was baptized, married and buried at Christ Church. Here, troops of Girl Scouts enter the Church for her funeral in 1927.

The plaque commemorating Bishop Reese is located in the north aisle of the Church, near those of his Episcopal colleagues in the Diocese of Georgia.

The memorial tablet was put in place a year after the war's end, where it still reminds us of the thirteen sons of the parish who gave their lives.

Activities similar to these, related to the war and the special needs it created, continued through the next several years. The war itself was relentless in its demands as the daily headlines made apparent enough. One could almost suppose they were attempting systematically to exhaust the entire catalogue of bad news possibilities. Perhaps it was a need to think of something else, at least for a moment, that explains the refreshing break from wartime routine the parish enjoyed in the spring of 1943. So unusual was the occasion that labels to describe it suitably are a bit scarce. What does one call an event which combines an exhibit of rather loosely related historical memorabilia with an heirloom tea and childrens' carnival? The visitors enjoyed it in any case as they viewed "a vest of Napoleon," a bit of "sunglass brought to this country on the *Mayflower*," and a "coral stick-pin owned by the Empress Carlotta of Mexico," plus an assortment of christening gowns, snuff boxes, handwoven rugs, and "other cherished and valuable belongings of old Savannah houses." Especially featured at this mid-war "happening" were the heirloom dresses, "exhibited on living models," at the tea — the models being ladies of Christ Church. Judging from the press coverage, this last feature was surely the highlight of the whole event for it merited several paragraphs in the Sunday society column, "Nobody's Business."[1120]

The festive affair provided pleasant distraction from a war that was only then beginning to produce a few victories to brighten its long list of defeats. Costly triumphs at Guadalcanal and Stalingrad, in the weeks just prior to the event, had to share headlines with contests yet undecided in North Africa and the Aleutians. But not all of the combat took place on those distant fields and islands. A fray of another sort broke out in the parish when Dr. Wright again submitted his resignation in May of 1943. Having continued some 18 months after resigning the first time, he now proposed to retire from the active ministry — and really do it this time. His intention was to winter in Savannah and summer at his family home near Hendersonville, N.C. Everyone knew the parting would be painful — he was, after all, now in his 20th year as Rector. The young people of the diocese especially would miss him at Camp Reese, where his varied experience and personal style had long made him a favorite.[1121] Yet along with everything else, the last year and a half had at least given a little time for people, including Dr. Wright, to get used to the idea of his retirement and to accept the inevitable. Even so the Vestry accepted his decision "with regret."[1122]

As assistant Mr. Snowden also resigned, somewhat startled to find himself so suddenly without a job.[1123] Still the resignation was only a formality, he thought, and some action to retain his services would follow shortly. It didn't. The Vestry accepted his resignation, too, and that was when the battle began. It grew more strident through the spring and summer as Mr. Snowden rehearsed his irritation at this turn of events. Not only was the resignation, which he expected to be merely a formality, accepted, but even his claim for a vacation after 14 months on the job was rejected. He expressed his gross indignation in a letter to Senior Warden T.M. Johnson, which he vowed to read from the pulpit Sunday morning.[1124]

He was a good as his word. There is no record of the congregation's reaction, but in his own response the Senior Warden explained the Vestry's position. They felt that Mr. Snowden had actually forced Dr. Wright's resignation by raising tension against him and even going to the extreme of approaching them to complain of the Rector's methods.[1125] The parish as a whole may have felt much the same way, for when the smoke cleared it was Dr. Wright who was still on the job. Indeed, he continued to serve for still another year, into the autumn of 1944, when his labors were taken up by a series of temporary clergy — J.B. Walthour, C.H. Dickens, and B.T. Tyler.[1126]

The first of these, the Rev. J.B. Walthour, was the most likely successor to Dr. Wright. In fact, it was actually agreed that he should be called and Mr. Walthour, a son of the parish, wanted to accept. But there were many delicacies involved in arranging a separation from his position as Chaplain at West

From cigar factory to parish house! A plaque outside of the Parish House invites passersby to take note of the unique weathervane atop the building.

Point. The strategy adopted relied on the intercession of the Presiding Bishop to arrange that part, which was not an easy task in the midst of war. Instead of writing to Bishop Sherrill as planned, however, the letter from Bishop Barnwell's office was somehow misdirected to General Arnold, the Army's Chief of Chaplains. The necessary delicacies had not been observed. The mix-up effectively quashed the whole scheme,[1127] and forced the search committee to resume its work.[1128]

Although attention had been distracted for the moment, the war was still there — persistent and unforgiving. At least, by the autumn of 1944 it was going better, if "better" refers to the balance of victories vs. defeats. But with 136 stars on the parish service flag, including 4 gold ones, even "victory" had become difficult to define. Amid such a war, ministry became more important than definition, which was why the men's club made it a policy to designate one member as godfather to each parishioner in the service.[1129]

152

One of several services commemorating the 200th anniversary of Georgia and the parish.

The end result: the labor of a decade.

IX
An Era of Crisis: Race, Politics and Worship

The outlook continued to improve throughout the winter of 1944-45 so that, despite some setbacks, by early February of 1945 the outcome of the war no longer seemed in doubt — only the timetable. So confident was the mood, in fact, that Senior Warden T.M. Johnson had already appointed a committee on returning veterans "to advise and assist these men and women (Christ Church's 126 blue stars) in assuming their proper places in civilian life."[1130]

Adding bouyancy to the rising spirits of the day was the news from the search committee that they had persuaded the candidate of their choice to become Rector of the parish. Indeed, when the committee visited him in Washington, D.C., they were so impressed that he was right for Christ Church that they pooled their cash on the spot and bought rail tickets and reservations for him and his wife to insure their early visit to Savannah![1130a] Their instincts proved sound, as the Rev. Dr. Francis Bland Tucker had been well prepared by experience to serve a parish at war, but anxious for peace. His fifty years included an undergraduate degree at the University of Virginia (1914), two years in Kyoto, Japan, teaching English, and service with the AEF during World War I — in a French evacuation hospital near Verdun. Returning from France in 1918, he resumed studies at Virginia Theological Seminary which culminated in his ordination in 1920. Then came nearly 25 years of parish experience (20 of it at St. John's, Georgetown, District of Columbia,)[1131] and recognition through a Doctor of Divinity degree awarded to him in 1942 by his beloved seminary. Knowing only this much about him, the large congregation was especially pleased to hear his first sermon as he spoke of the great heritage of the parish and asked their prayers and cooperation in making the "future worthy of the past." No doubt they were also pleased to hear, as did a visiting journalist, "his strong voice and splendid delivery."[1132]

Dr. Tucker's style proved both winsome and salutary. He had a unique way of cutting through the smoke and haze that so often surround issues and moving directly to the point. Once he had clarified the matter, it might seem simple enough; anyone else could have done the same, . . . but usually didn't. For instance, when speaking on Confederate Memorial Day to a local Rotary group, he pointed out that the purpose of such an observance was "not to renew old bitterness." "We are not here to impugn the motives of the men who fought for the North, . . . rather it is for the lessons of devotion, of courage and endurance, of sacrifice that we look back to them." They help us to recognize the great value of "dedication of self to a cause greater than self."[1133] More often than not his comments on such an occasion would center on some aspect of the life and character of Robert E. Lee, or on the value of family. Interestingly, with all his practical insight and ability to speak persuasively to the public, even to a public which did not share his approach to life, Dr. Tucker was also a poet and scholar. He had served on the board of editors to revise the *Hymnal*, a few years before coming to Savannah, and in that function had made a number of notable contributions to the 1940 edition. Several of these texts were translations from Greek, and from classical or medieval Latin, while others were of his own composition.[1134]

If this appealing diversity had a secret additive that made all work together for good, surely it was his sense of humor. Not only did he use it to help others maintain their perspective on life, he did the same for himself. Thus, while he approached his calling and its labors very responsibly, he never took himself too seriously. Possibly this was a gift from his ancient Virginia ancestry, for he delighted to recall how his mother, Anna Maria Washington, frequently would introduce herself as "just a farmer's daughter." Only rarely would she go on to reveal that the "farm" was Mt. Vernon! In the same vein, when asked if he were related to Henry St. George Tucker, the former Presiding Bishop, Dr. Tucker's favorite response was "yes, . . . distantly . . .' Then with a twinkle he would add that Henry was the eldest and he youngest of 13 children in the family.[1134.a]

Perhaps it was his deep sense of his own humanity which, added to his other qualities, so endeared the new Rector to his parishioners and which expressed itself so naturally in countless forms of community service. Building on the parish's long tradition of service, for example, Dr. Tucker encouraged his flock to continue in that path in the firm belief that "service to the community is service to the Church."[1135] It is also why the Diocese of Western North Carolina found him so attractive as to elect him Bishop in 1948, and why he declined that honor because he felt there was still "much to do in his work here."[1136]

Certainly he was right in his judgment about the work to be done at Christ Church. The war brought many changes to American society and seemed to set the stage for even greater ones in its aftermath. Among the first issues to demand conscious attention after the war was race. Looking back, it is easy to see that in its long history the racial question had never stood still for long. It was no different in the 1930's either. Indeed, the issue of race had reached a very uncomfortable stage by the time World War II began. At the General Convention in 1940, for examle, Georgia's Bishop Barnwell was among those arguing for separate "Negro Missionary Districts" as a means to offer Black churchmen "opportunity" for expression and advancement, "not restriction".[1137] But years of desperate combat against Hitler's racial madness made it simply impossible to return to the American scene and look upon the old problem in the old way. The contradiction had become unacceptable, and with the Bishop's support Dr. Tucker led the movement to eliminate it in the Diocese of Georgia. Although a newcomer, it was he who made the motion at the 1946 convention to dissolve the separate "Council of Colored Churchmen," and give Black clergy and parishes full representation and privileges in the Diocese.[1138]

That was only the beginning, however, and slowly other signs of change appeared. Dr. Tucker also spearheaded the formation and became first president of a new and unsegregated organization of clergy in the city.[1140] But most of the process was anything but sensational and could not be cast in terms of unique events. It was just a long, slow, and often painful time of change for all concerned. As desegregation continued through the uneasy 1950's Dr. Tucker remained a prominent figure — sometimes representing and sometimes leading his congregation into the unknown.

Nationally his leadership was also recognized, when he was asked to chair the House of Deputies' sub-committee on race relations at the General Convention (1958),[1141] but it was on the local level that his "soothing presence" was most notably effective. That was the level on which controversies could grow like mushrooms, overnight, and where it was so easy to lose perspective on their significance. Typical was the anxiety raised over the "new Camp Reese," later known as Honey Creek, when it was being readied for use in 1958. The question arose as to whether the new facility would be run on a segregated basis, and it was decided that the parish's financial support should depend on the answer.[1142] Similarly, some of the congregation had difficulty with the fact that the local Council on Human Relations had been allowed to use the Parish House for its meetings and offered "severe criticism" to the Vestry.[1143] Understandably, views on race relations varied widely within the parish. Of itself, that is neither surprising nor necessarily unhealthy, but the situation certainly did offer its fair share of administrative challenges.

At the end of the decade the desegregation pilgrimage reached a particularly crucial stage, which at least one observer thought portended the "probable collapse of the state educational system." In his public comments Bishop Stuart alerted local churchmen to their responsibility both to work to keep the public schools open during the present crisis and to prepare to fill the gap that would be created should they close. It might even be, he speculated, that God "is calling us in this strange development . . . to resume a vocation and function we have surrendered too completely to the State."[1144] The Diocese had actually given some thought to founding an Episcopal school in 1955, when the public system first seemed threatened by the stir that followed the suit of *Brown v. Board of Education, Topeka*.[1145] It proved to be several years, however, before the implications of that case were felt sharply on the local level. But by 1960 the situation had grown so uncertain that the Vestry of Christ Church began making preparation to set up a day school should closure of the public schools become a reality.[1146]

That was the same year in which the desegregation movement took a new turn. During the summer teams of Black worshippers began "kneel-in" demonstrations, attending traditionally white churches to challenge the Sunday morning color line. Christ Church's turn began in August when Dr. Tucker was away on vacation and the Assistant Rector, the Rev. Thomas Hastings, was in charge. News of the visit was quickly communicated to the Rector who responded by requesting the Vestry "not to pass any resolution or take any action that would prevent the entry of any person into the house of God." Eliminating any doubt about the strength of his feeling in the matter, he added that "he would take a reduction in salary to offset any loss in pledges that might result from our taking this position."[1147] On returning from vacation the Rector commended all on the manner in which the demonstrations had been handled.[1148] Then seeking to place his earlier remarks in perspective, he counseled "I would not presume to examine the motive of anyone who wished to attend a service at Christ Church, . . . not even my own parishioners."[1149]

Eventually an uneasy calm settled over the community, but the doubt, fear, and impatience raised by desegregation would not be quickly dispelled. A process had begun whose course would have to be measured in decades, not in moments of resolution or pastoral advice alone. Attention again centered on Christ Church, for instance, eight years later when the Rev. Martin Luther King, Jr. was assassinated, and questions arose about services at the Church. By this time it was not the presence of a racially mixed congregation, but the crowds anticipated and the consequent potential for disorder and even violence that gave cause for concern.[1150]

The uneasy calm returned slowly, until it was broken again in 1971. That was when a major court decision on school desegregation set-off a decade of turmoil in the local educational structure and closure of the schools once again seemed a live possibility. Emergency plans were revived and Bishop Stuart, along with other leaders, exhorted the community not to lose sight of the goal of the plan — quality education for all — or the law of the land.[1151]

Another noteworthy milestone along the arduous road toward better relations between the races was passed a few years later, on 7 July 1980. On that day was celebrated the 230th anniversary of the baptism of a Black women in "Christ Church" — the first such baptism recorded in the history of the parish. To commemorate the event of 1750, twelve members of St. Matthew's and Mt. Bartholomew's congregations were prepared for baptism in Christ Church by the Rev. Charles L. Hoskins, their Rector, with the Rev. Thomason Newcomb (then Assistant Rector of Christ Church) assisting.[1151a]

Another area of significant change following the war was in the shape of the city itself. Automobile use became all but universal and Savannah followed the pattern of American cities generally by spreading far beyond its old confines to develop new neighborhoods at distances never before imagined. This trend raised the need for new churches and thus Christ Church's tradition of support for diocesan missions began a new chapter. St. Thomas, opened just prior to American entry into the war,[1152] was merely the first of a whole series of neighbohood missions which were begun in outlying areas with support from the parish. Organized effort began in earnest in January of 1949 when a new committee of the Diocese met in Christ Church to lay plans for a $75,000 missions fund campaign.[1153] Among the first expenditures in this new missions effort were funds derived from the sale of Christ Church's old St. Andrew's property, which went to make improvements in the Sunday School at St. Thomas.[1154] Through the next decade missions were also set out at Tybee,[1155] in the new southside where the Church of the Holy Apostles was begun,[1156] and even further south in Windsor Forest where St. George's was established.[1157]

Not surprisingly, such support for local missions did not emanate from a languid parish, but from one throbbing with vitality. Indeed, it was so filled with life and activity that Dr. Tucker soon found that he could not handle Sunday morning liturgical functions without help. To deal with the situation he requested Walter Nelson, a warden at the time, to take orders as a perpetual deacon.[1158] Then, spearheading an active neighborhood ministry were the Women of the Church who carried on several activities of particular value to the community. One of these was the Houston St. Nursery School which was then housed in the old Kate Baldwin Kindergarten Building. The Christ Church Guild had carried on this essential work since before the war when it was begun with WPA support to serve children living in the vicinity. After the WPA program closed down in 1943 other forms of federal and community support were found, but at times the ladies were forced to carry on alone. At the end of the war, however, it was still flourishing — caring for 35 children from 8:15 A.M. until 6:15 P.M., six days a week.[1159] Through the years the Nursery proved itself to be a durable good work. It has continued to serve the neighborhood and the parish has continued to support it.[1160]

The women of the parish also continued, and even expanded, the now traditional tour of homes, which in its first year after the war seemed to take on special sparkle. One factor heightening interest in the 1946 tour was the participation of a number of delegates to the International Monetary Conference then underway in the city. Proceeding by auto caravan to a dozen or more locations ranging from River Street to Wormsloe Gardens, the delegates especially were charmed by the hostesses in ante-bellum costumes who greeted visitors at each stop on the Tour.[1161]

Through the next four decades the annual spring Tour grew into one of the largest programs carried out by the Women of Christ Church. Yet even more impressive than the enormous amount of planning and volunteer labor required to execute the tour has been the women's creative use of the revenue generated — significant especially because it represents what is probably the greatest source of funds not previously assigned to meet some budgeted obligation.[1161a]

An equally successful enterprise of the Women's organization was preparation of a "Christ Church Cookbook" for publication in 1956. Surprisingly durable, this collection of local recipes is now in its sixth printing and continues to prove attractive to buyers nationwide.

Another vital ministry to the community was carried on through the "Boys Club of Christ Episcopal Church." Reorganized in the spring of 1946, it boasted a membership of 39 boys, largely from the Old Fort neighborhood. The Club opened each evening from 7 to 11 P.M., except Sundays, for ping pong, pool, and a variety of other games or just plain socializing, and it fielded its own baseball team in the city-wide Church League — the "Old Fort Sluggers." Typical of its social life was a dance held that first spring which featured crepe paper decorations, refreshments furnished by the mothers of the boys and parishioners, and music from a borrowed Victrola.[1162] The Men's Club, too, was active and frequently took direct interest in the activities and needs of the Boy's Club.[1163]

Elsewhere in the spectrum of parish life signs of real vitality were plentiful. Certainly, one thing that added to the sense of health and vigor was the fact that the Bishop maintained his Savannah offices in the Church during these post-war years, and continued to do so until the diocese obtained space in the renovated Trustees' Garden, in 1956.[1164] The Bishop's presence always added something extra whether he was merely keeping routine office hours or was here to join one of the parish's frequent guests for special services.[1165] But the same vibrancy and sense of expectation could also be felt by sitting in on a meeting of the Girls Friendly Society as they pressed their work with underprivileged girls in the city's poorer neighborhoods,[1166] or by hearing the report of the "Torch Bearers Club," formed to take young boys (aged 9-12) living downtown off the streets and interest them in athletics.[1167] It could also be sensed in the enthusiasm of Young People's Supervisor Harry Zeigler as he spoke about the idea of a "junior vestry."

The interior of the Church after the installation of the new organ in 1973.

Bishop Barnwell, too, is commemorated by a plaque in the Church's north aisle.

Another plaque commemorates Mr. Lynah's bequest of 1942 and the many projects it has facilitated since then.

The plan was intended "to prepare younger members of the Church for future participation in [its] activities."[1168]

Of special interest were the programs of the "Christ Church Experts." Under this title a series of public discussions were led by prominent Savannahians who were selected for their technical knowledge in topics of vital interest to the nation. The sessions, which aired such controversial issues as the Taft-Hartley and Wagner Acts, federal credit control, prepaid medical insurance, and universal military training, were organized by the Men's Club in response to a request for public debate made by President Truman[1169] A similarly ambitious attempt to minister to the broader needs of American society took the form of weekly radio programs dramatizing typical family problems. The Women of Christ Church joined with their counterparts in the other city parishes to sponsor the 13-week series which was intended to help listeners better cope with the difficulties of family life in the 1950's.[1170]

Sensational as were some of these undertakings, it should be noted that they were additions to the more usual forms of parish activity, not substitutes for it. One project particularly dear to Christ Church folks was the memorial to Bishop Walthour. Having been for many years a member of the parish and ordained a deacon here in 1931, the young Walthour attended college and seminary at the University of the South before becoming chaplain to the U.S. Military Academy at West Point. After the war he became Dean of St. Philip's Cathedral, Atlanta, and was later elected bishop of the diocese. Now, in the late 1950's the parish wished to celebrate his memory by donating the entry to the south aisle of All Saints Chapel at Sewanee.[1171]

Through these same middle decades of the century the musical side of things was not without a little sensation of its own. The organ's need of attention was certainly no surprise,[1172] but when it was discovered to be haunted by rats that was news! Fortunately, for all involved with the music of the Church, and for the organ, Orkin agreed to keep them out for $6.00 per month.[1173] With this problem overcome the musical life of the parish continued in the pattern established after the war, which usually included a major choral offering each spring in addition to the Christmas *Messiah*.[1174] Palm Sunday performances of standard works, for example DuBois' *Seven Last Words*, or new compositions such as *Gethsemane to Golgotha*, by H. Alexander Matthews, drew considerable attention from the community.[1175] There were also special musical events from time to time, some from very unexpected sources. For instance, during the Korean War years two enlisted men from the U.S. Marine Corps, one an organist and the other a tenor, were very well received for their recital of works by Handel, Brahms, Buxtehude, Bach, etc.[1176]

The same spirit which fostered this varied community ministry and the music also created the need for an additional service each Sunday morning. Set at 10:00 A.M., the new Service was begun in the autumn of 1952 and "filled a real need" in the Rector's opinion.[1177] This schedule of services, however, placed heavy demands on the lay readers and clergy who filled in for Dr. Tucker the next year when an extended illness kept him out of the pulpit for about ten months.[1178] When the Rector returned efforts were pressed to find an assistant who could carry some of the load. That search brought John L. Kelly to the parish early in 1954.[1179] The young assistant proved invaluable. Not only did he carry his assigned duties well, but he and a team of lay readers performed virtually all duties during a second major period of disability for the Rector, in 1955.[1180]

Happily, Mr. Kelly remained at his post for over three years, to the great satisfaction of all. Indeed, he was so successful that when he departed in 1957, to become headmaster of a boy's school in Tennessee, there was no question but that he must be replaced with another capable assistant. In fact, since Kelly's time the line of assistants has been virtually unbroken.[1181]

Certainly it was fortunate that good assistants and lay readers were both plentiful and willing,[1182] because activity of all sorts seemed to accelerate with each passing year during the 1950's and into the '60's. Not only did the parish continue to support long term community programs, such as the Kate Baldwin Nursery School,[1182a] but new needs were constantly emerging, too. One of these was the "surplus food program" of the federal government then under consideration by the Chatham County Commission. To study the question of local participation the commissioners appointed a committee with Dr. Tucker as chairman.[1182b] Then, in a particularly imaginative fund raising effort, the Women of Christ Church created a *Color Savannah* book for children. Plans called for it to be marketed through the "Factors' Fair," coordinated with the 1967 spring Tour of Homes. Best of all, the young artist who sketched the familiar Savannah scenes in the book asked only a hand-knitted ski sweater, ready "by Thanksgiving", as his fee![1182c]

Within the parish, no doubt the area most in need of major attention, because so long overdue, was building repair and modernization. Significant work had been all but impossible during the depression and war years,[1183] and little had been attempted during the years of post-war adjustment.[1184] Somehow, other projects always seemd to claim priority, but now several needs presented themselves with undeniable urgency. Thus, it was in the mid 1950's that momentum began to gather to deal with one of the most urgent needs: the parish house. Numerous plans to increase space through purchase, or alteration of the existing building, were considered.[1185] When the decision was finally made to add a new wing to the existing structure that left only one problem: where to find the estimated $165,000 to $170,000 needed with only $7000 in sight![1186] But the need was simply too great even for difficulties of that magnitude to block the project. One capital funds drive and one year later the "new" parish house was ready for use.[1187] On the 8th of May, 1955, the new "Tucker Building" was dedicated with special ceremonies and a most satisfying "house warming."[1188] The new facilities were put to the test, for the Sunday School was flourishing under Director Elizabeth Fuller (Mrs. Ford) and superintendent Monteith Capps, and it continued to do so after Frank S. Bryson, Jr., took over the superintendent's job in 1959.[1189]

With parish house modernization at last behind them the congregation could, with a clearer conscience, return to another long deferred ambition — to air condition the Church. This was finally accomplished during the spring and summer of 1955 to the great refreshment of worshipers,[1190] but that was soon outdone by a special project which drew considerable attention in the broader community. This was the creation of a chapel in the basement of the Church, dedicated to the memory of Raymond M. Demere.[1191] Built in the central area of the ground floor in space formerly used by the Sunday School, the new chapel was intended for small weddings and funerals, and to be open at all times for private meditation and prayer. Architect Edward V. Jones, of Albany, Ga., prepared plans, inspired by the Greek revival style of the Church itself, with Ionic columns arranged so as to highlight the central circular ceiling design. The chancel also was flanked by Ionic columns which were made compatible with the style of the altar and font — the "original" ones, removed from the Church after the 1897 fire. The floor was laid in Italian marble.[1192] When the chapel was dedicated, a year after it was begun, both Bishops Stuart and Barnwell were present and assisting, as was also the Rev. Charles Demere. Those attending the service heard Dr. Tucker liken the columns supporting the ceiling to the personal qualities of faith, ardor, and magnamity displayed by Mr. Demere himself.[1193]

Through the years that followed, several other repair and maintenance projects were undertaken, most of them routine, until by 1963 sentiment began to build for interior renovation of the Church itself.[1194] In the plan finally adopted, the most visible change was in the new pews. They looked much more like the original 1840 version than the elaborately carved scroll-top victorian seating they replaced — lacking only the entry doors. Yet in their classic simplicity and combination of natural mahogany with off-white painted surfaces it was thought that they would blend more suitably with the architecture of the Church.[1195] Final touches this time took the form of a memorial plaque honoring James Lynah, whose bequest many years earlier had made possible so much of the work on the building, and new slates on the porch of the Church.[1196]

Happily, most of this work was completed in time for a most unusual service in the spring of 1965: a quintuple ordination. Assisting Bishop Stuart at this unique event in the history of the Diocese was Bishop Henry I. Loutit (of South Florida), father of one of the five ordinands. In his sermon, Bishop Loutit reminded the new priests that their charge was to lead the Church "not to save itself, but to serve and save God's world!"[1197]

Collectively, the community service programs, Sunday School doings, and the construction and renovation projects, etc., represent a fairly normal assortment of parish activities. But the 1960's were in no way a normal decade! The era became one of high controversy, both within and outside the churches. Questions in great variety arose — something to suit every taste — from theological and liturgical to social and political. In 1962, for instance, concern was expressed by some at the swing toward "high churchmanship" which they feared was sweeping the Episcopal Church from the Diocese all the way to the national level.[1198] About the same time, Bishop Pike, of San Francisco, provoked a general furor with a number of widely read articles and letters on theological issues, which he published in the New York *Times* and *Christian Century.*[1199]

But such rumblings proved to be only the advanced signs of a greater storm approaching. Soon, controversy took a pew in Christ Church in the form of growing concern over actions of the National Council of Churches.[1200] By October of 1964 the Council's active involvement in political causes, such as advocating repeal of portions of the Taft-Hartley Act, brought the Vestry to be "of one mind" that the congregation needed some "explanation of our affiliation."[1201] Dr. Tucker, away in St. Louis attending General Convention, was contacted and made aware "that quite a lot of resentment is building up among very good and dedicated members of our congregation" over our affiliation with the N.C.C.[1202]

A Vestry committee, appointed to investigate, tried to put the matter in perspective in its report. While agreeing that Council thinking had "out-paced" that of its member bodies and that its recent actions had at times been "unwise" and "intemperate", and even "politically meddlesome," the committee also noted its many positive achievements. Specifically, they cited the Council's coordination of world wide missionary efforts, its work with displaced persons and food distribution to the world's hungry, and its fostering of such a significant scholarly achievement as the Revised Standard Version of the Bible, in addition to all of the obvious advantages of interchurch cooperation. The report also recalled for its readers that the General Convention, only a few days before, had formally scolded the N.C.C., urging that it "rid itself of . . . self-assumed encyclical authority [and] and resume its role as an active, . . . challenging Christian forum." As a final comfort to parishioners the committee then pointed out that although their irritation might be great, the problem was not — less than 1/1000 of the 1964 budget of the parish had gone to the N.C.C., only 7¢ out of every $100.[1203] Feeling that reform would best come from within, the report suggested that pressure applied through member churches would be the most effective means of recalling the Council to its "proper mission." Change came slower than desired, however, and the controversy remained active into the summer of 1965. At that point the Vestry, with the urging and support of many in the congregation, began to press for a resolution by the Executive Council of the Episcopal Church. The intent was to make a matter of record the displeasure felt by Episcopalians generally at the activities of the Council, and to suggest that withholding of funds would be considered unless change for the better were soon discernible.[1204]

The National Council of Churches was still a point of issue the following Winter, 1966. The convention of the Diocese of Georgia voted a resolution of support for the Council, but urged it to refrain from attempts to influence specific legislation, except regarding issues on which the Episcopal Church has taken a stand.[1205] Then, still attempting to come to grips with the slippery issue, the Men's Club invited the N.C.C.'s

Close-up views of the organ console and the seal of the Diocese.

163

The new "Tucker Building was dedicated in 1955 and soon put to good use!

Associate Executive director, Dr. Conrad Hoyer, to speak to its April meeting. It was a "pleasant meeting," but one filled with questions directed to Dr. Hoyer. Their urgency was driven home by St. John's recent withdrawal from the Diocese and the nearly coincident withdrawal of several local Presbyterian congregations from their denomination, partly over the N.C.C. issue.[1206]

As the N.C.C. furor slowly subsided, the distressing issue of St. John's Church increasingly commanded the attention of folks at Christ Church. Loss of this sister congregation was deeply painful, but as they had labored to bring St. John's into being 125 years before, they now worked for its return. Thus at the 1966 convention of the Diocese, it was Malcolm Bell, Jr., who introduced a motion designed to facilitate St. John's return;[1207] and Dr. Tucker was appointed to chair the committee created to maintain communicaiton with the congregation. Certainly Tucker diplomacy also had a great deal to do with the "real progress" reported by the committee the next year.[1208] But it was the reconciliation, effected in 1970 with St. John's return to the Diocese, which was the true reward for their effort. In September, the service of installation for the new Rector at St. John's featured special music by Dale Fleck, organist at Christ Church, and the combined choirs of Christ and First Baptist Churches.[1209]

Although everyone realized the time would have to come, few were prepared for it when the moment actually arrived, in the midst of the St. John's affair. Dr. Tucker reached the mandatory age of retirement. He tendered his resignation in February of 1967, although he agreed to stay on as "supply minister" until April "or such time as a new Rector is here."[1211] It was with "deep regret" that the Vestry accepted, but they gave the occasion a positive twist by initiating a scholarship fund in his name at Virginia Theological Seminary.[1212] They also offered him use of the York Street Rectory for life, since he planned to remain in the Parish after retirement. All of these things helped make the loss of the beloved Rector a little easier to cope with.

Suitable candidates to replace Dr. Tucker proved to be scarce, but after much searching a promising possibility was located at St. Andrew's Church, Marysville, Tennessee. Finally, in the first days of May, the Rev. Mr. Warren E. Haynes accepted the call and agreed to take up his duties during the summer. The new Rector expected to bring his wife, Paula, and three daughters from Marysville (near Knoxville) to Savannah in time for him to lead services on 2 July 1967. Meanwhile, the *Morning News* did what it could to acquaint the local public with the new arrivals. Mr. Haynes, they reported, had done his basic theological study at Vanderbilt University, then added some graduate work at the University of the South, Sewanee, Tennessee, before his ordination in 1956. He was also a Fellow of the College of Preachers at the National Cathedral, Washington, D.C.[1213] Knowing little more than this, the sense of expectancy in the Church grew as July approached. But it worked both ways. For his part, Mr. Haynes felt "humbled to have been called to follow so beloved and fine a man as Dr. Tucker and to become Rector of such a venerable parish." Then surveying the work ahead, he wrote

> *Ours is no small task. Our world is undergoing great change. People and nations face enormous problems. Our young are restless and seeking purpose for their lives. Our old are often forlorn. Despairing men walk the city streets. Each of us knows the growing question, "What is the meaning of it all?" In the Church itself, there are ferment and confusion.*
>
> *I wish that I had the answers to these immense problems facing us in the Body of Christ. I do not. I do believe that this is the world God made, the world God loves, the world into which God came to be with us, and the world in which "God is working His purpose out." My only credentials are a desire to know and do the will of this God, and a faith in the lordship of Christ, His Son.*[1214]

The Haynes' arrival on the first of July finally relieved Dr. Tucker and Mr. Dawson Teague, who had also carried many

pastoral duties through the spring, of their nearly full-time responsibilities. It also freed Mr. Teague to return to his education,[1215] and Dr. Tucker to begin at least semi-retirement. Now that he was fully in charge, one of Mr. Haynes' first jobs was to find a replacement for organist and choirmistress Mrs. Addie Mae Jackson. That was not destined to be an easy task, for she had served more than 41 years in what the Rector described as "truly a ministry in the name of Christ."[1216] After much searching, however, replacements were found in the persons of Conrad C. Morgan and his associate, Dale Fleck. The two had worked together in Lincoln, Nebraska, in a large Presbyterian congregation, and Mr. Morgan presented an impressive resume which featured music degrees from the University of Colorado and advanced study in Europe.[1217]

Another early duty of Mr. Haynes was to lead the congregation through the year of "trial use" — the first public step in the development of a revised Prayer Book.[1218] The new Eucharistic rite was introduced to the Diocese at the Thanksgiving Day service in Christ Church, 1967, with Bishop Stuart as celebrant. A few days earlier the Bishop had alerted the women of the parish that "you have to be on your toes.... We are doing this service together. It is demonstrative of the corporate pattern of the whole Church." When the Rector was asked, as frequently he was, "Why change?" his response was twofold. "The faith never changes," he said, but "in each age the Church seeks to express its ancient and changless faith in terms which can be understood."[1219] As Thanksgiving Day drew near, the article announcing the forthcoming service found it worthy of note that the Epistle would be read from the lectern, "in front of the altar rail," and the Gospel from the "ornate brass pulpit, which is also forward in the nave."[1220] As happens so often in human affairs, what is most noteworthy now is what *they* found noteworthy then! Finally, as the year of "trial" neared its end, the Rector placed a little note in the Sunday bulletin which was designed to put the controversy it generated into perspective. Under the headline "New Service Arouses Opposition" appeared the following quotation.

WhitSunday came, the new liturgy was used in the churches. Although my own part in it was only that of translator and editor, I could not help exulting over the accomplishment. My self-congratulation was short-lived. The first reports I had of the [new prayer] book's reception were disturbing and as the week went on the news became worse and worse. The dissatisfied were not content to protest, they turned to violence. A priest in Devon was surrounded by his congregation carrying pitchforks and scythes and compelled under threat of personal injury to revert to the old liturgy. Armed revolt spread quickly through the western counties, and, while hasty preparations were made to deal with it, similar outbreaks followed in places as far as York and Norfolk.[1221]

Only at the end did readers learn that the words were from the 1549 diary of Thomas Cramer, Archbishop of Canterbury. They were written about events surrounding introduction of the first *Book of Common Prayer* in the English language. The Rector might have gone on to point out that after using the new book only a few years, people went to the stake rather than give it up!

Meanwhile, despite the storm, the ship of the Church continued to make good headway along the traditional course of parish work. Perhaps the best reading of its direction at the time is to be had by sitting in at the annual meeting of January 1968, Mr. Haynes' first as Rector. That meeting, as it turned out, virtually wrote the agenda for Warren Haynes' years at Christ Church. Participants discussed the possibility of redoing the undercroft, sponsoring a housing project for senior citizens, engagement of Jeanne Garlington (Mrs. Henry F.) as the new Director of Religious Education to replace Libby Fuller, and designation of laymen to administer the chalice — the Rector having expressed his wish to have two for each Sunday service. Over-reaching all was their effort to assess anew the general situation and mission of a downtown parish.[1222]

Work on the undercroft project began immediately. Ultimately, partitions were rearranged, ceilings lowered, and lavatory facilities modernized in the effort to create new usable space in the ground floor of the church building. After more than two years of planning and labor the undercroft was at last ready for use during the Spring of 1970. Although some work had yet to be done it was soon obvious that the effort had been worthwhile, for the new space was devoted to kitchen and reception areas as well as vesting and choir rooms.[1223] Even while the undercroft modification was underway a number of additional physical changes were made around the Church as well. Although none were on a like scale, several were highly visible. For instance, this is when the handsome ancient weathervane was brought by Lester Karow from General Oglethorpe's Church in Cranham, Essex, and placed atop the parish house, and when the Bishop's chair was removed to the Parish House from the chancel in the Church where it had resided for 80 years.[1224] It was also when the Washington Avenue rectory was purchased, and when the bronze plaque which repeats the information on the corner stone of the 1803 Church was placed on the West porch where readers could see it.[1225]

So well did Mr. Haynes gain the confidence of his flock during his first two years as Rector, that when Bishop Stuart asked the Diocese to elect a co-adjutor in 1969 the parish delegation was instructed to vote for him so long as his candidacy appeared hopeful.[1226] When the Rev. George Paul Reeves was elected instead, Mr. Haynes quickly sent to the Bishop-elect a very warm invitation offering Christ Church as the site for his consecration.[1227] It was astonishingly effective. Not only did Mr. Reeves accept, but so did eighteen other bishops who joined in his consecration on the 30th of September 1969.

The procession passing through Reynolds Square, on its way to the Church from the parish house, was more than 200

A typical Sunday morning procession in the mid 1950's with Dr. Tucker and Mr. Kelly bringing up the rear.

strong! Included were lay and clerical representatives of the Diocese and all its parishes, both local college presidents, the mayor, chairman of the county commission, and a rainbow of clergy representing denominations from Greek Orthodox and Roman Catholic to the further end of the Protestant spectrum. The whole impressive company was led by the Rector, who acted as Master of Ceremonies. Inside the Church nearly a thousand had gathered, filling every inch of space, as a multi-parish choir was led by Mr. Morgan and the Rt. Rev. Stephen Bayne preached on "Faith-Not Formulas."[1228]

In the parish, the level of activity had now reached the point where it was time to think once again about hiring an assistant to the Rector. January, 1970, marked the 50th anniversary of Dr. Tucker's ordination and, in his mid-70's, he was beginning to slow down . . . a little, but still anxious to be helpful without appearing to peek over Mr. Haynes' shoulder.[1229] The search brought young Mr. James P. Nichols, Jr., to be the new assistant beginning in July 1970,[1230] and he soon became much involved in the youth and community ministries that had so often engaged the parish in the past. In fact, it was his active work along these lines, especially in generating plans for the Mayor's Youth Council, that explains one of the unusual features of his ordination a year later. One of the three lessons in the service was read by Mayor John Rousakis.[1231] It was also the first ordination service in Savannah celebrated according to the "trial use." Only two weeks after that, Mr. Nichols left to assume a position at St. Bartholomew's, White Plains, N.Y., and an old friend of the parish, the Rev. Dawson Teague, filled in for the summer.[1232] By autumn, however, Mr. Clifford Pike was on hand to take up the task.[1233]

Also during 1970-71, the parish was visited by a team from the National Episcopal Church. Their report was discussed at the annual meeting of the parish, in January, 1971, where the Rector indicated he would appoint a committee to review and respond to their observations. Actually, neither the visitors' points nor the committee's evaluation of them offered any surprises, for they were the same ones that most parishes would raise of themselves in moments of self-examination. There were the expected appeals for renewed leadership in the community and well aimed community programs, reproof for low stewardship and weak adult education, plus suggestions regarding the need for lay evangelism, etc. Out of it all, came a new Parish Planning Committee[1234] and a fresh examination of the proper mission of the church. The simple act of thinking through the question of purpose, not simple at all, of course, may actually have proven helpful. For the process produced a solid statement — perhaps a predictable one — that the mission of

Christ Church is to proclaim the Gospel of Jesus Christ to all men, to be a guide for those within the Church to enable them to lead a more Christian life, to spread the Christian faith to those within the community beyond the parish membership, and to act as an institution to carry out Christian work within the community to all in need.[1235]

Once the parish had placed its priorities in clearer perspective, a number of other points seemed to follow inescapably, points which reveal a great deal about what had been troubling both Rector and congregation. For instance, the same meeting at which the Vestry adopted the statement of purpose also saw passed resolutions that they would discuss actions of the national and diocesan leadership of the Episcopal Church when either take positions contrary to

> *What we believe are in the best interest of our Church. If either goes against what we feel are the wishes of the great majority of our congregation, the Vestry will review the amount given by Christ Church to the Diocese and the National Church, and should that amount be reduced, the same amount will be given to other programs selected by the Vestry.*[1236]

It is easier to see now that the parish, like the nation, was passing through what may well have been the most distressing internal crisis of this century. Indeed, not for a hundred years — since the 1860's — had our society been so beset with doubt and distrust, albeit for somewhat different reasons this time. True, we have had problems in the 20th century, war and depression aplenty; but nearly all Americans were on the same side then, working for a common cause. But it was not so in the 1960's and 1970's. Households of every sort were divided — familial, social, corporate, political. Rank and file distrusted leadership, and leaders replied with scorn. And as it was in the nation, torn by controversy over Vietnam and scandal in Washington, so it was in the Church and in relationships of every kind, where little Vietnams and Watergates bedeviled all. It was a time of troubles and of great unpleasantness, there being no easy cure for mistrust. A bold step toward rebuilding was taken by Mr. Haynes when he arranged "A Weekend with the Presiding Bishop" and encouraged members of the congregation — "however they polarized over Mr. Hines' tenure as head of the Church" — to use this opportunity to talk with him.[1237]

More specific local concerns were voiced over the condition of the Church's youth program, which some felt compared unfavorably to others,[1238] and over the rising use of drugs and the parish's role in dealing with the problem.[1239] But whatever doubts were held about the Church's national leadership, there was never doubt that community ministry was an essential part of parish life. In the Tour of Homes in 1972, for example, leaders recognized that the enterprise had become "a cooperative community endeavor" and that "Christ Church has a feeling of responsibility" that all funds raised should "go back out into the community" with none spent for projects within the parish.[1240] This was altogether in keeping with the parish's established record of involvement in such projects as the Inner-City Mission, begun in 1969 by the Episcopal Order of the Holy Cross, the Savannah Nursery School, and the work of the Association for Children with Severe Learning Disabilities, Inc.[1241] That ministry carried also into the realm of the elderly in 1972, in a special effort to involve them more fully in the life of the parish.[1242]

Very normal, too, was the fact that the aging 1920 Austin organ was fast approaching the point of no repair. Suspecting the high, and probably uncontrollable, cost of rebuilding and maintaining the relic, the Vestry agreed to hear a proposal by Mr. Harrison.[1243] Clearly they were impressed with his proposal and with the fact that his bid was "by far the lowest."[1244] Shortly thereafter the deal must have been sealed, for all subsequent documents point to fears of rising costs and lengthening timetables.[1245]

Excitement grew as crates full of organ parts began arriving in the autumn of 1972 and the new pipes were stacked in the galleries to await installation. The next few months only added to the suspense. Choir and organ console were relocated to the west gallery, after nearly 70 years in the east end of the Church, and carpets were peeled back to improve sound.[1246] Also, about the time organ pipes began arriving from England so did the Rev. Mr. Harold Loasby. Despite appearances, he was here to look after the parish, not the pipes, while the Rector was in England.[1247] The Rector returned in time for the opening service in December, however, when the unfinished organ was first heard publicly.[1248] Grand as the occasion was, it was only a sample of what was to come.

The real climax occurred two months later, Sunday, the 4th of February 1973. On that day the Right Reverend Bishop of London, Robert Stopford, visited the parish to lead the grand celebration dedicating the new organ and simultaneously closing the convention which marked the 150th anniversary of the Diocese and the 240th of the parish.[1249] Then in the spring, this season of triumph was topped off with a sparkling concert on the 25th of April by the renowned organist, E. Power Biggs.[1250]

Amid all the excitement over the organ project a very important change had taken place with little notice and no furor. Having sent its first woman delegate to the Diocesan Convention a few years before,[1251] Christ Church elected its first woman to the Vestry in 1972.[1252] After her first year on the job, Eleanor Ormond (Mrs. Alex C.) recalled how, according to pleasant custom, the entire Vestry stood as she arrived at each meeting. More comfortable after her presence became less noteworthy, Mrs. Ormond declined such faddish touches as "Vestryperson" and seemed content just to be one of the board.[1253] When her three year term expired, in 1975, she was succeeded by Ashby Angell (Mrs. John H.) and she by other who soon came to represent a customary presence on the Vestry.[1254] Within a decade, election of women to the Vestry became so routine as to attract no special attention, even when their number approached 50% of the total.[1255]

The echo of celebration over the organ had hardly died away when events took such a surprising turn that many were shocked — just when life in the parish seemed once again restored to wholeness. In what appeared to be a sudden action, the Vestry dismissed the director of music and moved immediately to seek a replacement.[1256] Petitions, pleas, and appeals for reconsideration notwithstanding, the Vestry stood its ground and the Rector concurred.[1257] Although the specific substance of the dispute remained buried in obscurity, the distress engendered did not.

The same Vestry meeting which declined to act further regarding the musicians also received the news that the Rector had accepted a call to Calvary Church in Memphis. One month later Mr. Haynes left the parish in charge of the Assistant Rector, the Rev. Clifford Pike,[1258] who carried on through October and November, remaining long enough for the new Rector to become established in the parish.

The Rev. George M. Maxwell came to Christ Church from Sumter, South Carolina, where he had been heavily involved in community activities as Rector of the Church of the Holy Comforter since 1968.[1259] He arrived in time to preside at services for the first Sunday in Advent, 1973, and almost overnight his distinctive style became apparent as the parish moved rapidly into its 25th decade. Within two weeks he had made notable progress in procuring a new organist-choirmaster, and also moved to revise the schedule of Sunday services by increasing the frequency of Eucharistic celebration to the first and third Sundays each month. The latter change coincided with the Bishop's request that the "Green Book" be used in the parishes of the Diocese from January to May, 1974.[1260] The next month he proposed action on two additional matters of fundamental importance. One proposal would set a committee of the Vestry working on the constitution and by-laws of the parish, on the supposition of "there having been no revision of these, probably, in this century."[1261] The second, which suggested that the presidents of the Women of the Church and the EYC be given seats on the Vestry — voice without vote — received immediate and favorable action.[1262]

While still settling in as Rector, Mr. Maxwell turned serious attention to the necessary business of assembling a new staff. First to be added was the Rev. Jerome Meachen, a perpetual deacon who was called from Sarasota, Florida, to serve as assistant to the Rector, as well as organist and choirmaster.[1263] "Jerry" officially took over musical leadership of the parish in early February, 1974, almost in time to be late for his first special assignment, which was to help install Mr. Maxwell officially as the new Rector, on the 17th![1264]

The special quality that Mr. Meachen brought to the parish was his rare determination to offer music in liturgical perspective. Music was never allowed to dominate or presented simply as a "performance," either in the context of worship or even when it might be the major feature of a special celebration.[1265] This remained the case even after use of a variety of musical instruments in services became common in the later 1970's. At that time a small instrumental bay was created in the north gallery to accommodate a harpsichord, instrumentalists who support the weekly Eucharists of the 9:00 A.M. service (usually with guitars and recorders), and occasional brass or string ensembles.[1265a]

Another addition to the clerical staff was the Rev. Ralph Byrd, who came to Christ Church from St. Phillip's, Charleston, during the summer of 1974.[1266] Finally, Miss Mary Regina Puckett was hired to replace the retiring Jeanne Garlington as

Restoring the ceiling, what a mess!

Looking into Johnson Square from the portico of the Church.

Director of Religious Education. Although ordained a deacon a few days before assuming her post at Christ Church, it was agreed that the Rev. Miss Puckett would have "no liturgical function at this time."[1267] Like the Rector himself, and others he had gathered, "Gina" was concerned "to see her Church more and more committed to the community."[1268]

Innovations in liturgical style were generally introduced at a moderate pace, in part perhaps because the "Green Book" provided conversation enough through the spring and summer of Mr. Maxwell's first year. By autumn, however, the Rector was ready to seek further enrichment of the parish's liturgical life and gained Vestry agreement to purchase a Paschal candlestick for use the next Easter season.[1269] Next, the decision was made to restore baptisms to the context of Sunday morning worship where, according to the ancient custom of the Church, the congregation could do its part by accepting a share of responsibility for these new members of the Body.[1270] There were indeed many changes, yet it was certainly not the case that everything the Rector suggested was adopted without question — not at all. Some proposals for liturgical change were tabled, while others, such as the use of young women as acolytes, were postponed indefinitely — until a clearer view could be had of the issues involved and of parish opinion about them.[1272] Then on some occasions the Rector simply abandoned his point and acceded to the wishes of the congregation.[1273] Yet through it all, the many innovations did not seem to disturb parish style so much as they marked the stages of its growth. The Maxwell style proved to be firm, decisive, and reassuring. For most it provided an effective antedote to the disturbances of the years just past and the upsetting events coincident with Mr. Haynes' departure. This was so despite continuing discomfort with the "Green Book" and growing apprehension that use of the *Book of Common Prayer* (1928) might soon be lost.[1274]

Significantly, Miss Puckett's arrival in the parish had coincided with the rising controversy over ordination of women in the Episcopal Church. Only months before she came, the

Women of the Church had sponsored a debate on the topic,[1275] which was destined to continue for years to come. Two years of rising "interest" in the question culminated in a visit by the Presiding Bishop, the Most Reverend John Allin, who was here to speak to the Diocesan Convention, in an attempt to help all gain clearer perspective the matter.[1276] The following autumn, the issue again arose at the Church's triennial convention in Minneapolis, where women's ordination was approved by a narrow margin. Even the Archbishop of Canterbury became involved when he arrived at the tense gathering there and spoke in favor of the change.[1277] But the action at Minneapolis did not fully settle the issue. In Georgia, Bishop Reeves adopted a "wait and see" stance for the Diocese, although he made no secret of his own views on the questions.[1278] "In my opinion," he told the next convention of the Diocese, "the provision for the ordination of women probably was the most serious single mistake the Episcopal Church has made in the nearly 200 years of its history."[1279]

At the peak of the controversy the Rev. Miss Puckett left Christ Church to become associate minister at a church in Vancouver, B.C., where she could be involved in the liturgical action of the parish.[1280] Her work in the Sunday School was missed, of course, and the Vestry commended her for it,[1281] but her major impact on the parish may well have been of another sort entirely. While she never became openly involved in the controversy over ordination of women, for many she became the one thing they knew for certain amid a storm that obscured most other points of reference. Her effective work and calm, sunny, devoted style seemed to bring reassurance to many that, whatever else, nothing subversive was happening. It may even be that her example was in part responsible for the rather quiet acceptance, several years later, of two Christ Church women as postulants for the diaconate.[1282]

One more feature of Mr. Maxwell's impact on Christ Church which should be noted is the greatly increased use of lay readers. Although certainly not new to the parish — lay readers had been used extensively at several periods in its history — their visibility and numbers had considerably declined during the controversial years of the 1960's. With Mr. Maxwell in charge, however, that trend was reversed. First signs of the change appeared only a few weeks after he arrived in the parish, with announcement of a meeting to which all former and prospective lay readers were invited.[1283] The movement developed rapidly and achieved solid form when the first readers began service on the Sunday after Easter, 1974.[1284] In 1980, the Rector announced that a number of women would soon be training to be used as lay readers at the 9:00 A.M. service. Although some concern was voiced at this innovation, it does not appear to have been deep-rooted, for within a short while women had become an important part of the parish's corps of lay readers.[1285]

A more rigorous test of leadership began in the autumn of 1976 when plans were first laid to commence regular use of the Proposed *Book of Common Prayer*. Actually, the timetable did not call for introduction of the new rites until October of 1977, one year hence, but in the meantime there was much to do. The proposed version of the Prayer book had to be ordered,[1286] and a series of events were scheduled to introduce the congregation to its arrangement and use.[1287] Most clergy had to wait until the Diocesan Convention (1977) to get their first look at the proposed Book.[1288] At the time, Bishop Reeves expressed his full support and even relief at the publication of the new book. He commended its content and flexibility, and especially its inclusion of "forms that many of us previously had to borrow from unauthorized sources." Finally, in the autumn of 1977, the proposed *Book of Common Prayer* appeared in the pews of Christ Church, and with that began another year of exploration, instruction, and misgivings.[1289]

It is fair to say that the pleasure felt by Bishop Reeves at the sight of the new Prayer book was not shared universally. What delighted him produced apprehension in others. Few on either side remembered, as did Dr. Tucker, the anxiety that accompanied introduction of the 1928 book or the furor that surrounded its predecessor in 1892.[1290] After a year of trial use, opinion within the parish was divided, but the majority polled favored the old (1928) Prayer book.[1291] For that reason it was decided to retain the use of both versions, at least until the General Convention might decree otherwise. Meanwhile, to minimize the impact of division, the Rector urged all of the Vestry to read I Corinthians 12-14. Further, "he cautioned those present that the leadership of the Vestry and clergy in the coming year will determine whether the Church becomes a divided body or one body of diverse opinions."[1292]

Some of the explosive potential of the issue was diffused when the General Convention not only approved the new Prayer book but authorized continued use of texts (including entire services) from the 1928 version as well. One day it may be more obvious than it is now that both sides in the controversy perhaps overestimated the powers of the "Book". Those who viewed it negatively seemed to credit the new Prayer Book with being the source, or at least the symptom, of all the church's troubles and controversies over the past two decades. Thus, they scorned it and sought to avoid any contact, in the hope that this too would pass.[1293] Advocates, on the other hand, looked at the same book and saw in it the Church's salvation from many of those same troubles. But expectations so great were also vulnerable. Thus, it was with disappointment that Bishop Reeves observed, a few years later, that what began as reform and revitalization had in some cases become little more than "orchestrated camaraderie."[1294] Presumably, the Bishop was referring, to the "passing of the peace," which the new prayer book restored after centuries of disuse. It is a tragic irony that the very liturgical act to which he alluded with evident disappointment remains the primary stumbling-block for many parishioners who dislike the new book. As for Christ Church, the approach taken followed the traditional Anglican way, and the example of the General Convention. The parish chose to embrace diversity and continue the use of both books.[1295]

Fortunately, there were numerous aspects of parish life which were noncontroversial during these years. Under the combined leadership of the Rev. Ralph Byrd, the Rev. Regina

Puckett, and Jeanne Garlington, youth activities flourished. The calendar seemed filled with "hungerthons" to dramatize the food distribution problem and raise money for world relief, retreats, and backpacking trips in North Carolina, Lenten dramas, and Shrove Tuesday Pancake Suppers.[1296] When most of this leadership team moved to other positions in 1977 and were replaced by Emmeline Cooper (Mrs. Robert S.), as lay assistant, and the Rev. Thomason Newcomb as assistant Rector,[1297] the pace of activity never slackened. Only the character of it changed a bit to reflect the new personalities involved. Now the schedule sparkled with monthly "Sundae Mondays" (featuring ice cream and singing) in the undercroft,[1298] "Advent Events," a "Merry Berry Ice Cream Outing" at Point Pleasant, and "Wonderful Weeks in August", held for children during their late summer doldrums. Then, for the parish as a whole there were annual "birthday" oyster roasts, plus an assortment of other parties and picnics designed to bring the entire body together.[1299] These were all in addition to the normal retreats and quiet days, the continued Shrove Tuesday Suppers, and the enduring concern with hunger — both in the community and world-wide.[1300]

Influencing both Sunday School activities and popular perception of the liturgical changes of the late 1970's was another side of the "renewal movement."[1300a] Liturgical renewal, as we have seen, had been a topic of conversation and controversy for at least a decade as the Episcopal Church slowly worked its way toward introduction of a new *Prayer Book*. But now new forces emerging within the parish complicated the chronic anxiety over liturgical matters and provoked the Rector to take action. His course was to renew the search begun by his predecessor for ways to divert into productive channels the energy stirred up by this era of controversy. That energy had been too often dissipated fruitlessly in recent years, and to aid in harnessing it he sought, as did Mr. Haynes, opinion of a parish planning consultant.[1301]

Whether by cause or coincidence, things began to happen almost instantly![1302] The parish newspaper was revived, for instance, and under the editorial hand of Regina Puckett, the first issue of *Columns* appeared in May of 1976[1303] Interestingly, that first number also contained an extensive article by the Rector on the many facets of the renewal movement as it was developing in the Episcopal Church. Among his most notable points was the rather startling observation that, contrary to much of Anglican tradition, the great emphasis of the movement was evangelical: that is, rather than assuming "conversion" among churchmen, the renewal movement presumed the need of it.[1304]

Simultaneously, a Renewal Committee was created which immediately began making plans for a future preaching mission[1305] and parish involvement in the Diocese's first "Cursillo," which was being introduced by Bishop Reeves.[1306] A dozen parishioners participated in that first Cursillo, or "little course," in the summer of 1976. While their reactions varied, the quality of the experience is made clear enough in the words of a participant.

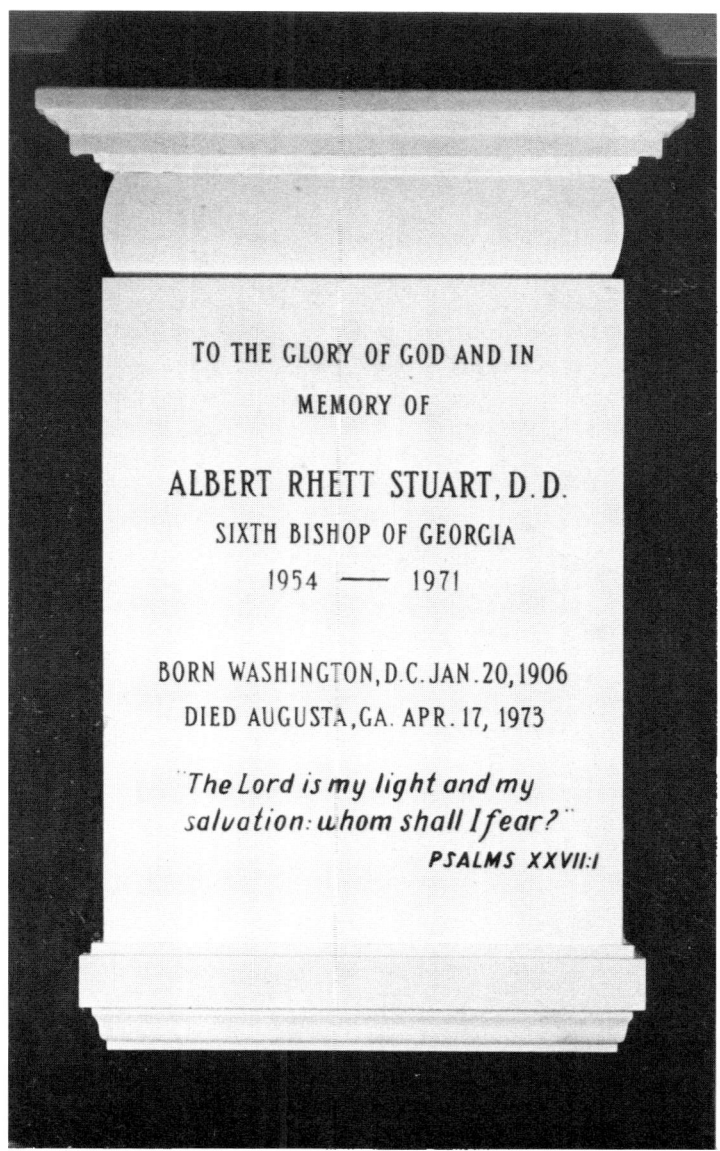

Bishop Stuart's plaque was placed beside those of his Episcopal predecessors.

We took a serious look at the teachings of the Church and their meaning — intellectually, emotionally, and personally. We studied, discussed, and examined our basic beliefs and feelings. We were led to a deeper understanding of the form and content of our worship and the meaning of the sacraments. There was singing and stillness, and lots of laughter and a warming sense of sharing and of community, of God's love shown and felt through the love of each other.

Since that first experience, many more members of the parish have become involved in the movement. Few who have undergone the very intense three-day spiritual experience have come away unmoved. Indeed, most have brought back from Cursillo fresh determination that its exhilaration and promise of spiritual growth will be successfully carried over and fulfilled through the "fourth day" — the cursillistos' expression for the remainder of one's life.[1307]

There is no question that the renewal movements — liturgical and evangelical — have had significant impact on the life of the parish. For instance, out of that first Cursillo came the urge to begin weeknight services on a trial basis. Although, at first, the idea evoked much discussion within the Vestry and some opposition, Thursday night Eucharists were begun as a special devotion during the following Easter season (1977).[1308] They proved so popular that they were resumed the following autumn and thereafter became a weekly feature of the church's calendar.[1309]

Two other manifestations of the renewal movement in the parish were special preaching missions, begun on a regular basis during the Lent of 1977, and "Parish Weekends" for families at Honey Creek, the Diocesan Conference Center. For these occasions special leaders were sometimes imported, such as the Rev. Richard Copeland (Rector, Church of the Redeemer, Dallas), who led the first one, followed by the Very Rev. David Collins (Dean, St. Philip's Cathedral, Atlanta), and the Rev. Everett L. (Terry) Fullam, Rector of St. Paul's Church in Darien, Connecticut, who led a subsequent one in 1978.[1310] By the 1980's these special missions and weekends had expanded to the point where they sometimes drew their leadership from the "Renewal Ministries" of the National Church,[1311] and involved dozens of parish families at a time. Indeed, sometimes they were so fully enrolled as to have waiting lists.[1313] One outgrowth of the Cursillos and Parish Weekends was the formation of numerous small groups in the parish. Usually gathering no more than 5-10 individuals on a weekly basis the groups met for study, prayer, counsel, sharing, and fellowship, and above all to press their quest for spiritual insight beyond the point where the weekend left it. By 1983, more than twenty such groups were active in the parish in their attempt to transform the event of renewal into a pattern of sustained growth.[1313a]

Small fellowship groups have not been the only manifestation of the renewal movement. Interest of adults in Sunday School classes is another. In recent years, approximately 100 adults have attended classes on a regular basis, comprising nearly 40% of the total Sunday school enrollment.[1313b] Perhaps an even more significant indication of a new level of commitment to serious churchmanship within the parish is evident in the popularity of the program called Education for Ministry.[1313c] Involving seminary-level extension courses in biblical, historical, and theological studies, EFM is intended to help Episcopalians "link faith to life" in daily experience. So far, about 20 parishioners have completed the entire four-year curriculum and a similar number are either in process or poised to begin.[1313d]

It is no wonder that by this time the renewal's influence had become visible in the operating style of the Women of the Church, the Vestry, and other parish groups. The Women of Christ Church, for example, despite their already fine tradition of efficient and productive organization, showed many signs of renewed strength and determination to put the language of ministry into action. During the 1980's this was manifest through some 25 active committees which attended everything from the traditional flower, altar, and hospitality tasks, and the Tour of Homes, to operating the parish library, caring for the Church and parish house gardens, looking after assorted Church housekeeping jobs, managing the United Thank Offering, and choir "mothering." Beyond these, other committees carried out a variety of special ministries: visiting the hospitalized and those recently released to care for their unique needs, as well as visiting and providing transportation to long term shut-ins, visiting new mothers, and helping to incorporate newcomers into the parish and identify "sponsors" for them. Still other committees are devoted to planning program and retreat functions, providing an important linkage with the "clothes closet" operated by the Social Apostolate, and to maintaining the prayer chain which has come to involve some 40 to 50 in daily prayer for those in need and which reaches "far beyond our own parish."[1314]

Especially interesting is the impact of renewal on the Vestry, since this is the very body which for a century after the Revolution actually barred the Rector from its meetings. Only in the days of Thomas Boone, in the late 1870's, was that tradition broken as he began to attend meetings and soon to open them with prayer. That pattern held for another century until the Rector, George Maxwell, in the late 1970's began the practice of establishing the context and setting the tone for each meeting with teaching and discussion of some spiritual discipline — a pattern which apparently was as novel to him as it was to the Vestry.[1315]

It may be even more important in the long run that, concurrently with these developments, a profound change in the operating pattern of the parish itself was subtly taking place — one which can, with legitimacy, be described as a "20th Century Reformation." The style of churchmanship that had grown up since the Rev. Mr. Boone's day had gradually transformed the position of Rector into the executive office of the congregation. It was a style which tended to foster a "leave it all to the professionals" attitude. One result of this was that each of Mr. Boone's successors increasingly became not only executive officer, but also chief planner, recruiter, organizer, fund raiser, and general cheerleader, in addition to being

liturgical president. The renewal of the 1970's, however, among other things, helped to bring about a sharp reformation of that attitude through greatly increased lay involvement. Although nothing changed officially, ministry increasingly became a parish activity, not simply a clerical one. The motive power of the congregation began to emanate from the entire body, not just from its head.

This fundamental power inversion, and the collective events of the 25th decade, do more than describe the recent history of the parish. They exemplify a corporate experience which has proven to be of great interest outside it. Surely this was what moved the Canadian Broadcasting Corporation to feature Christ Church in its "Testament" series, aired nationally in 1983, and why the hour-long broadcast centered on this period of inner struggle with the renewal phenomenon.[1315a]

Yet another indication of the combined effect of recent developments in the parish is to be seen in the pattern of stewardship. In September of 1981, the Vestry went on record as accepting "the tithe as the Christian standard by which we gauge our giving."[1316] Such words might be described as "bold," "optimistic", `or even "unrealistic", but they were followed by an act that can only be called "brave." The Rector, Wardens, and Vestry of the Church decided to reverse the usual order of things: and carry out the annual canvass for funds *first*. Only after that would they establish a budget.[1317] This change may have been as revolutionary as were earlier decisions to replace tax-support with pew rentals, and rents on pews with voluntary contributions.[1318]

Whatever else, the stresses that have accompanied the movements of the last decade represent symptoms of new life — troublesome at times, to be sure, but more appealing than the alternative. Furthermore, no matter how one judges these years — as a time of deterioration or of growing pains, or

Memorial plaques throughout the Church recall some of the parish's many twentieth century laborers. Below, Mr. Gawin Corbin is perhaps Christ Church's oldest living communicant.

merely as a time of change — distress has never dominated the scene. Nor has it ever shattered the parish's fundamental unity and its ability to function as a body. More important than any of the controversies have been other signs of life exemplified in the congregation's efforts in two significant areas. One of these can be seen in a campaign of many years, one shared by parishioners of all shades of opinion, to repair and restore the Church building. The monumental effort has brought the structure to its finest condition, both physically and aesthetically, since 1840.

It all began simply enough with preparation of a proposal to place the Church on the National Register in 1974.[1319] From this small beginning plans began to take shape over the next several years to work on the dark, cramped, uninviting narthex, the interior of the Church, and also on the parish house.[1320] Finally, by 1978, earlier piecemeal plans had begun to coalesce into a single comprehensive and multi-phased project.[1321]

As developed by early 1979, plans called for repairing, renovating, and restoring virtually the entire Church structure from the undercroft of the belfry. Specifically envisioned were such things as replacing existing windows with new mullioned ones, removing exterior shutters and substituting interior ones, enlarging the narthex, replacing the black and white tile floors with pine, and discarding the old "railway station" ceiling globes in favor of more suitable interior lighting — including, perhaps, a central chandelier. All of this would, of course, be in addition to the full range of plastering and painting that goes with every restoration of a building.[1322] Altogether, nearly three years of thought, consultation, and planning preceded the first visible signs of progress, in mid-1979.[1323]

Through the next three years work progressed normally — that is, more slowly than anyone wished, but more rapidly than it might have done — treating the window and exterior lighting phases of the work. At last, by the summer of 1982, it was time to begin renovation of the narthex "without further delay." This phase of the work was notable both because of its high visibility and because it involved some rather daring moves. Among other things it meant pushing the narthex partition eastward for several feet, at the sacrifice of one row of pews; bringing the gallery steps into the Church so as to diminish noise from outside and simplify their ascent; and a very risky treatment of the great doors at the entry to the Church. It also required matching existing moldings around the narthex with newly carved pieces to accommodate the enlarged dimensions of the space.[1324]

While major restoration work was still in mid-course, several individual contributions added special touches. One of these was a new portable baptismal font dedicated to Ben Washington, longtime sexton of the Church.[1325] But it is to the parish as a whole, and especially to the Restoration Committee, that credit must be given for bringing the restoration so far along in so few years.[1327]

Even though the goal of completing the gigantic task in time for the Church's 250th anniversary was not achieved, enough was done by 1983 that the end result could easily be envisioned by all. The main things still to be done were laying of the pine flooring, recarpeting in green, and carrying out the recommendation on interior lighting arrangements.[1328]

Another vital concern which demonstrates the fundamental unity of the parish is that of community ministry. Few things have been more consistently represented throughout the parish's 250 years than this. Consciously or otherwise, each generation has sought its own way of matching the Church's obligation to serve with the peculiar needs of the community. In that tradition, when he first became Rector, Mr. Maxwell asked for suggestions as to "ways in which the Church could be used during the week for the benefit of the downtown community."[1329] Developments in the parish since that time have given new impetus to this strong tradition.

One of the first responses was to take the Church out *into* the community. To do this the Women of the Church donated funds generated by the Tour of Homes to purchase sound equipment which could broadcast into Johnson Square music performed inside the building.[1330] Noonday organ concerts soon began to serenade the crowds of office workers who gathered there for lunch. "Thursday Events", as they came to be called, achieved such popularity that they became a year round feature of the downtown neighborhood, and were sometimes supplemented by concerts on other days.[1331]

Equally important, however, was the effort in the opposite direction, to make the Church more inviting to those who wished to come in. Aware of the widespread interest among visitors to the city, as well as among those who live and work here, in the historic building and in "Wesley's Church," a Guild of Vergers was formed in 1980. Under the zealous leadership of parishioner Brendan Galloway, the Guild's 35 members began in December 1980 to keep the Church open two days per week to visitors of all kinds.[1332]

Perhaps two of the most unusual community projects in the entire history of the parish have emerged in recent times to treat one of the oldest problems. Because of abnormally high unemployment during the late 1970's, there was an urgent need for food, and the most direct approach to meeting that need was to grow it. With that end in mind Christ Church joined forces with several other churches and organizations in the downtown area to support the expertise of Ian Robertson as he coached needy families on the fine art of transforming vacant city lots into productive gardens. In their first year the seven original plots produced enough to sustain 46 families, plus a good many of their friends, through the entire summer with a generous surplus.[1333] Over the next few years the garden project grew vigorously. A government agency took on responsibility for Mr. Robertson's salary in 1977 and other groups, including the city and the county, joined in as the merits of his enterprise became better known. Then in 1978 the project really moved into high gear as it continued to expand and also began to diversify. Raised plots were prepared for cultivation by wheelchair gardeners, while others were worked by mentally handicapped growers, thus enriching the value of the whole program. But surely the most massive infusion of new activity that year was added by still another group — a prize team of 200,000 earthworms, purchased especially for the gardens![1334]

For needy families who had homes, and vacant lots available in their neighborhoods, the garden project was a boon. Those who had less, however, needed more. For them the creation of a local Food Bank branch offered brighter hope. The Savannah chapter was organized in 1980 by a coalition of downtown groups — churches, including Christ Church, public agencies, etc. Basically, its purpose was to gather surplus or threatened food stocks from any source available, food which would otherwise be discarded and lost, and to channel it to those in need. Government surplus stock, Ian Robertson's gardens, passing ships and trucks which had to discharge their supplies, as well as local restaurants and markets were all potential sources. Clearly, the bank's "depositors" were there, but to be successful the Food Bank needed also to locate warehouse space and to cultivate community awareness, both of the need and the potential for salvage. Finally, the task of orchestrating all the parts had to be accomplished — a huge logistical and public relations challenge.[1335]

Once established, the Food Bank rather naturally invited thoughts of the next step in the process of food distribution: a soup kitchen. The idea emerged from the extended meditation and prayer of one of the small groups within the Women's organization of the Church. As they pondered the message of "feed my sheep" plans began to take shape which gained momentum when taken up by the Women's Urban Ministries Committee.[1336] Several churches in the central area of the city also saw the need and soon had a moving kitchen in operation, serving one day a week from each church. Before long it became apparent, however, that a kitchen could be more effectively and efficiently run from a permanent home. Plans were then made to operate "Emmaus House" in the Christ Church parish house, which was especially fitted for the task through a $5000 grant from the Women of the Church and support from the other participating churches.[1337] The first meals were served from the newly equipped parish house kitchen in September, 1982. Within a few months Emmaus House was feeding more than 90 each day, and doing it at an average cost of only 26¢ per person![1338]

These rather unusual attempts to deal with very practical needs in the community were accompanied by many additional forms of outreach — less sensational perhaps, but equally indicative of the motivation behind them. They ranged from helping to found the "Chatham Academy" in 1978, designed to treat children with learning disabilities,[1339] to furnishing funds, meeting space, or facilities for such worthy enterprises of SAFE Shelter, HOSPICE, AA, the Savannah Nursery School and the Abrahams Home, the restoration of Nicholsonboro Baptist Church, Royce Reading Center, the Savannah Symphony, Parents Anonymous, and the Presiding Bishop's Fund for World Relief.[1340]

With such a list before us it seems as though, in some senses at least, the parish completed its first 250 years in the place it began — immersed in ministry to the community

This memorial of Dr. Tucker is in the south aisle of the Church.

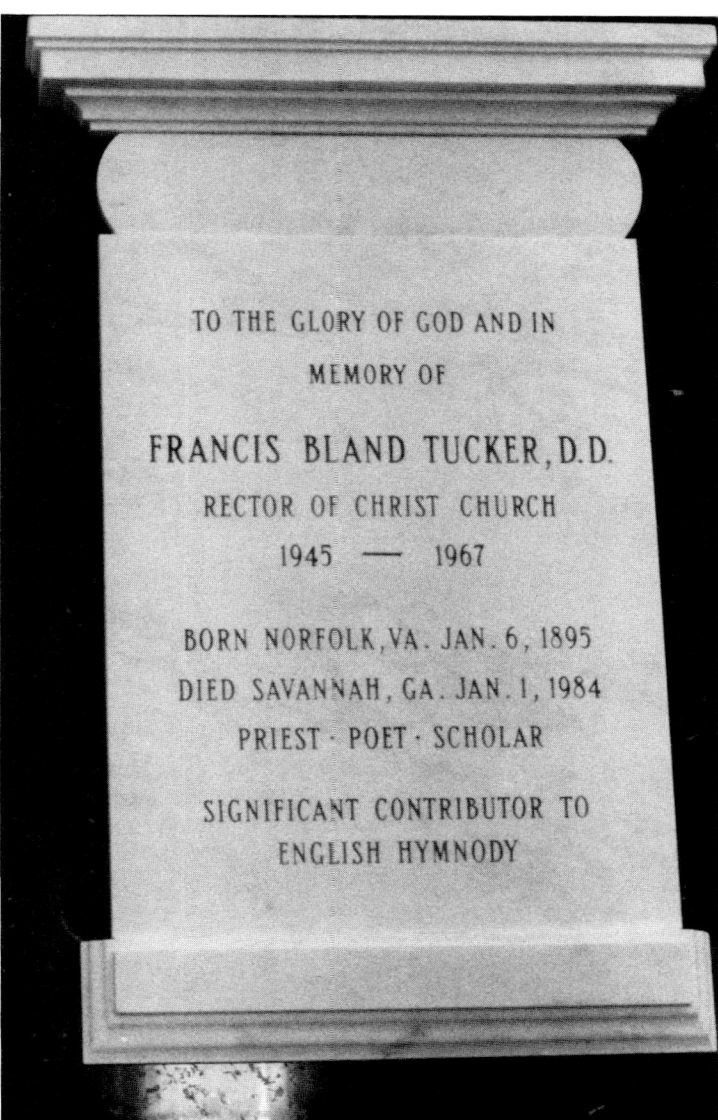

Another Tucker plaque is presently mounted outside Demere Chapel. Below Dr. Tucker's funeral, January 4, 1984.

around it. In most ways, however, the situation in 1983 differed so markedly from that of 1733 that the two virtually defy comparison. Little wonder is it. Between those dates have passed some ten or eleven generations and as many wars, two dozen depressions, and forty rectors (more or less), and all have wrought their changes. Certainly one thing that would not have taken place in 1733 was a visit from the Archbishop of Canterbury — or any other bishop for that matter. Yet the pilgrimage from Canterbury was only one of the events envisioned by planners of the parish's semiquincentennial observance.[1341] Together with completion of the restoration work on the Church, these things would indeed make 1983 a year of celebration.

Even though restoration plans did not progress according to the timetable first conceived, the year was quite full enough in any case. Christ Church hosted the annual convention of the Diocese in February, which brought the Most Rev. John Allin, Presiding Bishop, to be its featured Speaker, and opened jubilantly with a Festival Evensong in the jampacked Church.[1342] Then a special anniversary service on the Sunday following, provided the liturgical climax, with the Rev. David Collins, Dean of St. Philip's Cathedral, Atlanta, preaching. After that came the Birthday Party itself which featured a large cake decorated to read "For 250 years a community of the New Covenant." Countless parishioners squeezed into the undercroft to continue the celebration and enjoy the cake before all retired to the final event of the day, an oyster roast at Bluffton.[1343]

The year also became one of significant changes as both Messrs. Meachen and Newcomb departed for other fields of labor. As a deacon, Mr. Meachen had carried a double function, and since the new director of music would most likely not be ordained, the Rector announced his intention to instruct four lay readers as chalice bearers and seek their licensure by the Bishop.[1344] As Mr. Meachen was in the process of leaving, in mid-June, Mr. Newcomb told the Vestry that he had accepted a call to become Rector of St. Timothy's Church in Fairfield, Connecticut, ending a successful five years at Christ Church.[1345] Finally, the year neared its end the way it had begun, in the midst of planning. This time to consecrate the man destined to become the eighth Bishop of Georgia. The Rev. Harry Shipps, elected coadjutor at a special September session of the Diocese, would be the fourth of its Bishop's to be consecrated in Christ Church.[1346]

Ending this year of milestones was perhaps the most touching one of all, the death of Francis Bland Tucker on the first day of the new year, 1 January 1984. Although well into his 80's, and physically burdened during his last years, Dr. Tucker's mind and spirit were in no way diminished, nor was his devotion to the parish or to the Church and its music. He had remained very active in translating and paraphrasing ancient hymn texts and in composing new ones of his own. With his background and long-time membership on the Church's Commission on Church Music — one of those specifically charged with the task of revising the *Hymnal*[1347] — Dr. Tucker had a keener sense than most of what was needed to accommodate the new *Book of Common Prayer* and the general stylistic changes in churchmanship over the last forty years. He gave the final strength of his life almost totally to finishing that work. Indeed, when the committee on texts met for their last editorial session, it was at his home on York Street that they gathered from across the nation, because by that time he was too feeble to travel well.

Because of his singular devotion and the extraordinary quality of his work, Dr. Erik Routley described him on that occasion as "one of the greatest American hymn writers."[1348] It is these attributes, plus many more — represented in the extravagant admiration of the Christ Church congregation and Savannah community for the man and his memory — that account for the dedication of this volume to him.[1349] In its way the General Convention of the Church, which met in New Orleans in October 1982, made it evident that such admiration is not confined to this parish and city. For not only was the work of the committee approved, but Dr. Tucker and his achievement were also thunderously celebrated as he was introduced to both Houses of the Convention.[1350]

Nearly forty years before, when Dr. Tucker arrived in the parish to become its Rector, he expressed a hope that is as apropos of the parish's 250th anniversary as it was of the context in which he offered it: "May our future be worthy of our past." May it indeed be so until that day when, in the words of his translation of the *Didache*,

As grain once scattered on the hillsides
Is in this broken bread made one,
So from all lands Thy Church be gathered
Into Thy Kingdom by Thy Son.[1351]

Detail of the altar

References

Important Dates

1733	The Colony of Georgia and Christ Church are founded.
1736	The Rev. John Wesley becomes the minister. While here, he starts America's first Sunday School and publishes the first English hymnal for use in America.
1738	The Rev. George Whitefield becomes the minister.
1740	Mr. Whitefield lays the cornerstone for Bethesda Orphanage.
1744	Cornerstone of the first church laid by Mr. Bosomworth.
1750	The first church is dedicated.
1758	The cemetery, now known as Colonial Park, is vested in Christ Church.
1796	The church is burned in the great fire which destroys most of the city.
1803	The second church is begun.
1804	A great hurricane destroys the unfinished church.
1815	The second church is consecrated.
1837	The second church is pulled down.
1840	The third and present church is consecrated.
1841	The first Bishop of Georgia, The Rt. Rev. Stephen Elliott, is consecrated in Christ Church.
1841	The parish is divided. All families south of Oglethorpe Avenue will be in a new parish to be known as "St. John's."
1908	Frederick F. Reese is consecrated the fourth Bishop of Georgia.
1927	Juliette Gordon Low is buried from Christ Church, her home parish.
1969	Paul Reeves is consecrated Bishop Coadjutor of Georgia.
1973	The Bishop of London attends the Sesquicentennial of the Diocese of Georgia and dedicates the new organ in Christ Church.

Rectors of Christ Church

1733	Henry Herbert
1733-35	Samuel Quincy
1736-37	John Wesley
1738, 1739-40	George Whitefield
1738-39	William Norris
1740	William Metcalf (appointed, but died before he could depart England for Georgia)
1741-42	Christopher Orton
1744-45	Thomas Bosomworth
1745-66	Bartholomew Zouberbuhler
1767-71	Samuel Frink
1771-73	Timothy Lowten
1773-75	Haddon Smith
1776	John Rennie
1779-80	Edward Jenkins
1780-81	James Brown
1781-82	John Stuart
1783?-84	John Holmes
1786-87	William Nixon
1787-92?	Benjamin Lindsay
1793-95	Edward Ellington
1804-07	William Best
1810-14	John Bartow
1815-22	Walter Cranston
1822-27	Abiel Carter
1827-51	Edward Neufville
1851-52	Abram Beech Carter
1852-59, 1861-66	Stephen Elliott
1860	L.P. Balch
1867-68	Charles H. Coley, (having served also as Bishop Elliott's assistant since 1861.)
1868-72	John M. Mitchell
1873-74	John W. Beckwith
1874-77	George D.E. Mortimer
1877-88	Thomas Boone
1889-1905	Robb White
1906-14	Francis Brown
1915-23	John Durham Wing
1924-44	David Cady Wright
1945-67	Francis Bland Tucker
1967-73	Warren E. Haynes
1973-	George M. Maxwell

Bishops of the Diocese of Georgia

The Right Reverend
Stephen Elliott D.D.

The Right Reverend
John Watrous Beckwith, D.D.

The Right Reverend
Cleland Kinloch Nelson D.D.

The Right Reverend
Frederick Focke Reese, D.D.

The Right Reverend
Middleton Stuart Barnwell, D.D.

The Right Reverend
Albert Rhett Stuart

The Right Reverend
Paul Reeves

The Right Reverend
Harry Woolston Shipps

They Gave Their Last Full Measure of Devotion

From Christ Church — Those Who Died in Wars

The information for this section was gathered by David C. Barrow Jr., a former Christ Church Vestryman, from available records.

Mexican War

May 26, 1848 Buried: Capt. George S. Welcher, USA
June 1, 1848 Buried: Capt. John Mackay, USA

War Between The States
1861-1865

From Parish Register — Burials — On micro-film at Georgia Historical Society, Hodgson Hall, Savannah, Georgia

From May 3, 1860 up to April, 1861, no records are found of burials from Christ Church Parish, during which interval, the Parish was without a regular rector, the needs of the parish being served by the Assistant Rector, The Rev. C. H. Coley.

June 16, 1861 Buried: Enoch Brady, private in Volunteer Co., the "Joe Browns."
June 28, 1861 Buried from Christ Church: Acting Brig. Gen. Francis S. Bartow, who was killed at the Battle of Manassas Junction. General Bartow was the son of Dr. Theodosius Bartow, former Warden of Christ Church and "as gallant a spirit as ever lived."
Sept. 12, 1861 Buried: Charles Bevis, a soldier of the regular Confederate Army from the Oglethorpe Barracks, Savannah.
Sept. 20, 1861 Buried: Alexander Gardner, private, 1st Regiment, Georgia Regulars, Co. D., C St., Oglethorpe Barracks, Savannah.
Jan. 7, 1862 Buried: James Griff, Savannah Volunteer Guards, Drowned at Green Island, Dec. 23, 1861.
Dec. 25, 1862 Buried on Christmas Day from Christ Church: Capt. Henry Lord King, aide de camp to General McLaws, who fell in the Battle of Fredericksburg, Dec. 13, 1862.
May 17, 1863 Buried: Lieut. Frederick A. Habersham; killed at battle of Mary's Heights.
June 8, 1863 Buried from Christ Church: Lieut. Edward Padelford Jr., Savannah Volunteer Guards.
July 6, 1863 Buried from St. John's Church, Savannah: Major John R. Giles, of Col. Gordon's Regiment, Phoenix Riflemen.
July 13, 1863 Buried: Julian Santina, killed in Battle on Morris Island, S.C.
July 13, 1863 Buried: Edward Postell, killed in battle on Morris Island, S.C.
Dec. 18, 1863 Buried: Lieut. S. Breck Parkman, killed Sept. 1862, at the Battle of Sharpsburg.
Jan. 7, 1864 Buried: William W. Spaulding, Sergeant Major of Captain Maxwell's light battery.
June 4, 1864 Buried from Christ Church: Wright R. Jones, a seaman of Gunboat Georgia, C.S.N., killed in capture of U. S. Steamer "Water Witch."
June 4, 1864 Buried from Christ Church: Thomas F. Pelot, Lieut. in C. S. Navy, killed while leading the boarding party which captured the U.S. Steamer "Water Witch."
July 27, 1864 Buried from Christ Church: Capt. Joseph C. Habersham, killed in battle at Atlanta, July 22, 1864; Aide de Camp to Gen. F. R. Gist, of S.C.
July 27, 1864 Buried from Christ Church: Lieut. John Potter, died of a wound received in Battle of Atlanta, July 22, 1864.
August 3, 1864 Buried from the Confederate Hospital: Joseph Padger.
August 3, 1864 Buried from the Confederate Hospital: A. Jenkins.
August 18, 1864 William Neyle Habersham Jr., killed in battle near Atlanta, July 22, 1864.
August 28, 1864 Buried: Thomas Y. Simons, of Charleston, S.C., Ashley Dragoons.
Sept. 14, 1864 Buried: I. G. Rosler, born in Norway, Master Mate of C. S. Gunboat Sampson.
Oct. 8, 1864 Buried from Christ Church: Major Joseph S. Socke, Commissary of the Confederate States for the State of Georgia.
Nov. 21, 1864 Buried: T. S. Palmer, Private, C. S. A.
    A. I. Williams, Private, C. S. A.
    S. T. Witherspoon, Private, C. S. A.
    W. W. Spinks, Private, C. S. A.
    C. F. Palmer, Private, C. S. A.
    Maxwell Johnson, Private, C. S. A.
    A. A. Coats, Private, C. S. A.
    N. I. Newcomb, Private, C. S. A.
    T. I. James, Private, C. S. A.
Nov. 23, 1864 Buried: G. A. Lawson, Private, C. S. A.
Dec. 12, 1864 Buried: Major Ferdinand W. C. Cook, Athens Battalion, killed in the lines before Savannah.
Dec. 29, 1865 Buried: William Grant, Lieut., Savannah Volunteer Guards; killed at Battle of Sayler's Creek, Va., April, 1865.
Jan. 21, 1866 Buried: Charles Barney Postell, Private, Savannah Volunteer Guards.
Feb. 9, 1866 Buried: Lieut. Frederick Bliss, 8th Ga. Reg't., C. S. A.

World War I

Casualties from Christ Church Parish — Information from Parish Register.

October 2, 1918 Buried: George S. Inglesby, United States Army, Bonaventure Cemetery.
October 6, 1918 Buried: Thomas L. Davis, Sergeant, U. S. Army, Laurel Grove Cemetery.

World War II
1941-1945

From Parish Register (Burials) and marble tablet in Nave of Christ Church.
Charles Greenlee Rowland
Joel Atwood Merriman Jr.
Frank Bernard Bragg Jr.

World War II continued

Robert Francis Jones Jr.
Louis Marcel LeHardy Jr.
Edward McGuire Gordon
Walter Scott Nelson Jr.
Cresswell Garlington Jr.
Mark William Johnson
Justin Lowe Jackson
Carl Scales Reitzel Jr.
Ralph Meldrim Jones
John Helm Maclean

Korea and Vietnam

From Parish Register (Burials)

April 1952 Lieut. (j.g.) F. K. Wolfe Jr. (Navy) Lost at sea, (Korea)
March 15, 1967 Lieut. (j.g.) Dean Smith Jr., (KIA — Vietnam)
December 7, 1967 Lieut. John Woodward Sognier Jr., (KIA — Vietnam)

Selected Bibliography

Primary Sources

Manuscripts

"Account of Designs for the Colony [of Georgia], 1732." Sloane MS 3986, f. 38. British Library, London, England.

"Address of the Assembly to the Governor [of Georgia], 1774." MS 21672, ff. 227-229. British Library, London, England.

Beckwith, John W. Papers. MS 64. Georgia Historical Society, Savannah, Georgia.

"Charter for Establishing the Colony of Georgia." MS 17477, f. 100. British Library, London, England.

Christ Church Collection. MS 978, Georgia Historical Society, Savannah, Georgia. The Collection includes, *inter alia*, a rich assortment of parish registers (baptisms, marriages, burials, communicants, etc.) which are virtually complete beginning with 1822. Vestry minutes are also nearly complete from 1839 to the present. Fragmentary records of the vestry, including correspondence, minutes, pew charts, financial records, etc., dating back to the 1760's also survive there. In addition, MS 978 contains transcriptions of minutes, journals, and letters relating to Christ Church in the archives of the Society for the Propagation of the Gospel in Foreign Parts (SPG), the Society for Promoting Christian Knowledge (SPCK), the Associates of Dr. Bray, and in the libraries at Fulham and Lambeth Palaces and the British Public Records Office.

"Copy of the Answers of James Wright, Esquire, Governor of Georgia, to the Queries Proposed by the Lords of Trade, 29 Nov. 1766." Kings MS 205, f. 305. British Library, London, England.

DeBrahm, William. "Report of the General Survey in the Southern District of North America, June 1772." Kings MS 210, f. 42. British Library, London, England.

Elliott, Stephen. Papers. MS 846. Georgia Historical Society, Savannah, Georgia.

"Establishment of the Colony of Georgia, ca. 1751, 1754." MS 33029, ff. 71-76, 122. British Library, London, England.

Hartridge Collection. Uncatalogued manuscripts. Georgia Historical Society, Savannah, Georgia.

Little, Lewis. Papers. Privately held. Savannah, Georgia.

"Minutes and Correspondence of the Trustees, 1743-1747." MS 27990, f. 71. British Library, London, England.

"Minutes of [the Savannah] City Council." Municipal Research Library. Savannah, Georgia.

"Papers Relating to the British Colony of Georgia." MS 23789, ff. 228-233 (1733); MS 35909, f. 74 (1737); MS 35910, f. 134 (1763). British Library, London, England.

"Reports on the State of Georgia, 1766-1768." Kings MS 206, ff. 5, 33b, 69, 84. British Library, London, England.

Savannah Historical Research Association Papers. MS 994. Georgia Historical Society, Savannah, Georgia.

"Warrant for a Charter Establishing the Colony of Georgia. . .1732." MS 36130, f. 69. British Library, London, England.

"Mr. Woodmason's Account of South Carolina, North Carolina, and Georgia. . .1766." Transcript of a MS in the Fulham Palace Library, made by Walter C. Hartridge. Hartridge Collection. Georgia Historical Society, Savannah, Georgia.

Newspapers & Journals

Kollock, Susan M., ed. "Letters of the Kollock and Allied Families." *Georgia Historical Quarterly* 33 (1949): 331-354; 34 (1950): 36-73, 126-156, 227-257, 313-327, 35 (1951): 60-75.

(N.B. All newspapers are Savannah publications unless otherwise noted.)

American Patriot. 1812.
Columbian Museum and Savannah Advertiser. 1796-1817, 1820.
Columbian Museum and Savannah (Daily) Gazette. 1817-1820.
Columns (Christ Church). 1976-1983.
Daily Morning News. 1850-1866.
Daily News and Herald. 1866-1868.
The Episcopal Church in Georgia (Diocese of Georgia). 1943.
Gazette of the State of Georgia. 1783-1788.
Georgia Gazette. 1763-1776, 1788-1802.
Georgia Journal & Independent Federal Register. 1793.
Georgian Republican. 1806.
Georgian Republican & State Intellingencer. 1804-1805.
Georgian and Evening Advertiser. 1821.
New York Times. 1926-1927.
Parish Helper (Christ Church). 1906.
Patriot and Commercial Advertiser. 1807.
Republican and Savannah Evening Ledger. 1807-1816.
Royal Gazette of Georgia. 1779-1782.
(Savannah Daily) Georgian. 1820-1854.
Savannah Daily Herald. 1866.
Savannah Daily Republican. 1840-1842.
Savannah (Evening) Press. 1903-1983.
Savannah Morning News. 1868-1983.
Savannah Museum. 1822.
[Charlestown] South Carolina Gazette. 1732-1733.
Southern Patriot. 1806-1807.
Sunday Morning Telegram. 1881-1883.
Times (London). 1791.

Books

An Account, Showing the Progress of the Colony of Georgia in America, From Its First Establishment (published per order of the Honourable Trustees). London, 1741, as reprinted at Annapolis, 1742.

Candler, Allen D., et al., eds. *Colonial Records of the State of Georgia.* 38 vols. Atlanta, 1904 ff.

Candler, Allen D., ed. *Confederate Records of the State of Georgia, 1860-1868.* 6 vols. New York, 1909 ff.

Candler, Allen D., ed. *Revolutionary Records of the State of Georgia.* 3 vols. Atlanta, 1908.

[Christ Church]. *Yearbook of Christ Church.* Savannah, 1918.

[Christ Church]. *Yearbook and Directory.* Savannah, 1927.

Classified Digest of Records of the Society for Propagation of the Gospel in Foreign Parts, 1701 ff. Fifth edition. London, 1805.

Coulter, E. Merton, *The Journal of Peter Gordon.* Athens, Georgia, 1963.

Coulter, E. Merton, ed. *The Journal of William Stephens, 1741-1745.* 2 vols. Athens, Georgia, 1958-59.

Coulter, E. Merton and Saye, Albert B., eds. *A List of the Early Settlers of Georgia.* Athens, Georgia, 1949.

Diary of Viscount Percival, Afterwards First Earl of Egmont, 1730-1749. 3 vols. London, 1920-23.

Force, Peter, ed. *Tracts and Other Papers Relating Principally to the Origin, Settlement, and Progress of the Colonies in North America from the Discovery of the Country to the Year 1776.* Volume 1. Washington, 1836.

Habersham, James. *Letters, 1756-1775.* Vol. 6 of the *Collections of the Georgia Historical Society.* Savannah, 1904.

Jones, George Fenwick, et al. trans and ed. *Detailed Reports on the Salzburger Emigrants Who Settled in America. . . Edited by Samuel Urlsperger.* 8 volumes to date. Athens, Georgia, 1968ff.

Jones, George Fenwick, ed. *Henry Newman's Salzburger Letterbooks.* Athens, Ga, 1966.

Journal of the Proceedings of the . . .Convention of the Protestant Episcopal Church in. . .Georgia. Published annually by the Episcopal Diocese of Georgia, 1823-1983.

Leigh, Frances Butler. *Ten Years on a Georgia Plantation*. London, 1883.

McPherson, Robert G., ed. *Journal of the Earl of Egmont, 1732-1738*. Athens, Georgia, 1962.

Marbury, Horatio and Crawford, William, compilers. *A Digest of the Laws of the State of Georgia, . . .1755. . .to 1800*. Savannah, 1802.

Montgomery, Robert, bart. *A Discourse Concerning the Designed Establishment of a New Colony to the South of Carolina in the Most Delightful Country of the Universe*. London, 1717.

Oglethorpe, James Edward. *Letters of General Oglethorpe*. Vol. 3 of the *Collections of the Georgia Historical Society*. Savannah, 1873.

Oglethorpe, James Edward. *A New and Accurate Account of the Provinces of South Carolina and Georgia: with Many Curious and Useful Observations on the Trade, Navigation, and Plantations of Great Britain Compared with Her Most Powerful Maritime Neighbors in Ancient and Modern Times*. London, 1732.

The Siege of Savannah. Albany, 1866; reprint ed., Spartanburg, South Carolina, 1975.

"A State of the Province of Georgia Attested Upon Oath in the Court of Savannah Nov. 10th, 1740." London, 1742. (Reprinted in the *Collections of the Georgia Historical Society*. Vol. 2: 67-85.) Savannah, 1842.

Tailfer, Pat. et al. *A True & Historical Narrative of the Colony of Georgia, with Comments by the Earl of Egmont*. Edited by Clarence L. Ver Steeg. Athens, Georgia, 1960.

Washington, George. *The Diary of George Washington (1789-1791)*. Edited by Benson J. Lossing. Richmond, 1861.

Watkins, Robert and George, compilers. *A Digest of the Laws of the State of Georgia*. Philadelphia, 1800.

Wesley, Charles. *The Journal of the Rev. Charles Wesley, M.A.* Edited by John Telford. London: Robert Culley, n.d.

Wesley, John. *A Collection of Psalms and Hymns*. Charles-Town, 1737 (facsimile edition in Georgia Historical Society Library, Savannah, Georgia.)

Wesley, John. *The Journal of the Rev. John Wesley, A.M.* Edited by Nehemiah Curnock. 8 vols. London, 1938.

Wesley, John. *The Letters of the Rev. John Wesley, A.M.* Edited by John Telford. 8 vols. London, 1931.

Wesley, John. *Works*. Edited by John Emory. 7 vols. New York and Cincinnati, n.d.

Whitefield, George. *Journals*. London, 1960.

Whitefield, George. *The Works of the Rev. George Whitefield, M.A.* 6 vols. London and Edinburgh, 1771.

Secondary Sources

Unpublished Works

Collins, Doris Kirk. "The Episcopal Church in Georgia from the Revolutionary War to 1860." M.A. thesis. Emory University, 1957.

Douglas, W. Walter. "Christ Church, Savannah, Georgia," Paper in Georgia Historical Society, Savannah, Georgia, 1951.

Hauton, Richard. "Savannah in the 1850's." Ph.D. dissertation. Emory University, 1968.

Mitchell, Robert Gary. "Loyalist Georgia." Ph.D. dissertation. Tulane University, 1964.

Books

Atwell, James S. *A Brief Historical Sketch of St. Stephen's Parish, Savannah, Georgia*. New York, 1874.

Catalogue of the Wymberly Jones DeRenne Georgia Library, . .1700-1929, 3 Vols. Wormsloe (Savannah), Georgia, 1930.

Coleman, Kenneth. *The American Revolution in Georgia*. Athens, Georgia, 1958.

Coleman, Kenneth. *Colonial Georgia: A History*. New York, 1976.

Coulter, E. Merton. *Georgia: A Short History*. Chapel Hill, North Carolina, 1960.

Coulter, E. Merton. *Wormsloe*. Athens, Georgia, 1955.

Crandall, Marjorie Lyle. *Confederate Imprints*. 2 vols. Boston, 1955.

Dallimore, Arnold A. *George Whitefield*. Vol. 1. London, 1970.

Davis, Harold E. *The Fledgling Province: Social and Cultural Life in Colonial Georgia, 1733-1776*. Chapel Hill, North Carolina, 1976.

Fries, Adelaide L. *The Moravians in Georgia*. Raleigh, North Carolina, 1905.

Gamble, Thomas. *A History of the City Government of Savannah, Georgia, 1790-1901*. Savannah, 1901.

Harden, William. *History of Savannah and South Georgia*. 2 vols. Chicago and New York, 1913.

"A History of the Erection and Dedication of the Monument to Gen'l James Edward Oglethorpe." Vol. 7 of the *Collections of the Georgia Historical Society*. Savannah, 1911.

Hoskins, Charles L. *Black Episcopalians in Georgia*. Savannah, 1980.

Hoskins, Charles L. *Black Episcopalians in Savannah*. Savannah, 1983.

Lane, Mills. *Savannah Revisited*. Second edition. Savannah, 1973.

Lee, F.D. and Agnew, J.L. *Historical Record of the City of Savannah*. Savannah, 1869.

Malone, Henry T. *The Episcopal Church in Georgia 1733-1957*. Atlanta, 1960.

Perry, William Stevens. *The History of the American Episcopal Church, 1587-1883*. Vol. 1 Boston, 1883.

Rubin, Saul J. *Third to None: the Saga of Savannah Jewry, 1733-1983*. Savannah, 1983.

Spalding, Phinizy. *Oglethorpe in America*. Chicago, 1977.

Sprague, William Buell. *Annals of the American Pulpit*. Vol. 5 (Episcopalians). New York, 1859.

Stevens, William B. *Early History of the Church in Georgia*. Philadelphia, 1873.

Stevens, William B. *A History of Georgia*. 2 vols. Philadelphia, 1847; and New York, 1859.

Stickney, Edward C. and Evelyn. *Revere Bells*. Revised edition. By the authors, 1961.

Strickland, Reba C. *Religion and State in Eighteenth Century Georgia*. New York, 1939.

White, George, ed. *Historical Collections of Georgia*. New York, 1855.

White, George. *Statistics of the State of Georgia*. Savannah, 1849.

Woolverton, John F. *Colonial Anglicanism in North America*. Detroit, 1984.

Periodicals

Corbin, Gawin L. "First List of Pew Holders of Christ Church, Savannah." *Georgia Historical Quarterly* 50 (1966): 74-86.

Davis, Mollie C. "Whitefield's Attempt to Establish a College in Georgia." *Georgia Historical Quarterly* 55 (1971): 459-470.

Lawrence, J.B. "Religious Education of the Negro in the Colony of Georgia." *Georgia Historical Quarterly* 14 (1930): 41-57.

Mikell, H.J. "The Founding of the Church in Georgia." *Georgia Historical Quarterly* 17 (1933): 77-90.

Monger, Dwyn. "History as Interpreted by Stephen Elliott." *Historical Magazine of the Protestant Episcopal Church* 44 (1975): 285-317.

Pennington, Edward. "The Reverend Bartholomew Zouberbuhler." *Georgia Historical Quarterly* 18 (1934): 354-363.

Strickland, Reba C. "Building a Colonial Church." *Georgia Historical Quarterly* 17 (1933): 276-285.

Footnotes

[a] *Journal 1872*, p. 27

[b] *Savannah Morning News* 6 May 1881 (4-6). The *Journal of 1882* reported its completion the following year, by a layman under Mr. Boone's supervision.

[c] *Vestry Minutes*, 6 Feb 1890. See also 9 Jan. 1919, 18 Oct. 1949, and 21 May 1968.

[d] *Vestry Minutes* 13 May 1974.

[e] Miss Johnston's notebook and photographs, many of which are reproduced in this volume, is now in MS. 978, f. 127.

[f] *Vestry Minutes*, 11 May 1981.

Chapter One

[1] The warrant for the charter is dated 25 April 1732. MS 36130, f. 69ff., in the British Library.

[2] Ibid, f. 80. The charter itself follows the language of the warrant precisely in this. MS 17, 477 f. 112 (British Library).

[3] *Journal of the Earl of Egmont*, (ed. Robert G. McPherson), Abstract of the Trustees Proceedings for Establishing the Colony of Georgia, 1732-1738. p. 8. (1 Nov. 1732).

[3a] *Journal of Peter Gordon*, ed. E.M. Coulter. See the entries for 21st November and 26th November (1732), pp. 29, 30.

[3b] Reported in the *South Carolina Gazette*, 13-20 Jan. 1732 (3-1). The modernized date is, of course, 1733, which will be used hereinafter. The daily calendar would also be altered, eleven days later if modernized, but since the date is the key to the citation in this case, it has been left in the "old style."

[3c] *South Carolina Gazette*, 24-30 March 1732/3 (2-1 ff.). The Rev'd Mr. Lewis Jones was Rector of St. Helena's, Beaufort.

[3d] *Journal of Peter Gordon*, entry for Sunday, 4 February (old style), p. 37.

[3e] *South Carolina Gazette* 26 May to 2 June 1733 (3-1). This meeting was considered so important that the *Gazette* devoted some five full columns to its coverage. The peculiar tense of the final sentence is due to its having passed from the mouth of the Creek spokesman, to the translator, to the reporter, to the editor. How reliable are translator John Musgrove and the others?

[4] Egmont's *Journal* 8 Nov. 1732.

[5] Egmont's *Journal* p. 11 (28 Dec., 1732).

[6] Egmont's *Journal* p. 9 (23 Nov. 1732).

[6a] Egmont's *Journal*, 21 Dec. 1732.

[6b] Egmont's *Journal*, p. 8.

[7] Letter to Oglethorpe from the Trustees dated 4 April 1733 in *Colonial Records of Georgia*, vol. 29, p. 17 (hereinafter abbreviated as CR).

[8] *The Journal of Peter Gordon*, p. 46. The *List of Early Settlers* says it was 21 July. Quincy is number 1193.

[9] CR vol. 29, p. 41. Letters from Trustees' secretary, Mr. Benjamin Martyn, to General Oglethorpe dated 22 Nov. 1733.

[10] With much vexation the letter from the Trustees pointed to their "surprise that they have never in all this time heard from you of the state of your parish" in CR, vol. 29, p. 77.

[11] CR vol. 20, pp. 207-209.

[12] CR vol. 20, p. 209.

[13] Egmont's *Journal* 28 June 1735 (p. 95), See also CR, vol. 20, pp. 408-411.

[13a] *Diary of Viscount Percival, Afterward First Earl of Egmont*, vol. 2, p. 329.

[14] Egmont's *Journal*, 2 July 1735 (p. 96).

[14a] Cited in Phinizy Spalding, *Oglethorpe in America* p. 16.

[15] Egmont's *Journal*, 20 August 1735 (p. 103).

[16] Egmont's *Journal*, 10 October 1735 (p. 108). The Trustees also sought to have his £50 salary now given to his successor instead, see pp. 120 and 124.

[17] CR vol. 29, p. 165. The letter is dated 10 October 1735. In Mr. Quincy's defense it should be noted that the S.P.G. took a much more apreciative view of him. Under their auspices he served for several years at St. John's, Colleton, at St. George's, Dorchester, and at St. Philips until his return to Boston in 1748. Stevens also attributes his departure to the "insolent and tyrannical magistrate to whom the government of the colony was committed". W.B. Stevens, *History of Georgia*, I, 320 ff. Alexander Garden also considered most of the complaints "frivolous and groundless". Fulham Palace Papers contain Mr. Garden's letter to his superior, the Bishop of London, dated 4 June 1736. Copy in Georgia Historical Society MS 978, file 113.

[18] Egmont's *Journal*, 10 October 1735 (p. 108).

[19] Egmont's *Journal*, 20 October 1736, (p. 207 f.). Egmont, whose journal provides us so much insight into the growing disaffection between the Trustees and Quincy, does not elaborate on this final encounter.

[20] Wesley, John, *Works*, ed. John Emory. Volume III is devoted entirely to Wesley's journal, but since there is another standard edition commonly available, entries will usually be shown by date.

[21] Wesley, *Works*, see entries for 17-20th March 1735.

[22] Wesley, *Works*, 25 January 1736, vol. 3, p. 17.

[23] Wesley, *Works*, 26 January 1736. vol. 3, p. 17.

[24] Wesley, *Works*, vol. 3, p. 18.

[24a] *The Letters of the Rev. John Wesley, A.M.*, ed. John Telford, vol. 1, p. 196. Letter from Savannah, 18 March 1736.

[25] Wesley, *Works* vol 3 pages 18-21.

[26] An ill, eleven day old infant named Mary Welch. *Ibid*.

[27] *The Journal of the Rev. John Wesley, A.M.*, ed. Nehemiah Curnock, 5 May 1736, vol. 1, p. 210f. Pastor Bolzius, of the Salzburger community, also noted that "the people [in Savannah] are much displeased that Mr. [Wesley] does not wish to baptize other than by immersing." Samuel Urlsperger, ed., *Detailed Reports on the Salzburger Emmigrants Who Settled in America*, translated and edited by George Fenwick Jones, *et al*. vol. 4, page 6 (13 Jan. 1737).

[28] Wesley, *Works*, vol. 2, pp. 208-210f.

[29] Wesley, *Works*, vol. 3, p. 40 (7 August 1737).

[30] Wesley, *Works*, 9 May 1736, vol. 3 p. 24. The Evening Service was held at 7 P.M. during the week because, as Wesley noted years later, in Savannah "The generality of people rose at 7 or 8 in the morning and [worked] till six in the evening. Thus the hours of services were selected to avoid interference with that pattern. See *Works*, Vol. 5, p. 92.

[31] Wesley, *Works*, 10 May 1736 vol. 3, p. 24f.

[32] Wesley, *Works*, 4 April 1737, vol. 3, p. 35.

[33] CR, vol. 21, p. 220f.

[34] Wesley, *Works*, vol. 3, p. 44.

[35] Wesley, *Works*, vol. 3, p.44f.

[36] In a summary of his Georgia experience composed some time after the fact, Wesley included a useful description of the layout, distance and direction to numerous towns and other sites in the area. Of special interest is his note on the Indian town of Irene, where, a furlong away stand "a house built for an Indian school in the year 1736 . . . on a small round hill in a little piece of fruitful ground, given by the Indians to Mr. Ingham." Wesley, *Works*, vol. 3, p. 48.

[37] Wesley, *Works*, 1 August 1737, vol. 3, p. 40.

[38] See especially the entries for 22 June, 26 July, and 25-31 October 1736 in Wesley's *Works* vol. 3 pp. 26 ff.

[39] *Works*, vol. 3, p. 23. Ideally suited for travel in the coastal marshes, a pettiawga was a flat-bottomed craft, variable length to as much as thirty feet.

[40] *Works*, 2 August 1736 (vol. 3, p. 31) Moderns will find it enjoyable as well as painfully amusing to realize also how little some things change — for contemporary records of such adventures contain many references to recognizable landmarks and channels along with irritated condemnations of the ubiquitous mosquitoes, sandflies, and tiny red vermin that attack the unwary in the woods.

[41] *Works*, 12 April 1737, vol. 3, p. 35. His visit on this occasion was to Mr. Alexander Garden, the official representative of the Bishop of London.

[42] *Journal*, 14 October 1735, p. 114.

[43] Wesley, *Works*, vol. 3, p. 23f.

[44] Wesley, *Works*, 30 June 1736, vol. 3, p. 27.

[45] Wesley's *Journal*, vol. 1, p. 160 (14 Feb. 1736).

[46] Egmont's *Journal*, p. 177f, and Wesley's *Works*, vol. 3, pp. 28-30, record a fascinating interview with a group of Chicka-

⁴⁷ Wesley, *Works*, 23 November 1736, vol. 3, p. 32f. Although this is only Wesley's version of the dispute, it is entirely compatible with the scattered references that appear elsewhere in journals, Oglethorpe's correspondence, Trustees' records, etc. See, for example, the ministerial plan for the colony sketched by Lord Percival in his *Diary*, vol. 2, p. 365 (8 March 1737). Percival's understanding of the plan makes it clear that Wesley's expectation of being freed to preach to the Indians is not simply the product of his own imagination.

⁴⁸ Wesley, *Letters*, 10 October 1735, to Dr. Burton at Corpus Christi College, Oxford. Vol. 1, pp. 188ff.

⁴⁹ There is some evidence that the controversy over introduction of slavery, which proved so divisive later, may already have raised tempers and polarized opinion, and that it may have also been one of the quarrels which so vexed some against Wesley. This deserves further investigation, but see CR, vol. 6, pp. 273-293.

⁵⁰ Wesley, *Works*, 2 Dec. 1737 vol. 3, p. 45. It is almost painfully ironic that Wesley came as close to the Indians as he was ever to come only a few hours after arriving in Savannah. The one he met and chatted with on that occasion, Tomochichi, he could have met had he never left England! See Egmont's *Journal*, 14 Feb. 1736 (p. 131 f.)

⁵⁰ᵃ Quoted in H.J. Mikell, "The Founding of the Church in Georgia," *Georgia Historical Quarterly*, vol. 17, (1933), p. 81, from a contemporary, but uncited source.

⁵¹ Egmont's *Journal*, p. 216 (Dec. 1736).

⁵¹ᵃ *Fulham Palace Papers* (archives of the Bp. of London), in a letter dated 22 Dec. 1737 (from a transcript in MS 978, f. 112.)

⁵² *Journals*, 2 June 1738, p. 157.

⁵³ *Times*, 4 May 1791, p. 3 col. 1. The obituary is, of course, speaking not specifically of Wesley's work in Georgia, but of his career in general. See also the *Georgia Gazette*, 26 May 1791 (3-1).

⁵⁴ Egmont's *Journal*, 15-29 June 1737, pp. 284, 286.

⁵⁵ Egmont's *Journal*, 16 May 1738, p. 358.

⁵⁶ CR, vol. 29, p. 520, in a letter from the Trustees to William Stephens (20 May 1738).

⁵⁷ Whitefield, *Journals*, Monday, 8 May 1738, p. 155.

⁵⁸ CR, vol. 29, p. 561 f. 28 June 1738.

⁵⁹ CR, vol. 30, p. 17 and vol. 4, p. 212

⁶⁰ CR, vol. 4 p. 219 f. Stephens' *Journal*, 30 October 1738.

⁶⁰ᵃ *Detailed Reports* vol. 5, p. 252 (25 Oct. 1738). Dr. Jones appropriately suggests that Pastor Bolzius' prejudice most likely was transmitted via James Habersham, who was indeed among Norris' most avid tormentors. See also p. 263 f.

⁶¹ Stephens' *Journal* 18 November 1738. CR vol. 4, p. 229 f. As for the priesthood, however, Whitefield intended that from the beginning. Even before his arrival in Georgia, he wrote to a "Mrs. H[utton]" that he intended returning "to England about Christmas next" for ordination. George Whitefield, *Works*, vol 1, p. 42. (Letter 37, 14 April 1738, written while "at Sea," underway from Gibraltar to Savannah.)

⁶² CR, vol. 4, p. 255 (Stephens' *Journal*, 31 Dec. 1738).

⁶³ CR, vol. 4, p. 255.

⁶⁴ CR, vol. 4, p. 487 (Stephens' *Journal* 11 January, 1740).

⁶⁵ CR, vol. 4, 489 f. (13, January 1740) There is some confusion regarding who was really assigned where, but a report from Pastor Bolzius seems to clear it. He recounted (31 July 1739) that "Mr. Norris showed me two letters from the Lord Trustees wherein he [was] asked to take on the office of minister in Frederica." *Detailed Reports*, vol. 6, p. 170 f. This seems a likely explanation, because by May Norris was already directing his attention to the troops at Ft. Frederica "for the better opportunity of exercising my ministry." There was even hope, if Oglethorpe's arms should be successful, "of enlightening the poor benighted Spaniards and bringing them to worship the *True God* after a true manner." (This letter from Mr. Norris, dated 5 May 1740, is included in the collection of SPG Correspondence, vol. B-7, p. 263. Copy at G.H.S., MS 978, f. 106.)

⁶⁵ᵃ CR, vol. 4, p. 528 (Stephens' journal for 7 March 1740).

⁶⁶ CR, vol. 30, p. 288. The letter from the Trustees, dated 8 July 1740, tells us little more about Metcalf except that he was living at Immingham, near Caster, Lincolnshire.

⁶⁷ Whitefield, *Journal*, 29 December 1740 (p. 500).

⁶⁸ CR vol. 22 (Part I), p. 751 in a letter dated 12 Dec. 1738.

⁶⁹ CR vol 22 (Part I) p. 354.

⁷⁰ CR, vol. 22 (Part I), p. 352.

⁷¹ *Journal*, 6 June 1737, p. 277.

⁷² CR, vol. 22 (Part I), pp. 351-353.

⁷³ Perhaps Savannahians can even take some comfort from the observation that some of what Mr. Norris feared here did indeed happen in England — at least in the sense that the Church of England was split. He saw accurately the issue that would do it and the rock on which it would occur — only the labels for each will still be debated.

⁷⁴ *Journal* of William Stephens, 4 April 1740, in CR, vol. 4, p. 548.

⁷⁴ᵃ In a letter dated 28 May 1742 at Frederica. *The Letters of General Oglethorpe*, published as the *Collections of the Georgia Historical Society*, vol. III, p. 120 f.

⁷⁵ *[The] State of the Province of Georgia . . .* (London, 1742), p. 3.

⁷⁶ Ibid, p. 4.

⁷⁷ Whitefield, *Journals*, 29 January 1740, p. 396.

⁷⁸ 9 October 1740, CR, vol. 4, page 9. Regarding Whitefield's liturgical irregularity, see also William Stephens *Journal*, 30 October 1738.

⁷⁹ *A Collection of Psalms and Hymn*, Charles-Town: Lewis Timothy, 1737. Along with the slightly earlier, but similar, collections of Tate and Brady, Isaac Watts, and the contemporary Augustus Montague Toplady (all dissenters), Wesley's publication signals a major departure in that it was not only the first Anglican hymnal, but also the first English-language collection published in America. See also Curnock's notes in Wesley's *Journal*, Vol. 1, p. 114 regarding other hymnals Wesley possibly had at hand. It is also intriguing to note that only a few blocks removed from the shop where Mr. Timothy was setting Wesley's pioneer hymnal to print lived Carl Theodor Pachelbel, organist at St. Philips Church. Carl's father, Johann, was one of the most celebrated organists and composers of the age, and a major figure in the Lutheran musical tradition — indeed, a favorite of J.S. Bach. It seems quite plausible to speculate that the younger Pachelbel further reinforced Wesley's already vigorous admiration for German piety and sacred chorales, and may well have influenced the contents of the new hymnal.

⁷⁹ᵃ *Journal* (Curnock) 5 and 7 May 1736, vol. 1 p. 211 f.

⁷⁹ᵇ CR vol. 6, p. 101. Apparently the job was not only considered important enough to pay for, but even to pay a substitute if need be. Interestingly, Thomas Lee himself received 25 shillings per quarter for the same job!

⁷⁹ᶜ Urlsperger, ed., *Detailed Reports of the Salzburger Emigrants* vol. 4, p. 135. See also pp. 102 and 117.

⁸⁰ Specifically, it was charged that Wesley had introduced "into the Church and Service at the alter compositions of Psalms and hymns not inspected or authorized by any proper judicature." The indictment against Wesley is most readily accessible in CR, vol. 4, p. 19ff. (notes), and Wesley, *Works*, vol. 3, pp. 42-44. See also Dr. Tucker's discussion of Wesley's role as reported in the *Savannah Morning News* 29 Jan. 1967 (1-1ff.).

⁸¹ Stephens' *Journal* in CR vol 4 (Part 2), p. 58, 21 December 1740.

⁸² CR, vol. 4, p. 61. Refusal to take note of "popish feasts and fasts" had become a hallmark of the Presbyterians and Calvinist tradition generally.

⁸³ CR, vol. 4, p. 63, 20 December 1740.

⁸³ᵃ Stephen's *Journal* 16 November 1745 (vol. 2, p. 251 f.)

⁸⁴ Stephens' *Journal* 31 May 1742 vol. 1, p. 87. The *Journal* also notes the completion of the work on the roof one month later, 26 June, p. 99.

⁸⁵ Dec. 1732 The silver followed, thanks to Mr. Wesley's mediation, in April 1733. CR, vol. 3, pp. 20-23. The Rector of Epworth's interest in Georgia enterprise is well documented in contemporary correspondence, leaving little doubt that it was the father, and not the eldest of the brothers, both named Samuel, who was instrumental in the donation of the silver.

See, for example, his correspondence with Oglethorpe in November and December of 1734 in *Henry Newman's Salzburger Letterbooks* transcribed and edited by Geroge Fenwick Jones. (Athens: 1966) pp. 514f and 517-519.

[86] CR vol. 30, p. 108 in a letter to Wm. Stephens dated 14 July 1739.

[87] Whitefield, *Journals*, 11 March 1740, p. 399.

[88] *Journal*, 25 March 1744 (Easter Day), vol. 2, p. 86

[89] *Journal*, 25 March 1744 (Easter Day), vol. 2, p. 86

[90] *Journal*, 19 April 1742, Vol. 1, p. 67.

[91] Wesley, *Journal* (Curnock), vol. 1 pp. 421 ff. (1 February 1738).

[92] vol. 2, page 112.

[92a] Noted in the *Minute Book, 1729-35* as enacted 2 July 1733,. From a copy in MS 978, folio 114, at Georgia Historical Society.

[93] Numerous lists are to be found, but a sizable and representative collection is easily accessible in CR, vol. 3, pp. 20-23.

[94] See, for example, CR vol. 29, p. 216; and *Journal* (Curnock) where Wesley notes "by Mr. Ingham I writ to the Founders of Parochial Libraries "who sent a library to Savannah in the latter end of last year."

[95] CR, vol. 31, p. 325. Dr. Crow was rector of St. Botolph's, Bishopsgate, London.

[96] Wesley, *Letters*, vol. 1, p. 211, and 214; 16 February 1737 and 26 February

[97] CR, vol. 22, part I, p. 354 (Dec. 1738).

[98] Whitefield, *Journals*, 12 June 1738, p. 158

[99] *The Journal of the Rev. Charles Wesley, M.A.*, ed. John Telford. (London: Robert Culley, n.d.) 2 Nov. 1737, p. 129.

[100] In a letter to a friend dated at Bethesda, Ga., 21 March 1746, cited in Georgia White, *Historical Collections of Georgia*, p. 329. This particular source, confirmed by others, is of special interest in that it includes a good description of the produce of Bethesda, and a full list of past and present orphans, as of its date of publication, 1855.

[101] Dalimore, *George Whitefield* vol. 1, p. 453. See also Egmont's *Journal*, 13 December 1738, p. 512.

[102] Whitefield, *Journals*, 19 May 1738, p. 156.

[103] Whitefield, *Journals*, 11 July 1738, p. 159; and also *Detailed Reports*, vol. 5, p. 152 f.

[104] Whitefield, *Journals*, 9, May 1739, p. 263; See also CR, vol. 5 p. 166.

[105] Whitefield, *Journals*, 9 May 1739, p. 263. This represents 7680 halfpenny coins! Can we presume that each halfpenny represents an individual contributor? If so, it tends to increase our trust of Whitefield's estimates of the size of the crowds he attracted.

[106] Whitefield, *Journals*, 13 May 1739, p. 263.

[107] Ibid.

[108] CR, vol. 5, p. 166.

[109] Whitefield, *Journals*, 11 January 1740, p. 395.

[110] Ibid.

[111] Whitefield, *Journals*, 24 January 1740.

[112] Whitefield, *Journals*, 29 January 1740.

[113] Whitefield, *Journals*, 29 January 1740, p. 396.

[114] Whitefield, *Journals*, 6 June 1740, p. 432.

[115] Whitefield, *Journals*, 30 January 1740, p. 396.

[116] Whitefield, *Journals*, 30 January 1740, p. 396.

[117] Whitefield, *Journals*, 30 January 1740, p. 396.

[118] Whitefield, *Journals*, 25 March 1740, vol. 2 p. 403. A few months later he wrote a friend complaining that the orphan house would have been finished already "if the Spaniards had not taken a schooner loaded with bricks and other provisions" intended for the work. Written from Good-Hope (South Carolina), 1 January 1741. George Whitefield, *Works*, vol. 1, p. 230.

[119] Whitefield, *Works*, vol. 1, p. 85 cited in A.A. Dallimore, *George Whitefield*, p. 448f.

[120] In this regard, Whitefield's exhuberant outburst on hearing of Oglethorpe's repulsion of the Spaniards in 1742 makes the point with gusto! "The deliverance of Georgia from the Spaniards is such as cannot be paralleled but by some instances out of the Old Testament!" The remark is quoted by Walter G. Charlton in an address dedicating the Oglethorpe monument in Chippewa Square, Savannah, November 1910. Unfortunately, no source is indicated in the printed edition, (*Collections of the GHS*, vol. 7, part 2, p. 36.)

[121] Wesley, *Letters*, vol. 6, p. 41, dated September 1773.

[122] White, *Historical Collections of Georgia*, pp. 228-230, dated 3 June 1773. The letter goes on to note that while a little furniture and a few books were saved, such treasures as Whitefield's effigy in wax, his picture, and a "neat brass branch" were lost — all melted in the flames.

[123] Cited in Dallimore, *George Whitefield* p. 446, is the infirmary he had set up in a house (rented from a Mr. Bradley) with medicines he had bought from England. Placed in charge was Patrick Hunter, described by Egmont as an "experienced apothecary and surgeon of good substance."

[124] CR, vol. 33, p. 115f.

[125] Beneath this small point in our narrative lurks a very large and amusing iceberg. It seems that Whitefield was "bound over" in Charlestown for his outspoken "libel" of clergy and opposing views. CR vol. 4 (Part 2), p. 75 and vol. 5, p. 421. He was also cited by the Rev. Mr. Alexander Garden, Commissary for the Bishop of London, for "preaching false doctrine," a net with which Whitefield would rather have seen others ensnared, suggested Garden, and "irregular practices." (30 June 1740. CR, vol. 5, p. 380.) Both actions are illuminated when we note a small item published in Savannah that same year entitled *A Letter from the Rev. Mr. Whitefield . . . Wherein He Vindicates His Asserting That Abp. Bishop Tillotson [of Canterbury] Knew No More of Christianity Than Mahomet.* (Recalled in Sprague, *Annals of the American Pulpit*, vol. 5, p. 40, in the article on Alexander Garden.) Nevertheless, Whitefield complained to the Bishop that Mr. Garden had proceeded against him in ecclesiastical court, and that he had been obliged to preach in a "meeting house" because Garden would not permit him use of his Church, St. Philips! Ten years later, while reflecting on his experience in Charlestown, Garden recalled that he had been obliged to proceed against only four clergymen while he was commissary. One of these was Whitefield, whom he had suspended from office only, "being a vagabond clergyman and having no Benefice to be suspended from." (Both letters, dated 8 September 1740 and 1 February 1750, are among the Fulham Palace Papers, with copies held in MS 978, f. 113, at the Georgia Historical Society.)

[126] CR vol. 33, p. 150.

[127] Letter to the Trustees, date 4 April 1741. CR, vol. 23, p, 7.

[128] CR, vol. 33, p. 180f. By the same action, Sept. 1741, the Trustees again revoked Whitefield's commission to perform in Savannah. See also CR vol. 30, p. 369.

[129] By the Bishop of St. David's at the Chapel Royal, St. James, Westminster. CR, vol. 33, p. 179.

[130] William Stephens' *Journal*, vol. 1, p. 14.

[131] Stephens' *Journal*, vol. 1, p. 16.

[132] Stephens' *Journal*, vol. 1, p. 30 (11 January 1742).

[133] Ibid.

[134] Bosomworth in fact recorded it at Stephens' request as a way of protecting young Orton from the worst effects of such "rude treatment."

[135] For the theologically minded, it will also be noteworthy that unlike Wesley and his followers, and Anglicanism in general at the time, Whitefield's belief was vigorously Calvinistic — hence the salience of the predestination issue.

[136] In a letter to the Trustees dated 4 March 1742 CR vol. 23, p. 228.

[137] *Journal* vol. 1, p. 69 (25 April 1742).

[138] *Journal*, vol. 1, p. 119. (12 August 1742).

[139] 26 February 1744, vol. 2, p. 75 in Stephens' *Journal*.

[140] Stephens' *Journal*, vol. 2, p. 75f.

[141] Stephens' *Journal*, vol. 2, p. 77.

[142] Stephens' *Journal*, vol. 2, p. 90ff.

[143] Stephens' *Journal*, 21 July 1744, vol. 2, p. 127.

[144] Stephens' *Journal*, vol. 2, p. 131.

[145] They were eventually awarded St. Catherine's. Bosomworth reappears only briefly in 1749 and again in 1752 — long enough to ask help from the vestry. He sought their endorsement of an affadavit that he had always been dutiful and loyal to the prince and "strictly conformed to the liturgy of the Church of England . . ." these five years past. See CR, vol. 27, pp. 475 and 491. Eventually the Colonial Privy Council formalized the nearly universal dissat-

isfaction with his performance, charging that he "deserted his ministry, . . . going up with his wife into the Creek Nation without any license from the Trustees." MS 978, folder 116.

[146] The ordinations took place in the Chapel-Royal, Whitehall, 22 September and 20 October 1745, and arrangements to transfer SPG support to the new missionary were made in November. British (Museum) Library MS 27990, *Minutes and Correspondence of the Trustees 1743-1747*, folio 71ff. See also CR vol. 33, pp. 311-321, and vol. 31, p. 51f.

[147] *Minutes and Correspondence*, folio 71ff. This is the same "Bartholomäus Zoberbiller" who had begun preaching to the Reformed people of Purrysburg (S.C.) in the place of his recently deceased father. The *Detailed Reports* of the Ebenezer Salzurger clergy describe him as a "theological student." vol. 6, p. 268 (3 Nov. 1739).

[148] *Minutes and Correspondence*, folio 71ff.

[149] CR vol. 33, p. 373.

[150] CR vol. 33, p. 469. The questions arose in 1750. Incidently, Mr. Zouberbuhler was the last of the SPG missionaries to serve both Savannah and Frederica on a regular basis.

[151] In a letter to the Trustees dated 11 May 1747, from Savannah. CR vol. 25, p. 177.

[152] Letter of 8 August 1748. CR vol. 25, p. 315. The rector also reports 46 baptisms, including 9 in the last six months.

[153] 7 July 1745, vol. 2, p. 224.

[154] Letter from the Trustees to officials in Savannah dated 16 March 1747. CR vol. 31, p. 106f. The Trustees had earlier offered to pay for a servant for Zouberbuhler if he would agree to pay Zubly £10/annum to officiate at Vernonburgh and Acton. CR, vol. 2, 478 (16 Feb. 1747).

[155] Letter to the Trustees, 11 May 1747 CR vol. 25, p. 178.

[156] In a letter dated 8 August 1748. CR vol. 25, p. 316.

[157] In a letter dated 24 January 1733, CR vol. 29, p. 6. The accounts of the Trustees note an expenditure "for the Religious uses of the Colony" of some £50 "for . . . the building of a Tabernacle of Split Boards, 36 ft. long by 12 ft. wide, for Divine Service, and building an House for the Minister." (See Mr. Verelst's statement of accounts for 1734-35, found in CR, vol. 3, p. 87.) This is probably the dual purpose Tabernacle-Courthouse shown on the 1734 view of Savannah sketched by Peter Gordon, standing on the rear of the lot now occupied by the Customs House. (The rectory is shown, too, east of the church lot, making it then the only dwelling house beyond Drayton St.) Clearly, however, a hybrid structure did not satisfy the desire to have a real church. Contemporary records make virtually no mention of it as a tabernacle, but always refer to it as the courthouse.

[158] Expressed in a personal letter to Oglethorpe dated at Charlestown 19 October 1734, CR vol. 20, p. 640ff. from a Mr. Samuel Eveleigh.

[159] Typical of these notes is that found in CR vol 29, p. 280, which confirms donations from several benefactors and requests plans and cost estimates from Oglethorpe, 1736.

[160] Egmont's *Journal*, 31 March 1736, p. 145.

[161] Given by a Mr. John Tuckwell and noted in Egmont's *Journal*, 26 March 1735, p. 79. No further mention of the clock has been discovered. Its donor, on the other hand, was noted as an ironmonger from Wallingford, Oxfordshire. At one point he was even granted 50 acc. in Georgia, but was later excused from going over. *Diary of Viscount Percival*, vol. 2, p. 198f. (2 Oct. 1735).

[162] CR, vol. 5, p. 383 and CR, vol. 22 (part 2), pp. 358-360 in a letter from Whitefield to the Trustees dated at Savannah, 10 March 1740.

[163] Council Minutes of 6 April 1741, CR vol. 2, p. 365. The affair dragged on through another three years and many lawyers before the account was finally settled. See, for example CR, vol. 5, pp. 629, 698, 714.

[164] In a letter penned by Mr. Harman Verelst, CR, vol. 5, p. 488 (6 April 1741).

[164a] Adding to the mystery, the pile included blocks from a "quarry of ironstone — which was . . . looked upon as a rarity," found in a 5 acre lot near Saannah. (CR vol. 4, p. 603f., June 25, 1740). It was probably this accumulation of materials that inspired the Trustees, with misleading optimism, to claim that "a Church is at present building." See the *Account Showing the Progress of the Colony of Georgia in America From Its First Establishment* (London, 1741; reprinted and sold by James Green, at his Printing Office in Annapolis, 1742), published per order of the Honourable Trustees, p. 32.

[165] Egmont's *Journal*, p. 287.

[166] Egmont's *Journal* 12 April 1738, p. 345. What appears to be the bill of lading for this order also survives and appears in the CR vol. 29, p. 531. The list of materials shipped is a more detailed version which specifies their use for building the church at Savannah along with lumber from another source. Craftsmen will enjoy the inventory of supplies and tools on pp. 541-543 of the volume.

[167] Egmont's *Journal* for this period, pp. 360-363, is especially informative; see also the Trustee's letter to Whitefield dated 11 June 1740, CR vol. 30, p. 270.

[168] Letter from the Trustees to Wm. Stephens, 11 June 1740, cited in E.M. Coulter, *Wormsloe*, p. 95.

[169] G. Whitefield, *Journals* for 6 June 1740, p. 431f.

[170] Dated 1 January 1741 CR vol. 22 (part 2), p. 482.

[171] CR, vol. 30, p. 270.

[172] In a letter to the Trustees dated at Savannah, 14 December 1742, CR vol. 23, p. 453.

[173] Stephens' *Journal* vol. 2, p. 50f. The "Covent Garden Church" is the one known by its association with the names of St. Paul and Eliza Doolittle (*My Fair Lady*). With that structure and the present Christ Church building in mind, the details of Stephens' remarks take on considerable interest.

[174] Stephens' *Journal*, vol 2, p. 69.

[175] Stephens' *Journal*, vol. 2, p. 75.

[176] Stephens' *Journal*, 5 March 1744 vol. 2, p. 77f.

[177] Stephens' *Journal*, 28th March 1744, vol. 2, p. 87.

[178] Stephens' *Journal*, vol. 2, p. 95.

[179] *Ibid*.

[180] Stephens' *Journal*, 16 May 1744, vol. 2, p. 103.

[181] *Journal*, 28 July 1744, vol. 2, p. 129.

[182] Stephens' *Journal*, 6-7 September, 1744, vol. 2, p. 143.

[183] Stephens' *Journal*, 22 october 1744, vol. 2, p. 158ff.

[184] Stephens' *Journal*, 9 October 1744, vol. 2, p. 155.

[185] *Journal*, 3 Dec. 1745, vol. 2, p. 257ff.

[186] CR, vol. 31, p. 109.

[187] Noted in a letter to officials in Savannah which includes unusual detail about the nature of the paint and the proper technique of its application. CR vol. 31, p. 143f.

[188] Minutes of 18 August 1747, CR vol. 6, p. 188f. It is interesting to compare the structure actually built with the one envisioned by the Trustees. Several years earlier, they had thought in terms of a building 40 × 80 ft. with a tower 20 ft. square and 40 ft. high; walls 3 brick thick to ten feet, and then 2½ above that, with no windows for 10 ft. above ground level, but with loopholes for muskets; all white washed inside and furnished with a pulpit, reading desk, communion rail and table, plus benches "as at Tunbridge." [*Diary of Viscount Percival*, vol. 2, p. 415 (22 June 1737.)] A further comparison may be made with the rather crude depiction, c. 1779, reproduced in Mills B. Lane, *Savannah Revisited* (2nd edition), pp. 36-37, from a manuscript in the Newberry Library, Chicago.

[189] Letter of 16 March 1747, CR, vol. 31, p. 109.

[190] Letter from Zouberbuhler to the Trustees, 11 May 1747, CR vol. 25, pp. 177-179.

[191] Letter from the President and Assistants in Savannah to the Trustees, 5 May 1749, CR vol. 6, p. 247. By that time the "Crowne Glass" ordered for the Church and the minister's house apparently was in place. Unfortunately the dates regarding the order of 280 squares for the Church — "200 for the sides and 80 for the end windows, including spares" — are now lost, although the order survives. CR vol. 31, p. 325f.

[192] Letter dated 2 October 1747, CR vol. 25, pp. 225-237.

[193] *SPG Correspondence*, Vol. B-18, p. 197, 20 Dec. 1750. (Transcript in MS. 978, f. 108.) Zouberbuhler's letter also noted how the occasion was made especially joyous by their coincidental celebration of several colonists' "invitation to the happy privileges of British subjects", and the tenth anniversary of "our great and wonderful deliverence out of the bloody hands of the Spaniards." See also Edgar L. Pennington, "The Rev. Bartholomew Zouberbuhler", GHQ, vol. 18, no. 4 (Dec. 1934), p. 359.

[193a] In his "Religious Education of the Negro in the Colony of Georgia," GHQ, vol. 14, (1930), p. 51, J. Lawrence suggested this may have been the first Negro baptism in Georgia. This study has discovered none earlier.

Chapter Two

[193.2] Appointed 15 Feb. *S.P.G. Correspondence* in MS 978, f. 109 at Georgia Historical Society.

[193.3] *SPG Correspondence*, B-19, p. 149. 9 September 1751 (MS 978, folder 109).

[193.4] Ibid.

[193.5] *SPG Correspondence*, vol. B, 2 June 1752, in a letter to the Rev. Mr. Smith at All Hallows-London Wall, MS 978, folder 109.

[193.6] In a letter of 19 Nov. 1753, found in the same collection.

[193.7] *SPG Journal*, vol. 12, in a letter dated 20 July 1753 (In MS 978, f. 110.)

[193.8] *Letters of the Honorable James Habersham (G.H.S. Collections VI)* p. 95, dated 26 Nov. 1770. See also the letter to the S.P.C.K. secretary of 1 Dec. 1770, p. 99f.

[193.9] *Georgia Gazette*, 10 June 1767 (3-2); 6 July 1768 (3-2); 30 August 1769 (2-2).

[193.91] Cited in W.B. Stevens, *A History of Georgia* vol. 1, p. 310 from a Whitefield letter to the Trustees, 6 Dec. 1748.

[193.92] Cited in Stevens, *History of Georgia*, vol. 1, p. 309, from Whitefield's *Journals*.

[194] Dated 6 August 1754, #75. CR vol. 34, p. 67.

[195] Ibid, *Royal Instructions* 76-78.

[196] This function continued primarily in ecclesiastical hands, established and otherwise, until the beginning of the twentieth century. The period 1890-1920 saw the gradual assumption of these duties by state and county agencies created specifically for the purpose. Chatham county is exceptional in this regard, having begun the change over the first decade of the nineteenth century. Specifics of Georgia's royal charter may be found in CR, vol. 13, pp. 156-159, 260, 265ff., 295, 481, etc.,

[197] Instruction #85. CR vol. 34, p. 70

[198] CR vol. 13, p. 596 (16 Nov. 1761)

[199] "Colonial Cemetery", as it is now known, passed into the care of the vestry as a part of the "Act for Constituting . . . the Several District of the Province into Parishes and for Establishing of Religious Worship therein according to the Rites and Ceremonies of the Church of England . . .". Thus, as with "establishment", it took effect 1 March 1758. See CR, vol. 18, p. 260f.

[200] CR vol. 13, p. 720 (9 November 1762).

[201] CR vol. 18, p. 568f. 7 April 1763, where the site is described as being at the corner of Abercorn and South Broad Sts., containing 380' × 210'.

[202] Remembering that the entire Church building finally cost c.£400, one is impressed with the extremity of the problem presented 18 Feb. 1767. CR vol. 14, p. 39.

[203] For example, see the *Georgia Gazette* 5 March 1789 (2-1) and 24 September 1789 (2-2), which listed Leonard Cecil and John Habersham as wardens.

[204] CR, vol. 19 (Part 1), pp. 137-140 (27 Feb. 1770).

[205] CR vol. 19 (Part 1), p. 181f.

[206] 17 June 1767 (3-1)

[207] Council Minutes for 18 April 1755 in CR, vol. 7, p. 172f.

[208] 30 November 1758, CR, vol. 13, p. 331.

[209] Report by Mr. Ottolenghe read 17 January 1759, CR, vol. 13, pp. 345-347.

[210] To Wright Square. This proposal would have had the further impact of forcing relocation of the market then in Wright Square to the middle of Ellis Square. CR vol. 13, p. 749f.

[211] CR vol. 28 (Part 2), p. 51 f.; see also vol. 14, pp. 95, 130, and vol. 17, pp 98f., 101, 110.

[212] The "appropriations bill" for the fiscal year 29 Sept. 1763-29 September 1764 included £130 for "repairs to the Church made last year." CR, vol. 14, p. 103.

[213] Imagine what monuments could be erected if only we could tax video-game dens! It would hardly matter that the revenue might have to be divided, as in this case, between repair of the Church and the upkeep of Tybee Light, "An Act to Defray the Expense of Repairing the Church in Savannah" 27 March 1759, CR, vol. 18, p. 308 ff.

[214] 30 June 1763 (3-1).

[215] *Georgia Gazette*, 7 July 1763 (4-2).

[216] *Georgia Gazette*, 5 September 1765, (3-1).

[217] *Georgia Gazette*, 21 November 1765 (3-2).

[218] In the *Georgia Gazette*, 17 June (3-1) and 1 July 1767 (4-2).

[219] *Early History of the Church in Georgia*, p. 8.

[220] "Mr. Woodmason's Account of South Carolina, North Carolina and Georgia . . . 1766", p. 3f. Extract from a MS in Fulham Palace made by Walter C. Hartridge, and now in the Hartridge Collection at the Georgia Historical Society.

[221] Pennington, p. 356 f. The precise date of the comments is not cited. Zouberbuhler's death on the 11th was noted in the *Georgia Gazette* of 17 Dec. 1766 (2-2).

[223] "Woodmason's Account . . .", p. 3f.

[224] Some of his comments do tend to raise doubts about his willingness to deal accurately, however. At one point he asserts that "the Provincial allowance to clergy is £25" and that "there are no churches or parsonages yet built." The first statement is misleading at best, and the second is plainly false as his next statement recognizes. Ibid.

[225] Ibid.

[226] The assertion of wealth is not without some foundation. Zouberbuhler's Will (Chatham County Superior Court, Will Book "A", 184-188), reveals his title to more than 3000 acres of land, which was devoted largely to the Church, and to Bethesda on his death. However, the will also makes clear enough that for the rector, as for so many Colonials, land alone did not constitute real wealth. What they too often lacked in the early years were the means to make it fully productive. This fact is underscored by his prolonged and unsuccessful attempts to sell portions of his holdings. See, for example, the *Georgia Gazette* issues of 10 Nov. 1763 (3-2), 14 Nov. 1765 (3-1), and 29 October 1766 (3-1).

[227] *SPG Journal*, vol. 15, 16 July 1762.

[228] 18 April 1765 (2-2).

[228a] William DeBrahm, *Report of the General Survey in the Southern District in North America, June 1772*, p. 63b. British (Museum) Library, London. Kings MS 210.

[229] *SPG. Journal*, 17, letters of 26 Jan. and 23 February 1767 (entered 15 May 1767).

[230] *SPG Journal*, 17, action of 12 June 1767; see also W.B. Stevens, *Early History of the Church in Georgia*, p. 50 f.

[231] *Georgia Gazette* 25 April 1765 (3-1).

[232] *SPG Journal*, 17, in a letter from Frink dated January 26, 1767 (entered 10 April).

[233] *Georgia Gazette* 28 January 1767, (3-1) and 14 January (3-1).

[234] *Georgia Gazette*, 8 July 1767 (2-2) to the Courts of Oyer and Terminer.

[235] *Georgia Gazette*, 23 Dec. 1767 (3-2), 7 Dec. 1768 (3-1), 20 Dec 1769 (2-2), etc.

[236] *SPG Journal* 17, 15 May 1767 (letter of 24 February 1767).

[237] *Georgia Gazette*, 2 Nov. 1768 (2-2), solicits bids for the work, e.g., but the burial ground repeatedly was a thorn in the flesh of rector, wardens, and vestry alike for many years.

[238] *SPG Journal*, 17, 16 October 1767 (Frink letter of 3 July).

[239] *SPG Journal*, 18, 15 Sept. 1769 (letter of 29 June 1769).

[240] 1 November 1764 (1-2).

[241] *SPG Journal*, 15, 15 July 1763 (letter from Zouberbuhler dated 14 March 1763), and in vol. 16, 19 April 1765 (in a letter of 31 December 1764).

[242] *SPG Journal*, 19, 21 April 1769 (in a letter of 4 January 1769).

[243] 22 March 1764 (2-1).

[244] Stated by Reba Strickland in *Religion and the State in Georgia in the 18th Century* p. 626. The author cites a letter from Zubly as her source; and such an act does not seem out of character.

[245] Ibid. Mr. Ellington had been Mr. Frink's successor at St. Paul's, Augusta, but moved to Bethesda after a short stay. In 1792 he followed his path once again to become rector of Christ Church.

[246] Reported by the *Georgia Gazzette* 29 March 1769 (3-1), the affair marked the anniversary of the Orphan House with the founding of its academy.

[245] *SPG Journal*, 18, in a letter dated 6 July 1770 (entered 19 October).

[248] (2-1)

[249] *Georgia Gazette*, 31 January 1770, (2-1).

[250] *Georgia Gazette*, 7 February, 1770, (2-2). "Frontiniak" denotes frontignan, a popular muscatel.

[251] Ibid.

[252] See, for example, 21 March (2-1) and 28 March (3-1 and 2).

[253] Reported in Stevens, *Early History*, p. 33.

[254] *SPG Journral* 19, in a letter dated 3 January 1771 (entered 19 April 1771).

[255] Habersham *Letters*, p. 225, (dated 5 April 1773). Piercy and Eccles were both connected with Bethesda at the time.

[257] *SPG Journal* 19, in a letter of 10 October 1771 (entered 17 January 1772).

[258] When he had been stranded making his way to an assignment in E. Florida, St. John's was so impressed they persuaded him to stay. *SPG Journal* 19, in a letter from Mr. Frink dated 8 July 1771 (entered 8 October).

[259] Although SPG documents make it seem unlikely, CR, vol. 12, p. 320 suggests he may also have had some connection with St. Philips about this time.

[260] *Letters* dated 12 March 1772 to Gov. James Wright.

[261] Habersham, *Letters* to Gov. Wright, dated 30 March 1772.

[262] *SPG Journal*, 19, Letters from the Wardens dated 1 January 1772, (entered 20 March 1772).

[263] Implied by a letter from Habersham to William Knox, secretary to the Earl of Hillsborough. The writer expresses his confidence that "Mr. Lowten will be no loser by the Society withdrawing their salary." *Letters*, 13 June 1772.

[264] Stevens, *Early History*, p. 59.

[265] *Georgia Gazette* 27 July 1774 (2-1).

[266] The date is inferred from an affadavit sworn amid controversy the following year by the Sexton, John Neidlinger, and published in the *Georgia Gazette* 14 December 1774 (2-2).

[267] On the other hand, among the churches with a background of establishments such as Anglican, Lutheran, etc., there was little of the ecclesiology of the "gathered" or "covenant" congregation. The distinction is more than academic. It had profound affect on their response to social issues and relations to government as well as on their "self-image."

[268] Coleman, *American Revolution in Georgia*, p. 222 f.

[269] Noted in a letter from James Habersham to the Rt. Hon., the Earl of Hillsborough, 15 June 1772. MS. 978, file 87, a transcript of an original in the Colonial Office.

[270] For example, *Georgia Gazette*, 10 May 1769 (3-1) See also 16 May 1770 (2-1).

[271] Rates in 1765, for example, were set at: 3^d per 100 acc. of land; 3^d in slaves per head; 6^d per £100 at interest or stock-in-trade; plus 1/8 of the general tax paid on lots in Savannah. *Georgia Gazette*, 2 May 1765 (5-2).

[272] First generation alien immigrants could appreciate their situation, for they too had sworn to be loyal subjects of King George when they entered the colonies.

[273] *Georgia Gazette* issues of 10, 17, 24, and 31 August, and September 14, 21 and 28 carried the first of the series.

[274] Recorded in a sworn statement which the *Gazette* published 14 December 1774 (2-2).

[275] *Georgia Gazette*, 14 December 1774 (2-1).

[276] Printed by the *Georgia Gazette* 21 December 1774 (2-2).

[277] Ibid.

[278] *Georgia Gazette* 28 December 1774 (4-2).

[279] *Georgia Gazette* 11 January 1775 (4-1).

[280] *Georgia Gazette* 1 February 1775 (2-1).

[281] Coulter, *Georgia, A Short History*, p. 123.

[281a] Tondee's was on the northwest corner of Broughton and Whitaker Streets.

[282] The proclamation was printed in the *Georgia Gazette*, 12 July 1775 (2-2).

[283] The Provincial Congress was viewed by many as an unconstitutional body, like the Council of Safety and the Parochial Committee, and therefore possessed of no legal authority. Sometime after the furor, when petitioning the King for compensation, Smith gave this account of the ordeal. See CR, vol. 39, pp. 413-419, especially p. 416.

[284] *Revolutionary Records of Georgia*, vol. I p. 258.

[285] CR vol. 38 (Part I), p. 531f., and vol. 39, p. 416.

[286] CR vol. 38 (Part I), p. 531 f.

[287] Reported in a Deposition sworn out by Mr. Smith 25 July 1775, now found among the *Fulham Palace Papers*, MS 978, f. 113, at Georgia Historical Society.

[288] CR vol. 39, p. 417

[289] From a deposition sworn 7 August 1775 by Haddon Smith, before leaving Georgia, in CR vol. 38 (Part 1), p. 544 f.

[290] Written to Gov. Wright, the petition appears in CR, vol. 38 (Part 2) pp. 18-21; a deposition to the same effect by Anthony Stokes, Chief Justice of Georgia and signer of the petition, complements it nicely. CR vol. 38 (Part 1) p. 580. Vestry lists are in the *Georgia Gazette* issues of 6 April 1774 (2-2) and 19 April 1775 (2-2). Later in the revolution the Langworthy mentioned was elected a delegate to Congress along with Edward Telfair and John Houstoun. *Revolutionary Records of Georgia*, vol. 2, p. 175. Minutes of the Executive Council for 31 August 1779.

[291] CR vol. 38 (Part 1), p. 532

[292] *Georgia Gazette*, 23 August 1775, (3-1).

[293] *Georgia Gazette* 1 November 1775 (2-2). In an odd twist, Smith's sister arrived at Tybee only three weeks after his departure, having had no chance to hear news of the summer's events until then. *Georgia Gazette*, 20 September 1775 (3-1).

[294] Quoted in Coulter, *Georgia, A Short History*, p. 130 f.

[295] *Revolutionary Records of Georgia*, vol. I, p. 97.

[295.1] Reba Strickland, *Religion and State in 18th Century Georgia*, p. 157 f.

[295.2] Loyalist Claims (Georgia) 13-35 and 13-36a, in MS 978, f. 103 f.

[296] See Coulter, *Georgia, A Short History*, p. 150

[298] *Royal Gazette of Georgia*. 11 March 1779 (1-2) The appointment was made one week earlier, on the 4th.

[299] Gov. Wright's statement was made in an affadavit sworn some years after the events described in support of Jenkins' claim against the British government. It is now in the Public Record Office among the records of the Audit Office, *Loyalist Claims*, vol. 13, item 130. (transcript in the Georgia Historical Society MS. 978, folder 104)

[300] *SPG Journal*, vol. 22, under 21 July 1780. The information was itself abstracted from correspondence received from another SPG missionary, Rev. Mr. James Brown, dated 15 April 1780.

[301] *SPG Journal*, vol. 22 The words are those of the SPG secretary who recorded this summary of his correspondent's remarks under the date 21 July 1780.

[302] *SPG Journal*, vol. 21, entered 21 September 1781.

[303] Ibid. and CR vol. 12, p. 320.

[304] *SPG Journal*, vol. 21, summary of a letter from Seymour dated 26 April 1781, entered 21 September 1781.

[305] *SPG Journal* vol. 21, recorded 15 Feb. 1782 from a letter dated at Charleston, 29 Dec. 1781.

[306] *SPG Journal*, vol. 21 entered 21 June 1782 from correspondence dated 14 March. Our next glimpse of Mr. Seymour finds him in St. Augustine relieving a colleague there during the final days of British control. *SPG Journal*, vol. 21, recorded 21 Nov. 1783.

[307] *Revolutionary Records of Georgia*, vol. III, p. 122. See also W.B. Stevens, *Early History of the Church in Georgia*, p. 61. The "House of Assembly" was created by the revolutionary constitution of 1777 as the successor to the old "Commons House of Assembly" which had existed under royal government.

[308] *Gazette of the State of Georgia*, 1 April (2-3), and 8 April (1-1), 1784.

[309] *Gazette of the State of Georgia*, 8 April 1784, (1-1).

[310] *Vestry Minutes*, 15 May 1783, MS 978, folder 4.

Chapter Three

[308] That is, the German or Lutheran Church, *Gazette of the State of Georgia*, 15 April 1784 (4-2).

[309] *Gazette of the State of Georgia*, 26 January 1786, (2-2). There is no mention of a Rector in these routine notices, but Mr. Holmes may nonetheless have had an early successor of some sort. The same newspaper, just a month earlier, had advertised that Lodge #42 (Ancient York Masons) would celebrate the Feast of St. John the Evangelist "at their room in Mrs. Eppinger's house. . . . from whence the Lodge will proceed in form to Christ Church where a sermon will be delivered . . . by the Rev. Mr. Lucas." 22 December 1785 (4-1).

[310] *Gazette of the State of Georgia*, 20 July 1786 (2-2).

[311] *Gazette of the State of Georgia*, 17 August 1786 (4-1).

[312] Letter dated 20 June 1787, MS 978, folder 131 (copy made by T.F. Screven; original now lost.)

[313] He seems not to have found one; for as advertisements and surviving letters make clear, he was bedeviled by debt and debtors until death brought him relief in 1801. *Columbia Museum and Savannah Advertiser*, 18 September 1801 (3-5). See also *Gazette of the State of Georgia*, 22 May 1788 (2-3) and MS 978, folder 4, for a letter of 20 August 1797.

[314] *Gazette of the State of Georgia*, 1 November 1787 (3-2). Notices dealing with the parish after this date presume it well known that Mr. Lindsay is in charge.

[315] *Gazette of the State of Georgia*, 19 June 1788 (2-3).

[316] *Georgia Gazette*, 25 October 1788 (1-3).

[317] *Georgia Gazette*, 25 October 1788 (1-3). Actually Mr. Lindsay may have been following a well established tradition among Christ Church Rectors — at least there is ancient precedent. We have record of a special sermon to the Masons as early as 25 June 1739. CR, vol. 4, p. 361.

[318] Virtually every *Gazette* issue during the late summer contained an ad for the new school which would emphasize Greek, Latin, French, Mathematics, English, and Writing.

[319] *Vestry Minutes*, 22 January 1789.

[320] *Georgia Gazette*, 18 November 1790 (2-1).

[321] *Georgia Gazette*, 25 March 1790 (3-3).

[322] *Columbian Museum and Savannah Advertiser*, 18 June 1802 (3-2).

[323] *Gazette of the State of Georgia*, 13 March 1788 (2-1). See also 10 July (2-1).

[324] From a letter in the Hartridge Collection (uncatalogued), Georgia Historical Society, dated 2 September 1789.

[325] *Georgia Gazette*, 19 August 1790 (2-1).

[326] *Gazette of the State of Georgia*, 10 July 1788 (3-1).

[327] For example, see the *Georgia Gazette* 6 August 1795 (1-1).

[328] *Vestry Minutes*, 22 January 1789.

[329] Watkins', *Digest of the Laws of the State of Georgia* (1800), p. 410 (23 December 1789). Three Churches (Christ, Kioka Anabaptist in Richmond County, and St. Paul's, Augusta) were all chartered the same date, making them the first in Georgia to be incorporated.

[329.1] *Georgia Gazette*, 19 May 1791, as reproduced in William Harden's *History of Savannah and South Georgia* vol. 1, p. 261.

[330] Malone, *Episcopal Church in Georgia*, p. 53, apparently quoting from early vestry minutes.

[331] Based chiefly on inference from the *Cash Book, 1782-1815*, p. 6f. MS. 978.

[332] His letter of acceptance to the Wardens, William Stephens and Dr. George Jones, 4 May 1792, is still extant in the Hartridge Collection at Georgia Historical Society.

[333] *Georgia Gazette*, 14 Oct. 1767 (3-1).

[334] *SPG Journals*, vol. 18, record (under 20 April 1770) a letter from Ellington, dated 10 Feb., which informs the Society of his acceptance.

[335] Still the subject of considerable debate, it seems quite probable that the adjective "Protestant" was added in order to distinguish the Americanized offspring of the Church of England from the "other" episcopal church in the old colonies, i.e., the Roman. Interestingly, the term appears first in Maryland, about 1780, where some distinguishing terminology was needed. In any case, the "Protestant" soon proved useful also to distinguish the Church from the organized Wesleyan societies which became the "Methodist Episcopal" Church in 1784.

[336] *Georgia Gazette*, 8 May 1794 (3-3).

[337] *Georgia Gazette* 5 November (3-2), and 3 December 1795 (2-3) and (3-1).

[338] *Columbia Museum and Savannah Advertiser* 24 January (3-2) and 31 January (3-4) 1796.

[339] *Georgia Gazette*, 14 April 1796 (3-1), reported the death on April 1st. Indeed, he seemed still to be acting as Rector the following December when he officiated at a parish wedding at Beth Abraham, the late Bartholomew Zouberbuhler's plantation. *Columbian Museum and Savannah Advertiser*, 16 December 1796 (3-2).

[340] *Columbian Museum and Savannah Advertiser*, 29 November 1796 (2-1). The Newspaper counted 229 significant buildings destroyed, leaving only 171 standing in the city.

[341] *Columbian Museum and Savannah Advertiser*, 9 December 1796 (3-3). The second fire appears only relatively small — destroying one entire residential block (i.e. a full tithing block of 10 city lots) containing about 20 houses.

[342] *Columbian Museum and Savannah Advertiser*, 14 April 1797 (3-4).

[343] *Georgia Gazette* 9 August 1799 (3-1) and *Columbian Museum and Savannah Advertiser*, 13 July 1798 (3-5) and 20 April 1798 (3-3).

[344] 22 August 1799 (2-2), This one was for 200,000 bricks.

[345] *Georgia Gazette* 15 January 1801 (2-2) and *Columbian Museum and Savannah Advertiser* 20 March 1801 (4-1), etc. Entries related to building materials begin to show in the *Cash Book* in March of 1801.

[346] *Georgia Gazette*, 22 August 1799 (2-2), and *Columbian Museum and Savannah Advertiser*, 11 January 1802 (4-5) and 10 March 1804 (3-3), respectively.

[347] *Deed* V 457, Superior Court of Chatham County, conveyed the "300 acres, more or less," along the Savannah River to William Hobkirk.

[348] MS. 978, f. 16 and 17.

[348] MS. 978, f. 16. This stone is now set in the exterior east wall of the Church, some 15 feet above street level, where it was placed in 1875 through the generosity of W. J. DeRenne. *Vestry Minutes*, 20 May 1875. Although bids on the construction project from Adrian Boucher and Amos Scudder are extant, it appears that the architect chosen was named Bale and the masons were Tucker and Ludlow.

[349] *Columbian Museum and Savannah Advertiser*, 11 April 1804 (3-5). It was traditional for the Lutherans to hold only monthly services in town.

[350] *Columbian Museum and Savannah Advertiser*, 31 March 1804 (3-4)

[351] *Columbian Museum and Savannah Advertiser*, 22 September 1804 (3-4).

[352] *Columbian Museum and Savannah Advertiser*, 12 September 1804 (3-4f.)

[353] *Vestry Minutes*, 2 April 1806. MS 978, f. 19

[354] Typically his contract had run from Easter to Easter, and an ad in the *Columbian Museum and Savannah Advertiser*, 4 August 1807 (2-5), offered the house "lately occupied by the Rev. Dr. Best" for rent. Similar news notes about that time reported his performing marriages, etc. at St. Simon's. Christ Church, St. Simon's, was then a mission of Christ Church, Savannah, and Best would necessarily have become well acquainted with it in carrying out his duties as Rector. Malone's, *Episcopal Church in Georgia*, cites Best for leading the island mission into a new era of prosperity as a parish (p. 55). Apparently Best remained in that area, for his wife died in Camden County according to the *American Patriot*, 14 April 1812 (3-4). Oddly enough, surviving *Vestry Minutes* or other records do not mention their departure.

[355] The actual text of the legislative act is most easily found in the 1812, Augusta, edition of Watkin's, *Digest of the Laws of Georgia*.

[356] MS 978 folder 23, A letter from Thos. Mendenhall to Messrs. G. and R. Waite, 30 June 1808, laid out a plan for the lottery, complete with ticket prices, prizes, etc. See also *Vestry Minutes* for 14 July 1808.

[357] *Columbian Museum and Savannah Advertiser* 14 May 1810 (2-1).

[358] 19 April 1810 (3-3).

[359] *Columbian Museum and Savannah Advertiser*, 14 May 1810 (2-1)

[360] These were 9 × 3 × 4½", "the size of Charleston bricks," costing $11.50 per thousand. Thus wrote Mordecai Sheftall to the building committee of John Grimes, Benj. Ansley, and James Johnston, 18 May 1810. MS 978, folder 26.

[361] The correspondence between the supplier, Mr. Fred Ball, and the wardens and Vestry is still in the Christ Church Collection, dated 11 Dec. 1810. It contains some interesting specifics of architectural details in the building under construction. MS 978, folder 26.

[362] *Republican and Savannah Evening Ledger*, 5 Jan 1811 (3-1). Similar notices appeared throughout the year. Although little record of his activities survives, Mr. Bartow appears to have remained Rector until 1 May 1815, when final salary payment was made. MS 978, f. 33. Indeed, record of J. V. Bartow is so cloudy that his name has often been confused with those of other Bartows: viz., Dr. Theodosius Bartow, a physician, and a prominent member of the congregation at the time; and Theodore B. Bartow, his

son, who grew up in Christ Church, became a priest, and served elsewhere in the Diocese of Georgia through the middle decades of the century.

[363] 28 Feb. 1811 (3-2).

[364] Sale was announced in the *Columbian Museum* 19 March 1812 (2-1), and also in other newspapers in the weeks following. Within six weeks sales convinced the wardens to continue the project. *Republican*, 2 May 1812 (3-3), *American Patriot*, 1 May 1812 (4-4), etc.

[365] *Savannah Republican and Evening Ledger*, 26 Jan 1813 (1-4).

[367] Of special interest is the painting (1818) which included: "bricks painted red and 'penciled' white, stone work painted white, the pews of the gallery painted and numbered, the plaster work round the outside of the Church painted & penciled, gelding the ball at the top of the church, burnishing the doors, painting the sides of the galleries white, painting roof of portico and cornice . . ." *Vestry Records* 10 April 1818) MS 978 folder 93.

[368] Such occasions were announced in the newspapers, typically with each charity receiving its share of attention annually through the early decades of the 19th century.

[369] *Vestry Records* MS 978, folder 33.

[370] In a letter from the wardens and vestry. *Vestry Minutes*, 26 December 1814, MS 978, folder 31.

[370a] Based on a copy of the entry in the *Vestry Minutes* for April (?), 1815 (?) (MS978, folder 32) as submitted to local newspapers. The date of the consecration cannot be fixed with precision from local sources since this copy, which carries neither a month nor a year, is all that survives. The original *Vestry Minutes* are now lost, and the story does not appear among extant newspaper editions. A search of Charleston news sources might, however, bring good results. Until this is done, the safest way would seem to be to rely on Bp. Nathaniel Bowen's address to the Georgia Diocesan Convention of 1825. In his recollection the Bishop states that the consecration took place in the spring of 1815. (*Journal 1825*, p. 7f).

[370b] According to Bp. Bowen these were the first "episcopal acts" ever performed in the Church. Previous episcopal care had been exercised via correspondence, *Journal*, 1825 p. 8.

[371] Based on an early biographical sketch in Sprague, *Annals of the American Pulpit*, vol. 5, p. 581. However, that biographer's timetable does not entirely square with local records. Its author recalls that it was during Cranston's visit to his old friend, Dehon, now Bishop in Charleston, that he came to Christ Church to preach. Cranston was thereupon invited to take charge even though only a deacon at the time. This, according to the sketch in Sprague, did not occur until the autumn of 1815. Cranston was subsequently ordained by Bp. Hobart in New Haven the following year.

[372] The colleague was Dr. Kollock, brother of the minister at the Independent Presbyterian Church. From a letter by Kollock in MS 978, folder 34.

[373] *Columbian Museum and Savannah Daily Gazette*, 15 April 1817 (3-3).

[374] *Daily Georgian*, 4 May 1818 (2-5) and *Columbian Museum and Savannah Daily Gazette*, 3 May 1818 (2-1).

[375] *Vestry Minutes* 22 September 1819. MS 978, f. 34. According to Edward C. and Evelyn Stickney, *Revere Bells* (rev. ed. 1961, published privately) only about one hundred recognized Revere bells still survive in the nation. The one in Christ Church, one of only four located outside New England, is inscribed "Revere and Sons, Boston, 1819." The bell has continued to cause waves of excitement as later generations have "discovered" it anew in the tower of the Church. See, for example, *Savannah Morning News* 18 February 1943 (9-5) and 10 March 1943 (12-2).

[375a] Quoted in Sprague, *Annals*, vol. 5, p. 582.

[376] The *Georgian*, 17 January 1820 (2-4f.) Forced by the fire to suspend publication for a time, the *Georgian* reported a week late: 321 wooden buildings and 45 of brick destroyed by the fire. See also *Columbian Museum and Savannah Advertiser*, 13 January 1820 (2-4).

[377] *Daily Georgian*, 27 January 1820 (3-1), 19 February (3-2), etc. The St. Simon's donation is attested by correspondence dated 31 January 1820 in MS 978, f. 36.

[378] *Daily Georgian*, 28 November 1820 (2-5).

[379] MS 978, f 34, has an extensive description of the design and detail of the structure envisioned.

[380] At least one local churchgoer thought so! He offered to sell or exchange his pew *on the middle aisle* in the Presbyterian Church for a pew in Christ Church. *The Savannah Museum*, 1 January 1822 (1-3).

[381] *Savannah Museum*, 10 August 1822 (3-2). The obituary suggests he was much older, but Sprague's *Annals* (based on Harvard College records), his graduation date of 1810, and his professional career at the College tend to support 32. Sprague also says he made use of Christ Church's own records, family manuscripts, an obituary in *Churchman's Magazine*, and papers of I. K. Tefft.

[382] The *Georgian*, 25 November 1822 (2-3)

[383] *Savannah Georgian* 5 Nov. 1827 (3-3). See also Sprague, *Annals*, p. 584.

[384] From a eulogy on Mr. Carter delivered by the Rev. Mr. Lot Jones in Christ Church, December 1827, and now in the Christ Church archives. MS 978, folder 118.

[385] *The Georgian*, 27 Nov. 1822 (2-1).

[386] *The Georgian*, 21 March (2-2), 7 April (2-1), 18 April (3-1), 19 April (2-5), 25 Sept. (3-3), all in 1823, 12 July 1825 (2-5) and many more!

[387] Typical are the "gossip notices" in The *Georgian* 17 June 1823 (3-2), 15 July 1824 (3-2),

[388] *Savannah Georgian*, 17 Sept. 1825 (3-3)

[389] See the *Georgian*, 28 June 1823 (3-1).

[390] *Savannah Georgian*, 22 June (2-1) and 6 July (2-1) 1826.

[391] *The Savannah Georgian*, 24 March 1825 (2-1f.)

[392] The sermon was soon printed and sold by W. T. Williams. See the *Savannah Georgian*, 25 April 1825 (2-6), for a typical notice of sale. The space itself, for many years after this dedication, was popularly called "Monument Square."

[392a] Many thanks to Gordon Smith for pointing out this little gem in the *Savannah Morning News*, 22 June 1884 (4-6). Mr. Smith, a Savannah attorney and ardent historical researcher, is confident that R.W.H. is Richard West Habersham, and that Mrs. E. is Mrs. Eppinger.

[393] In the *Georgian*, 1 February 1823 (2-3)

[394] *Journal 1823*, p. 3. Also see, for example, the *Georgian*, 3 May 1824 (2-1)

[395] The *Georgian* reported that in 1822 there were 26 Episcopal clergy in South Carolina, 28 in Virginia, 55 in Maryland, 28 in Pennsylvania, 85 in New York, and 16 even in (ex-)puritan Massachusetts. Only North Carolina's 9 resembled Georgia's 3. 16 March (2-4).

[396] Malone reports that the Rev. J. V. Bartow attended the General Convention of 1811 in New Haven. Presenting himself as representative of the Episcopal Church in Savannah, he was given an honorary seat, but could not be admitted as a member since Georgia was not an organized element of PECUSA. *The Episcopal Church in Georgia*, p. 57.

[397] For details of the growth of the Church in Georgia, and of Christ Church's role in it see Malone, *The Episcopal Church in Georgia*, passim.

[397a] Mr. Carter was appointed to help draw a constitution for the new missionary organization, and James Bond Read, of Christ Church, was made its treasurer. *Journal 1823* pp. 11, 16. The rather surprising urgency felt for the Georgia missionary cause at this juncture, after so many years of no apparent concern, is not without reason. To place it in context Georgians must recall that it was only in 1821 that the state expanded to the south of the Altamaha River and west to the Flint. Then in 1824 the Creek land exchange opened all of their Georgia lands to settlement. Finally it was in 1835-1838 that the great Cherokee relocation finally created the Georgia we recognize on the map.

[398] See, for example, the issues of Dec. 18, 19, and 20, 1827 (all 3-2) and Dec. 25 and 26 (both 3-6).

[399] *The Daily Georgian*, 18 Nov. 1820 (2-4).

[400] *Savannah Georgian*, 19 July 1828 (2-6).

[401] *Savannah Georgian*, 22 July 1828 (3-2) See also 6 Dec. 1828 (2-5).

[401a] *Journal 1829*, p. 23 f.

[401a2] *Daily Georgian*, 24 April 1834 (2-3)

[401b] As they did in 1837 to elect directoresses. *Daily Georgian*, 27 November 1837 (3-2)

[401c] *Vestry Minutes*, meeting of 29 May 1839.

[401d] Notice of the charity sermon appeared in the *Georgian*, 18 June 1831 (2-2), and a letter of thanks in the edition of 18 August 1831 (2-1)

[401e] *Vestry Minutes*, 11 April 1835 (MS 978, f. 41.)

[401f] *Daily Georgian*, 12 May 1838 (2-6)

[403] See the *Journals* of the Diocese for 1825 and 1826, and also Malone, *Episcopal Church in Georgia*, p. 60 ff.

[404] *Savannah Georgian*, 29 April 1829 (2-1), 24 May 1830 (2-3).

[405] Malone, *Episcopal Church in Georgia*, p. 64, has collected evidence from numerous early *Journals* of the Diocese. About this time, too, the vestry was designated by the diocese to be trustee of the funds of the ladies' branch, "The Female Episcopal Society for the Advancement of Christianity in Georgia." (MS 978, f 41, no date is on the document.")

[406] *Savannah Georgian*, 23 December 1829 (3-6), repeated the next day. Two weeks later a "thank you" notice appeared indicating they had raised well over $600 — enough to support two missionary priests for a year, more or less!

[407] Sprague, *Annals*, vol. 5, pp. 584, 585, 586. See also the *Savannah Georgian*. 5 November 1827 (2-4). The Carters rest today in Colonial Cemetery. For his information Sprague relied on Carter's son, Abram Beach Carter, and Dr. Smith's funeral oration.

[409] MS 978, f. 46. See also Malone, *Episcopal Church in Georgia*, p. 61f.

[410] Biographical sketch is based on a eulogy given at the time of his death by Bp. Stephen Elliott in Christ Church, Jan. 1851. MS. 978, folder 120, contains Elliott's handwritten version. See also Sprague, *Annals*, vol. 5, p. 661f.

[411] *Savannah Georgian*, 6 June 1828 (3-1). The Rev. Hugh Smith of St. Paul's Augusta, performed the marriage. Mary was the daughter of long time vestryman and frequent warden, William Bulloch.

[411a] See Neufville's letter to the wardens and vestry dated 14 March 1835. MS 978, f 41.

[411b] Malone, *Episcopal Church in Georgia*, pp. 61-67. Christ Church's continued support of Georgia missions (for example, see the *Daily Georgian* 6 April 1833, 2-2) appears to have been reflective of the mind of the national Church as well. For contemporary with those nearby ventures, local newspapers reported the laying of the cornerstone for a Protestant Episcopal Church in Paris. (*Daily Georgian* 17 June 1833, 2-4.)

[412] *Savannah Georgian*, 23 February 1829 (3-1).

[413] *Savannah Georgian*, 3 April (2-1) and 4 April (2-4), both 1829.

[414] By order of the wardens and vestry each pew would have one vote, *Savannah Georgian* 11 December 1830 (2-6).

[414a] *Journal 1831*, p. 4.

[415] *The Georgian*, 26 February 1831 (2-2).

[416] *Georgian*, 22 March 1831 (2-1). The *Journal 1831*, p. 4, describes the entire gift as "presented to the Church" by the Ladies Beneficent Society.

[417] *Georgian*, 24 March 1831 (3-6).

[418] *Georgian*, 28 March 1831 (2-3). The same builder, responsible for the largest organ then constructed in the U.S., at St. Thomas' Church in New York, won several other commissions in Savannah as well.

[419] *Georgian*, 24 December 1833 (2-1).

[420] *Georgian*, 27 April 1830 (2-1).

[421] *Daily Georgian*, 3 September 1836 (2-3). Mr. White would soon become a familiar figure in Christ Church.

[422] As when the vestry "cheerfully consented" to his absence in the fall of 1832 to attend the General Convention in New York (*Vestry Minutes*, 28 September 1832; MS 978, f 38), and to address the Diocesan Convention in Macon, May, 1835 (*Daily Georgian*, 27 April 1835, 2-2).

[423] *Daily Georgian*, 14 May 1836 (2-5), quoting from the Charleston *Courier* and the Columbus *Herald*. MS 978, f.42, includes Neufville's letter of "resignation" from April to November, and the arrangement for soon-to-be-ordained George White to fill in for him.

[424] MS. 978, f 120, Bp. Elliott's eulogy on Neufville, 1851.

Chapter Four

[425] Mr. Neufville's note to the Wardens and Vestry 21 September 1833. MS. 978, folder 39.

[426] 27 December 1833 (2-1)

[427] Copy of entry, *Vestry Minutes* 11 March 1834 (MS, 978, folder 40), and the report of committeemen William T. Williams and A. Barclay, 24 March 1834 (folder 42).

[428] Letter from E. Bath, 6 November 1835, reporting the details of the problem to the Wardens and Vestry. MS 978, folder 41.

[429] Reports to the Wardens and Vestry 6 November 1835, MS 978, folder 41.

[430] Letter to the Vestry, 7 November 1835, the day following submission of the reports. MS 978, folder 41.

[431] Letter from Thomas Clark to the Rev. Mr. George White, filling in while Mr. Neufville undertook his mission to interior Georgia, 2 April 1836. MS. 978, folder 42.

[432] MS. 978, folder 42 contains several fragmentary notes, one of which appears to be a draft resolution to place before the Vestry. They express considerable doubt about the accuracy of preliminary building estimates and the determination of potential contributors to meet the challenge. Although undated, these appear to have originated in this winter of doubt, 1836.

[433] Copy of an entry in the *Vestry Minutes* 25 April 1836. MS 978, folder 42.

[434] Statement of James Marshall included in the *Vestry Minutes* of 25 April 1836.

[435] *Vestry Minutes* 21 Jan. 1840. The Minutes went on to contemplate with horror "if such an event had happened when the Congregation was assembled. . . ."

[436] Copy of entry, *Vestry Minutes*, 21 November 1836 MS. 978, folder 42.

[437] *Daily Georgian* 25 Nov. 1836 (2-7); also 26 November (2-6).

[438] Copy of entry, *Vestry Minutes*, 22 August 1836, MS 978, f. 42.

[438a] W.B. Stevens, *Early History of the Church in Georgia*, p. 6.

[439] Fortunately, the *Minutes* of that meeting of January 28th have survived in MS 978, folder 43.

[440] For example, *Daily Georgian*, 19 May 1832 (2-2); 29 March 1834 (2-4).

[441] 29 April 1836 (2-6 and 2-3).

[442] *Daily Georgian*, advertisements of 29 Nov. (3-1) and 4 Dec. (3-1).

[443] 23 January, 1838 (2-2).

[444] Inferred from an undated draft of a resolution before the Vestry. MS. 978, folder 45.

[445] *Daily Georgian*, 28 Nov. (2-6) and 3 December (2-7), 1838.

[446] The *Daily Georgian*, 27 Feb. 1838 (2-2), published a detailed description of the affair.

[447] The action of the Wardens and Vestry calling for the celebration and inviting the public to participate, and also specifying the contents of the inscription, survive in MS 978, folder 43, in a document dated 23 Feb. 1838. Notice in the *Daily Georgian* edition of 24th (2-5) and 26th (2-2) Feb. advertised the invitation prominently, and that of the 27th detailed the contents of the stone for the public.

[448] 27 February 1838 (2-2).

[449] The *Vestry Minutes* contain this memorial statement, inserted in secretary Anthony Bartow's hand following minutes for a meeting of 8 April 1839.

[450] For example two doors and stairways from the basement to the portico's side entrances were requested, as were iron railing and stone flagging or brick around the church. *Vestry Minutes*, 25 August and 1 Sept. 1839.

[451] *Vestry Minutes* 23 May 1839

[452] *Vestry Minutes*, 3 June and 19 June 1839, and a letter from Mr. Neufville to the Wardens and Vestry, dated 27 May 1839, make the confusion clear . . . for us. The Vestry had apparently given Mr. White some forewarning, but saw "little probability of any conflict."

[453] The usual announcement of pew sales and rentals makes completion sound imminent since pewholders "will have pews in the basement story assigned to them corresponding as near as practicable to their pews, until the Church shall be finished." *Daily Georgian*, 24 Nov. 1839 (3-2) and 8 Dec. (3-1).

[454] *Daily Georgian*, 23 March 1840. Happily, the clipping was pasted into the *Vestry Minutes* of the day, for the original newspaper is now lost.

[455] *Daily Georgian*, 23 March 1840

[456] *Vestry Minutes*, 23 March 1840. Interestingly, bills of sale, etc. still survive for these two items. They identify the table

[456] as the work of John Evans and Co. (77 Huntington Ave, Back Bay, Boston, Mass.), and the font as purchased from the Joseph Barnes Co. (Newport, R.I.) for $165! MS. 978, folders 45 & 46.

[457] *Vestry Minutes*, 23 March 1840. Specifically, they committed $500 from the Vestry and $500 additional from the congregation, assuming the rest would be raised elsewhere in the diocese.

[458] Malone, *The Episcopal Church in Georgia*, p. 69f.

[459] MS 978, folder 41. The proposal was presented to the annual convention of the diocese.

[460] *Vestry Minutes*, 1 September 1839. The Vestry met the day after word of the bishop's death reached Savannah. See the *Daily Georgian*, 30 August 1839 (2-4).

[461] *Vestry Minutes*, 22 April 1840.

[462] From a note appended at a later date to the minutes of the April 22nd meeting.

[463] *Savannah Daily Republican*, 2 Dec. 1840 (3-1). See also the *Daily Georgian* for the same date (2-6) and the following day, 3 Dec. (2-7).

[464] This was Mr. Neufville's assessment expressed in a letter written from the convention, 5 May 1840, and appended to the *Vestry Minutes* for 26 November.

[465] Quoted in a *Daily Georgian* article, 18 January 1841 (2-3).

[466] From a letter in Elliott's hand, dated 26 July 1840. MS. 978, folder 48.

[467] These opinions appear scattered through several letters, viz., 26 May (appended to the *Vestry Minutes* of 26 Nov.), 26 July (in MS 978, folder 48), and 15 Dec. (MS 978, folder 47).

[468] The service was originally scheduled for January 17th but had to be postponed "as the Rev. Bishops who were expected had not yet arrived." *Daily Georgian*, 18 January 1841 (2-3).

[469] *Daily Georgian*, 2 March 1841 (2-2). See also the Savannah *Daily Republican* of the same date (2-1). Vestry records further reveal that Paul Trapier was rector of St. Michael's (Charleston), William H. Barnwell of St. Peter's (Charleston), and that present also were the Rev. Messrs, Joseph Walker and C. C. Pinckney (both of S.C.), M. L. Forbes of Mississippi, and George White of Georgia.

[469a] The *Journal 1841*, p. 16 f., confirms that this was the first episcopal consecration south of Maryland. It also appears that considerable good fortune was involved in bringing the consecration to the diocese at all. First, there was the basic problem of getting three bishops together in 1841, because plans "often failed from the sickness of Bishops, or their refusing to leave home in the depth of winter . . ." Then in this instance, a missed rendezvous and other peculiar circumstances so complicated matters, causing at least one postponement, "that the ceremony might as easily have taken place at Baltimore or Richmond as in Savannah." This interesting detail, and much more is revealed in some correspondence of the Standing Committee which Mrs. Neufville turned over to the Historian of the Diocese in 1874. The historian's description of their contents appears in the *Journal 1874*. pp. 30-32.

[470] All of the quotes are snipped from the *Daily Georgian* article of 2 March (2-2) cited above.

[471] "The bell will not be rung tomorrow in consequence," reported the Savannah *Daily Republican*, 30 January 1841 (2-2).

[472] Vestry records in MS 978, folder 55, include the bill for services from Matthew Luffborrow, dated 11 Aug. 1846.

[473] *Vestry Minutes* 25 July 1847.

[474] *Vestry Minutes* 11 July 1847 and 30 April 1848.

[475] *Vestry Minutes* 12 April 1852.

[476] The Rector requested attention to heating, *Vestry Minutes*, 5 Nov. 1846. Vestry Records, MS 978, folder 55, include the original proposal from Mr. Norris, dated 27 Nov. 1846.

[477] *Vestry Minutes*, 9 June and 16 June 1850. Cost, including chandeliers, burners and all, was estimated not to exceed $500.

[478] *Vestry Minutes* 24 Nov. 1850.

[479] In a letter from Mr. Neufville to Wardens and Vestry, dated 4 Nov. 1846, MS. 978, folder 55. The Vestry's actions are recorded in the *Minutes* of 5 Nov. and 26 Nov. 1846.

[480] 23 February 1852.

[481] *Journal 1841*. pp. 8-10, Also, see the *Daily Georgian*, 12 July (2-6), 3 August (2-6), and 4 August (3-1) all in 1846, for example.

[482] *Daily Georgian*, 28 July 1843 (2-5).

[483] The intensity of the writers' feelings about the issue shows clearly. See, for example, the *Daily Georgian* editions of 21 July (2-5) and 3 August (2-4), 1843.

[484] *Daily Morning News*, 9 March 1853 (1-3). See also the *Dictionary of American Biography* (N.Y.: Chas. Scribner's Sons, 1932), vol. V, p. 521f., the entry for Levi Sullivan Ives.

[484a] The great intensity of the feelings evoked can be sensed by sampling Bp. Elliott's stinging comments on the matter to the 1853 Convention of the Diocese. There, after commenting on the death of Bp. Gadsden (S.C.), he went on to lament how yet "another of [the Church's] Bishops has gone, but, alas! not to his grave!" The threat of the "Roman apostasy," as he called it, was a theme to which he returned frequently during these years. See *Journal 1853*, p. 17 f.

[485] *Vestry Minutes*, 25 October 1856. This was the usual practice after 1840.

[486] *Daily Morning News,* 9 Dec. 1854 (1-1). Originally, posted at the opening of a new Episcopal Church in Davenport, Iowa.

[487] *Vestry Minutes*, 4 April 1844.

[488] *Vestry Records*, MS 978, folder 55, include the letter from Mr. Neufville, (dated 4 Nov. 1846), and the receipt from Mr. Richmond on behalf of his wife, who was hired for $50.

[489] *Vestry Minutes*, 24 Dec. 1844. Both also enjoyed the freedom to be absent three months during the summer or fall.

[490] *Vestry Minutes*, 27 August 1848, include this enthusiastic resolution of thanks to the departing Mr. Salisbury.

[491] *Vestry Minutes*, 9 Jan. 1851, also MS 978, folder 60, when a Mrs. Pond carried both assignments for a time.

[492] For example, the *Vestry Minutes* of 24 November 1850 indicate they considered hiring several individuals "as may be necessary to form an efficient choir". Yet two years later they took special care to thank "each and every member of the choir . . . for their valuable and voluntary services during the past season." *Vestry Minutes*, 18 July 1852.

[493] *Vestry Minutes*, 4 Dec. 1850.

[494] *Vestry Minutes*, 15 Feb. 1852.

[495] This report of the organ committee is undated, but they had done their homework fully before reporting to the Vestry, that almost certainly it belongs late in 1852. MS. 978 folder 41.

[496] The Vestry's appropriation of the $500 still needed, and the Committee's letter containing the suggestions on financing are included in the *Vestry Minutes* of 15 Dec. 1852. The detailed description of the Knauff organ is from the report cited above.

[497] *Daily Morning News*, 30 July 1853 (2-1). It was brought to Savannah aboard the *State of Georgia* in two separate shipments.

[498] *Daily Morning News*, 20, Aug. 1853 (2-1).

[499] The *Vestry Minutes* of 27 Nov. 1853 reported the choir's request for use of the Church, and the *Daily Morning News* of 24 Feb. 1853 (2-1) advertised the date, time, and ticket information to the public.

[500] *Minutes*, 5 Jan. 1854.

[501] See *Daily Morning News* for 7 June (2-1) and 11 Nov. (2-1) 1856.

[511] For example, see the *Daily Georgian* 30 January 1841 (3-1).

[512] *Daily Georgian*, 26 January 1842 (2-6).

[512a] *Daily Georgian*, 26 January 1844 (2-4f), 30 January (2-3), and 2 February (2-5), for example. J.F.O'N was clearly Father O'Neill of the local Roman Catholic Church.

[513] From a draft copy of the text given to the Convention of 1831(?). MS 978, f. 38.

[514] *Daily Morning News*, 23 July 1850 (2-2).

[514a] *Journal 1841*, p. 22

[515] *Daily Georgian*, 3 December 1840 (2-3); see also the Savannah *Daily Republican*, 31 December 1840 (2-1).

[516] The *Journals* of the Diocese of Georgia for 1841 and 1856 mark the life span of the Montpelier project, while that of 1842 includes the Bishop's enthusiastic description of the plan to support the Institute with income generated by a slave force cultivating its lands. (pp. 12-14).

[517] *Vestry Minutes* 7 April 1857.

[517a] *Savannah Morning News*, 31 August 1884 (8-5).

[518] *Daily Morning News*, 29 May 1857 (2-3).

[519] *Journal 1854*, p. 25. The fund itself was created by the benefaction of Dr. Ralph Elliott of Christ Church, who left $1000 in trust to the Bishop for the purpose.

[520] Appeared in the Savannah *Daily Republican* 22 December 1840 (2-7).

[521] Savannah *Daily Republican*, 23 December 1840 (2-4).

[522] Earliest evidence of this particular effort appears in a letter from Robert W. Habersham to Mr. Neufville, dated 16 March 1850, which offered money for support of the mission. The letter survives among Vestry Records in MS 978, f. 60.

[523] *The Daily Morning News* devoted an 8″ article to one missions program in Christ Church led by a converted Chinese, Tong Choo Keung. 14 February 1853 (2-1).

[524] Charles L. Hoskins, *Black Episcopalians in Savannah*, pp. 12-15. An interesting addendum to the story of St. Stephen's was offered by Dr. F. Bland Tucker, both in conversation and in an historical article, which appeared in *Columns*, vol. 3, no. 3, June 1978 (4-3). He felt rather strongly that the new mission to Savannah Blacks was named more for Stephen Elliott than for Stephen Martyr, out of appreciation for the bishop's special care for the welfare of Blacks in the Diocese. Unfortunately, he could no longer recall the sources that had given him this impression.

[524a] James S. Atwell, *A Brief Historical Sketch of St. Stephen's Parish*, pp. 5 and 11. Writing in 1874, this first historian of the parish was apparently quoting from notes or letters left by Kennerly himself, and from other contemporary sources. See also *Journal 1856*, p. 45.

[524b] Atwell, *A Brief Historical Sketch*, p. 11.

[525] *Daily Morning News*, 11 April 1860 (1-1).

[526] *Daily Morning News*, 3 May 1861 (2-1).

[526a] Atwell, *A Brief Historical Sketch*, p. 11.

[526a2] See *Journal 1854*, pp. 28, 45.

[526a3] Indeed, these parochial reports continue to show similar figures right through the war years and into the 1890's. See *Journals* for 1856 to 1891.

[526b] *Journal 1853*, pp. 39-41. The report of the Rev. Thomas L. Smith, missionary, identifies the sources, including $1225 raised "almost entirely [from] Christ Church."

[527] *Journal 1856*, pp. 46, 53. See also Malone, *Episcopal Church in Georgia*, p. 91.

[528] *Vestry Minutes*, 2 September 1844.

[529] Malone, *Episcopal Church in Georgia*, p. 86f. The *Daily Morning News* reported both the laying of the cornerstone for the Calhoun Square Church, 9 December 1857 (2-1), and the consecration of the completed structure, 27 May 1859 (2-1).

[530] *Vestry Records* (MS 978, f. 53) contain Mr. Neufville's letter of 22 June 1844 which states the plan, including his expectation that the candidate would be ordained early in July, about the time of his own departure. See also *Journal 1844*.

[531] *Vestry Minutes*, 23 May 1847 contain the request of the Vestry's agreement to the leave of five months. See *Journal 1847*, which indicates he was also nominated by the Diocese to be a trustee for the General Theological Seminary.

[532] *Vestry Records* in MS 978, folder 59, contain his letter to the Wardens and Vestry, dated 9 June 1849. This time he proposed to procure the Rev. Mr. Richard Johnson, "favorably known to the congregation," who had served also during the summer of 1847. That letter also makes clear that "duties" often included teaching all of the Sunday School classes as well as carrying the usual priestly responsibilities.

[533] A letter from Mr. Neufville to the Wardens and Vestry dated 4 Nov. 1846 at Savannah. MS. 978, folder 55.

[534] It was planned that the two men would then share a salary of $3000. *Vestry Minutes*, 4 December 1850.

[535] *Vestry Minutes*, 15 December 1850

[536] *Vestry Minutes*, 1 January 1851.

[537] The pages of the *Daily Morning News* for the first ten days of January are generously supplied with letters, verses, and encomia of great variety.

[537.a] Susan M. Kollock, ed., "Letters of the Kollock and Allied Families," in *Georgia Historical Quarterly*, vol. 34 (1950), p. 38. The particular letter cited was written by G. J. Kollock to his wife in Clarkesville, Georgia, dated at Savannah, 5 February 1851.

[537.b] Sprague, *Annals of the American Pulpit*, vol. 5, p. 662.

[538] *Daily Morning News*, 3 January (2-2) and 4 January (2-1 and 2-3), 1851.

[539] This account, found in MS 978, folder 120, appears to be the source of the more fragmentary accounts in the newspapers.

[540] From a printed copy of the eulogy in MS. 978, folder 120.

[541] In a letter written, to the "Wardens and Vestry of Christ Church", Festival of the Epiphany, 1851, in MS 978, folder 61.

[542] *Vestry Records* in MS. 978, folder 61, include the letter written from Columbus, 14 May 1851.

[543] This is the one which now hangs in the east wall of the Church on the Congress Street side. According to vestry records, it was cut in New York by a sculptor named Launitz for $125, and reached Savannah by ship in October of 1851.

Chapter Five

[544] Even in death, rest did not come easily. He was originally buried in Colonial Cemetery, but after three years was moved to Laurel Grove when the "old cemetery" was closed. His activity also continued in other ways. His will (file 46 at Chatham County Probate Court) listed several interesting bequests, including one to Bishop Elliott, which may well have provided a start for some of the special funds created by the diocese in the early 1850's.

[545] *Vestry Minutes*, 9 January 1851.

[546] *Vestry Minutes*, 16 February, 1851, record Dr. Elliott's letter.

[547] *Vestry Minutes*, 23 February 1851.

[548] *Daily Morning News*, 8 April 1851 (2-3)

[549] *Vestry Minutes*, 22 May 1851 include his letter dated at St. Ann's Church, Morrisania, New York.

[550] *Vestry Minutes*, 9 November 1851.

[551] *Vestry Minutes*, 22 June 1851.

[552] *Vestry Minutes*, 20 June 1852, include a copy of Mr. Carter's note explaining the problem.

[553] *Vestry Minutes*, 18 July 1852, contain the letter of resignation, dated 5 July, from New York.

[554] *Vestry Minutes*, 18 July 1852.

[555] *Daily Morning News*, 27 July 1852 (2-1) acknowledging and often quoting sentiments expressed in the *Republican*.

[556] *Vestry Minutes*, 18 July and 1 August, 1852, contain the terms and correspondence related to the call.

[557] *Vestry Minutes*, 1 Aug. 1852.

[558] *Vestry Minutes*, 1 July 1854.

[559] *Vestry Minutes*, 27 August 1854. The angel of mercy was W.L. Dickinson Dalzell, who was finally persuaded to accept a "service of silver" from the congregation "as a grateful testimonial for his pious and valuable services during the epidemic of 1854." *Vestry Minutes*, 29 April 1855.

[560] *Vestry Minutes*, 4 May 1856.

[561] The by-laws were included *in toto* in the *Vestry Minutes* of 22 June 1856.

[562] Record of Vestry consideration is found in the *Minutes* of 24 March, 27 April, and 16 November, all in 1856. The complete report of the legal history of the plot, compiled by R.R. Cuyler and George A. Gordon, appears in the April entry.

[563] See the editions of 28 May (2-5), 30 May (2-4), and 31 May (2-3), 1853 for their public correspondence.

[564] *Daily Morning News*, 7 Nov. 1853 (2-1).

[565] *Daily Morning News* 6 March 1856 (2-2), and 27 May (2-4).

[566] For example, the *Daily Morning News* announced a Wednesday afternoon lecture on *Acts* that appears to have been part of a series, 3 June 1854 (2-2).

[567] *Vestry Minutes*, 24 Feb. 1856.

[568] See the *Daily Morning News* 14 Feb. 1853 (1-1), 2 Aug. 1854 (2-6), and 17 Jan. 1857 (2-1) for a start.

[569] For example, see the *Vestry Minutes*, 7 April 1857.

[570] See the *Vestry Minutes* for 12 June and 15 June 1859.

[571] The *Vestry Minutes* of 4 Sept. 1859 include a copy of Bishop Elliott's letter of resignation dated 29 Aug. 1859.

[572] This extensive and rather confusing correspondence is recorded in the *Vestry Minutes* of many meetings through October, November, and December of 1859.

[573] This phase of the Balch rectorship is also represented by extensive and confusing correspondence, primarily in the *Vestry Minutes* of 29 February, 26 June and 8 August, 1860.

[574] *Vestry Minutes*, 26 June 1860, indicate the Bishop's approval of the arrangement, and

575 *The Vestry Minutes*, 15 January 1861, include the letter declining their offer from the Rev. Mr. J.T. Johnson of Alexandria, Va.

576 *Vestry Minutes*, 15 April 1861. Mr. Coley, from Athens, became a candidate for orders in 1856, and was ordained to the priesthood in 1858 or 1859. *Journal 1856*, p. 20, and for 1859, p. 19.

577 *Daily Georgian*, 20 July 1841 (2-6).

578 *Daily Morning News*, 13 Dec. 1854 (1-2), based its judgement on a letter to the editor of the *New York Churchman*, "for many years the leading organ of the Protestant Episcopal Church," which it found quoted in the Charleston *Mercury*. Significantly, this article was surrounded by others dealing with the slavery issue, including riots in Chicago, the status of Kansas, etc.

579 *Confederate Records of the State of Georgia*, ed. Allen D. Candler, (NY: AMS Press, 1911) vol. I, p. 61. These resolutions, amony others, were presented by a Mr. Hartridge on behalf of the County.

580 Malone, The *Episcopal Church in Georgia*, p.94.

581 *The Daily Morning News*, 6 April 1861 (2-1), cited this hope expressed in the *Church Journal* (N.Y.).

582 The one other bishop with considerable seniority, Leonidas Polk of Louisiana, was on active duty as a Confederate General. For a full account of Bishop Elliott's leadership during the war years, see Malone, *Episcopal Church in Georgia*, p. 93ff.

582a Title of a sermon heard in Christ Church on 18 September 1862 — a Thursday given over to "prayer and thanksgiving for our manifold victories" by proclamation of the President, C.S.A.

583 The appeal appeared in an "open letter" printed by the *Daily Morning News*, 6 August 1861 (1-3). He used almost identical words three years later, including the rather amusingly worded paraphrase of Admiral Nelson, in a widely circulated pastoral letter.

584 The *Daily Morning News*, 11 Dec. 1861 (2-4), took the trouble to itemize the donations of both the Association and the bishop.

585 *Daily Morning News*, 30 September 1863 (2-1). In this instance the donors were known as the "Christ Church Aid Society".

586 *Daily Morning News*, 28 June 1861 (2-1). The sermon was printed under the title "The Silver Trumpets of the Sanctuary."

587 See the *Daily Morning News* for 13 August (2-1) and 22 Aug. (2-1), both 1861.

588 Heavily excerpted in the *Daily Morning News* of 4 Nov. 1862 (1-2), this easily accessible example provides a nice glimpse of his sympathetic and eloquent style.

589 Robert Manson Myers, *Children of Pride*, includes this observation of C.C. Jones, Jr., in a letter to his mother, Mrs. Mary Jones, dated at Savannah, 22 August 1863.

589a The first three were preached on 8 April 1864, 21 August 1863, and 27 March 1864, respectively — all were Fridays appointed by the President, C.S.A. to be days of fasting, humiliation, and prayer.

590 The outline of the service (p.2, col.3) called for:
-Morning prayer as usual to the Psalter
-Psalms 27, 77, 130
-First Lesson: Isaiah 40
-Second Lesson: Romans 12
-Then, after the prayer for the President, CSA, to use the
-"Lesser Litany", and immediately before the General Thanksgiving to introduce
-the Confession which precedes the Epistle in the service for Ash Wednesday
-The Prayer quoted. (Parts of the text, unfortunately, are blurred in the microfilm copy.) A similar service was held the following spring (see *Daily Morning News*, 25 April 1862 (2-1). For contrast it is interesting to compare the exuberant celebration of "Prayer and Thanksgiving" that took place after a season of victories the following summer. The Bishop directed there should be:
-Morning Prayer as usual to the Venite
-Instead of the Venite, use the Psalm of Praise and Thanksgiving (to be found in "Forms of Prayer to be used at Sea") "If the Lord had not been on our side . . ." (said or sung.)
-Psalms 136, 144, 146
-Gloria in Excelsis
-Lesson I: II Chronicles 20:1-21
-Lesson II: I Timothy 6:1-17
-Before the General Thanksgiving introduce the collect for Victory (found in "Forms . . . for use at Sea") beginning "O, Almighty God, the Sovereign Commander of all the World" (but changing "this happy victory" into "these happy victories", etc.)
-Introduce the "Collect for Peace and Deliverance from our Enemies" (found among "Occasional Thanksgivings")
-Omit the Litany (this not being a Litany Day) and the prayer set forth by the Bishop to be used during the continuance of the War.
Daily Morning News, 15 Sept. 1862 (2-2).

591 *Daily Morning News*, 8 June 1863 (2-2).

592 *Daily Morning News*, 26 October 1863 (2-3) reported the ceremony which took place on the 22nd. Miss Tattnall was herself the daughter of a flag officer in the C.S. Navy.

593 *Daily Morning News*, 2 Nov. 1863 (2-1 and 2).

594 *The Vestry Minutes* of 29 June 1862 include this eloquent and touching memorial to their long time colleague who died in January at 69.

595 An amount sufficient, at that time, to build a substantial brick house.

596 The *Vestry Minutes* from 16 July 1862 through those of 20 April 1863 note the major steps in the Vestry's thinking.

597 "Objectionable", in this case, meant stockholders were subject to double liability for company losses. Further, the Vestry's "small print" expert found that the charter authorized creditors to select any stockholder against whom to proceed for recovery!

598 The *Vestry Minutes* of 18 Oct. 1863 record the surprise as well as the happy decision to use the funds to raise the salaries of the rector and assistant.

599 Since only a few days advanced notice were given, the Vestry had to think quickly how best to protect Church funds for the April 1st devaluation. See the *Vestry Minutes* of 20 March 1864.

600 Preached in Christ Church, 15 September, 1864. The date is supplied by the *Daily Morning News* ad for the printed copy, 1 Nov. 1864 (2-1).

601 *Vestry Minutes*, 22 Feb. 1863. As if to confirm their insecurity, this same session of the Vestry was notified by the Phoenix Assurance Co. (London) that coverage on the Church ($15000!) could not be renewed on expiration in June. They were unable to obtain coverage again until after the war. *Vestry Minutes*, 16 July 1865.

602 *Vestry Minutes*, 11 Dec. 1864.

603 *Vestry Minutes*, 4 February 1865.

604 *Vestry Mintues*, 4 February 1865. The phrase "state of the currency" covers a host of problems, including the question, whose currency? There were in circulation Confederate notes, Georgia notes, Federal greenbacks, several kinds of scrip, notes of particular banks, etc. These fluctuated greatly in value with every change in time or location, and even with the politics or personal whims of those involved in the transaction. The fact that you had the money offered no guarantee that the merchant with whom you hoped to trade would accept it, and no law effectively bound him to do so.

604a Thomas Gamble, *A History of the City Government of Savannah, Georgia*, p. 263.

604b Quoted in Gamble, *A History of the City Government of Savannah, Georgia*, p. 263f. The phrase "earlier kindness and liberality" recalls a shipment of rice sent by Savannahians to Boston during the tense summer of 1774.

605 *Vestry Minutes*, 17 April 1865.

606 *Vestry Minutes*, 24 April 1865.

607 The *Vestry Minutes* of April 24th identify the committeemen as "Messrs. Wm. P. Hunter, Wm. T. Williams, and H.D. Weed."

608 Belatedly reported in the *Vestry Minutes* of 9 July 1865.

609 *Vestry Minutes* 24 Nov. 1865. An additional $750 was paid six months later to help make-up for his loss.

610 *Vestry Minutes*, 4 February 1865. This is the earliest noted mention of the "pensioners."

611 Reported in the *Vestry Minutes* of 14 Jan. 1866.

612 *Vestry Minutes*, 2 April 1866. In some cases, as with the Central Rail Road and Banking Company, they applied for a new stock certificate and new scrip. Other stocks, such as the Planters' Bank, were "considered of no value and not worth the effort to . . . apply."

613 Those annual reports on

the special funds were attached, as usual, to the *Vestry Minutes* of the Easter Monday meeting, 2 April 1866.

[614] As reported in the *Vestry Minutes* of 10 October 1865.

[614a] Gamble, *History of the City Government of Savannah, Georgia*, p. 262-266. The City Council had already expressed great appreciation of General Geary in a glowing resolution last January, 1865. Things seemed to go well with his replacement, General Brannan, also. He had been most helpful in the city's efforts to cope with the smallpox of last summer, and it was his decision to turn the city back to the oversight of the Mayor and Aldermen.

[615] Invoices and Receipts for the work indicate that Laurent and Lifley installed the sixty new burners @ 25¢ each, November(?) 1865. MS 978, f. 63.

[616] *Vestry Minutes*, 21 June and 12 August 1866.

[617] *Vestry Minutes*, 23 September 1866. This was the A.A. Smett's house, located at the NE corner of Bull and Jones Sts. Interestingly, members of the Vestry were required to sign the rental agreement individually.

[618] A fact further confirmed by the annual list of pew rentals seen in the *Vestry Minutes* of 5 Dec. 1866, and by Malone, *Episcopal Church in Georgia*, p. 110, using outside sources.

[619] From the Bishop's "Address" to the Convention of the Diocese of Georgia, recorded in the *Journal 1866*, p. 17.

[620] Again, the words are Bishop Elliott's as recorded in the *Journal 1866*, p. 16.

[621] See, for example, in the *Savannah Daily Herald*, 31 Jan. 1866 (2-3), response to remarks about Bishop Elliott in a Philadelphia paper.

[622] Published in the *Savannah Daily Herald*, 2 Feb. 1866 (1-1), The actual letter was addressed to Bishop Johns of Virginia, who was senior among southern bishops after Bishop Elliott.

[623] *Savannah Daily Herald* 15 Feb. 1866 (3-1).

[624] Frances Butler Leigh, *Ten Years on a Georgia Plantation* p. 12. I am indebted to Malcolm Bell for pointing out this welcome visitor to Christ Church.

[625] *Journal 1866*, pp. 24-29. Malone, *The Episcopal Church in Georgia*, p. 111 f., has a fuller treatment of the Bishop's message to the 1866 Convention, held at St. John's Church, Savannah. Occasional public expressions also reveal similar thinking. For example, see the *Daily News and Herald*, 8 August 1866 (1-5), where the emphasis is on the success of the pre-war missions.

[626] *Daily News and Herald*, 7 July 1868 (3-1).

[627] *Daily News and Herald*, 22 December 1866 (2-1).

[628] The quoted portions of this description were recorded by Mr. Lincoln in the *Vestry Minutes* following the entry for 23 December 1866. In addition, the *Daily News and Herald* issues of 24 December 1866 (2-1), 3 January (2-3) and 5 January (2-3) 1867 all contain informative bits on funeral plans and the event itself, as do *Vestry Minutes* of 22 and 31 December 1866.

[629] *Vestry Minutes*, 31 December 1866. Finally, Bishop Wilmer (of Alabama) added yet another commendation in a commemorative sermon delivered in Christ Church on Sunday, 27 January 1867 at 10:30. *Daily News and Herald*, 26 January 1867 (2-1).

Chapter Six

[630] *Vestry Minutes* 7 January 1867.

[630a] *Journal, 1867*, p. 58. The report was submitted by Mr. James Porter, St. Stephen's very able lay reader.

[630b] *Journal, 1867*, p. 35.

[631] *Vestry Minutes* 4 August 1867.

[632] *Vestry Minutes* 18 August 1867.

[633] *Vestry Minutes* 29 September and 28 November 1867, respectively.

[634] *Daily News and Herald* 5 December 1867 (3-2).

[635] *Vestry Minutes* 19 Jnauary 1868.

[636] *Daily News and Herald*, 5 May 1868 (3-4); see also the edition of the following day (3-1).

[637] *Daily News and Herald*, 14 May 1868 (3-3).

[640] *Daily News and Herald*, 23 August 1867 (2-5); see also their edition of 8 July 1867 (2-2).

[641] *Vestry Minutes*, 5 January 1868.

[642] *Savannah Press*, 16 May 1908 (11-6). These interesting recollections were stimulated by the accidental discovery of a printed program for that occasion on the eve of Bishop Reese's consecration, forty years later. See also page 9, columns 2, 3, and 4.

[643] *Journal, 1868*, p. 19f.

[644] *Journal, 1868*, pp. 19-20, in the Bishop's first "Address" to the diocese.

[645] The letter from "Homewood" in Rome (Georgia) is included in the *Vestry Minutes* of 16 Aug. 1868.

[646] *Savannah Morning News* 17 October 1868 (3-1).

[647] *Vestry Minutes* 23 Nov. 1868.

[648] *Vestry Minutes*, 25 Feb. 1869. The letter, dated 28 January 1869, signed by A. Low, W.P. Hunter, W.W. Lincoln, J. Screven and others, is included in the *Minutes*.

[649] *Vestry Minutes*, 15 April 1869 and 14 March 1870.

[650] *Vestry Minutes*, 4 June 1869.

[651] *Vestry Minutes*, 7 July and 17 July 1869.

[652] *Savannah Morning News*, 8 November 1869 (3-1).

[653] *Savannah Morning News*, 8 November 1869 (3-1).

[654] *Vestry Minutes*, 14 March 1870.

[655] *Journal 1869*, p. 63 f., *Journal 1870*, p. 52; and *Savannah Morning News*, 20 March 1869 (2-1). The first source cited reveals that some funds were from outside the parish, too; e.g., the Bishop Elliott Sunday School Class at St. John's.

[656] *Savannah Morning News*, 25 December 1869 (7-2). Actually, the showing of the window was timed to coincide with the third anniversary of the Bishop's burial. The article described in considerable detail how in its great center panel the window depicted Jesus with a child in his arms and others standing at his feet, his right hand on one of their heads. The two side lights, flanking the center one, presented saintly figures of a male and a female leading more children to Him. Immediately above the head of Christ there was a representation of the Agnus Dei carrying a "Cross of Victory", while filling the rest of the top of the window were the symbols of the four gospel writers — the Angel, the Lion, the Ox, and the Eagle. Depicted at the bottom of the center light was a baptismal font surrounded by lilies, with the Holy Dove hovering over it. Beneath the three lights were the inscriptions: "They brought young children to Christ" (north); "He put his hands upon them and blessed them" (center); and "Of such is the kingdom of God" (south). Then, at the bottom of the entire arrangement was the memorial inscription to Bishop Elliott.

[657] This brought the number of pews on the ground floor to 90.

[658] *Savannah Morning News*, 15 November 1869 (3-1). The gas work was done by Mr. W.A. Thomas of Savannah. Special pride was taken in the sophisticated equipment which ran separate gas lines along each side of the Church to assure equal distribution.

[659] Virtually all of the renovation details, except those relating to the gas fixtures, are contained in the report of the Building Committee which is in MS 978, f.65, and is recorded in the *Vestry Minutes* of the 14 March 1870. The total cost of the work was $18,231.74.

[660] *Vestry Minutes*, 17 July 1869.

[661] *Vestry Minutes*, 23 December 1869; MS 978, f. 65, holds the note of thanks for the furnishings from St. John's.

[662] Vestry Records in MS 978, f.65, contain the note of invitation dated 11 May 1870.

[663] *Vestry Minutes*, 4 March 1871.

[664] *Savannah Morning News*, 10 July 1871 (3-3).

[665] *Savannah Morning News*, 16 Sept. 1869, (3-2).

[666] *Journal, 1871*, pp. 70-72.

[667] *Journal, 1871*, p. 72. See also Malone, *The Episcopal Church in Georgia*, p 121f. The "Ogeechee Mission," really "Missions," on the north bank of the Great Ogeechee River, have at various periods been known as St. James', St. Mark's, and, from the 1880's to the present, as St. Bartholomew's.

[668] *Vestry Minutes*, 2 June 1870. The plan didn't work so easily for St. John's resources were too fully committed already to a new parochial mission chapel, etc. Nevertheless, the Bishop did locate in Savannah thanks in some degree to Christ Church's support. See *Vestry Minutes*, for 30 Nov. 1870.

[669] Bequeathed to the parish many years earlier by Archibald Wilkins, the property was to pass to the parish on the death of his surviving heir, Mary L. She agreed, however, in return for certain considerations, to make the Warren Square property available before that time. Should it be rented or leased for income? Used as a rectory? Sold? These were all considered through

[669] an extended period, but see especially the *Vestry Minutes,* of 10 July and 21 July 1870.

[670] *Vestry Minutes,* 13 October 1870, and *Savannah Morning News,* 15 Oct. 1870 (3-2).

[671] *Savannah Morning News,* 16 June 1871 (2-5 and 3-3) and 17 June (3-1 and 2-1).

[672] *Christ Church Guild Minute Book,* pp. 3-7 especially. Founded at a "meeting in the basement of the Church," February 4th, the first few meetings were spent hammering out this statement of purpose. MS 978.

[673] *Savannah Morning News,* 9 January 1871 (3-2).

[674] *Savannah Morning News,* 10 April 1871 (3-1).

[675] *Savannah Morning News,* 10 April 1871 (3-4).

[676] *Vestry Minutes,* 3 June 1871.

[677] *Savannah Morning News,* 12 February 1872 (3-5).

[678] *Vestry Minutes* 22 April 1871. Unfortunately they give no clue as to their fears re the Book of Common Prayer, or their hopes regarding the creed.

[679] See, for example, the notice in the *Savannah Morning News* 27 November 1871 (3-6) advertising a lecture by Bishop Lynch of Charleston on "The Temporal Power of the Pope."

[680] *Vestry Minutes,* 11 April 1872.

[681] *Savannah Morning News,* 20 May 1872 (3-3). The residents, Mr. P. Maccumber and Dr. Horace Royall, lived in turn at 107 Congress St., across from the Church. *City Directory 1870,* p. 115 and *1871,* p. 122.

[682] *Vestry Minutes* 12 April 1872.

[683] *Vestry Minutes,* 22 and 29 April 1872.

[684] *Vestry Minutes* for meetings of 1 and 2 May 1872.

[685] *Vestry Minutes* 13 May 1872.

[686] The Vestry complied, but, still confident of Dr. Mitchell, resolved to pay him to 1 June. See *Vestry Minutes,* 15 May 1872.

[687] *Vestry Minutes,* 18 May 1872. See also the *Journal, 1873,* p. 12.

[688] The letter is included in the *Vestry Minutes* of the same date as the deposition.

[689] 20 May 1872 (3-3).

[690] *Vestry Minutes,* 30 May 1872.

[691] *Savannah Morning News,* 19 June (3-1) and 21 October (3-1), 1872.

[692] *Vestry Minutes,* 5 September 1872.

[693] *Vestry Minutes,* 25 December 1872.

[694] *Vestry Minutes,* 21 December 1872.

[695] *Vestry Minutes,* 19 February 1873.

[696] *Vestry Minutes,* 5 April 1873.

[697] *Journal 1873,* p. 27. The Finance Committee of the Diocese also discovered more than $1200 missing from its Mission Fund. This, the "late treasurer" vowed, "if his life is spared he will repay." (p. 36).

[698] The *Vestry Minutes* of 15 June and 30 August, 1873, and of 5 February 1880 indicate at least the early and final steps taken in pursuit of these questions.

[699] *Savannah Morning News,* 26 Feb. 1873 (3-1).

[700] *Journal 1873,* pp. 19 and 43.

[701] *Vestry Minutes,* 21 December 1872.

[702] *Journal 1873* in the Bishop's address to the Diocese p. 26f.

[703] The *Savannah Morning News,* 21 October 1872 (3-1).

[704] *Savannah Morning News,* 7 Jan. 1873 (3-3).

[705] The figures reported by parishes are included in the *Journal* of the convention each year, but a more confident statement is rendered impossible by the obviously incomplete records of 1860-1861.

[706] W. J. DeRenne even donated "one of the best pews in the middle aisle" for the exclusive use of the Bishop and his family *in perpetuity*! *Vestry Minutes,* 30 March 1873.

[707] *Journal 1873,* p. 43.

[708] *Savannah Morning News,* 29 Dec. 1873 (3-2) and the parochial report in the *Journal* of 1874 ff.

[709] *Vestry Minutes* 30 August 1873.

[710] *Vestry Minutes,* 29 Nov. 1873, record the renewed invitation which was apparently accepted. See Malone, *Episcopal Church in Georgia,* p. 120.

[711] *Vestry Minutes,* 4 Jan. 1874.

[712] *Vestry Minutes,* 29 Jan. 1874.

[713] The *Vestry Minutes* of 31 March 1874 record the call (at $3500 per annum, plus a house), while the *Savannah Morning News, 4 July 1874* (3-1), establishes his acceptance. The same *Minutes* also record the congregation's "grateful remembrance" of C.H. Coley, whose death just became known in Savannah. They recalled how "in peace and prosperity, in the trials of suffering and war, in the threatened disintegration of political and social law, in the agony and distress of our stricken congregation, . . . always when Christian souls yearned for consolation, they found it in . . . this tender Minister of Christ."

[714] *Journal 1875* and *1876.*

[715] For example, see the *Savannah Morning News,* 19 May 1875 (3-4). Mozart Hall was located on Whitaker St at St. Julian and Bryan Streets.

[716] 16 April 1876 (3-1).

[717] E.g., *Savannah Morning News,* 27 Dec. 1875 (3-2). These great services, often conducted jointly with St. John's became traditional. See the *Savannah Morning News,* 25 April 1878 (3-3) 18 April 1881 (3-4), 28 March 1883 (4-2), etc.

[718] *Savannah Morning News* 31 Dec. 1874. (3-2).

[719] *Journal 1876* p. 20.

[720] *Journal 1875,* p. 61, in the parochial reports.

[721] *Savannah Morning News,* 27 February 1875 (3-2).

[722] *Vestry Minutes,* 25 May 1874.

[723] *Vestry Minutes,* 5 Dec. 1874.

[724] *Journal 1874,* p. 24, and *Journal 1875* p. 19.

[725] *Journal 1874,* pp 22-27.

[726] See especially his addresses in the *Journals* of 1874, 1875, 1876, 1877, and 1880.

[727] *Savannah Morning News* editorial, 18 May 1877 (2-3).

[729] *Journal 1874,* p. 21f.

[730] *Journal 1874,* p. 20.

[731] *Vestry Minutes,* 10 July 1875.

[732] *Vestry Minutes,* 1 Dec. and 9 Dec., 1876. Conveniently, the *Savannah Morning News* lists the four singers by name, 8 Jan 1873 (3-1).

[733] *Vestry Minutes* 1 Dec. also 6 and 16 Dec., 1876, but reaching back as far as April 8 of the same year. Five vestry meetings in a single month give one some idea of the gravity of the crisis!

[734] *Savannah Morning News,* 9 Sept. 1876 (3-3). Cemetery reports, long ones, appeared daily throughout the worst period of the epidemic.

[735] *Vestry Minutes,* 11 December 1876. See also the *Morning News* notes of 3 Aug. (3-3), 6 Sept. (3-1), and 17 Oct. (3-3).

[736] *Vestry Minutes,* 30 Dec. 1876, recorded in response to Mr. Mortimer's letter of 23 Dec. 1876. The original document is in MS. 978, f. 67.

[737] *Vestry Minutes,* 25 Jan. 1877.

[738] *Vestry Minutes,* 14 and 20 March 1877.

[739] See, for example, the "Kollock Letters," found in the *Georgia Historical Quarterly,* vol. 34 (1950), p. 326, in the letter from Mrs. E.F. Neufville to Mr. G.J. Kollock, dated 7 April 1877.

[740] Made in his *first* letter of resignation, 23 Dec. 1876. and noted in the *Vestry Minutes,* 31 Dec. Note, this was prior to any formal request that he do so.

[741] *Vestry Minutes* 14 March 1877.

[742] That several persisted in their resignations would not seem to diminish the comfort brought by the vote, nor to damage the interpretation of its cause. See *Vestry Minutes,* 8 April 1877.

[743] *Savannah Morning News,* 30 April 1877 (3-3).

[744] *Savannah Morning News,* 30 April 1877 (3-6).

[745] 20 March 1877. (3-2).

[746] 1 May 1877 (3-3). The "west" turned out to be Grand Rapids, Michigan, where Mr. Mortimer became rector of St. Mark's Church.

[747] See, for example, the article of 11 Dec. 1880 (5-5), or that of 1 Jan. 1881 (3-3) which notes that on Christmas Day the Mortimers were presented with an elegant set of parlor furniture by the ladies of the parish.

[748] *Vestry Minutes,* 20 March 1877.

[748] See MS 978. "Christ Church Records," vol. 4, contains the service record for the period the rectorship was vacant. Such lapses were avoided thereafter, even when hard times struck, by Christ Chruch and St. John's working out a summer exchange. For example, in 1878 Christ Church folk went to St. John's during July and August, while their Rector vacationed, and St. John's worshippers came to Christ Church while Mr. Strong was away in September and October. *Vestry Minutes,* 8 July 1878.

[749] An editorial writer appears to be the first in print with this news on 4 August 1877 (3-3).

[750] Mr. Boone's letter of 18 July 1877, was copied into the *Vestry Minutes* of 9 August 1872.

[751] A second letter, dated 25

July is included also in the *Minutes* of 9 August. Thomas Boone was the son of the Rev. Mr. William J. Boone (of South Carolina) and Phoebe Elliott, sister of the late bishop and rector. The couple was also married by Bishop Elliott, probably in Christ Church, in 1844. Probate Court of Chatham County *Marriage Index (1806-51)*, p. 57, certificate #2649.

[752] See the letter from Mrs. E.F. Neufville to Mr. G.J. Kollock, dated 3 September 1877, in "The Kollock Letters," *Georgia Historical Quarterly* vol. 35 (1951), p. 60.

[753] *Vestry Minutes*, 17 August 1877.

[754] The *Journals* of the late 1870's and early 1880's show St. Philip's, Atlanta, now to have surpassed the rest, but Christ Church still slightly ahead of rapidly growing St. John's.

[755] Much of Mr. Foute's letter was incorporated right into the *Vestry Minutes*, 29 Jan. 1874.

[756] *Vestry Minutes*, 2 April 1874. This wording aims directly at one of the by laws of 1856.

[757] *Vestry Minutes* 7 Feb. 1878.

[758] *Vestry Minutes*, 4 April 1878.

[759] Judgement file 21176, Superior Court of Chatham County, 3 Oct. 1918.

[760] In a letter to the Vestry, dated 30 May, 1878, and incorporated into the *Minutes* of 4 June.

[761] *Vestry Minutes*, 6 June 1878.

[762] *Vestry Minutes* for 20 and 27 June 1878.

[763] *Savannah Morning News*, 9 November 1878 (3-2).

[764] See *Vestry Minutes* 5 June, 2 Oct., and 6 Nov. 1879.

[765] From the original *Minute Book* of the Society in MS. 978, f. 162. The records of the Altar Society, as the group was usually known after 1888, are in MS. 978, f. 160.

[766] These measurements are of particular interest architecturally because later alterations to the building's interior have made much of this information otherwise irrecoverable.

[767] *Vestry Minutes*, 6 May 1879.

[768] Offered by Emily C. Cuyler in memory of Robert M. The *Vestry Minutes* of 11 September 1881 note the donation, while those of 2 February 1882 record its arrival.

[769] *Savannah Morning News*, 24 May 1884 (4-3).

[770] It seems Mrs. Mann had given a font to the Independent Presbyterian Chruch in honor of her parents, Mr. & Mrs. Cumming. Her husband therefore deemed it an appropriate tribute to her for "Christ Church, of which she was a faithful and zealous member." The old 1840 font was subsequently loaned to a struggling parish in Sylvania, but eventually returned to Christ Church in the Demere Chapel. The *Vestry Minutes* of 13 March 1886 record the loan. Mr. Mann also donated his pew for the Vestry to use as they "think fit" when he was called from the city for an extended period. See *Vestry Minutes*, 10 Feb. 1887.

[771] *Vestry Minutes*, 5 March 1885.

[772] Stimultaneously, she gave additional altar brass in honor of Charlotte Tattnall and Mary Drayton Neufville.

[773] This is the property at 211 York St., east, which is now listed for sale. See especially item 3 in her will, f. 27, Probate Court of Chatham County, and the deed of conveyance, 5 M202, in the Superior Court. To place in perspective the value of this bequest, which totalled c.$12,600, one might recall that the annual salary for the Rector at this time hovered around $3500. See also the "Kollock Letters" in the *Georgia Historical Quarterly*, vol 35 (1951), p. 74.

[774] *Journal, 1884*, p. 61. See also *Vestry Minutes*, 21 October 1886 and 10 Feb. 1887. The will, read at Miss Young's decease early in the summer of 1883, obviously did much to improve the financial outlook of the parish. Not all the fiscal news was good, however. The parish lost some rounds, too, as when it was sued by the Hutton estate and found liable in court for $2000! *Vestry Minutes*, 10 June 1886.

[775] *Savannah Morning News*, 6 Dec. 1877 (3-2). She proposed "giving . . . private lessons and also class instructions [in the] Sunday School room." Interestingly, the budget for the entire musical operation: organist, quartet, repairs, etc. totalled $1550 for the year. *Vestry Minutes*, 19 Dec. 1877.

[776] *Savannah Morning News*, 7 May 1880 (3-4).

[777] *Savannah Morning News*, 27 Nov. 1880 (3-2). This composition by Mr. Frank Rebarer, was sung the same day at St. John's and St. John the Baptist, also.

[778] *Vestry Minutes* 29 Nov. 1877.

[779] *Vestry Minutes*, 1 May 1881.

[780] The culmination of the affair is found in the *Vestry Minutes* of 5 Oct. 1882, but those throughout 1880-1882 are replete with discussion and correspondence related to Mrs. Cleveland.

[781] Her arrival, too, was noted with delight in the *Savannah Morning News*, 5 Dec. 1882 (4-1)

[782] *Vestry Minutes* 5 October and 2 November 1882. Gradually, many of the duties formerly carried out by the Music Committee of the Vestry devolved upon the Rector. Ultimately, it was "RESOLVED: In pursuance of Canon XXIII of the General Canons of the Church, the Rector is fully empowered to determine all matters regarding the choir." *Vestry Minutes*, 4 Jan. 1883.

[783] *Savannah Morning News*, 2 May 1883 (4-1). Unlike some of the musicians, however, the organ had an excuse for its erratic behavior. It had been badly water-damaged by a hurricane in August of 1881. *Vestry Minutes*, 1 Feb. 1883.

[784] *Vestry Minutes*, 13 June 1883. Almost as certain was some trouble with Madam Bouligny, for the Rector made and then quickly seized the opportunity to accept her resignation. It was even worth paying her off himself with the sigh that "it was better to let her go and say *Amen*." *Vestry Minutes*, 4 Oct. 1883.

[785] *Savannah Morning News*, 29 October 1883 (4-1).

[786] *Savannah Morning News*, 13 October 1883 (4-1).

[787] *Journal 1884*, p. 61. The boys were reinforced later in the year with addition of an adult male quartet, hired on a three-month trial basis. *Vestry Minutes*, 6 Nov. 1884.

[788] *Vestry Minutes*, 4 Dec. 1884.

[789] *Vestry Minutes*, 7 July 1889.

[790] *Savannah Morning News*, 9 Dec. 1884 (4-1).

[791] *Savannah Morning News* 24 Dec. 1881 (4-1).

[792] *Savannah Morning News* 25 Dec. 1883 (4-1).

[793] And consciously ignoring the 1863 proclamation of President Lincoln setting aside the last Thursday in November. *Savannah Morning News*, 31 Aug. 1882 (4-1).

[794] The letter, signed by "Taty", first appeared in the Episcopal *Recorder and Covenant*, but an extract of it and the response by "Truth" were printed in the *Savannah Morning Telegram*, 20 Feb. 1881 (3-5,6). To be sure Taty's jabs provoked a vigorous response, but fair or not "his" description would not appear to be mere invention.[794]

[794.1] MS. 978, f.165 Interestingly, this same file contains a 1927 program for a Sunday School Easter celebration modeled on one done in 1871, for which the program had recently been discovered after 56 years.

[794.2] Although "resting upon the altar was a solid brass cross about three feet high, "during the services of Easter Day, 1885. *Savannah Morning News* 6 April 1885 (8-1,2)

[795] Delivered to the clergy at its 1888 Convention, the Bishop doubled the space normally given to the anti-Roman segment of his address. *Journal, 1888*, p. 35. The next step, he feared, would be "transubstantiation!" Thus, he cautioned, quoting a favorite saying of one of the apostolic Fathers, "do nothing without the Bishop!"

[796] *Savannah Morning News*, 13 August 1883 (4-2).

[797] And this despite the fact that it had been installed with the consent of the City. *Vestry Minutes*, 5 May 1887.

[798] *Savannah Morning News* 12 Feb. 1879 (3-2).

[799] *Savannah Morning News*, 23 March (4-1), 23 March (4-2), and 28 May (4-3) all in 1884.

[800] The activities of the Society are noted in the *Journals* each year as a part of the parochial report. The Society was limited to twelve active members who divided the city into six wards and set about serving need wherever they found it. Often it meant the society must make the garments and raise the money which they later distributed. *Rules and Regulations of the Bishop Elliott Society of Christ Church Parish*.

[801] *Savannah Morning News* 24 Dec. 1878 (3-3)

[802] *Savannah Morning News* 6 Feb 1880 (3-3).

[803] The Rector addressed the Union Society's 134th annual meeting at Bethesda. The WCTU, though not so conspicuously populated with Christ Church names as were other local groups, sometimes held its meetings at the Church. On the contrary, the White Cross Society, for baptized men and boys over 16,

attracted many members of Christ Church, including the Rector. *Savannah Morning News*, 24 April 1884 (4-3 and 5); 8 April 1890 (8-4); 27 Oct. (8-1) and 3 Nov. (8-4) in 1888.

[804] *Savannah Morning News* 11 Feb. 1884 (4-3 and 4). Among the officers and board members of the Port-Society are many Christ Church names.

[805] *Savannah Morning News*, 16 Feb. 1882 (4-1). This is the son of Stephen Elliott, the first Bishop of Georgia and former rector of the parish, who had recently been consecrated the first Bishop of Western Texas.

[806] *Savannah Morning News* 10 Jan. 1884 (4-2). The term "Gallicanism" calls to mind an ancient tradition of independent spirit among French speaking Roman Catholics. Presumably, however, this particular manifestation of that spirit, the Old Gallican Church, was one of several bodies that separated from Rome after the Vatican Council and the proclamation of papal infallibility. Today, these are still known collectively, as the "Old Catholic" Churches.

[807] *Vestry Minutes*, 31 March 1885. *Journals* of the years following 1885 confirm the change, although it could not be accomplished immediately — requiring, as it did, consent of renters or expiration of current contracts.

[808] *Journal 1882*, in the report of the Savannah Convocation. See also the *Journal 1880*, p. 72, and *Vestry Minutes* 8 Jan 1880, which show the Rector or his assistant, Mr. Barnwell, keeping the mission open for several months.

[809] *Journal 1883*, p. 26f., *Journal 1885*, p. 70, and *Journal 1884*, p. 61, respectively.

[810] *Journal 1881*, p. 55, details the parish expenditures. The items noted are, of course, in addition to the salaries of the Rector and Assistant. See also the *Vestry Minutes* for August 1880.

[811] Distilled from the parish reports in the *Journals* of 1884-1886.

[812] *Savannah Morning News*, 30 Dec. 1877 (3-2). This was probably sponsored jointly by several local churches. At least this had been the case earlier in the year when the ladies of Christ Church, St. John's and St. Matthew's joined to hold a fair at the Pavillion Hotel to raise money for repairs to the mission's structure. *Savannah Morning News*, 18 Jan 1877 (2-7). Interestingly, a similar appeal from the Bishop on behalf of St. Matthew's several years earlier had been given a negative response because of "the state of our finances." This was probably exceptional, however, since the appeal came just as the treasurer's misuse of funds was being uncovered.

[813] *Savannah Morning News*, 20 March 1882 (4-1); *Vestry Minutes*, 6 June 1889; *Savannah Morning News*, 7 Feb. 1889 (8-5).

[814] *Vestry Minutes*, 18 Dec. 1884.

[815] *Savannah Morning News*, 15 Feb. 1879 (3-2)

[816] All of the quotations are taken from a moving exchange of letters between the Rector and the Vestry recorded in the *Vestry Minutes* of 23 May and 2 June 1881. In refusing the call Boone defended the parish, whose troubled state was "largely inherited from evil times", with the affirmation that "I am not among those who despair of our ancient Zion."

[817] *Savannah Morning News*, 2 April 1883 (4-4).

[818] For example, *Savannah Morning News*, 25 April 1878 (3-3); 18 April 1881 (3-4); 28 March 1883 (4-2).

[819] Tiffany was Rector of Zion Church, New York City, but "the missions" unfortunately are unnamed in the article, *Savannah Morning News*, 2 April 1883 (4-2).

[819.1] Booked in Savannah for 21-28 March 1886. *Savannah Morning News* 20 Jan. 1886 (8-2).

[820] *Savannah Morning News*, 3 Jan. 1887 (8-2f.).

[821] *Savannah Morning News*, 6 Feb. 1888 (8-2).

[822] *Vestry Minutes*, 3 Feb. 1881.

[823] *Vestry Minutes*, 4 March 1880. Although the city had been memorialized a year earlier, there is no indication in the Church records that the problem had yet been given serious attention.

[824] *Vestry Minutes*, 9 June 1881.

[825] *Vestry Minutes*, 9 June and 28 June 1881.

[826] The *Savannah Morning News*, is full of stories relating details of the storm 29, 30 and 31 August 1881. Sometimes the later accounts, less frenzied and perhaps better informed, increase our sense of the storm's power — as when it was reported that, afterall, there was a portion of one house still standing on Cockspur Island.

[827] *Savannah Morning News*, 3 September 1881 (8-1).

[828] *Savannah Morning News* 17 Sept. 1881 (4-1).

[829] *Savannah Morning News* 5 October 1881 (4-1).

[830] *Vestry Minutes* 22 Nov. 1881.

[831] *Vestry Minutes*, 5 Jan. 1882. Specifically, they had their eye on the Oglethorpe Barracks block, where the DeSoto Hilton now stands. See also the *Sunday Morning Telegram*, 1 Jan. 1882 (3-3).

[832] *Vestry Minutes* for 2 March 1882 and for the congregational meeting of 16 April 1882. The contract for ceiling construction went to J.J. McMahon, with work to begin after closure of the Church on 1 July. *Vestry Minutes*, 16 June 1882.

[833] *Sunday Morning Telegram*, 29 October 1882 (3-1).

[834] *Vestry Minutes* 2 Nov. 1882.

[835] *Savannah Morning News*, 27 Jan. 1883 (4-2).

[836] *Savannah Morning News*, 27 Jan. 1883 (4-2). The elaborate decorative plan was carried out by J.J. Murtagh, an experienced painter in the employ of the Savannah, Florida, and Western Railway Co.

[837] *Sunday Morning Telegram*, 28 Jan. 1883 (3-2).

[838] *Sunday Morning Telegram*, 12 Aug. 1883 (4-2) The work, already begun when the article appeared, was expected to cost about $1000.

[839] *Vestry Minutes*, 9 April 1885.

[840] *Vestry Minutes*, 14 Dec. 1885.

[841] *Savannah Morning News*, 11 February 1886 (8-3).

[842] See, for example, the *Savannah Morning News* of 24 April 1887 (10-2), which records her involvement when the new building was begun at Liberty and Jefferson Sts., Mr. Boone conducting the cornerstone service; and 3 May 1887 (8-1), which cites her role in the May Ball held at the Guards' Arsenal to raise funds for the Orphanage.

[843] *Savannah Morning News*, 8 Sept. 1886 (8-1).

[844] See the prologue to the Nevitt Report in MS. 978, folder 70.

[845] *Savannah Morning News*, 11 Sept. 1886 (8-1).

[846] An interpretation which would seem to offer Savannahians the feeble comfort that Charlestonians, at least, were more sinful than they! See *Savannah Morning News*, 13 Sept. 1886 (8-2).

[847] One of these which especially catches the eye, no doubt well intended, is cast in such atrocious verse that for the afflicted its only effect can have been to intensify their suffering. See the *Savannah Morning News*, 7 Sept. 1886 (12-5).

[848] *Journal 1887*, p. 53.

[849] Taken from the original report of Mr. Nevitt in MS. 978, folder 70, which is dated 5 Nov. 1886.

[850] *Vestry Minutes*, 12 Nov. 1886.

[851] This would cut the music budget to $1500, including organ repairs. *Vestry Minutes*, 1 Sept. 1887.

[852] *Vestry Minutes*, 7 September 1887. The Rector had attended all Vestry meetings for several years, but by an odd coincidence, he had not attended them since the previous March — six months. With such poor communication, the Vestry perhaps assumed that Mr. Boone was merely making a point by resigning, as he had in the past. (In addition to the occasion noted above, see also *Vestry Minutes* for 30 October and 6 November 1884.)

[853] *Vestry Minutes*, 15 Dec. 1887.

[854] *Vestry Minutes*, 9 Jan. and 21 Jan. 1888.

[855] 27 Jan. 1888 (8-1).

[856] These words of George A Mercer were recorded in the *Savannah Morning News*, 30 Jan. 1888 (8-1f.).

[857] Interestingly, the previously cited article in the *Morning News* included all of these points, often appearing to quote many of the speakers literally.

[858] The *Vestry Minutes* of 1 Feb. 1888 show this successful motion to have been the work of Mr. H.D. Weed. See also the *Savannah Morning News* edition of the following day. 2 Feb. 1888 (8-3).

[859] *Savannah Morning News*, 11 Feb. 1888 (8-2).

[860] All we know for certain beyond this is that the Sr. Warden, Mr. J.R.F. Tattnall, who had presided at the last meeting of the congregation and appointed the fund raising committee, resigned in disgust the following June. He did so after no one but he appeared for a Vestry meeting despite the fact that five others had acknowledged the call. It is an interest-

[860] ing coincidence. . . . . See the *Vestry Minutes* for 7 and 18 June 1888.

[861] See *Vestry Minutes* of 11 October 1888 and the *Savannah Morning News* of 19 Oct. 1888 (8-1).

[862] *Vestry Minutes*, 3 May 1888. Mr. Nevitt was also a pew holder in Christ Church.

[863] *Vestry Minues*, 20 June 1888. It is intriguing to note that this meeting took place only two days after the Sr. Warden had resigned because no one else had attended a called meeting of the Vestry. The story becomes even more interesting in the first week of the new year, a few days after Mr. Boone's final departure. Mr. Tattnall was re-elected to fill the vacancy *he* had created seven months before! *Vestry Minutes*, 4 Jan. 1889. Certainly all of this is related in some way — though how is by no means clear — for it was not until the Sr. Warden's re-election that *Minutes* for the meetings of the previous seven months were confirmed.

Chapter Seven

[864] *Journal 1889*, pp. 16, 18, 66, and *Vestry Minutes*, 10 Jan. 1889. Mr. Coley was officially resident in the Diocese of Connecticut, but may well have been related to the parish's old friend, C.H. Coley.

[865] *Vestry Minutes*, 6 June 1889.

[866] *Savannah Morning News*, 21 Jan. 1889 (8-2). On this visit to Georgia, Canon Leigh resided with Gen. and Mrs. Henry R. Jackson, on their plantation near Darien.

[867] *Vestry Minutes*, 7 March 1889.

[868] *Vestry Minutes*, 10 April 1889.

[869] *Vestry Minutes*, 6 June 1889 and the *Savannah Morning News*, 16 June 1889 (8-4).

[869.1] *Savannah Morning News*, 28 March 1905 (5-1).

[870] Mr. White was expected here by 1 November, and presumably arrived about that time. In any case, he was here for the Davis service on the 11th of December when "the Church was draped in mourning and everything wore an air of solemnity." *Savannah Morning News*, 11 Dec. (2-4) and 12 Dec. (7-1), 1889.

[871] *Savannah Morning News*, 17 Feb. 1890 (8-1).

[872] *Vestry Minutes*, 6 March 1890.

[873] Based on the parochial reports in the *Journals* of 1889-1894.

[874] 11 March 1890 (8-4).

[875] *Vestry Minutes*, 5 June 1890.

[876] *Savannah Morning News* 10 April 1890 (8-4). The article went into detail about everything from the costliness of the presents to the hometowns of the attendants — Richmond, Baltimore, St. Paul, and Augusta — all matters of interest to social historians. More amusing than informative, however, was its standardized rhetoric which described the bride as "one of the most amiable young ladies in Savannah," and the groom as "one of the most energetic and pushing young businessmen."

[877] *Vestry Minutes*, 5 June 1890, indicate hope to use "Hunter Hall" in the school.

[878] *Vestry Minutes* 5 June 1890. The Vestry resolved to back them up so that the organ could be ordered immediately, assuming the ladies would make good on their pledge.

[879] *Savannah Morning News*, 23 July 1890 (8-3).

[880] According to Mr. R. Geissler at the Christian Art Institute of New York, where it was purchased, the pulpit was "an original design of which I never made a copy." MS. 978, f.73, contains Geissler's letter dated 18 November 1890. *The Vestry Minutes* of 10 December 1890 indicate that the pulpit was erected by the congregation as a memorial to the late Jane M. Young with a portion of her recent bequest to the Church.

[881] *Vestry Minutes*, 6 Dec. 1890, show the table to have been given by the Misses Johnstone in memory of W. Duncan Johnstone.

[882] MS 978, f. 74. Some doubt remains as to the date of the changes described, since the source is a newspaper article which was unfortunately clipped without its dateline. A pencilled "1890" on the clipping in f.74 appears to be in a more modern hand, but it nevertheless represents the best guess of its acutal date. The best confirmation of that date was discovered in the *Vestry Minutes* for 21 October 1891, in the report of the "Building Committee". The largely financial report notes $1405.44 paid to T. Markwalter for "marble columns and marble work in the chancel."

[883] MS. 978. f. 72, contains invoices dated 25 August, 5 September, 1890, and 18 March 1891. Similar documents establish that the work of interior decoration was subcontracted to L. Haberstroh of Boston.

[884] *Savannah Morning News*, 14 Feb. 1891 (8-2).

[885] *Savannah Morning News*, 6 March 1891 (8-2). Built by George S. Hutchings of Boston for $4300, the organ was a two manual, 24 rank, instrument. Happily, MS. 978, f. 74 contains the original memo of agreement showing full specifications for stops, couplers, etc. Persumably Mr. Hutchings was pleased with his work, for he brought his family to the DeSoto Hotel while he inspected the finished product. *Savannah Morning News*, 16 March 1891 (8-3).

[886] The *Vestry Minutes* of 12 March 1891 note the raise from $2500 to $3000 per annum, effective 1 March 1891.

[887] See for example, the *Savannah Morning News*, 1 Sept. 1887 (3-1f.), or the *Vestry Minutes* of 5 November 1887, 5 Jan 1888, and 3 May 1888.

[888] The *Vestry Minutes* of 5 July 1892 note the agreement. It must have been an interesting problem for those vestrymen who were also aldermen! See also the agreement itself, dated 5 July 1893, and signed by all vestrymen, which is in MS 978, f.76, and the *Minutes of the City Council*, 19 July 1893, p 26.

[889] The letter containing the suggestion, from Mr. William R. Lealan (?), dated 12 Feb. 1892, is in MS 978 f. 75. The Vestry obviously liked the idea, which was discussed at its meeting of 3 March 1892.

[890] *Vestry Minutes*, 3 Dec. 1893.

[891] To be sure, his predecessor had done the same in his day, but Mr. Boone's final years had been very strained and spirits had sagged considerably as a result — especially during the months between his resignation and his actual departure.

[892] Mr. White wrote a note of welcome to the bishop-elect in December, 1891, and the Vestry offered Christ Church for his consecration. See MS 978, f. 75 and the *Vestry Minutes* of 7 Jan 1892. Bishop Nelson, however, chose Atlanta as the location of both his consecration and his cathedral, feeling that the see should be in the state capital. Malone, *Episcopal Church in Georgia*, p. 140.

[893] From the *Vestry Minutes* of 25 April 1892.

[894] *Journal 1892*, p.41. Two years earlier, in the same context, Bishop Beckwith had sighed with disgust that "the changes have not been very important, while the improvements have been less so!" *Journal 1890*, p. 25f.

[895] *Journal*, *1892*, p. 41 f. in the "Bishop's Address" to the Convention.

[895.1] *Journal*, *1892*, p. 43.

[896] *Journal*, *1893*, p. 47.

[897] *Journal*, *1893*, pp 49 and 48. So pleased was Bishop Nelson with this development that he called for a branch of the "Women's Auxilliary" in every parish and mission.

[898] The *Journals* of the Diocese are perhaps the best source to document this year by year. For example, see the *Journal, 1900*, when the women made their eighth annual report, led by Mrs. William Elliott (President), Mrs. J.H. Johnson (Vice-President), Miss E.M. Bancroft (Secretary), and Mrs. Marshall (Treasurer). By that year there was also a "Babies Branch" with Mrs. P.A. Waring as its president. See also the *Journal, 1892*, p. 46, in which the Bishop acknowledged a $10,000 gift from Mrs. Houston Clinch of Christ Church to endow scholarships for theological education at Sewanee. The original *Record Book* of the Auxilliary pinpoints the group's first meeting as 16th May 1892.

[899] See especially the *Journal, 1895*, in the parochial report, p. 157.

[900] After the congregation was split in 1840 to form St. John's, Christ Church had been a force in the founding or survival of the Ogeechee River Mission (now known as St. Bartholomew's) and the Savannah River Mission as well as of St. Stephen's and St. Paul's Free Church — the latter two founded in the city proper in the 1850's.

[901] The *Journal, 1891*, p. 103, records the earliest reference to the plan for a chapel, and the *Vestry Minutes* follow soon with the details. See the *Minutes* for the meetings of 4 June, 4 July, 24 September, and 5 Nov., all 1891.

[902] *Savannah Morning News*, 17 July 1891 (8-3).

[903] The parochial report from Christ Church in the *Journal, 1892*, p. 121 f., records costs at $500 for the lot and $1521 for construction.

[904] *Vestry Minutes*, 13 April, 5 July, 1892, and others following.

[905] *Vestry Minutes*, 21 April 1892.

[906] Entries in the *Vestry Minutes* for 5 and 13 March 1894 are confirmed by contemporary correspondence in M.S. 978, f. 76. A rest of several months restored Mr. White's health, but whether it also brought an assistant to take over duties at St. Michael's is unclear. Certainly no name appears consistently in the record until the arrival of the Rev. Mr. Frederick A. Juny in 1897 or 1898. See the *Journal 1898*, p. 19, and the *Vestry Minutes* of 16 August 1899. (Thanks to Mr. Hugh Hill for the last reference.)

[907] The *Journals* of the Diocese and the *City Directories* provide the simplest means to trace these developments through the 20th century.

[908] Also identified as 566 York St., West.

[909] Sometimes identified as 527 Broughton St., west.

[910] Written for the *Parish Helper* by a charter member of the Brotherhood of St. Andrew. MS. 978, f. 76. St. Andrew's Chapel, like St. Michael's, can easily be traced as to location, etc., in the *Journals*, *City Directories*, and occasional news articles; but nowhere is it more fully set to print than here in this surviving number of Christ Church's own *Parish Helper*, vol. I, no 2 (Jan. 1906), p. 2, columns 1 and 2.

[911] See the *Vestry Minutes* of 7 April and 5 May 1892, and also the *Journal, 1892*, p. 125 f., which records St. Augustine's public thanks for the donation. See also Hoskins, *Black Episcopalians in Savannah*, p. 29. About the same time Christ Church reclaimed the old 1840 baptismal font, on loan in Sylvania, for use at St. Michaels. *Vestry Minutes*, 5 July 1892.

[912] Gamble, *History of the City Government of Savannah, Georgia, 1790-1901* p. 207 ff.

[913] Gamble, *History of the City Government of Savannah, Ga, 1790-1901*, p. 199.

[914] See, for example, the *Savannah Morning News* 15 July (4-4f.), 26 July (4-4), and 11 Nov. (4-4), all in 1881, as well as 9 June 1882 (4-3), 21 Feb. (4-4), 26 Feb. (4-5), in 1883, 4 Jan 1885 (8-3), and the *Sunday Morning Telegram* of 25 February 1883 (3-5). The fuss in the newspapers is readily confirmed by the *Vestry Minutes* throughout the period, 7 April 1869, 12 March 1871, 3 Nov. 1881, documenting the struggle as do items in MS. 978, f. 155. The neatest summary of the long process, written from the City's point of view, is in Gamble's *History of the City Government*, pp. 207-213.

[920] *Savannah Morning News*, 6 Jan. 1888 (4-2).

[921] One reason for the delay was that the judge at this level, Robert Falligant, a long-time vestryman at Christ Church, disqualified himself from the case. At this turn, Walter Charlton, Falligant's colleague of many years on the Vestry, quipped that his decree had disqualified the otherside," which set off a round of "good natured badinage." *Savannah Morning News*, 4 June 1889, (8-3). The same source records the progress of the case also in 31 Jan (2-3f), 1 Feb (4-3), 2 Feb (8-4), all 1888, and in 9 April 1889 (1-5). See also *Vestry Minutes* for 6 March 1888.

[922] A copy of the decree by Judge Falligant, dated 9 Nov. 1895, is in MS. 978, f. 155. The agreement also specifies that the City may not "convey or sell" the property, lay-off streets on it, or allow erection of any structure or building foreign to its function as a burial ground and park. It may, however, tear down the walls and lay-off walks, and it must preserve the "graves, tombstones, monuments, vaults, . . . as valued relics of public and historical interest." Violations of any of these conditions and convenants would "at once" return title to the 380' × 210' plot to the Wardens and Vestry of Christ Church in fee simple. See also the *Vestry Minutes* of 6 Nov. 1895, 2 Jan 1896, Gamble's *History of the City Government*, p. 393, and the year-end financial statement, dated 30 Nov. 1896, in MS. 978, f. 77. Money from the settlement appears to have been slow in coming, for a year later the Vestry was still so much in the grip of the three-year national depression that they were forced to cut the salaries of the choir, organist, and rector by 15-20%. See the *Vestry Minutes* of 7 Nov. 1896, and 22 May 1897.

[922.1] The words are quoted from the premable to a resolution asking the congregation to subscribe toward the cost of a new communion table. MS 978, f. 161.

[923] This informative article, full of description, shock, and speculation, is in the *Savannah Morning News*, 23 May 1897 (8-1 ff., and continued on 6-4). See also MS 978, f. 83, which contains an unidentified news clipping, dated 18 Jan. 1898.

[924] *Vestry Minutes* for 23 May 1897 record that letters had been received from Independent Presbyterian, St. John's Episcopal, Trinity Methodist, Ascension Lutheran, St. Paul's, St. Stephens, and St. Augustine's Episcopal Churches, St. Paul's Lutheran, Duffy St. Baptist, First Presbyterian, plus others from Atlanta, Macon and Augusta, and Boston. More condolences arrived from the Savannah Volunteer Guard, YMHA, YMCA, and the Odd Fellows, as well as the Protestant Ministers Association. Many of these included offers of space.

[925] The *Vestry Minutes* of 23 July 1897 record the text of the Vestry's note of thanks. Among other things it cited with special appreciation "the feelings of friendship and love, now so long existent between the two congregations." Along with expressions of sympathy and offers of help, the fire also raised once again the question of relocating the Church. That idea provoked a vigorous counterattack in several strongly worded "letters to the editor of the *Savannah Morning News*. See, for example, 30 May (16-4) and 5 June (3-1), 1897.

[926] *Vestry Minutes*, 6 July 1897. Apparently the plan involving St. John's and St. Paul's was considered so that each of their clergy could enjoy a vacation of four weeks without interrupting services, for any, but the *Vestry Minutes* of 22 Dec. 1897 affirm the return to I.P.C.

[927] A letter dated 25 June 1897 from Preston to C. Lucian Jones, chairman of the Building Committee, affirms his acceptance of the job and outlines his plans for the trip to Savannah. This now survives in MS. 978, f. 81.

[928] MS. 978, f. 82 contains an inventory of "contracts, estimates, bills," etc. dated 23 July 1897.

[929] See Preston's letter of 26 July 1897 in MS. 978, f. 81.

[930] In a letter to Preston from the Building Committee, dated 4 September 1897, now in MS. 978, f.81.

[931] Several letters in MS. 978, f. 81, are packed with such details. They were exchanged between John M. Bryan, the new chairman of the Building Committee, and Mr. Preston on 28 August, 4 September, 23 September, and 27 September 1897.

[932] See Preston's letters of 5 Aug. 1897 (MS. 978, f. 81) and 14 November 1897 (in MS 978, f.80). Many comparisons are made between the ceiling destroyed by the recent fire, the one now contemplated, and the one Preston did for Independent Presbyterian Church following their fire of 1889.

[933] With Stewart Construction Co. of Savannah on 22 Dec. 1897. MS. 978, f. 82. Mr. Preston had earlier indicated his intention to retain Mr. Henry Urban as his local supervisor "to see that that part of the work is properly put up." (Letter from Preston to John Bryan, 28 August 1897 in MS. 978, f. 81.) There is no further mention of Urban's name in this connection, however.

[934] *Vestry Minutes* 22 Dec. 1897. The latter could be the one described in a news clipping (in MS. 978, f. 83) as made of "antique oak and mosaic, ornamented with the Christian emblems" provided by the "ladies of the parish." See also MS. 978, f. 82.)

[935] "Visited with a dreadful calamity entailing the complete destruction by fire of the Cathedral," the Vestry sent its heartfelt sympathy to the clergy and congregation at the loss of their beautiful church. *Minutes* 7 Feb. 1898.

[936] *Vestry Minutes* 11 April 1898.

[937] 17 May 1898 (8-2).

[938] The same reviewer also noted several other changes for us, such as new and improved pews in the gallery, and three transoms over the vestibule doors. The middle one, which especially caught his eye, depicted a head of Christ with a cross, crown, and open book. *Savannah Morning News* 22 May 1898 (16-1ff.) A news clipping dated 18 Jan. 1898, otherwise unidentified but apparently from a Boston paper, is now in MS 978, f. 83. The writer, who was discussing Preston's work, reported that some of the woodwork would be in natural cypress and that the chancel area would be wainscotted in "a dark, mottled, Tennessee marble." Since there is no mention of these features in the finished building, they would appear to be among the many discarded ideas.

[939] Built by John Brown of Wilmington, Delaware, for $4300.

[940] MS. 978 f. 74. See also *Savannah Morning News* 22 May 1898 (16-5).

[941] *Savannah Morning News* 22 May 1898 (16-6) and 23 May (8-3). See also the *Journal, 1898*, p. 186.

[942] An original program booklet for the occasion survives in M.S. 978, f. 83. For the children, Bishop Nelson spoke on "Jacob's Ladder." The children's offering went toward renovation costs, to Christ Church, Cordele, and to Anvik, Alaska. *Savannah Morning News*, 23 May (8-3).

[943] *Vestry Minutes*, 25 April, and 3 October 1896.

[944] MS. 978, f. 79, contains correspondence on designs and prices from a number of major specialists in stained-glass: Geissler of New York, Royal Bavarian of Munich and London, Haberstroh and Phipps-Slocum (both of Boston), Tiffany, etc. The contract was finally awarded to Redding, Baird, & Co. of Boston, who would perform the work under Mr. Preston's supervision for $1250. See *Vestry Minutes* for 21 Jan 1898, and correspondence with Redding, Baird and Co., dated 25 Jan 1898, in MS. 978, f. 80.

[945] "In utrumque paratus agere et pati." (In all things, be prepared both to do and to persevere.) The text, sent to Redding, Baird, & Co., appears in undated documents preserved in MS. 978, f. 83. The same text appeared on the seal of the diocese for many years until Bishop Reeves changed it in the mid-1970's.

[946] Redding and Baird sent out a replacement piece to correct the problem. *Vestry Minutes*, 6 June 1898.

[947] The report, signed by Building Committee Chairman John M. Bryan and Senior Warden H.C. Cunningham, is in MS. 978, f. 82.

[948] *Vestry Minutes*, 11 April and 22 Nov. 1898.

[949] *Vestry Minutes*, 23, November 1898.

[950] Her letter making the donation, dated 16 Nov. 1900, is in MS. 978, f. 80.

[951] For example, a handsome brass "rubbing" was given by C. H. Cole and E. S. Elliott, as recorded in the *Vestry Minutes*, 8 Feb. 1900; and Methodist Bishop Hendricks (Kansas) raised the topic of a memorial to Wesley. See *Vestry Minutes*, 25 May 1903.

[952] Sketched on a note pad from the "Rector's Office", the plan identifies a specific subject for each of the seventeen windows. Presumably it was the Rector's idea, but that is far from certain. The accompanying catalogue from L. von Gerichten Art Glass Co. bears the signature of C. Lucian Jones, the Junior Warden. See M. 978, f. 80.

[953] See the *Journals* of 1902-1904, especially 1903.

[954] *Vestry Minutes*, 21 June 1898.

[955] The committee also included laymen from Macon and Atlanta. Malone, *Episcopal Church in Georgia*, p. 149.

[956] *Journal 1904*, p. 99-101. The Archdeacon was the Rev. Harry Cassil of Brunswick.

[957] *Journal, 1904*, p. 102.

[958] The *Journals* of 1903-1906 record the developments which culminated in the separate archdeaconry in 1906. Bishop Nelson asserted that "no efforts have been made to thrust them out" (*Journal, 1905*, p. 47), and that the action was, in fact, taken at the request of a committee of Black churchmen in hope that it would "encourage self-help." (*Journal, 1905* p. 115). The circumstances under which that request was made are obscure, however. All we know is that Christ Church was represented on the committee which drafted the segregation amendement to Article III of the diocesan constitution in the person of H.C. Cunningham (*Journal, 1905*, pp. 22, 29, and *Journal, 1906* p. 30.), and that the Bishop, too, seemed to favor this course. (*Journal, 1905*), p. 48.

[959] It is probable that alternative sources would prove helpful in exploring the later history of parish work in the Black community. Records at St. Matthew's and in the pages of the *Savannah Tribune* would seem the most promising places to begin, but the search will be a project of major proportions in itself. The most ambitious and successful effort carried out thus far is found in Charles L. Hoskins, *Black Episcopalians in Savannah*, pp. 35-68.

[960] *Vestry Minutes*, 28 April 1916; see also their letter to the Bishop, dated 16 May 1916.

[961] *Vestry Minutes*, 11 Jan. 1904, record the request, but make no reference to the location of the ceremony. The best bet is probably Virginia, the family home, and the state of young Robb's first charge as priest.

[962] The *Vestry Minutes* suggest this indirectly. After attending the November meeting he missed the December one, and by January appeared to be unavailable altogether. It was most unusual for him to miss a Vestry meeting if he was in the city.

[963] *Savannah Morning News*, 28 March 1905 (1-5). This informative article, which includes a photograph of Mr. White, and an undentified obituary pasted into the *Vestry Minutes* of 28 March 1905 account for all of the quotations in the paragraph.

[964] *Savannah Morning News*, 28 March 1905 (5-1).

[965] Invited to assist Mr. Strong at the memorial service were the Rectors of St. Paul's and of St. Mark's (Brunswick). The terms describing Mr. White were gleaned from many commentators, but especially from the several obituaries noted above, from the "Bishop's Address" as recorded in the *Journal 1905*, p. 41, and from the *Savannah Morning News* of 28 March 1905 (1-5 and 5-1). All are very much in the spirit of the commemorative plaque now mounted in the south wall of the Church. Mr. White was buried in Virginia "near the old home place" at Warrenton. *Savannah Morning News*, 29 March 1905 (5-1).

[966] It is no surprise that those who knew him best soon set out to create a lasting memorial to his life and ministry in Christ Church. Their choice was a design by Tiffany & Co. which was ready about Christmastide, 1907. Bishop Nelson was invited to dedicate it on 23 February 1908. See *Vestry Minutes* for 14 November and 12 December 1907 and 17 Feb. 1908. This memorial was replaced in the 1920's by the one now in the south wall.

[967] See *Vestry Minutes* for 18 August, 15 September, and 23 October 1905. Mr. Brown had been rector of the parish in Washington and Archdeacon of Augusta. *Savannah Morning News*, 16 July 1905 (30-1). He knew the parish well when he arrived, for he was himself the July fill-in that summer. Then he returned in September, presumably to make final arrangements regarding the rectorship, at which time he was the house guest of Mr. J. Moultrie Lee. The Sunday editions of the *Morning News* report the church services scheduled each week, but his stay with the Lee's appeared in the 1905 version of "Nobody's Business" on 16 Sept. (7-1) and his final arrival to take charge of the parish on 15 October (23-1).

[968] *Vestry Minutes*, 2 Nov. 1905.

[969] Noted in the *Vestry Minutes* of 19 Dec. 1905, the first issue of the *HELPER* must have appeared almost immediately. Fortunately, a copy of no. 2, dated January, 1906, survives in MS. 978, f. 163. Alas, this appears to be the only surviving copy. Is it? Or are there others hidden away in family archives and attics?

[970] *Savannah Morning News*, 14 October 1906 (36-1)

[971] *Savannah Morning News*, 28 Oct. 1906 (35-1). The intention was that "the old choir in the organ loft" would be maintained. Apparently it was, indeed. See the edition of 23 Dec. 1906 (32-1).

[972] *Savannah Morning News*, 11 Nov. 1906 (36-1). The newspaper varies in its rendition of Ms. Hill's name, but the director was probably the Winford T. Hill, also known as "Fannie," who is listed in the *City Directory, 1907* as a music teacher.

[973] It was surely more than coincidence, for instance, that a week after his September visit in 1905, a professional quartet was hired suddenly after a year of reliance on a voluntary choir. *Savannah Morning News*, 24 Sept. 1905 (30-1).

[974] *Vestry Records* contain a draft of the Rector's report. MS. 978, f. 74.

[975] This is the Austin Co. of Hartford, Ct. The $7100 price included the fancy new electric action.

[976] For just a few of the countless examples, see the *Vestry Minutes* of 10 Oct. 1914, 29 March 1916, and 10 January 1918.

[977] Malone, *The Episcopal Church in Georgia*, p. 156.

[978] The Vestry issued the invitation to Mr. Reese on 6 Feb. 1908 (see the *Vestry Minutes* of that date), and the consecration took place 20 May 1908.

[979] *Savannah Press*, 20 May 1908 (1-1, plus pictures in columns 3 and 4.) See also a related article in the *Press* on 16 May; pages 9 and 11 have extensive coverage of the approaching event, but of special interest is the photograph (on p. 11) of Bishop Tucker. Also

pictured are the other bishops participating: Nelson (Atlanta), Weed (Florida), and Bratton (Mississippi), as consecrators; Gailor (Tennessee), preacher; and Knight (Cuba) and Tucker, as presentors.

[980] Hours were regularly announced in the church columns of the *Savannah Morning News* as well as in parish bulletins each week.

[981] See the *Vestry Minutes* for the annual meeting of Jan. 1932, in the report on St. Andrew's, and also the minutes of 11 May 1911. Also of interest are Miss Sack's reminiscences as she approached her 90th birthday. *Columns*, vol. 2, no. 2, Nov. 1977 (7-2 ff.)

[981a] Christ Church was also involved in supporting missions in Thunderbolt and at Ft. Screven although not totally responsible for them.

[982] See the *Journals of 1910 and 1911*. Tables with these and other statistics are usually found on the last pages of each *Journal*.

[983] *Journal 1912*, in the statistical tables.

[984] *Journal 1913*. See the tables and the Rector's report.

[985] *Vestry Minutes*, 17 Jan. 1910.

[986] Letter from J.H. Gibboney to F.A. Brown, dated 8 March 1911 MS 978, f. 78.

[987] *Vestry Minutes*, 31 August 1914, contain his letter, dated 20th August at Coxsackie, N.Y.

[988] *Savannah Morning News*, 25 October 1914 (38-1f.) Later in the day, at evensong, choristers from St. John's and St. Paul's joined with the choir of Christ Church to give Mr. Brown a musical send off.

Chapter Eight

[989] See, for example, the schedule of the day outlined in the *Savannah Morning News* church column, 1 November 1914 (38-3). See also the schedules for 8 Nov. (29-1), 15 Nov. (40-3), 22 Nov. (38-4), and 29 Nov. (36-3f). Perhaps Mr. Spence's custom of publishing all of his sermon titles in advance in these notices helped to keep folks coming . . . In any case, the titles make it obvious that he presented two, or even three, different sermons each Sunday plus others for mid-week services!

[990] *Vestry Minutes* 8 February 1915. The next year, when the Bishop again asked to use the Church for services things were different. A new rector was in place by that time and he took pains to attack the problem early. Writing that "we, of course, welcome the services" and the Bishop, he expressed the hope that it would be found "convenient to have women at the services," and suggested that "the men might sit in the middle aisle and the women in the side aisles". It worked. *Vestry Minutes* 13 Jan. 1916.

[991] *Savannah Morning News*, 4 July 1915 (36-1 and 36-2). See also the *Vestry Minutes* for 28 April, 11 May, etc. Mr. Wing was born in Atlanta and pursued his education at William and Mary College before taking positions in Atlanta; Christ Church vestrymen visited him at Grace Church, Anniston, Alabama, before issuing their call. Interestingly, a standard reference work takes no note of his holding a position there but indicates that he came to this parish directly from the Church of the Incarnation in Atlanta. See *Who's Who in the South and Southwest*, (First edition, 1950), p. 808. See also *Who's Who in America*, 1940-41 (vol. 21), by the same publishers, p. 2799. In any case, it is interesting to ponder the claim that Mr. Wing was the first native Georgian to become Rector of Christ Church. Mr. Wing's historical sketch, which is printed in the *Church Directory - 1918*, makes the point and it may well be true. Too little is known of some of the late 18th and early 19th century rectors to be certain, but if true, it also means he would be the only Georgian *ever* to be Rector of the parish until the Rev. George Maxwell came in 1973. Another candidate who was called is of interest even though he declined; he was the Rev. David Cady Wright, who accepted a second call to Christ Church nine years later. *Vestry Minutes* 1 Dec. 1914 and 8 Feb. 1915.

[992] *Vestry Minutes*, 11 Nov. 1915.

[993] See *Vestry Minutes* for 9 March 1916.

[994] In the process of rebuilding the 1912 Austin Organ a fourth manual was added to accommodate the solo and echo organs. This addition of ten new ranks of pipes brought the total to about 46. Correspondence and other documents relating to the organs survive in MS. 978, f. 74.

[995] *Vestry Minutes*, 4 April 1917.

[996] *Savannah Morning News* 4 October 1914 (38-3 and 38-1); see also (38-5).

[997] *Journal 1917*, p. 58f. The Bishop picked up the spirit of President Wilson's point (in his "Declaration of War" speech to the joint session of Congress on April 2), which developed the theme that "we have no quarrel with the German people . . . it was not at their urging that their government acted . . ."

[998] *Vestry Minutes*, 15 June 1917. At his departure an offering was taken up in support of his work.

[999] *Vestry Minutes*, 22 March 1918 and after, suggest that he departed late in 1917 or early in 1918 and returned in September, 1918.

[1000] Services to those devastated, displaced, or otherwise affected by the war are abundantly reported in the daily newspapers throughout 1917 and 1918.

[1001] *Vestry Minutes* 22 March 1918.

[1002] *Vestry Minutes* 26 Sept 1918 and 12 June 1919.

[1003] *Vestry Minutes*, 28 Nov. 1918, at a specially called meeting. Thus it was that, this being Thanksgiving Day," $500 was given Mr. Wing as a "token of love and esteem" and in recognition of his tireless services "during all that dark and trying period." At times Mr. Wing's services must have gotten the better of him for he was prevented from fulfilling his normal duties through much of the autumn of 1917 by severe illness. The Assistant Rector, Nicholas Rightor, and the Bishop took his place most of that time. See *Vestry Minutes* for 5 Nov., 13 and 16 December 1917, and 10 Jan. 1918.

[1004] *Journal 1918*, p. 36 f.

[1005] Significantly, the "Act to Incorporate the Episcopal Church in Savannah, Called Christ Church," signed by Gov. Edward Telfair in December of 1789, defined the name and style of the body corporate strictly in terms of "the church wardens and vestrymen." There was no mention of the rector at all. Such an extreme position may have been adopted in conscious reaction to the colonial Act of Establishment (1758) which specified that "the rector . . . shall be one of the Vestry," and that "no Vestry shall make any Order without having first given timely notice to the . . . Rector to be there," CR, vol. 18, p. 267.

[1006] *Journal, 1892*, p. 41. This statement was part of Bishop Nelson's annual address to the diocese.

[1007] See Judgment File 21176, Superior Court, Chatham County, dated 3 October 1918. The amended charter also defined the "name and style" of the body corporate in terms of the "Rector, Church Wardens and Vestrymen . . ."

[1008] The *Georgia Gazette* religiously announced the dates and then published the results of the elections held annually on Easter Monday. The colonial Act of Establishment virtually assured turnover in wardens by specifying that no one could be fined "for not taking upon him the said Office oftener than once in Seven Years." Refusal to serve when his time came, however, would cost the unwilling Warden 40 shillings! CR. vol. 18, p. 267.

[1009] William Thorne Williams died after having "been for more than 50 years a vestryman of Christ Church" (*Vestry Minutes*, 11 October 1868); William P. Hunter resigned a few weeks before his death after more than 35 years (*Vestry Minutes*, 25 Feb. and 11 April 1869); and Robert Habersham died at 86 after nearly 50 years on the Vestry. (*Vestry Minutes*, 2 Feb. 1870.)

[1010] Mr. Hunter's statement was made in his letter of resignation from the Vestry (dated 1 Feb. 1869), which is included in the *Vestry Minutes* of 25 Feb. 1869.

[1011] *Vestry Minutes*, 7 May 1908.

[1012] See also the *Vestry Minutes* of 9 May and 24 Oct. 1918.

[1013] See Judgment File 25161, Superior Court, Chatham County. Also note the *Vestry Minutes* of 10 and 15 Jan. 1924.

[1013.1] See, for example, the *Vestry Minutes* of 11 Jan. 1937, and 9 May 1950.

[1014] CR, vol. 13, p. 596. Journal of the Commons House of Assembly for 16 Nov. 1761.

[1015] *Vestry Minutes*, 2 Sept. 1844.

[1016] *Vestry Minutes*, 7 Dec. 1893.

[1017] For example, the figures reported in the *Journal, 1909*, p. 102, show 234 "free" services and 458 with rented pews.

[1018] For example, see the *Vestry Minutes* of 7 Nov. 1896 and 2 Jan. 1897.

[1019] *Vestry Minutes*, 19 April 1917.

[1020] *Vestry Minutes*, 25 October 1917.

[1020.1] See *Vestry Minutes* for 15 Jan. 1919.

[1021] *Vestry Minutes*, 23 Dec. 1919. For as much as a year prior to this date the Vestry had carried on a campaign advocating the change and educating parishioners to the new look of their old responsibility. See the *Vestry Minutes* of 24 October 1918, 13 March 1919, etc.

[1022] According to Malone, *The Episcopal Church in Georgia*, p. 170, Christ Church was the last in the diocese to make the change.

[1022.1] See *Vestry Minutes* for 15 Jan. 1919.

[1023] See the *Vestry Minutes* of 20 Feb. 1920. which contain the letter from St. Michael's.

[1024] *Vestry Minutes*, 10 June 1920.

[1025] Thanks to the generosity of Thomas L. and Dr. John Dunn, who gave $1000 each toward acquisiton of the property. The Vestry of Christ Church supplied the remaining $340 balance to purchase a lot at Kline and Burroughs Sts. (SW corner). The Bishop Beckwith Society then took action to relocate a portable school house from St. Andrew's, to an adjacent lot, since it was contemplated to abandon that mission. The arrangement was that Christ Church was responsible for the fabric of House of Prayer mission and the Junior Auxilliary of St. Michael's looked after its spiritual program. In practice, however, the division of responsibility was never quite so neat. For instance, although the Auxilliary, under Miss Georgina Sack, founded House of Prayer (1910), it was Mr. Wing who organized a parochial Aid Society for the mission among the women of the neighborhood. See the *Vestry Minutes*, annual reports for Jan. 1921.

[1026] See the *Savannah Morning News*, 21 Jan. 1923 (44-3).

[1027] *Savannah Morning News*, 6 Jan. 1924, Section 3 (10-3). It was the Senior Warden, J. Randolph Anderson, who so described it in one of his annual reports to the congregation. See the *Vestry Minutes* for 12 January 1925.

[1028] *Savannah Morning News*, 13 May 1944 (12-1).

[1029] *Vestry Minutes* 10 and 16 January 1924.

[1030] *Vestry Minutes*, 31 January 1924.

[1031] *Vestry Minutes*, 25 July 1925. There was also a special appropriation of funds "to replace the memorial tablet to Robb White with a more suitable one, to be placed in a side wall." *Vestry Minutes*, 17 Sept. 1925.

[1032] Some emergency repair work was carried out in 1916 after fifty-one ladies of the Church expressed their anxiety over the widening cracks in the ceiling. A consultant agreed with the ladies, noting that "the plaster of the ceiling and cornices was so cracked that pieces were likely to fall at any time," and that their condition had worsened considerably since his last inspection. See the *Vestry Minutes* for 18 Jan., 16 Feb., and 9 March 1916.

[1033] *Savannah Morning News* 2 August 1925, Sec. 3 (9-2).

[1034] *Savannah Morning News*, 4 Oct. 1925, Sec. 3 (11-3). The following two Sundays it was the archdeacon who celebrated in the chapel as the Rector was away in New Orleans at the General Convention. During these weeks the congregation was again invited to St. Paul's for the 11:30 service. During this time the Sunday School was divided with some using the ground floor rooms in the Church and "the Junior and Senior Departments in the new parish house on Congress St." (between Drayton and Abercorn.) *Savannah Morning News*, 11 Oct., Sec. 4 (15-1) and 25 Oct., Sec. 4 (15-1), both in 1925.

[1035] Also in attendance were members of House of Prayer Chapel. Earlier that day, all four local chapters of the Daughters of the King had gathered there for their annual corporate communion. *Savannah Morning News*, 1 Nov. 1925, Sec. 3 (9-2).

[1036] It seems likely that this is the one which is extant in MS. 978. ff. 146-148.

[1037] Like many earlier renovations, this one too brought forth several significant memorial gifts, including the two prie-dieux now used by the clergy. The first was donated by Bishop Reese as a memorial to his wife (*Vestry Minutes* 16 Dec. 1925), and Mr. Harris King "offered a similar memorial" a few months later. (*Vestry Minutes* 11 March 1926.)

[1038] *Savannah Morning News*, 2 Nov. 1925, Sec. 1 (12-6). The article highlighted the presence of "one member of the congregation . . . who remembered when the building was put up!" It also noted the special interest taken in the project by architect, Albert Simmons of Charleston, and the untiring supervision of Senior Warden J. Randolph Anderson.

[1039] *Vestry Minutes*, 26 Feb. 1929.

[1040] *Vestry Minutes*, 30 Oct. 1929.

[1041] To consider this and the related points that follow it, i.e., see the calendars for Holy Week in these years which are in MS 978, f. 156, and also the appropriate newspaper columns.

[1042] For example, see the notices in the *Savannah Morning News* announcing the Christmas Eve service for 1916 in which St. Michael's joined, 19 Dec. (44-4 and 44-6).

[1043] Notice for the first such service appeared in the *Savannah Morning News*, 23 Dec. 1945 (35-1).

[1044] *Vestry Minutes*, 20 March 1924.

[1045] *Vestry Minutes*, 16 Jan 1924. Note that Mr. Wright had only been in town for two weeks at that point!

[1046] *Vestry Minutes*, 7 Feb. 1924. Some 63 responded that they would attend a men's class on Sunday morning! Ford P. Fuller agreed to act as president of the new group and suggested Joseph G. Stovall as secretary. The same entry in the *Minutes* reported that a class for women was also to begin the next week.

[1047] The "Annual Report" for 1927. The president of the new club was W.H. Myers. *Vestry Minutes*, Jan. 1928.

[1048] The troop first appears in the parish report recorded in the *Journal 1914*, p. 158.

[1049] *Vestry Minutes*, 11 Feb. 1927.

[1050] *Vestry Minutes*, 5 March 1928.

[1051] The total reported by the Rector was 14,695. Since it is unclear in the reports precisely what the figures include it may be more significant that the average attendance for the noonday services was reported to be 291. *Vestry Minutes*, 3 April 1929. The schedule of lenten services remained virtually unchanged through the 1930's. The only differences of note were the diminished congregations and the absence of guest preachers during the depression years. See the "Church Columns" of the *Savannah Morning News* each Sunday morning through the decade.

[1052] *Vestry Minutes*, 20 March 1924.

[1053] The Vestry authorized the purchase of 500 books early in the year. *Minutes* 10 Jan. 1929, and Mr. Charles Ellis donated another set of 500 later the same year. See the *Vestry Minutes* of 30 Oct. 1929.

[1054] Enrollment always exceeded 300 and often reached well over 400 during their years. Figures were derived from the parishes own reports, found in the *Journal* of the Diocese of Georgia each year.

[1055] Mr. Wright intended to pay her out of communion alms and the Vestry readily agreed to cover any deficit. *Vestry Minutes*, 22 May 1924. Mrs. Griffeth was no stranger to the Sunday school; her name appears on earlier teacher lists at least as far back as the autumn of 1919.

[1056] *Vestry Minutes*, 10 July 1924.

[1057] For her work she was to be paid $1000 per year, the same amount she made at Trinity Church, Asheville, when she went there. *Vestry Minutes*, 16 Dec. 1925.

[1057.1] *Vestry Minutes*, 22 May 1924.

[1057.2] There was also "a unique class of 18 colored nurses who bring their charges to the Church School on Sunday mornings and are then instructed and led by the colored nurse in charge." *Vestry Minutes*, 20 March 1924.

[1057.3] *Vestry Minutes*, 10 July 1924.

[1057.4] *Vestry Minutes*, 11 March 1926.

[1057.5] See the *Minutes* of 20 Feb. 1920.

[1057.6] See the *Vestry Minutes* of 7 February, 20 March and 22 May 1924.

[1057.7] The ladies had made the lunch room into quite a successful venture. The operation produced at least $3400 between Aug. of 1921 and May of 1923 which was turned over to the Church School Building Fund. The Fund report, dated 10 April 1924, is included in the *Vestry Minutes*.

[1057.8] *Vestry Minutes*, 25 July 1925.

[1057.9] *Vestry Minutes*, 11 March 1926.

[1057.91] *Vestry Minutes*, 14 Jan. 1929.

[1057.92] The Society had been inspired to life in the spring of 1916 by the visit of Mrs. Emily Tillotson, of Church Missions' House (New York). For several years the ladies kept to their

[1057] purpose, "to pray for missions, to study about missions, and to give to missions." Annual Meeting Report of the Women's Auxilliary, 1 April 1918.

[1058] The Senior Warden had made the specific needs known to the congregation in a Sunday morning statement (25 May 1924.) To the officers this seemed an appropriate use for the Society's funds, which had been held by the Vestry for some 2 or 3 years.

[1059] After 15 months of her leadership there were 29 active singers. Mrs. Jackson had begun her work on 1 October 1925. When T.M. Cunningham announced her employment to his Vestry colleagues, after several years of contentious and generally unsatisfactory arrangements, the haggard chairman of the "music committee" cautiously expressed his hope that "she might work out." *Vestry Minutes*, 13 May 1926. See also the *Yearbook and Directory–1927*, where the choir-membership is listed

[1060] *Yearbook and Directory–1927* (no pagination.)

[1061] The annual report from the House of Prayer, 1928, has been microfilmed among the *Vestry Minutes* of the same period.

[1061.1] The Rector was awarded the honorary degree, "Doctor of Divinity" by the University of Georgia in 1927.

[1062] Taken from the Guild's annual reports for 1927 and 1928, the Guild's first president was Addine Myers (Mrs. Wm. H.), whose husband was simultaneously presiding over the revived men's club.

[1063] See the Auxiliary's annual reports for 1927 and 1928, in the *Vestry Minutes* ending each year.

[1064] The year-end report for 1927, included in the *Vestry Minutes* of the day, lists *all* of these activities. There may have been more, but the original minutes were lost, according to Treasurer Pope Barrow, and this was everything that he and President Betty Peeples could remember at reporting time!

[1065] See the *Journal 1924* p. 165.

[1066] *The Journal 1914*, p. 158, lists both.

[1067] As reported in the *Savannah Morning News*, 24 Jan 1927 (5-6) along with all of the other scouting news of the day.

[1068] The troop's annual report for 1928 contains all of these tidbits, unless otherwise noted, and is embedded among the *Vestry Minutes* along with other group reports for the year.

[1068.1] See the *Vestry Minutes* of Jan. 1930, where the annual report of 1929 appears. The Auxiliary was organized under the presidency of Mr. Noble Jones. So fondly were those good years recalled that the troop was revived for a time a generation later, in the 1950's.

[1069] Mrs. Low's confirmation, marriage, and burial in 1927 are all noted in the *Register* of Christ Church.

[1070] Neither the newspapers of the day, which celebrated her work, nor Church records indicate any direct involvement of the parish with her work. See, for example, the *Savannah Morning News* 12 Feb. 1926 (12-4 ff.), 18 Jan. 1927 (6-2), 19 Jan. 1927 (16-3 ff.), *Savannah Evening Press*, 18 Jan. 1927 (4-5), and the New York *Times*, 18 Jan. 1927 (25-3).

[1071] Foundation dates of new groups are deduced from their first appearance on the list reported by the Rector to the Diocese, and printed in the *Journal* each year.

[1072] From the Society's annual report for 1928, in the *Vestry Minutes*.

[1073] *Vestry Minutes* Jan. 1932, among the annual reports for 1931.

[1074] *Vestry Minutes*, 28 June and 29 Sept. 1932.

[1075] *Vestry Minutes*, 4 Nov. 1932.

[1076] *Vestry Minutes* 19 Feb. 1932. Unfortunately the committee is not named in the *Minutes*. All we know is that the Rector was its chairman and that the Christ Church Guild was requested to help.

[1077] Final plans are detailed in the *Vestry Minutes* of 27 Jan. 1933 and the primary news account the day after the celebration is in the *Savannah Morning News* 13 Feb. 1933 (10-1). See also the newspaper's announcement of the day's events on 12 Feb. (B 12-1) and (B 9-5). The final reference confirms the presence of the Rev. Robb White, Jr., son of the former Rector and now of Thomasville, among the clergy in procession.

[1078] *Savannah Morning News* 12 Feb. 1933 (B12-3).

[1079] All of the sermons, speeches, names, and liturgy of the day were printed in the *Georgia Historical Quarterly*, vol. 17 (1933), pp. 77-149, and also preserved in the *Vestry Minutes*. General thanks was publicly given to Dr. Wright who arranged the services "as nearly perfect as possible," according to Bishop Reese. *Savannah Morning News* 14 Feb. 1933 (B7-5).

[1080] *Vestry Minutes*, Jan. 1935, among the annual reports for 1934.

[1081] *Vestry Minutes*, Jan. 1935, among the annual reports for 1934.

[1082] See the report of the Women's Guild for 1934, among the *Vestry Minutes* for Jan. 1935.

[1083] Not to be confused with a much earlier Women's Auxiliary which was devoted to missions, the new version was created in March, 1934, under the presidency of Addine Myers (Mrs. Wm. H.). See the group's first report in the *Vestry Minutes* of Jan. 1935.

[1084] *Vestry Minutes*, 5 Feb. 1934.

[1085] *Vestry Minutes*, 2 Nov. 1934.

[1086] Altar Guild report for 1935, in the *Vestry Minutes* of Jan. 1936.

[1087] The actions of the annual meeting are recorded in the *Vestry Minutes*, 20 Jan. 1936.

[1088] All of the territory from a line some 30 miles east of the Rhine River westward to Germany's borders with Holland, Belgium, and France was officially "demilitarized" under terms of the Versailles Treaty ending World War I.

[1089] *Vestry Minutes*, 12 Nov. 1936. The Vestry, too, may have been adrift in the same spiritual swamp that had engulfed Rector and congregation, for they had met only once during the previous eight months and had made no progress whatsoever on the issues raised at the beginning of the year.

[1090] *Vestry Minutes*, 30 Dec. 1936. Needless to say, the benefactors who disposed of the $12500 debt, mostly anonymous, were given an enthusiastic resolution of thanks.

[1091] *Vestry Minutes*, 11 Jan. 1937, in Mr. Anderson's report to the congregation. A coincidence of circumstances made this the ideal time for the move. The parish "Widows and Orphan's Fund" currently had only one beneficiary, Miss Jane Boone, and she could be cared for by other means. The Church Pension Fund was now in place to cover all future cases. Cf. Mr. Anderson's annual report for 1928 in the *Vestry Minutes*, Jan. 1929.

[1092] The report of the Senior Warden on 10 Jan. 1938 showed the corpus to have grown to $17,000 by its first birthday. See the *Vestry Minutes* of that date. The Lynah bequest augmented the fund with cash plus 300 shares of General Motors stock. See *Vestry Minutes* of 23 June 1942.

[1093] *Vestry Minutes*, 6 Dec. 1937.

[1094] *Vestry Minutes*, 16 May 1938, and 24 Jan. 1939.

[1095] *Vestry Minutes*, 6 Oct. 1938.

[1096] *Savannah Morning News*, 31 May 1938 (14-5). She was buried near their home in Flat Rock, N.C.

[1097] *Vestry Minutes*, 22 Nov. and 13 Dec. 1938.

[1098] The *Vestry Minutes* of 16 May, 6 Oct. and 22 Nov. 1938, and the *Savannah Morning News*, 10 Jan. 1939 (14-4) trace the development of the new organization from its conception through the kick-off dinner at the DeSoto Hotel for 75¢ a plate, to its final realization as a working group. The three leaders named were respectively the group's president, vice president, and secretary-treasurer.

[1099] Minutes of the Annual Meeting *(Vestry Minutes)* 9 Jan. 1939.

[1100] The *Vestry Minutes* of 31 May and 2 July 1940 record W. Dewey Cooke's announcement, as chairman of the Music Committee, that the paid members of the choir for the coming year would be Mrs. Gawin Corbin (soprano), Miss Quint (contralto), Mr. Charles Whitfield (tenor), and Messrs. John Y. Dyer and James Morrell (basses).

[1101] The *Savannah Morning News*, 25 Nov. 1939 (12-2), recorded the dedication in honor of Mrs. Valmore W. Lebey, and noted the prayer, singing, lighting of the fireplace, transfer of keys, and tea which highlighted the celebration.

[1102] *Vestry Minutes*, 8 March 1940, and *Savannah Morning News*, 18 March 1940 (12-3).

[1103] Expressed, for example, in the Vestry's resolution to seek property near the church as far back as 1920.

[1104] *Vestry Minutes*, 11 April 1939.

[1105] *Vestry Minutes*, 7 August 1940.

[1106] *Savannah Morning News*,

[1106] 11 Oct. 1940 (18-6).

[1107] *Vestry Minutes* 4 Dec. 1940 and 4 March 1941. See especially the *Savannah Morning News* coverage of the dedication 5 March 1941 (16-5) and (7-4). Keep in mind that in those days the dining room was upstairs in the cottage on Bay Lane. Food had to be carried from the kitchen in the parish house, then taken up via dumb waiter, and dirty dishes returned the same way. Nonetheless, they often served 250 for Church functions while using fine china and silver to do it! [Read Mrs. Eloise Duncan's fascinating reminiscences of her 35 years as parish housekeeper in *Columns*, vol. 6, no. 3, Oct. 1981 (6-1ff.)

[1108] *Vestry Minutes*, 14 June 1941.

[1109] *Vestry Minutes* include Dr. Wright's note to the Vestry dated 22 Oct. 1941, with the news of Dr. Moultrie Lee's diagnosis and recommendation.

[1110] *Vestry Minutes* of 22 October 1941 and 4 May 1942 make clear that Dr. Wright even offered to pay the assistant himself.

[1111] Dr. Wright's letter to the Vestry stating his decision, and the effective date of 1 Jan. 1942, is dated 28 Oct. 1941 and was incorporated into the *Vestry Minutes* of that date.

[1112] *Vestry Minutes*, 5 Jan. 1942.

[1113] See the *Savannah Morning News* coverage 15 May 1942 (2-4). At the time of his acceptance, Mr. Snowden was Rector of St. Mary's Albany, N.Y., having taken his B.A. and B.D. degrees from Sewanee and done additional work at the Graduate School of Religion in Cincinnati. See also the *Vestry Minutes* of 4 May and Mr. Snowden's letter of acceptance, dated 12 May 1942.

[1114] Noted in the *Savannah Morning News*, 11 Oct. 1940 (18-6).

[1115] *Journal 1941*, p. 38.

[1116] *Savannah Morning News* 14 Jan. 1942 (14-5, 7-4).

[1117] *Savannah Morning News* 12 Oct. 1942 (12-2).

[1118] *Vestry Minutes* Jan. 1943, among the reports for 1942.

[1119] *Vestry Minutes*, 1942 annual reports (Jan. 1943).

[1120] *Savannah Morning News*, 7 March 1943 (21-4). See also *The Church in Georgia*, Vol. VII, no. 2, April 1943 (1-3).

[1121] *Savannah Morning News*, 13 May 1943 (12-1).

[1122] *Vestry Minutes*, 11 May 1943. Adding to the loss was the resignation of Rita Griffeth from her position in the Sunday School just three weeks before.

[1123] The wording of Mr. Snowden's note, incorporated into the *Vestry Minutes* of 11 May, suggests that he had been led to believe his resignation was expected in this situation.

[1124] The letter is in the *Vestry Minutes* of 28 August 1943.

[1125] *Vestry Minutes*, 2 Sept. 1943.

[1126] *Vestry Minutes*, 4 Nov. and 19 Dec. 1944, and *Savannah Morning News*, 2 Nov. 1944 (7-1, 2-2) and 1 Jan. 1945 (10-3).

[1127] *Vestry Minutes*, 16 Nov. 1944.

[1128] It is interesting to note that the Women's Auxiliary was asked to appoint two of their number to work with the Vestry in the search for a new Rector. (See the *Vestry Minutes* of 7 Oct. 1943); but it is even more noteworthy to see the ladies decline because they "think this impractical at this time." (Stated in the Auxiliary's letter responding to the Vestry, 1 Nov. 1943.)

[1129] *Vestry Minutes*, 4 Apr. 1944. It is a grim reminder that the war was far from over that in its last year or so, the number of gold stars grew from four to thirteen. The memorial plaque in the south aisle of the Church was dedicated Sun. 3 Nov. 1946. See *Savannah Morning News* 4 Nov. (10-6) also 17 June (2-7). 1946.

Chapter Nine

[1130] *Minutes* of the Annual Meeting, in the report of the Sr. Warden. 9 Jan. 1945.

[1130a] In a series of reminiscences which appeared in *Columns*, vol. 3, no. 4, Sept. 1978 (3-5), Mr. Hugh ("Buck") Hill recalled the incident involving himself, J. Cheshire Nash, Tom Johnson, and Walter Nelson.

[1131] *Savannah Morning News*, 11 Feb. 1945 (24-3), also an editorial filled with praise and great expectancy on 6-1. See also *Columns*, vol. 5, no. 2, March 1980 (6-1ff), for an interesting interview and reminiscence.

[1132] *Savannah Morning News*, 13 Feb. 1945. (8-2).

[1133] *Savannah Morning News*, 27 April 1948 (18-4 and 11-1f).

[1134] Especially noteworthy are the kerygmatic gems from the *Epistle to Diognetus* and the *Didache*, which he set for the *Hymnal 1940* (nos. 298 and 195, respectively), and his own prayer for family (no. 504). Alone among the 1940 editors, he also served to revise and prepare the next edition, *Hymnbook 1982*. The new one contains several more of his compositions and translations.

[1134.a] The new Rector's wife, Mary Goldsborough Laird Tucker, but far better known as "Polly," had a style, too! She was herself the youngest of twelve children and the daughter of a clergyman, and through her years in Savannah became "a familiar figure on her bicycle as she rode all over Chatham County, long before the current revival of cycling." Eventually, "the congregation gave her a motorized bicycle." "Downtown residents also knew her for the flowers and shrubs she planted along the sidewalks and lanes in her neighborhood." [*Savannah Morning News* 16 Feb. 1972 (7A-3).] She was also an accomplished poet, a talent both Tuckers continued to develop through their years together. In fact, a volume of their poems was published the day after her death in 1972, at 81. A particularly touching feature of the book is the way it highlights one of Polly's poems, entitled "The Wall." In it she speculated how probably the vision of the deceased would have no trouble piercing "the wall" which separates and hides them from the living. [*Savannah Morning News*, 1 April 1972 (6A-1).]

[1135] *Savannah Morning News*, 15 Jan. 1947 (12-4). See also the article, 18 Feb. 1949 (28-2), reporting the Rector's election as president of "Family Service of Savannah," a post in which he succeeded Wm. J. Robertson editor of the paper and a vestryman of the parish.

[1136] Reported in the *Savannah Morning News*, were his election, 15 Jan. 1948 (16-1), and his decision on 4 Feb. 1948 (16-3). The latter also evoked a supportive editorial on the same date (6-1).

[1137] The Bishop's words were part of an animated discussion at the Kansas City meeting which finally defeated the separatist motion in a fairly close vote. *Savannah Morning News*, 17 October 1940 (16-5).

[1138] *Journal 1946*, p. 22. See also Hoskins, *Black Episcopalians in Georgia*, p. 150 f. and the *Savannah Morning News*, 8 May (14-2) and 9 May (16-1), 1946. The Diocese was among the very last to complete such adjustments when it confirmed the constitutional changes at the following convention. *Journal 1947*, p. 31. Relying on the figures in the *Journals* of 1909 (i.e. after division of the Diocese) and 1947, it is interesting to note that during the life of the Council the number of Black communicants increased 14.5%, whereas white communicants in the Diocese increased nearly 61%.

[1140] This was the Chatham County Christian Ministerial Association. *Savannah Morning News*, 5 Feb. 1956 (24-4). Significantly, the Rector had already been recognized as a leader when the established Savannah Protestant Ministers' Union elected him president several years before. *Savannah Morning News*, 6 May 1952 (18-2).

[1141] *Vestry Minutes*, 21 Oct. 1958.

[1142] *Vestry Minutes*, 11 Nov. and 3 Dec. 1958 record the question and reveal that it was to be segregated. The same source shows a significant change in views five years later as the movement grew to desegregate the camp. See the *Vestry Minutes* for 19 March 1963.

[1143] *Vestry Minutes*, 19 March 1963.

[1144] See his address to the Diocese at its 1959 Convention, *Journal 1959*, p. 45, and the *Savannah Morning News*, 30 Jan. 1960 (6B-1).

[1145] *Savannah Morning News*, 13 Jan. 1955 (28-6).

[1146] *Vestry Minutes*, 21 March 1960. Apparently, the controversy also affected contributions to the Diocese, for it was notably short of meeting its quota to the National Church. At that point Christ Church and others, including St. John's jumped in to fill the embarrassing gap. *Journal 1960*, p. 37.

[1147] The *Vestry Minutes* of 26 August 1960 include Dr. Tucker's remarks. Visitors Claudia Quarterman and Carrie Orr reported they were "treated graciously" and "invited to return." *Savannah Morning News*, 22 Aug. 1960 (10B-3f.)

[1148] *Vestry Minutes*, 20 Sept. 1960.

[1149] Numerous members of the congregation have recalled his words on that occasion for the author. Their comments usually emphasize such points as the value of the Rector's "soothing presence" during those confused years (Mrs. Robert Giffen) and his ability "to embrace the most liberal views, or befriend the most eccentric or despised without becoming suspect by those with less courage." (Mrs. Leopold Adler II).

[1150] The matter became controversial when Bishop Stuart offered local Episcopal churches as sites for a community service "to pray for peace and harmony between the races," but local newspapers announced the gathering as a "memorial service." The latter, it was feared would probably draw a much larger crowd than could be accommodated and create a potentially violent situation. *Vestry Minutes*, 6 April and 15 April 1968. The bi-racial and interfaith service was, nevertheless, held as announced in Christ Church with a very large congregation in attendance, and without incident. *Savannah Morning News* 8 April 1968 (10 B-3).

[1151] *Savannah Morning News*, 5 June 1971 (7A-5).

[1152] Plans also called for use of the rite current in 1750 for the ceremony. *Savannah Morning News*, 5 July 1980 (7A-4f), and Hoskins, *Black Episcopalians in Georgia*, p. 158.

[1152] In 1940, St. Thomas was listed in the *City Directory* with Dr. Wright as Rector, p. 31.

[1153] See the *Vestry Minutes* for 17 Jan. 1949 and the *Savannah Morning News*, 30 Jan. 1949 (32-1). The new organization involved many from Christ Church, including Senior Warden W. Dewey Cooke and Dr. Tucker.

[1154] *Vestry Minutes*, 15 Nov. 1949.

[1155] The *Vestry Minutes* of 5 May 1955 indicate growing interest and those of 21 April and 19 May 1959 record donations of communion silver and candle branches to the new congregation from Christ Church people.

[1156] *Vestry Minutes* of 2 and 14 March 1955 and 26 Jan. 1956 (Sr. Warden's Report) record both land and money given to this new enterprise. See also the *Savannah Morning News* of 18 May 1955 (24-3).

[1157] Again, Christ Church purchased the lot and offered substantial initial help to get the new mission underway. See the *Vestry Minutes* of 11 March and 29 May 1958 as well as the Sr. Warden's report in those of 29 Jan. 1959.

[1158] Mr. Nelson agreed and fulfilled his special role with great vigor and devotion until near the end of his life, in 1979. Appropriately, he was buried in his deacon's vestments. *Columns*, vol. 4, no. 1, Feb., 1979 (2-3f.).

[1159] And did it all with qualified teachers for only a small tuition. *Savannah Morning News*, 17 Aug. 1945 (14-2).

[1160] See, for example, the *Vestry Minutes*, 25 Aug. 1958 17 Feb. and 27 Oct. 1959, 15 May 1962, and 10 June 1974. Parish support has come in a variety of ways ranging from furnishing a "communications system", which turned out to be a bell donated by the Men's Club, to purchasing adjacent property and paying for major construction projects. Much of the major funding has been derived from revenue raised by the ladies' Tour of Homes.

[1161] Directing the 1946 Tour of Homes for the Women's Auxiliary was Mrs. Thomas Hilton. See the *Savannah Morning News* 11 Mar. 1946 (10-2; 4-5) and 12 March 1946 (14-2).

[1161a] Examples of such uses are sprinkled throughout the rest of this chapter.

[1162] *Savannah Morning News*, 19 May 1946 (28-4). Directed by Mr. Pope Freeman, the Club elected its own officers and had strict rules of conduct enforced by the Club's "court."

[1163] *Savannah Morning News*, 22 May 1946 (14-2).

[1164] For example, see *Journal 1947*, pp. 5 and 21. See also the *Journal 1956*, p. 104 f. When the offices relocated, Mr. Hansell Hillyer, owner of the property, commented on the suitability of the move: how after more than 200 years three of General Oglethorpe's prime institutions were finally brought together again with the Fort, the Church, and the first Botanical Garden in America.

[1165] Usually the visitors came to lead Lenten Services, but not always. Guests for the 1947 Lenten services, listed in the *Savannah Morning News* of 4 Feb. 1947 (7-3), included Walter Russell Bowie and a number of other local and national notables. A similarly impressive list for the following year, published by the same source on 9 Feb. 1948 (14-6), included the Bishop of Pennsylvania. This tradition of worthy visitors seems to have continued throughout the Tucker years. See, for example, the *Vestry Minutes* of 29 Jan. 1959 (Sr. Warden's report.) and *Savannah Morning News*, 10 Feb. 1954 (20-5).

[1166] *Vestry Minutes*, 9 Jan. 1950, in the G.F.S. annual report.

[1167] *Vestry Minutes*, 10 Jan. 1952.

[1168] Authorized at the annual meeting; see the *Vestry Minutes* for 9 Jan. 1950. Ziegler also hoped to organize a junior choir, a junior altar guild, and a junior women's auxiliary.

[1169] *Savannah Morning News*, 9 Feb. 1949 (9-2).

[1170] The series featured actress Peggy Wood and the work of Dora Chaplin, noted authority and writer on family life. See the *Savannah Morning News*, 30 Oct. 1954 (2-8).

[1171] The university was pressing to complete the chapel in time for its cenntennial anniversary in 1958. *Vestry Minutes*, 11 Dec. 1956, and *Savannah Morning News*, 30 Jan. 1957 (22-1).

[1172] For example, see the *Vestry Minutes* of 24 Oct. 1941 and the *Savannah Morning News* of 11 Jan. 1948 (7-2).

[1173] *Vestry Minutes*, 14 Nov. 1950. Interestingly, it was soon thought advisable to replace the sexton, whom the Vestry described as "ineffective." They may have supposed a connection between his performance and the organ's unwelcome inhabitants. Mr. Ben Washington was employed to replace him and the problem was never again noted in the records. See the *Vestry Minutes*, 11 Dec. 1951.

[1174] See, for example, the *Savannah Morning News*, 18 Dec. 1950 (5-5), and 15 Dec. 1952 (18-5).

[1175] *Savannah Morning News*, 22 March 1948, (3-2) and 12 April 1954 (20-3) The latter was of special interest locally, not only because of its very recent premier at St. Johns, Philadelphia, but because it included a medieval hymn text translated by Dr. Tucker. *Savannah Morning News*, 12 Feb. 1954 (32-4).

[1176] *Savannah Morning News*, 17 March 1952 (18-6). See also the *Vestry Minutes* of 10 Oct. 1961 for another type of musical event altogether.

[1177] *Vestry Minutes* 15 Jan. 1953 (Annual Meeting). It certainly helped to relieve crowding at the 11:30 hour, which had become acute despite the absence of 29 sons and daughters of the parish in military service.

[1178] *Savannah Morning News* 2 Nov. 1953 (20-5). Despite an improvement he considered to be miraculous, after his first frightening diagnosis at Emory Chest Clinic, the Rector still had to face a very restrictive rest and recouperation program which kept him away from the Church from February until November 1953. During that prolonged absence he maintained contact with the congregation through frequent pastoral letters which were later published as *More Than Conquerors* (Forward Movement Publications, 1966). Clerical substitutes during those months included the Rev. Mr. Tyng, recently retired as Rector of St. Stephens in E. New Market, Maryland, who served for four months. *Savannah Morning News* 29 June 1953 (16-1).

[1179] *Vestry Minutes*, 13 Jan 1954. Young Mr. Kelly's letter of acceptance is dated 9 June 1954. He was ordained by Bishop Barnwell in October of the same year. *Savannah Morning News*, 18 Oct. 1954 (18-5).

[1180] *Vestry Minutes* 26 Jan. 1956. See especially Sr. Warden Joe Harrison's report to the annual meeting.

[1181] *Savannah Morning News* 30 Oct. 1957 announced the arrival of Kelly's successor, the Rev. Thomas L. Hastings. See also the *Vestry Minutes* of 8 Oct. 1957. Mr. Hastings stayed four years, into the autumn of 1961, when he became Vicar of St. Francis, Macon. *Savannah Morning News*, 26 Oct. 1961 (4D-3), and *Vestry Minutes* for 13 Nov. 1961. He was in turn replaced by the Rev. Richard H. Baker, Jr., son of the Bishop of North Carolina. *Savannah Morning News* 12 Dec. 1961 (5B-3). After two years Mr. Baker, too, departed, he to become chaplain at the Univ. of Virginia. Succeeding him was the Rev. Mr. Allie Washington Frazier, a fellow Virginian for Dr. Tucker to enjoy during his final years before retirement, *Savannah Morning News* 8 Jan. 1964 (5B-6).

[1182] The Rector reported 14 active lay readers in 1962 (*Vestry Minutes* 16 Jan.) and the *Journals* of the Diocese show figures ranging from 11 to as high as 18 for the years 1953 to 1963.

[1182a] *Vestry Minutes* 16 Jan. 1962.

[1182b] *Savannah Morning News* 19 April 1961 (10 B-2).

[1182c] *Savannah Morning News* 13 Nov. 1966 (1E-1ff.)

1183 Even the few projects that had been undertaken during those years of scarcity were themselves now in need of repair. This was the case with the elevator installed in 1939 in the northeastern corner of the Church through the gift of Miss Caroline L. Woodbridge. (See the *Vestry Minutes* of 11 April 1939.) The same was true of the parish house, which had scarcely been touched since its opening in 1940.

1184 A few relatively minor jobs were done in the years following the war, however, which were highly visible. One of these was the tile floor in the Church. (*Vestry Minutes* 24 July 1950.) A contemporary project mounted four bronze lanterns outside the front of the Church in place of the old gas lamps. These were given as memorials to Mrs. Sarah Clayton Walthour and Henry Dana Stevens. *Savannah Morning News* 5 Dec. 1950 (18-6).

1185 See, for example, the *Vestry Minutes* of 31 March 1953, and 22 Jan. 1954, as well as the *Savannah Morning News* of 22 Jan. (37-6) and 9 March (20-4), 1954.

1186 *Vestry Minutes*, 18 May 1954.

1187 See the *Vestry Minutes*, 26 May and 22 Sept. 1954, and the *Savannah Morning News*, 24 Sept. 1954 (32-5).

1188 *Savannah Morning News* 9 May 1955 (20-2) and *Vestry Minutes* 5 May 1955. The new arrangement included two chapels, one named in honor of Jane Wright (wife of the former Rector for whom the demolished building on the lane had been named, and the other called St. Andrew's Chapel, and dedicated with memorial services to six young Savannahians who had died since World War II.

1189 *Vestry Minutes* 19 May 1959. Relying on the figures reported each year to the Diocese, and published in the *Journal*, enrollments generally hovered in the range of 290 to 340 during the 1950's and early 1960's.

1190 It is all very well to be duly mindful of the perils of hell, but why volunteer for them prematurely when modern technology offers a reasonable alternative? The bid of the Mingledorff Co. was accepted in the spring, the same month the renovated parish house was dedicated. *Vestry Minutes* 20 May 1955.

1191 See the *Savannah Morning News* 16 Nov. 1955 (16-2).

1192 See the *Savannah Morning News* articles of 20 Nov. (28-6) and 22 Nov. (36-3), both 1956, as well as an extensive article in *Columns*, vol. 1, no. 4, Nov. 1976 (3-1ff.), commemorating the 20th anniversary of the chapel.

1193 *Savannah Morning News*, 24 Nov. 1956 (20-4). The Rev. Mr. Demere, son of the chapel's namesake, was Rector of St. Ann's, Tifton, Georgia, at the time. See also the *Vestry Minutes* of 2 Nov. and 11 Dec. 1956.

1194 Exterior painting of the Church in the spring of 1958 was followed by floodlighting of the Ascension window, over the altar, a year later (thanks to the cooperation of the John Wesley Hotel management). Such projects were coupled with the usual roof repairs and the rather unusual combination of damages caused to the parish house by vandals and hard use. See *Vestry Minutes* 6 Aug. 1958, 24 Apr. and 24 Sept. 1959, 23 Aug. 1962, and 13 Feb. 1963.

1195 Development of renovation plans can be traced through the *Vestry Minutes* of 13 Feb. and 10 Dec. 1963, and 10 March, 14 April, 23 June, and 15 Sept. 1964. Final form of the plans is best seen in a letter addressed to parishioners by the Rector and Wardens (Lewis Little and Malcolm Bell, Jr.), dated 15 July 1964.

1196 According to a letter from John McGowan to Lewis Little, dated 24 June 1965, the plaque was to be made compatible with the others in the Church and placed on the wall opposite the World War II memorial. Replacement of the porch slates, which had deteriorated to the point that walking on them had become unsafe, was the subject of a letter between H.H. Kleinsteuber of Cut-Art Stone Co., and Wesley Espy, 25 Sept. 1964. Both letters are in private hands. At present, these and a handful of related letters are the only sources available to document the 1964 work since *Vestry Minutes* for 1964 to 1967 are missing.

1197 *Savannah Morning News* 26 April 1965 (7A-2). Also present: Dr. Tucker, the Rev. Harry Shipps (future Bishop of the Diocese,) both assisting, and representatives of Greek Orthodox, Roman Catholic, and several protestant denominations.

1198 *Vestry Minutes* 15 May 1962.

1199 See the *Savannah Morning News* coverage 20 Jan. 1961 (10B-1).

1200 Earliest mention of the Council in this regard appears in the *Vestry Minutes* of April 1962.

1201 *Vestry Minutes* 8 Oct. 1964.

1202 The letter from Senior Warden Lewis Little to Dr. Tucker, dated 20 Oct. 1964, is in private hands.

1203 That is, the parish contributed $50 from a budget of $72,350. The committee's report to the Sr. Warden, dated 3 Nov. 1964, was signed by John McGowan, Malcolm Bell, Jr., Joseph Harrison, and Hugh Hill.

1204 Extensive correspondence dealing with the controversy and the campaign to obtain a resolution survives in private hands. It begins with the Vestry resolution of 6 July 1965 (see *Minutes* of that date) and continues through the following October when the draft resolution was presented. Involved at various points were Lewis Little, Hugh Hill, Dr. Tucker, Mr. Prime Osborne of Jacksonville (this Province's representative on the Executive Council of the Church), Bishop Stuart, Sen. Herman Talmadge, the Rev. Canon Charles M. Guilbert, and the Rt. Rev. William Crittenden (Bishop of Erie). See also the *Savannah Morning News* 27 July 1965 (4B-4).

1205 *Savannah Morning News* 6 Feb. 1966 (1B-1ff.).

1206 *Savannah Morning News* 27 april 1966 (8B-1ff.)

1207 *Savannah Morning News*, 6 Feb. 1966 (1 B-1 ff.) Mr. Bell was both a Warden of Christ Church and treasurer of the Diocese at the time.

1208 *Savannah Morning News* 5 Feb. 1967 (3 D-5).

1209 *Savannah Morning News*, 22 Sept. 1970 (1B-5). Another Christ Church figure who played a significant role in the cause of reconciliation was Malcolm Maclean, Chancellor of the Diocese.

1211 The letter from Dr. Tucker to Malcolm Bell, Jr., the Senior Warden, is dated 6 Feb 1967 and included in the *Vestry Minutes*.

1212 See the *Vestry Minutes* of 14 Feb and 28 March 1967. A measure of the congregation's esteem for Dr. Tucker is revealed by the rapid growth of the fund to nearly $13,000 in its first four months. *Vestry Minutes*, 27 June 1967. Interesting reading also is in *Columns*, vol. 1, no. 4, Nov. 1976 (2-3ff), an article lifted directly from the *Virginia Seminary Journal*.

1213 *Savannah Morning News*, 2 May 1967 (5B-2). Mr. Haynes' Bishop in Tennessee, the Rt. Rev. John Vander Horst, took the trouble to fill in many details about the new Rector's wife, Paula, and the family — all of it warmly appreciative. Commendatory letters written to Lewis Little (now in private hands), dated 24 and 26 July, expressed "every confidence" in the future Rector and his "dedicated ability," and noted his "sweetness of the best sort which gives him that quality of compassion that enables him to walk along side."

1214 This letter from Mr. Haynes to the "Church Wardens and Vestrymen of Christ Church" is dated 4 May 1967 and is copied into the *Vestry Minutes*.

1215 *Vestry Minutes*, 27 June 1967.

1216 *Savannah Morning News*, 13 Aug. 1967 (8B-8). The newspaper incorrectly states the year of her arrival as 1928. She came to Christ Church in 1926, and that was after 15 years at Mickve Israel, and some time at Wesley Monumental Church as well.

1217 *Vestry Minutes*, 18 July 1969.

1218 The *Vestry Minutes* of 24 Oct. 1967 note the coming experiment.

1219 *Savannah Morning News* 18 Nov. 1967 (6A-1ff.)

1220 The same article goes on to specify that the readers were Mr. Malcolm Maclean, Chancellor of the Diocese, and Deacon James Tiller, Jr.

1221 *Bulletin* for the twenty-first Sunday after Trinity, 3 Nov. 1968.

1222 *Minutes* for the annual meeting (no specific date shown) and the following Vestry meeting, 30 Jan. 1968, spell out the details of these reflections. The meeting also welcomed the new Rector, and even the new Christ Church *Cookbook* edition.

1223 Based on invoices and disbursements to contractor Olaf Otto, dated 30 April 1970. *Vestry Minutes* of 30 Jan. 1968 indicate thought of designating the entire project a memorial to the men of Christ Church who had died in national service in Korea and Vietnam. The overall cost of the work eventually totalled about $74,000. *Vestry Minutes* 21 Oct. 1969 and 23 Oct. 1970.

1224 See the *Vestry Minutes* of 30 Jan. 1968 and 18 March 1969, respectively.

[1225] *Vestry Minutes* of 15 April and 21 May 1968, respectively. This is also when, largely through an international effort of the Methodist Church, but with a substantial contribution from Christ Church, the statue of John Wesley was placed in Reynolds Square. *Vestry Minutes* 21 May 1968.

[1226] *Vestry Minutes* 20 May 1969. Should it appear he would not be elected, the delegates were further instructed to consider a candidate "who appears to be of moderate or low church leanings."

[1227] *Vestry Minutes*. The Rector's invitation is recorded there under the date 3 June 1969.

[1228] *Savannah Morning News* 1 Oct. 1969 (1A-1ff.). Coverage is extensive and includes many pictures. Bishop Stuart wrote a note of thanks to the "Rector, Wardens, and Vestry" a few days afterward which especially commended the Rector "for a remarkably fine piece of work." The letter, included in the *Vestry Minutes*, is dated. 6 Oct. 1969. Bishop Bayne had held several high posts in the Episcopal Church since becoming Bishop of Olympia (1947), but at the time of this visit he was "First Vice President and Deputy for Program" and operating out of National Church headquarters in New York.

[1229] *Vestry Minutes* 16 Dec. 1969. One other priest helped out at times and functioned as an assistant, but he too was retired. See the *Minutes* of 5 Sept. 1968.

[1230] *Vestry Minutes* 15, June 1970.

[1231] Equally unusual, was that another of the lessons was read by the Rev. Thomas Paris, of St. Paul's Greek Orthodox Church in Savannah. *Savannah Morning News* 15 May 1971 (6A-1).

[1232] *Vestry Minutes* 17 May 1971.

[1233] *Vestry Minutes* 18 Oct. 1971.

[1234] See the *Vestry Minutes* of 11 Jan. and 15 Feb. 1971.

[1235] Adopted at a special meeting of the Vestry and entered in the *Minutes* of 29 Sept. 1971.

[1236] Not surprisingly, what clarified for some clouded for others! The Vestry received a "number of letters in response," but decided to issue no further statement in an attempt to clarify its position. *Vestry Minutes* 8 Nov. 1971.

[1237] *Savannah Morning News* 25 March 1973 (1C-1ff.). Also invited to meet with the Bishop were members of other congregations and faiths.

[1238] *Vestry Minutes*, 14 Feb. 1972. It was James Hungerpiller who suggested we might learn much from the "Young Life" program.

[1239] *Vestry Minutes* 23 April 1972.

[1240] *Savannah Morning News* 1 June 1972 (10A-5). The $10,000 raised that year went to St. Matthew's Church, for their "Project Outreach" program, to the Historic Savannah Foundation for Georgia Day educational programs, to the Savannah Nursery School, to Episcopal Youth and Childrens' services for scholarships, etc.

[1241] *Savannah Morning News* 11 April 1969 (10 D-1 ff.). Involvement in the latter two enterprises is confirmed by letters in the *Vestry Minutes* from Lewis Little to G.L. Corbin (dated 7 Feb. 1969) and R.S. Carney to Mr. Haynes (dated 12 Aug. 1970.)

[1242] The proposal was presented to the Vestry by the Women of Christ Church, according to *Vestry Minutes*, 15 Jan. 1973.

[1243] *Vestry Minutes* 20 April 1970. Mr. Harrison was representing one of England's best known builders of instruments, Harrison and Harrison of Durham.

[1244] *Vestry Minutes* 11 May 1970.

[1245] *Vestry Minutes* 21 Sept. 1970 and 21 April 1971. The Vestry asked Mr. Malcolm Maclean to call upon the builders at their factory during his visit to England. Other problems eluded such direct treatment. "Music and choir expense," for example, virtually tripled the budgeted amount without warning or ready explanation. (See the budgetary statement in the *Vestry Minutes* through 1970.) Even more difficult to reconcile than account books were disputes between the "directors of music" and the former organist, who had been granted organ privileges to work with her students when she retired. See the Rector's letter to Mrs. Addie Mae Jackson, dated 5 Oct. 1970, in the *Vestry Minutes* and also the record of the next annual meeting, 11 Jan. 1971.

[1246] The *Vestry Minutes* of 11 Sept., 16 Oct., 13 Nov., and 11 Dec. 1972 tell the tale.

[1247] *Vestry Minutes* 11 Sept. 1972.

[1248] The *Bulletin* for Sunday, 17 December 1972, contains many details about the voicing and structure of the new instrument, for the service, and the entire effort. See also the notes "from the Organ Gallery" written by Conrad Morgan for the *Bulletin* of 15 Oct. 1972 and those of 22 Oct. 1972 and 11 Feb. 1973, which add further information about the organ and its builders.

[1249] A program for the multiple celebration can be seen in MS. 978, f. 163.

[1250] *Vestry Minutes* of 9 April 1973 and the *Savannah Morning News* of 22 April 1973 (7 A-1) describe the plans and the public reaction. All was not well within, however, for apparently the whole arrangement was booked and commitments made without either Vestry approval or notice. *Vestry Minutes* 14 May 1973.

[1251] See the *Vestry Minutes* 19 Nov. 1968 and the annual meeting of Jan. 1969.

[1252] *Minutes* for the annual meeting of 5 Jan. 1972. A few days later the Vestry asked her to chair its Special Projects Committee. *Vestry Minutes* 10 Jan. 1972.

[1253] See the *Vestry Minutes* for Jan. 1973, which include those of the annual meeting of the congregation.

[1254] *Vestry Minutes* 12 Jan. 1975, and 20 Dec. 1976.

[1255] Although it falls beyond the scope of this history, there is value in noting that the parish went on to elect its first female warden, Franklin Traub (Mrs. Herbert S., Jr.), to take office in Jan. 1985. She was warmly welcomed to the office of Junior Warden, but her premature death, shortly before the term was to begin, precluded her serving.

[1256] *Vestry Minutes* 9 July 1973.

[1257] Some even appeared before the Vestry in person. The Vestry, however, appeared to feel that their authority had been repeatedly usurped by the musician, and that further leniency would merely invite more of the same. Thus, they chose not to reconsider. *Vestry Minutes*, 13 Aug. 1973.

[1258] Stated in a letter from the Rector to members of the parish and in the *Vestry Minutes* of 13 Aug. and 10 Sept. 1973.

[1259] Reported in the *Savannah Morning News*, 17 Nov. 1973 (6A-3, includes a photo), which also notes that the new Rector was born in Augusta, Georgia, had attended Virginia Military Institute and Virginia Theological Seminary on his way to the priesthood. He also had spent four years in the family furniture business and a similar span in the military service. To Savannah he brought his wife, Virginia, and three children. See also the *Vestry Minutes* of 8 and 16 October and 12 Nov. 1973.

[1260] *Vestry Minutes* 10 Dec. 1973. The Green Book, remember, included the refined version of the "Trial Liturgy" used some years before, and represented the next stage in development of a major revision of the *Book of Common Prayer*.

[1261] *Vestry Minutes*, 14 Jan. 1974. It had indeed been 60 years or more. Not since 1923 had there been any modification, and no major revision since 1918.

[1262] *Vestry Minutes*, 14 Jan. 1974. The *Minutes* of the following meeting, 11 Feb., reveal the two pioneers to have been Ashby Angell (Mrs. John H.) and Miss Margaret Carswell, daughter of Jr. Warden John Carswell, who made the motion favoring the change.

[1263] *Vestry Minutes* 13 Dec. 1973

[1264] *Vestry Minutes* 11 Feb. 1974. He was himself to be installed three weeks later, on 10 March, in a ceremony which was accompanied by a major recital.

[1265] Special music was usually offered at the great festivals, but with some frequency there was also special music on such occasions as All Saints Day (1974), when the whole Savannah Convocation gathered at Christ Church to celebrate, and for festival Evensong with St. John's (April, 1975) or St. Michael's (Nov., 1977). The last of these was indeed special with the combined choirs of the two parishes offering Buxtehude's 1673 cantata *Rejoice Beloved Christians*. The singers were joined by a string ensemble from the Savannah Symphony and Sue Guerry, assistant organist at Christ Church. *Savannah Morning News*, 19 Nov. 1977 (6 A-6).

[1265a] The harpsichord, gift of a parishioner, is a two manual instrument made by Sabathil & Son.

[1266] Rather against his wishes, the uniquely talented assistant soon become known as "Big Byrd" to the youth of the parish, who were his special charges. Sa-

vannah Morning News, 29 June 1974 (7 A-1 ff, with a photograph), notes his educational background which included a B.A. from The Citadel and a Master of Divinity degree from Virginia Theological Seminary. See also *Vestry Minutes* 12 Aug. 1974.

[1267] *Vesty Minutes* 12 Aug. and 9 Sept. 1974.

[1268] *Savannah Morning News* 19 Oct. 1974 (6 A-1), with photograph.

[1269] *Vestry Minutes* 14 Oct. 1974.

[1270] *Vestry Minutes* 11 Nov. 1974.

[1272] *Vestry Minutes* 15 March 1976. The question was actually raised this time not by the Rector, but in a letter addressed to the Worship Committee from a Mr. Ackerman (not further identified).

[1273] For example, Mr. Maxwell proposed to reschedule the Christmas pageant from its traditional time on Christmas Eve to the Sunday before. *Vestry Minutes* 11 Nov. and 9 Dec. 1974.

[1274] The *Vestry Minutes* of 8 April, 13 May, and 10 June note that questionnaires were circulated in the congregation which sampled opinion and requested response to the trial rites. The 55 responses, which were forwarded to the Diocese, were overwhelmingly pro-1928. *Vestry Minutes* 12 August 1974.

[1275] *Vestry Minutes* 11 Feb. 1974.

[1276] *Savannah Morning News* 7 Feb. 1976 (1B -1 ff.) Bishop Allin's other mission was to defuse some of the reaction building up over proposed changes in the Prayer Book.

[1277] *Savannah Morning News*, 17 Sept. 1976 (1 A-3 ff.). The vote in Minneapolis reversed those of the two previous triennial meetings.

[1278] *Savannah Morning News*, 15 Dec. 1976 (5 D - 1 f.), reported on the content of the Bishop's recent pastoral letter.

[1279] *Journal 1977* p. 34. The remarks were made in the context of the Bishop's address to the convention. It did not help to clarify the issue in the public mind, however, when the news write-up reported, in the same article, the Diocese's action on the issue of homosexuals and the priesthood. *Savannah Morning News*, 13 Feb. (1 C- 6) and 16 Feb. (10 D-2) 1977.

[1280] *Columns*, vol. 1, no. 4, Nov. 1976 (3-4); also *Savannah Morning News*, 23 Oct. 1976 (6 A-6). Both articles are illustrated.

[1281] *Vestry Minutes*, 8 Nov. 1976.

[1282] The two are Susan Harrison, (Mrs. Robert L.) and Susan Dulany (Mrs. F. Reed, Jr.), and Vestry action on the question was unanimous. *Vestry Minutes* 14 Nov. 1983.

[1283] *Vestry Minutes* 14 Jan., 1974. The Rector also moved to survey congregational opinion regarding the use of lay readers to administer the chalice. *Vestry Minutes* 11 Feb. and 14 Mar. 1974.

[1284] *Vestry Minutes*, 8 April 1974, indicate the first readers were scheduled for service on the 21st following.

[1285] The Rector's announcement at first generated a lengthy discussion concerning the feelings of the Vestry, but there is no indication of further comment or change of plans. *Vestry Mintues* 15 Sept. 1980.

[1286] *Vestry Minutes* 11 Oct. 1976.

[1287] For example, see the *Vestry Minutes*, 8 Nov. 1976, which note the visit of the Rev. John Jenkins of St. Thomas' Church to talk about the proposed book to the Women of the Church.

[1288] At least Bishop Reeves supposed this to be the case when he addressed the Convention. *Journal 1977*, p. 35.

[1289] The general plan was to use Rite I, the one most similar to the 1928 rite, at the 11:15 A.M. Sunday service and to experiment with the less formal Rite II at Wednesday noon and Thursday evening services. *Columns*, Vol. 2, no. 2, Nov. 1977 (5-3) and also *Vestry Minutes* 13 March 1978. One "casualty" of the new schedule was the coffee and fellowship hour which traditionally followed the 11:15 service. With the new schedule in place such gatherings were practical only on the special occasions when the two major services were unified.

[1290] On several occasions Dr. Tucker compared, with distressed amusement, the events of 1978 to those of 1928 and 1892. The earlier furor, of course, he did not remember personally, but knew intimately enough through the recollections of his clerical uncles and father.

[1291] In the spring of 1978 a questionnaire was circulated to all "confirmed communicants in good standing" with the following results: 309 for the 1928 book, 216 for the proposed book, and 32 no opinion. *Vestry Minutes* 4 April and 8 May 1978.

[1292] *Vestry Minutes* 12 June 1978.

[1293] The *Vestry Minutes* of 16 Jan. 1978, for example, record the sentiments of one parishioner who was so unhappy at the "changes recently" and the support she "had observed at Christ Church for the new *Book of Common Prayer*" that she decided to change parishes. (Her action, incidentally, foreshadowed a fairly brisk two-way traffic.)

[1294] *Journal 1982*, p. 30.

[1295] Although controversial in itself, the two prayer book system had worked reasonably well. The 1979 version is used for the weekly Eucharists at the 9:00 A.M. service each Sunday and for special feasts, and the *Book of Common Prayer* (1928) is used at the 8:00 A.M. and 11:15 services. Expecting this diversity to continue indefinitely, the Vestry accepted a donation of 500 new prayer books (1928). *Vestry Minutes* 13 Dec. 1982.

[1296] See for example, the *Vestry Minutes* of 14 April and 9 June 1975, and 9 Jan. 1977.

[1297] *Vestry Minutes*, 11 April, 13 June, and 14 Nov. 1977; also 8 May 1978. Mr. Byrd became assistant to the Bishop of Western North Carolina, in charge of youth activities.

[1298] See *Vestry Minutes* 14 May and 8 Oct. 1979.

[1299] *Vestry Minutes* 14 April and 11 Aug. 1980, for example.

[1300] See, for example, the *Vestry Minutes* of 8 June 1981, 11 and 20 Feb. 1980, and 12 Nov. 1979.

[1300a] This would seem the appropriate place to point out that the term "renewal" is used hereafter in a simple, descriptive sense — much as one might use the term "Reformation" — to identify a recognizable movement in church history. Its use implies no value judgment whatsoever about the movement, those who are involved in it, or those who disclaim it — just as its 16th Century prototype need not be intended to connote who was reformed or who needed reforming.

[1301] *Vestry Minutes* 10 Nov. 1975 and 12 Jan. 1976.

[1302] *Vestry Minutes* 15 March 1976.

[1303] The second issue appeared during the summer, by which time Lee Giffen had become editor. *Columns*, Vol. 1. no. 2, Summer, 1976 (2-1f.).

[1304] Mr. Maxwell also noted that, in his judgment, the movement was already making its impact on the Sunday School. *Columns*, Vol. 1, no. 1, Spring 1976 (1-3ff.) Another article in the same issue, by Mrs. Charlton Theus discussed some of the more traditional exercises in renewal, such as monastic retreats, that had been carried out over the past year by the Women of the Church and the E.Y.C. (1-2 and 3-3f).

[1305] *Vestry Minutes* 12 April 1976.

[1306] *Vestry Minutes* 14 June 1976.

[1307] Names of participants from Christ Church appeared in the summer issue of *Columns*, vol. 1, no. 2 (1-2ff.), along with the other general information about Cursillo. An illuminating interpretation of the experience can be found in the following issue, vol. 1, no. 3, Fall 1976 (2-1f). Written by Elizabeth Sprague (Mrs. William), the article touches everything from her own prior misgivings and the content of "the course" itself to the camaraderie of the corporate experience. Another article of great interest recounted the history of the Cursillo movement from its Spanish origin in 1949, through many stages until its importation to the U.S. via San Antonio in 1957, and its subsequent spread into the Episcopal Church. *Columns*, vol., 8, no. 1, Feb. 1982 (2-3 ff. and 7-1 f.)

[1308] *Vestry Minutes* 8 Nov. 1976. The controversial nature of the question was clearly reflected in the vote: 5 in favor, 3 opposed, and 2 abstentions. See also *Vestry Minutes* for 11 April 1977.

[1309] *Columns*, vol 2, no. 2, Nov. 1977 (4-1ff.).

[1310] See *Columns*, vol. 1, no. 5, Feb. 1977 (1-1 ff.); *Vestry Minutes* of 13 March 1978, 14 Aug. 1978; *Columns*, vol. 3, no. 4, Sept. 1978 (1-1f., 2-3f.)

[1311] *Columns*, vol. 6, no. 1, Mar. 1981 (1-1 ff.) According to the Rector, by this date close to 100 parishioners had participated in Cursillos. Parish weekends usually involved a similar number.

[1313] *Vestry Minutes* 8 Aug. 1982 and 10 Oct. 1983.

[1313a] The figures are based on an unofficial count by the Rector.

[1313b] Based on the parochial reports published annually in

the *Journal* of the Diocese.

[1313c] The EFM program is operated through the School of Theology, University of the South, Sewanee, Tennessee. See *Columns* vol. 7, no. 2, June 1982 (7-1 f.)

[1313d] Figures cited are provided by Jeanne Garlington, a "Mentor" in the program, and its Diocesan Coordinator.

[1314] The annual reports of the Women of Christ Church for 1982 and 1983 (20 Jan. 1983 and 19 Jan. 1984, respectively) contain a wealth of detail about the breadth and vigor of their ministry. Already mentioned, but also important to this list, is the work of those who train vergers (fifty of them in 1983 alone) to welcome weekday visitors to the Church, and those who carryout the "tape ministry," which each year prepares 500 to 600 tapes of services, sermons, etc., to distribute among shut-ins, and loans many more from the tape library.

[1315] *Vestry Minutes* from 1977-80 show the development of this pattern as teaching and meditation was added to the traditional prayer. See also *Columns*, vol. 6, no. 1, March 1981 (2-1f.), in the Rector's column.

[1315a] Mr. Donald Mowatt of the CBC spent considerable time in Savannah and interviewed numerous individuals in an attempt to capture the spirit of the parish and to understand better the nature of its experience. The broadcast tape is available in the parish.

[1316] *Vestry Minutes* 15 Sept. 1981. For an earlier attempt to use the same idea, see the *Minutes* 16-23 Oct. 1954.

[1317] That plan was tried first in the 1982 fiscal year. See the *Vestry Minutes* of 8 Nov. 1982. See also *Columns*, vol. 7, no. 3, Oct. 1982 (1-1ff.).

[1318] For the parish's 250th anniversary year, 1983 pledges topped $300,000 for the first time. *Columns*, vol. 8, no. 1, March 1983 (1-1f.) Inflation, of course, always claims a share of the credit for any "record high" in money matters. But this figure would seem to represent a real increase, nevertheless, since it runs counter to a 9% decrease in communicant membership from 1975 to 1983. The secret is probably revealed in a realistic statistic which reports attendance at four key services each year. That figure has risen by nearly 38% over the same period. *Journals*, 1975-1983.

[1319] *Savannah Morning News* 1 April 1974 (1 B-4ff.) The proposal was the joint effort of Mrs. Lilla Hawes, Director of Georgia Historical Society, Dr. Tucker, and Mrs. Oscar Sims. See also the *Vestry Minutes* of 9 Dec. 1974 and 9 and 25 June 1975 for an indication of work done to illuminate and make emergency repairs to the Ascension window at this time.

[1320] See the *Vestry Minutes* for 9 Aug. and 13 Sept. 1976.

[1321] *Vestry Minutes* 16 Jan and 13 Mar. 1978. Building Committee Chairman John Miller reported on the cost analysis underway for the overall project. Ultimately, although some work was done on the parish house, e.g. in renovating the Jane Wright chapel and placing it "once again in use," [*Columns* vol. 2, no. 2, Nov. 1977 (8-1ff.)] most of that particular project was delayed for many years. The main reason for postponing it was the lingering hope that the Manger Hotel parking lot (across Congress St.) would be offered for sale after years of teasing, and thus allow erection of a facility nearer to the Church. *Vestry Minutes* 13 March 1978 and 12 Dec. 1983.

[1322] For the complete list of items under consideration at this early stage, see the *Vestry Minutes* of 23 Jan. 1979 and also the write-up in *Columns*, vol. 4, no. 2, June 1979 (1-1ff.).

[1323] Preliminary work included a major air conditioning and humidity control project which was intended to protect both the interior of the building and the organ by reducing maintenance and increasing longevity. The contract for this work was awarded to Erickson's, Inc., for just over $150,000. (*Vestry Minutes* 14 Aug. 1978.) Architectural work was hardly noticeable for the first year or more. The Restoration Committee, led by Mary Lee Lebey (Mrs. Clifford S., Jr.), met and corresponded repeatedly with consultant J. Everette Fauber (of Lynchburg, Virginia.) to clarify ideas, process plans through the Historic Review Board, and scale countless other obstacles in the path. See, for example, the *Vestry Minutes* of 4 April, 14 Aug. and 10 Oct. 1978.

[1324] *Columns*, vol. 7, no 2, June 1982 (1-1f.) For an interim report see Mrs. Lebey's remarks in the *Vestry Minutes* 11 May 1981.

[1325] Mr. Washington died of cancer in 1978. [*Columns*, vol. 3, no. 4, Sept. 1978 (5-5).] Crafted in hardwoods, with the central shaft enameled in white, the font is compatible with the other woodwork in the Church. [*Columns*, vol. 6, no. 1, March 1981 (5-4f.)] The idea for such a font had been suggested three years earlier by Dr. Tucker. His thought was that the existing font, being immobile, was less functional liturgically since many in the congregation could not see it and therefore could not really share in the act of baptism. Although the offer was "received with happiness and respect" it was decided that further discussion and thought should be given the matter. *Vestry Minutes* 16 Jan. 1978.

[1327] A successful fund drive, the Lynah Fund, an enormous boost in the health of the Endowment Fund, and sale of the Washington Ave. rectory also helped. *Vestry Minutes* 9 Aug. 1976, 12 Feb. 1979, and 16 Dec. 1980.

[1328] Progress on the floors was slowed when it was discovered that the existing tiles were underlain by several layers of old tile, plus asbestos. The cost and hazards of their removal introduced a whole new set of problems and worries. *Vestry Minutes* 14 Nov. 1983 and 12 Sept. and 12 Dec. 1983.

[1329] *Vestry Minutes* 11 Mar. 1974.

[1330] *Vestry Minutes* 15 May 1974.

[1331] Especially on the Saturdays which coincided with the local arts and crafts market on River St. — "First Saturday" *Columns*, vol. 1, no. 2, Summer 1976 (4-4f.) and vol. 1, no. 4 Nov. 1976 (7-1 ff.). The "Events" also became more elaborate and involved a variety of local musicians, eventually developing into a weekly feature of local public radio broadcasting via WSVH. A second way of carrying the Church to others was through a "tape ministry" in which Sunday Services and other occasions could be shared by those unable to be present. *Vestry Minutes* 14 Oct. 1974.

[1332] *Columns*, vol. 5, no. 3, Dec. 1980 (1-1ff.). See also vol. 5, no. 2, July 1980 (7-4ff.) for the letter which inspired the organization, and vol. 6, no. 2, June 1981 (3-2ff.) for a few of the rapidly growing anthology of "vergers' tales."

[1333] *Vestry Minutes*, 9 Feb. 1976, and *Columns*, vol. 1, no. 4, Nov. 1976 (5-1ff.). Christ Church furnished some 75% of the funds to begin the project, largely from revenue raised through the Tour of Homes.

[1334] *Vestry Minutes* 11 Sept. 1978, and *Columns* vol. 3, no. 1, March 1978 (4-4f.)

[1335] Especially helpful in executing this crucial phase of the plan were the organizational talents of parishioner Franklin Traub (Mrs. Herbert S. Jr.) and of grocer David Rosenzweig. An informative article about the development of the Food Bank appeared in *Columns*, vol. 6, no. 1, March 1981 (3-1 ff.).

[1336] See *Columns*, vol. 8, no. 1, March 1983 (6-1), in an article by Susan Dunlany (Mrs. F. Reed, Jr.) When the idea appeared in the *Vestry Minutes* of 19 April 1982, positive contacts had been made with Ascension Lutheran, First Baptist, and First Presbyterian Churches. Within the next month the Cathedral parish of St. John the Baptist was added to the list. *Vestry Minutes*, 10 May 1982.

[1337] Most of the money granted by Christ Church was revenue raised by Cookbook sales. See the annual report of the Women of Christ Church, 20 Jan. 1983, and *Vestry Minutes* 14 June 1982.

[1338] *Vestry Minutes* 14 Feb. 1983. The number of participating churches had also grown by this time, reaching seven according to the *Vestry Minutes* of 21 March 1983. See also the article on the development of the concept in *Columns*, vol. 8, no. 1, March 1983 (6-1ff.).

[1339] Again, the key grant of $10,000 was given by the Women of the Church. *Columns* vol. 4, no. 1, Feb. 1979 (5-1).

[1340] The list is much longer, but these will serve to illustrate the variety of projects supported. See, for example, the *Savannah Morning News* 20 May 1978 (6 A-3); or *Columns*, vol. 7, no. 2, June 1982 (1-1ff.), both of which deal specifically with uses of TOUR funds. (The Women of the Church began to share responsibility for TOUR operations with Historic Savannah Foundation in 1976, but this did not effect use of their portion of the revenues generated). The *Vestry Minutes* throughout the period reflect the full range of programs supported by the parish. There were also new thoughts of creating an Episcopal retirement home, or perhaps a bookstore, but despite great investment of time and effort, those have remained only ideas. See the *Vestry Minutes* of 14 June 1976, 16 Jan. and 10 Oct. 1978, and 12 Feb. 1979 for some of the hopes and problems involved.

[1341] The Rector also raised the possibility of a published history of the parish to mark the occasion. *Vestry Minutes*, 9 March 1981, note the invitation to the Archbishop and those of 11 May record his polite refusal — although far different than his predecessor of 1733 would have offered. Also in the latter *Minutes*, Lorton Livingston was named chairman of the planning committee for the 250th.

[1342] *Journal* 1983, p. 22.
[1343] *Columns*, vol 8, no. 1, March 1983 (1-1f. and 8-1ff.). Coverage includes pictures of the scene at the oyster roast, which was hosted by Dr. and Mrs. William Miller at their residence in Bluffton, S.C.
[1344] Notice of the Rector's intention and of the Vestry's approval is recorded in the *Vestry Minutes* of 11 April 1983.
[1345] *Vestry Minutes* 13 June 1983. His leaving was set for late July. See also *Columns*, vol. 8, no. 2, June 1983 (1-1ff.)
[1346] The consecration actually took place on Epiphany, 1984. See the *Vestry Minutes* of 12 Dec. 1983, and the *Journal 1984*, p. 24.
[1347] He was in fact the only member of the Commission who had served on it during the *previous* revision. See also *Columns*, vol. 6, no. 3, Oct. 1981 (3-4ff.)
[1348] *Columns*, vol. 7, no. 1, Feb. 1982 (3-1f.) In fact, Dr. Tucker is one of the greatest single contributors to the new hymnal.
[1349] A commemorative plaque honoring Dr. Tucker was placed in the south aisle of the Church during the spring of 1985.
[1350] *Columns*, vol. 7, no. 3, Oct. 1982 (2-3ff.)
[1351] *The Hymnal 1940*, # 195

Index

– A –
ABC With the Church, 23
Abercorn, Village of, 15
Acton, Village of, 15, 27, 28
Adam, Mr., 59
Aiken, Captain, 47
Air Conditioning of Church (1955), 162
Allin, The Rt. Rev. John, 172, 179
Altar Society, 118, 121, 144, 145, 147
American Episcopal Convention, Philadelphia, 54
American Independence, 54
Anderson, J. Randolph (Warden), 133, 145
Anderson, James (Sexton), 102, 103
Angell, Ashby (Mrs. John), 168
Anglican Worship, 16, 28
Annapolis, 60
Anne (Ship), 11, 23
Appollonian Society, 57
Archdeacon of Savannah, 123
Archer, Frederick, English organist, 116
Arnold, General, 152
Atkinson, Prof. William, choirmaster, 108
Augusta, Town of, 28, 60, 63

– B –
Balch, The Rev. L. P., 84
Baptism, 15
Baptist Congregation, 15, 56
Barbadoes, 39
Barber, Mr., Chaplain at Bethesda, 27
Barnard, Edward, 38
Barnwell, Rt. Rev. M. S., 147, 148, 156, 162
Barnwell, R. H., 106
Barnwell, Rev. William H., 73
Bartow, Mrs. Francis S., 76
Bartow, Rev. John V., 56, 57
Bartow, Dr. Theodosius, 65, 70, 73
Bayne, Rt. Rev. Stephen, 167
Beaufort, S. C., 11
Beckwith, Rt. Rev. John W., 95, 96, 97, 98, 100, 102, 103, 107, 109, 117
Bell, Malcolm, 164
Best, Rev. Dr. William, 55
Bethesda Orphanage, 23, 24, 25, 53
Bible and Prayer Book Society, 102, 118
Biddulph, Mr., 46
Biggs, E. Power, 168
Bishop Beckwith Society, 118
Bishop Elliott Society, 102, 109, 118, 144, 145, 147
Bishop's Fund, 76
Blodgett and Williams Schoolhouse, 68, 69
Bolzius, Pastor, 21
Bolton, Robert, 38
Book of Common Prayer, 23, 54, 117
Bonds, Confederate (1863), 86, 91
Boone, The Rev. Thomas, 105, 106, 107, 109, 110, 111, 113, 115, 123, 131, 136, 174
Boone, The Rev. William T., 110
Boone, Bishop (First Missionary Bp. of Shanghai), 110
Bosomworth, Rev. Thomas, 22, 27, 31
Boston 39, 89
Bouligny, Mme. Margaret, 107, 108
Bowen, Bishop (South Carolina), 65, 73
Bowen, Oliver, 46
Box, Philip (Warden), 38
Boy Scout Troup, 140, 142, 143, 147
Boys' Club, 157
Bragg, General Braxton, 86
Bragg, The Rev. Seneca, 70
Bray, Dr., 23
Brasch, Mr., Organist, 59
Brotherhood of St. Andrew, 118
Brown, The Rev. Francis Alan, 128, 130, 131, 140
Brown, Rev. James, 48, 50
Brush Electric Light & Power Co., 111
Bryson, Frank S., Jr., 161
Bulloch, Mary (Mrs. Edward Neufville), 65
Bulloch, William, 63, 70
Bunker Hill, 46
Business Women's League, 144
Butler, Gilbert, 70
Byrd, The Rev. Ralph, 169, 172

– C –
Calvinism, 28
Cambell, Colonel, 47
Camp Reese (Honey Creek), 156
Canadian Broadcasting Corp, 175
Canterbury, Abp. of, 23, 179
Capps, Monteith, 161
Carswell, J. D., 115
Carter, The Rev. Abiel, 61, 62, 63, 64
Carter, The Rev. Abram Beach, 76, 83
Carter, Maria Beach, 61, 64
Carter, Miss Sybil, 110
Causton, Mr., 14
Cemetery, Old, 118
Central of Georgia Railroad, 85, 90
Chadwell, George H., 106
Chancellorsville, Virginia, 89
Charleston, South Carolina (also Charlestown), 11, 16, 64
Charleston Mercury (Newspaper), 73
Charlton, W. G., 120
Chase, Bishop of Illinois, 70
Chatham Academy, 84, 116
Chickamauga, 89
Christ Church Association (1861), 85
Christ Church Club, 115
Christ Church Cookbook, 157
Christ Church Guild, 98
Christ Church, Macon, Georgia, 64
Christ Church, St. Simons Is., Georgia (Frederica), 63, 109
Christian Social Service, 145
Church of England, 14, 15, 16, 19, 28, 36, 40, 43, 54
Cincinnati, Society of, 54
City Exchange, 62
Clarkesville, Georgia, 65
Cleveland, Mrs. Annie T., 107
Cobb, Colonel Howell, 64
Coburn, Moses (Organist), 75
Cockspur Island, 13
Coley, Rev. Mr. Charles H., 85, 90, 93, 96, 100, 102
Coley, The Rev. Edward Huntingdon, 115
Collins, The Rev. David, 174, 179
Colonial Cemetery, 118
Colonial Park, 84
Color Savannah, Children's Book, 161
"Colored Work", 126
Columbian Museum (Newspaper), 56
Community Chest, 142
Concord Bridge, Battle of, 46
Concord, New Hampshire, 61
Confederate Veterans, 142
Consecration of 1840 Church, 70
Continental Army, 46
Continental Congress, 46
Convention, General, in Philadelphia, (1844) 79; (1865) 91
Cooper, Emmeline (Mrs. Robert S.), 173
Copeland, The Rev. Richard, 174
Corbin, Gawin, 147, 175
Cornerstone, Laying of, 1838, 69
Council of Colored Churchmen, 126, 156
Couper, James Hamilton, 67, 70
Cowes, England, 39
Crane, John, 41
Cranston, The Rev. Walter, 57, 59, 60, 61, 63
Crittenden Home Circle, 144

215

Cross, Altar-brass, 107
Crow, Dr., 23
Cuba, 84
Cunningham, H. C., 123
Cursillo, 173, 174
Cuyler, George A., 196
Cuyler, R. R., 70, 89
Cuyler Family, 107

– D –
Dalzell, Rev. W. L. Dickinson, 84
Daniel, R. E. L., 115
Dartmouth College, 40, 61
Dasher, Francis, 143
Daughters of the King, 145
Davis, Jefferson, 86, 115
Declaration of Independence, 47
Dehon, The Rt. Rev. Theodore, 57
Delamotte, Charles, 13, 16, 23
Demere Chapel (Christ Church), 162
Demere, Edward, 109
Dickens, C. H., 151
Didache, 179
Diocesan Council, 126
Dissenters, 16, 28
Doble, The Rev. Mr., 21
Dominicoi, 39
Driesler, Rev., 27
Duncanson, Rev. Mr., 39
Dulany, Susan (Mrs. F. Reed, Jr.), 172 (n. 1282)
Dunkirk, Battle of, 147, 148

– E –
Easter, 22, 53, 54, 56, 70
Ebenezer, Town of, 15, 19
Eccles, Rev. Mr., 42
Eckstein, Jerry, 143
Education for Ministry (EFM), 174
Egmont, Earl of, 12, 16, 18, 19
Ellington, The Rev. Edward, 40, 41, 42, 54, 55
Elliott, Miss Phoebe, 147
Elliot, Mrs. Stephen, 95
Elliott, The Rev. R. W. B. (later, Bishop), 98, 109
Elliot, The Rt. Rev. Stephen, Bishop of Georgia, 65, 70, 73, 76, 79, 83, 84, 85, 86, 89, 90, 93, 95, 96, 97, 123, 130
Ellis, Charles, Jr., 115
Ellis, Henry, 38
Emery, Miss, 117
Emmaus House, 177
Episcopal Orphan Asylum, 76, 95, 103, 109, 111
Erben, Mr., 65
Erben Organ (1831), 75
Establishment of the Church of England, 27
Ewen, William, 38, 43

– F –
Fallowfield, John, 29
Female Asylum, 61, 64
Finney, B. F., 120
Fire (1796) 55, (1897) 120
Fisher, Mr., 75
Fleck, Dale, 164
Flitchcroft, Mr., 29
Florida, Diocese of, 73

Font, Baptismal (Angel and Shell), 106, 107
Food Bank, 177
Fosbroke, Dean of General Theological Seminary, 140
Foute, The Rev. R. C., 102, 105
French (language), 15
French Settlers, 15
Friends of Seamen, 76
Frink, The Rev. Samuel, 35, 39, 40, 41, 42, 54
Frazer, The Rev. Charles S., 131
Frederica, Settlement at, 15, 18, 19, 27, 28, 63
Fort Pulaski, (Georgia), 90, 110
Fort Ticonderoga, 46
Fuller, Mrs. Elizabeth, 161
Fullam, The Rev. Everett L. (Terry), 174
Fund for the Relief of Widows and Orphans, 101

– G –
Gadsden, The Rt. Rev. Christopher, 57, 73
Gallaudet, The Rev. Dr., 108
Galloway, Brendan, 176
Garden, The Rev. Alexander, 18
Garlington, Jeanne (Mrs. Henry F.), 166, 169, 172
George, III, King of England, 47
Georgetown, South Carolina, 60
Georgia Bible Society, 61
Georgia, Diocese of, 63, 64, 65, 128
Georgia Episcopal Institute and Montpelier College, 76
Georgia Historical Society, 84
Georgia Militia, 61
Georgia Relief and Hospital Association (1861), 85
Georgia, Secession of, 85
German (language), 13, 15
Germans, 13, 15, 39
Gettysburg, Battle of, 89
Gibboney, The Rev. J. Hoffer, 131
Gibbons, William, 43
Gilmore, General, 90
Girl Guides (Girl Scouts), 128, 143, 147
Girls' Friendly Society, 142, 143, 157
Glover, J. N., 147
Gnospelius, Mr., 75
Goose Creek, South Carolina, 54
Gordon, Colonel George A., 134
Gordon, Mr. George A., 85
Gordon, Colonel W. W., 116
Grace Church, Clarkesville, Georgia, 73, 74
Graham, The Rev. William, 115
"Green Book," 171
Greene, Nathanael (Monument), 62, 89
Grenada, 39
Griffeth, Rita, 140, 146
Groover, General, 90
Guadaloupe, 39

– H –
Habersham, James, 24, 25, 27, 35, 42
Habersham, Mrs. L., 106
Habersham, Robert, 70
Habersham, William Neyle, 123
Hale and Revere, Founders, 59
Hamlin, Hannibal, 85
Hampstead, Village of, 15, 19, 23
Harrison and Harrison Organ (1973), 168
Harrison, Joseph, 147
Harrison, Susan (Mrs. Robert L.), 172 (n. 1282)
Harvard College, 57
Hastings, The Rev. Thomas, 156
Haynes, The Rev. Warren E., 164, 166, 173
Herbert, The Rev. Mr. Henry, 11, 12
Hibernian Society, 61, 62
Highgate, Village of, 15, 19, 23
Hill, W. T., 128
Hilton, Mr. Thomas, 147
Hines, Bishop, 168
Hitler, Adolph, 145, 147, 148, 156
Hobart, Bishop, 61
Holmes, The Rev. John, 50, 51
Holy Apostles, Church of the, 157
Honduras, Bay of, 39
Hornbook, 23
Hoskins, The Rev. Charles L., 157
Hospice, 177
Hough, Edward, 89
Howard, (ship), 61
Hoyer, Dr. Conrad, 164
Hulbert, The Rev. Irwin, Jr., 147
Hull, Misses Albert and Elise, 116
Hull-McLeod Wedding, 115
Hunter, Patrick, 27
Hunter, William P., 70, 89, 136
Huntingdon, Countess of, 25
Hussars (Georgia), 65
Hyacinthe, Pere, 109
Hymnal, 1940, 156, 179

– I –
Independent Presbyterian Church, 57, 115, 116
Indians, 16, 17
Ingham, Benjamin, 12, 16
Inner City Mission, 168
Isle of Hope, 98
Isle of Wight, 11, 39
Italian (language), 15
Ives, Bishop of North Carolina, 70, 73, 74

– J –
Jackson, Mrs. Addie May, 142, 166
Jackson, James, 79
Jamaica, 39, 53
James, George, M.D., 70
Jenkins, Rev. Edward, 47, 48
Jewish Parishioners, 15
Joe, (brigantine), 47
Johnson, Governor of South Carolina, 11
Johnson, H. M., 134

Johnson, T. M., 151, 155
Johnston, James, 47
Jones, Edward V., 162
Jones, Master George, 70
Jones, The Rev. Mr. Lewis, 11
Jones, The Rev. Mr. Lot, 65
Jones, Noble, 12
Jones, Ralph and Fenwick, Eagle Scouts, 143
Joubert, Peter, 29, 31

– K –
Karow, Lester, 166
Kate Baldwin Nursery School, 157, 161, 177
Kelly, The Rev. John, 161
Kennerly, The Rev. Mr. S. W., 76
Kennington Common, 36
Kimber, The Rev. Joshua, 110
King, The Rev. Martin Luther (assasination), 156
Knauff, Mr. H., 75, 130
Kollock, Rev. Dr., 57, 59, 60, 63
Kollock, Dr. Phineas M., 70, 83, 101
Kollock, Mrs. P. M., 77

– L –
Ladies' Missionary Society, 141
Lafayette, General, 61, 62
Langworthy, Edward, 47
Laurel Grove Cemetery, 84, 90, 118
Lay Readers, 118
Laymen's League, 147
Lebey, Mary, cottage, 147
Lectern (Brass Eagle), 107
Lee, Robert E., 97, 98, 156
Lee, Thomas, 21
Leigh, The Rev. Canon, 115
Lenten Services (1927), 140
Levy, B. H., 143
Lewis' Catechism with Explanations, 23
Lexington Green, Battle of, 46
Lincoln, Abraham, 85
Lincoln, W. W., 100
Lindsay, Rev. Benjamin, 53, 54
Lloyd, Captain, 54
Lookout Mountain, 89
Loutit, The Rt. Rev. Henry I., 162
Low, Juliette Gordon, 128, 143, 149
Lowten, Mrs. Elizabeth, 42
Lowten, Rev. Timothy, 42
Luffburrow, Matthew, 67
Lutheran Church, 55, 56
Lynah, James, 162

– M –
Mann, T. Grayson, 107
Margaret Street Mission, 118
Marine Hospital Service (WWI), 134, 142
Marshall, Mrs. Mary, 70
Masons (Masonic Order), 53, 61, 76
Matthews, Mary Musgrove, 27
Maundy Thursday Service (1919), 140
Maxwell, The Rev. George M., 169, 171, 172, 174
Meachen, The Rev. Jerome, Organist, 169, 179

Meade, Bishop of Virginia, 73, 85
Mehrtens, Professor (Organist and Choirmaster), 107
Men's Club (Men of Christ Church), 140, 141, 143, 147, 161, 162
Metcalfe, The Rev. Mr. William, 19, 25
Methodism, 12, 16, 27
Middletown, Connecticut, 60
Mikell, Bishop, 144
Milledgeville, Georgia, 65
Miller, John F. (Architect), 96
Missionary Ridge, 89
Missionary Society, 118
Mitchell, The Rev. John M., 96, 97, 98, 100
Monroe, President, 59
Moorfields, 24
Moravians, 13, 15
Morgan, Conrad (Organist), 166
Mortimer, The Rev. George D. E., 102, 103, 104
Musgrove, Mr., 11

– Mc –
McCoy, Mrs. J. J., 123
McLeod, Richard, 116

– N –
National Council of Churches, 162
Negro Missionary Districts, 156
Neidlinger, John (Sexton), 43, 46
Neighborhood Woman's Club, 145
Nelson, The Rt. Rev. Cleland Kinlock, 116, 117, 136
Nelson, The Rev. Walter, 147, 157
Neufville, The Rev. Mr. Edward, 65, 67, 69, 70, 73, 74, 75, 76, 79, 81, 83
Neufville, Edward F., Marriage to Mary D. Tattnall (1863), 86
Nevitt, John (Architect), 111, 112, 113, 116
New York, N. Y., 39, 89
Newcomb, The Rev. Thomason, 157, 173, 179
Nichols, George (Printer), 85
Nichols, The Rev. James P., Jr., 167
Nixon, Rev. William, 53, 55
Norris, John (Architect), 74
Norris, William, 18, 19, 23

– O –
Ogeechee Mission, 97
Oglethorpe, General James, 11, 12, 15, 16, 17, 18, 20, 22, 23, 29, 43, 123
Ordination of Women, 172
Ormond, Eleanor (Mrs. Alex C.), 168
Orphan Home Society, 118
Orton, The Rev. Mr. Christopher, 27
Ossabaw Island, 27
Ottolenghe, Joseph (Catechist), 35
Owens, T. Lloyd, 120

– P –
Parish Helper, The, 128
Parish House (Cortez Cigar Co.), 147
Parish Weekends, 174
Parker, Mr. and Mrs., 14
Parochial Aid Society (1893), 116
Pearl Harbor, 148
Penfield, Mr., 74, 102, 103
Pew Holders (1802), 61
Pews, Free, 137
Philadelphia, 39, 89
Philadelphia Inquirer (newspaper), 75
Philbrick, Samuel, 65
Picayune (newspaper, New Orleans), 95
Pierce, Honorable William, 54
Piercy, Rev., 42, 47
Pike, Bishop of California, 162
Pike The Rev. Clifford, 167
Port Royal, South Carolina, 71
Potter, Bishop of Pennsylvania, 84
Potter, James, 86
Powell, James, 47
Presbyterian Congregation, 28, 55, 56
Preston, William Gibbons (Architect), 116, 121, 123
Primate of Ireland, 18
Prince William Parish (Sheldon, South Carolina), 65
Proposed Book of Common Prayer (1976), 172
Protestant Episcopal Church, 54, 63
Provinical Congress, 47
Providence, Rhode Island, 39
Puckett, Mary Regina, 169, 171, 172, 173
Pulaski Guards (1861), 83, 85
Pulpit, Brass (1890), 116
Puseyism (Oxford Movement), 74

– Q, R –
Quincy, Samuel, 12, 18, 22
Racial Missionary District, 126
Read, J. B., 38, 59
Rebecca Clyde (ship), 89
Red Cross, 148
Reese, The Rt. Rev. F. F., 130, 133, 134, 139, 144, 145, 150
Reeves, The Rt. Rev. George Paul, 166, 172, 173
Renewal Ministries, 174
Rennie, The Rev. Mr. John, 47
Repair and Restoration of Church (1978), 176
Restoration of Christ Church (1897 and 1925), 139
Revere, Paul, Ride of, 46
Revere Bell (Hale and Revere), 59
Reynolds, Governor John, 35
Rinkie Dinks, 142
Robertson, Ian, 176
Ross Water Engine, 123
Routley, Dr. Erik, 179
Royall, Dr., 100

– S –
Sack, Miss Georgina, 130
Sacristan Society, 106
SAFE Shelter, 177
St. Andrews Chapel, 123, 137, 157
St. Augustine's, 109, 118
St. Barnabas Guild for Nurses, 144
St. Bartholomew's, 157
St. Catherine's Island, Georgia, 27
St. George's (Savannah), 157
St. George's, South Carolina, 48
St. John the Baptist, Cathedral of, 98, 107, 121, 122, 123
St. John's, Fayetteville, North Carolina, 64
St. John's, Georgetown, Maryland, 155
St. John's (Savannah), 73, 75, 77, 79, 83, 84, 95, 96, 97, 107, 109, 110, 121, 123, 164
St. Luke's Hospital, Japan, 142
St. Luke's Hospital, Richmond, Virginia, 126
St. Matthew's (Savannah), 109, 110, 157
St. Michael's Chapel (Savannah), 118, 121, 123, 130, 131, 137
St. Michael's (Charleston, South Carolina), 65
St. Patrick's Day, 62
St. Patrick's Total Abstinence Society, 95
St. Paul's (Augusta, Georgia), 39, 50, 63
St. Paul's (Chattanooga, Tennessee), 137
St. Paul's "Free Chapel" (Savannah), 77, 95
St. Paul's (Louisville, Kentucky), 137
St. Paul's (Savannah), 121, 123
St. Philips, Parish of (Georgia), 47
St. Philip's (Charleston, South Carolina), 64
St. Simon's Island, 16, 55
St. Stephen's (Savannah), 76, 77, 109
St. Thomas', Isle of Hope (Savannah), 157
Salzburgers, 15
San Jacinto (steamer), 97
Sapelo Island (Georgia), 27
Savannah (ship), 59
Savannah, Albany and Gulf Railroad, 84
Savannah Bible Society, 76
Savannah Convocation, 99, 109
Savannah Female Asylum, 57, 61
Savannah Free School, 57, 64
Savannah Medical College, 84
Savannah Port Society, 98, 109, 115
Savannah River, 13
Savannah Volunteer Guard, 62
Scarborough, William, 70
Scholl, Charles (Architect), 74
Schreiner, H. L. (Choir Director), 102
Schwaab, Augustus (Architect), 96
Scudder, Amos, 61, 67, 70

Seabury, The Rt. Rev. Samuel, 55
Sephardim, 15
Seymour, The Rev. James, 48, 50
Sheftall, Mordecai, 54
Sherman, General, 89
Sherrill, The Rt. Rev. Henry Knox, 152
Shipps, The Rt. Rev. Harry W., 179
Simmonds (ship), 13
Skidaway Island (Georgia), 15
Smith, The Rev. Mr. Haddon, 42, 43, 46, 47, 50
Smith, John, 38
Snowden, The Rev. Charles M., 148, 151
Society for Promoting Christian Knowledge (S.P.C.K.), 23
Society for Propogation of the Gospel in Foreign Parts (S.P.G.), 12, 23, 28, 35, 39, 40, 42, 48, 50, 54, 83
Spangenburg, August Gottlieb, 14, 15
Spear, The Rev. William, 70
Spence, The Rev. H. Percival, 133
Spotsylvania, Battle of, 89
Stephens, Hugh, 143
Stephens, William, 19, 20, 21, 22, 27, 28, 29, 31, 32
Stevens, Bishop, 39
Stevens, John, Jr., (Organist), 38
Steward, Professor (Organist), 115
Stoddard, A. H., 143
Stopford, the Rt. Rev. Robert, Bishop of London, 168
Strong, The Rev. C. H., 126
Stuart, The Rt. Rev. Albert Rhett, 156, 157, 162, 166
Stuart, The Rev. Mr. John, 50
Sturges, Oliver, 61
Sunbury, Town of, 42
Sunday School, 95, 102, 109, 110, 118, 133, 140, 141, 143, 147, 174
Swiss Settlers, 15

– T –
Tattnall, Miss Henriette, 107
Tattnall, Josiah, 47, 98
Tattnall, Mary D., Marriage to Edward F. Neufville, 86
Tax Act, 38
Teague, The Rev. Dawson, 164, 166, 167
Telfair, Edward, 46
Telfair, William, 38
Temperance Society, 76
Thomas, Captain, 29
Thunderbold Mission (Georgia), 118
Thunderbold, Town of (Georgia), 21
Tiffany, The Rev. Mr., 110
Tomochichi, 11
Tondee, Peter, 46
Tondee's Tavern, 46
Tour of Homes, 145, 157, 161, 168
Trapier, The Rev. Paul, 73

217

Trinity Church (Pittsburg, Pennsylvania), 61
Troup Ward Mission (1860), 170
Trustees, Colony of Georgia, 11, 12, 13, 16, 17, 18, 19, 20, 22, 23, 24, 29, 32, 35
Tucker, The Rt. Rev. Beverly Dandridge, 130
Tucker Building (North Wing of Parish House), 161
Tucker, The Rev. Francis Bland, 155, 156, 157, 161, 162, 164, 166, 172, 177, 178, 179
Tucker, F. Bland, Scholarship, 164
Tucker, Henry St. George (Pres. Bp), 156
Tunbridge Chapel (England), 29
Turner, William H., 70
Two Brothers (ship), 18
Tybee (ship), 65
Tybee Island (Georgia), 13
Tyler, B. T., 151

– U, V –

Union Society, 57, 61, 64, 109
Unitarians, 69
University of the South (Sewanee), 109
Urban, Henry (Architect), 116
Vergers, Guild of, 176
Vernonburgh, Village of, 15, 27, 28
Vincent, The Rt. Rev. Boyd, 144
Virginia Theological Seminary, 155
Vogel, Otto, 107

– W, X, Y, Z –

Wachtel, Leo, 143
Waldburg, Jacob, 101
Walthour, The Rev. J. B. (later Bishop), 151, 161
Walton, George, 46
Waring, Mrs. Pinckney, 134, 139, 140, 146
Washington, Anna Maria, 156
Washington, Ben, 176
Washington, George, 46, 54
Washington, Mrs. George (funeral), 54
Watson, Charles, 38
Weed, Joseph D., 115
Wesley, The Rev. Charles, 13, 15, 16, 18, 23
Wesley, The Rev. John, 12, 13, 14, 15, 16, 17, 18, 19, 20, 21, 22, 23, 25, 36, 39, 123
Wesley, The Rev. Samuel, 22
Wheelock's Indian School (Dartmouth College), 40
White Cross Society, 109
White, The Rev. George, 65, 70
White, The Rev. Robb, 115, 116, 121, 123, 126, 131, 136, 140
White, The Rev. Robb, Jr., 126
White, The Rev. Rufus, 79, 83
White, The Rt. Rev. William, 61, 68
Whitefield, The Rev. George, 18, 19, 20, 21, 22, 23, 24, 25, 27, 29, 35, 39, 40, 41, 42, 54
Widows and Orphan's Fund (1866), 76
Wilkins, Archibald, 77
Wilkins, Miss Martha, 65
Williams, William Thorne, 70
Wilson, Woodrow, 134
Wing, The Rev. John Durham (later Bp. of S. Florida), 133, 134, 136, 137, 140, 144
Winter, Cornelius, 35
Women's Auxiliary, Christ Church, 117, 118, 142, 145, 157, 169, 172
Women's Christian Temperance Union, 109
Women's Guild, 142, 145, 158
Women's Urban Ministries Committee, 177
Woodmason, Mr., 39
World War II Dead, Christ Church, 150
Wright, Ambrose, 41
Wright Cottage, Camp Reese (Honey Creek), 145
Wright, Mrs. David Cady, 147
Wright, The Rev. David Cady, 137, 139, 140, 144, 145, 147, 148, 151
Wright, Sir James, Governor of Colonial Georgia, 39, 46, 47, 48
Yamacraw Bluff (Georgia), 11
Young People's Service League, 142, 168
Zeigler, Harry, 157
Zouberbuhler, The Rev. Bartholomew, 27, 28, 29, 31, 32, 33, 35, 37, 38, 39, 40, 42, 43, 97
Zubly, The Rev. J. J., 28, 35